I0709651

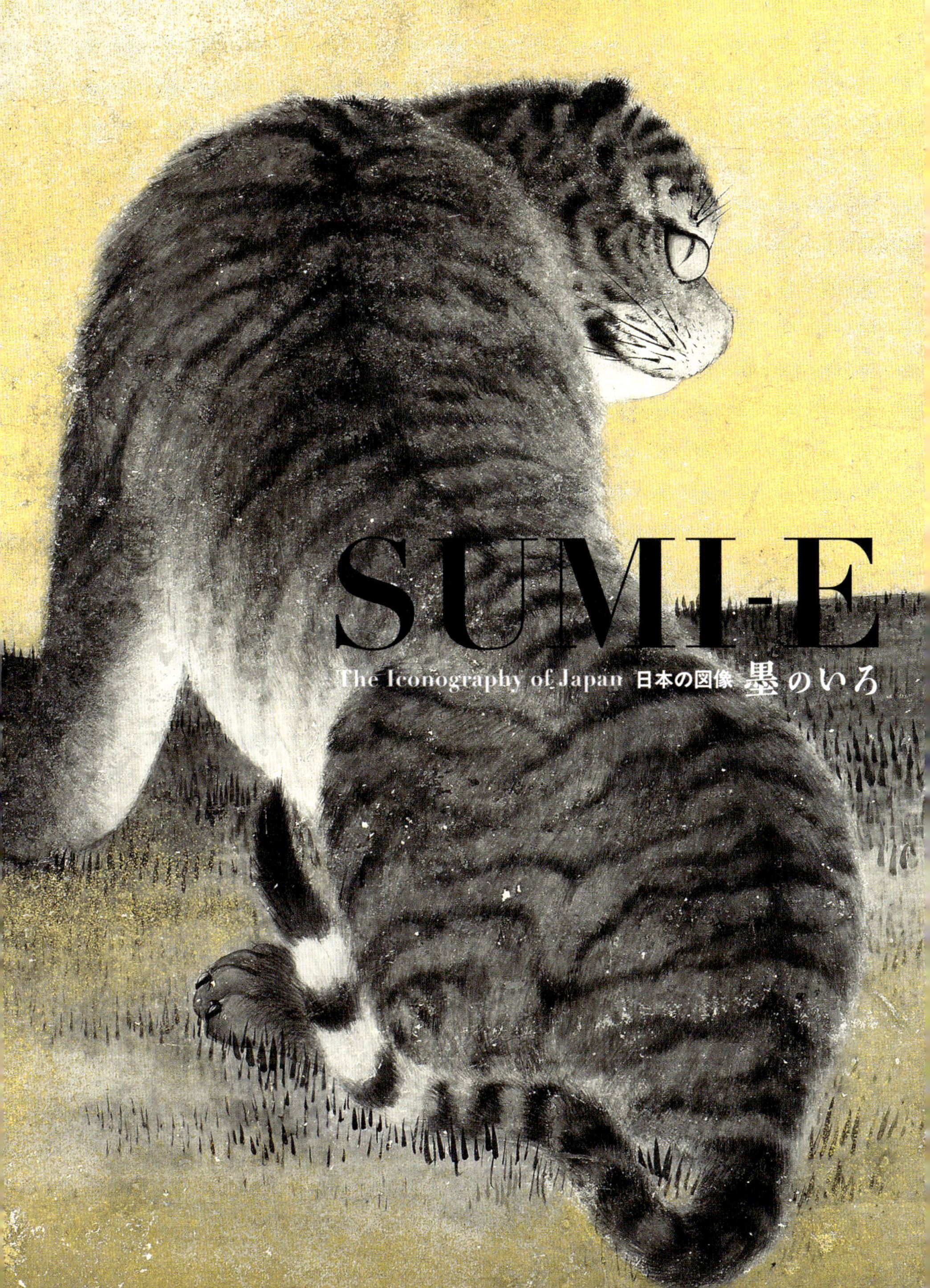

SUMI-E
The Iconography of Japan 日本の図像 墨のいろ

<h1>はじめに</h1>

　水墨画は中国の唐代中期に誕生した、東洋における絵画である。わが国には禅宗とともに鎌倉時代中期に宋時代の成熟した水墨画が渡来し、室町時代に隆盛をみた。それまでの精神文化や美術の世界にあたえた影響ははかり知れない。ことに絵画では中世以降の展開の大きな軸をなすといってもいい。

　水墨画は写実的な描きかたの技法ではなく、主題や構図、技法、鑑賞形式などがまとまったかたちであり、完成された絵画形式として受け入れられた。また色彩を用いずに墨の濃淡や暈し、滲みなどでかたちをとらえる表現形式は、それまでの線描中心の画法を一変させ、着色画とは一味違った造形の世界をつくり出したのである。

　初期の水墨画は南宋画を習得することから始まった。南北朝時代の禅宗・可翁仁賀や黙庵霊淵ら高僧画家たちはその初期にはすでに完成した作品を遺した。それらはやがて明兆や如拙、周文たちの活躍を経て、室町水墨画を大成させた雪舟へと受け継がれていった。

　そして戦国時代には雪舟の弟子や武人画家たちの登場により、それまで禅寺に限られていた水墨画が日本各地へと広められて行った。この時代はいままでの禅宗的な画題から、山水や花鳥などのはなやかな画題へと好みが変わり、着実に水墨画が日本文化に溶け込んでいった転換期でもあった。この時代の代表作は長谷川等伯の「松林図屏風」であり、主題と技量ともに中国画に対抗できる水墨画が誕生した。

　また狩野派では、室町時代後期から桃山・江戸時代初期にかけて幕府お抱えの御用絵師として社寺仏閣をはじめ、大坂城、聚楽第、御所などの障壁画に腕を振るっていたため、その結果、次第にマンネリズムに陥ちこみ衰退していく時期でもあった。

　この時代は封建社会の悪癖として人々の自由を束縛したため、絵画の世界では「奇想派」と呼ばれる画家たちが生まれた。そのなかの曾我蕭白や長澤蘆雪の描く作品は超現実的世界を見せてくれた。

　この息苦しい状況のなか再び日本の水墨画に新たな息吹を吹き込んだのが、蕪村や大雅をはじめとする南画家たちだった。彼らはまだ見ぬ中国の情景を想いを込めて描き、ロマンにあふれる桃源郷の世界をみごとに描き出した。

　本書では、約五百年にわたる水墨画の歴史を紹介し、それらの作品を通して日本の水墨画の特質を探り、さらにわが国の美術史、文化史に果たした役割や意義などを考えてみたい。

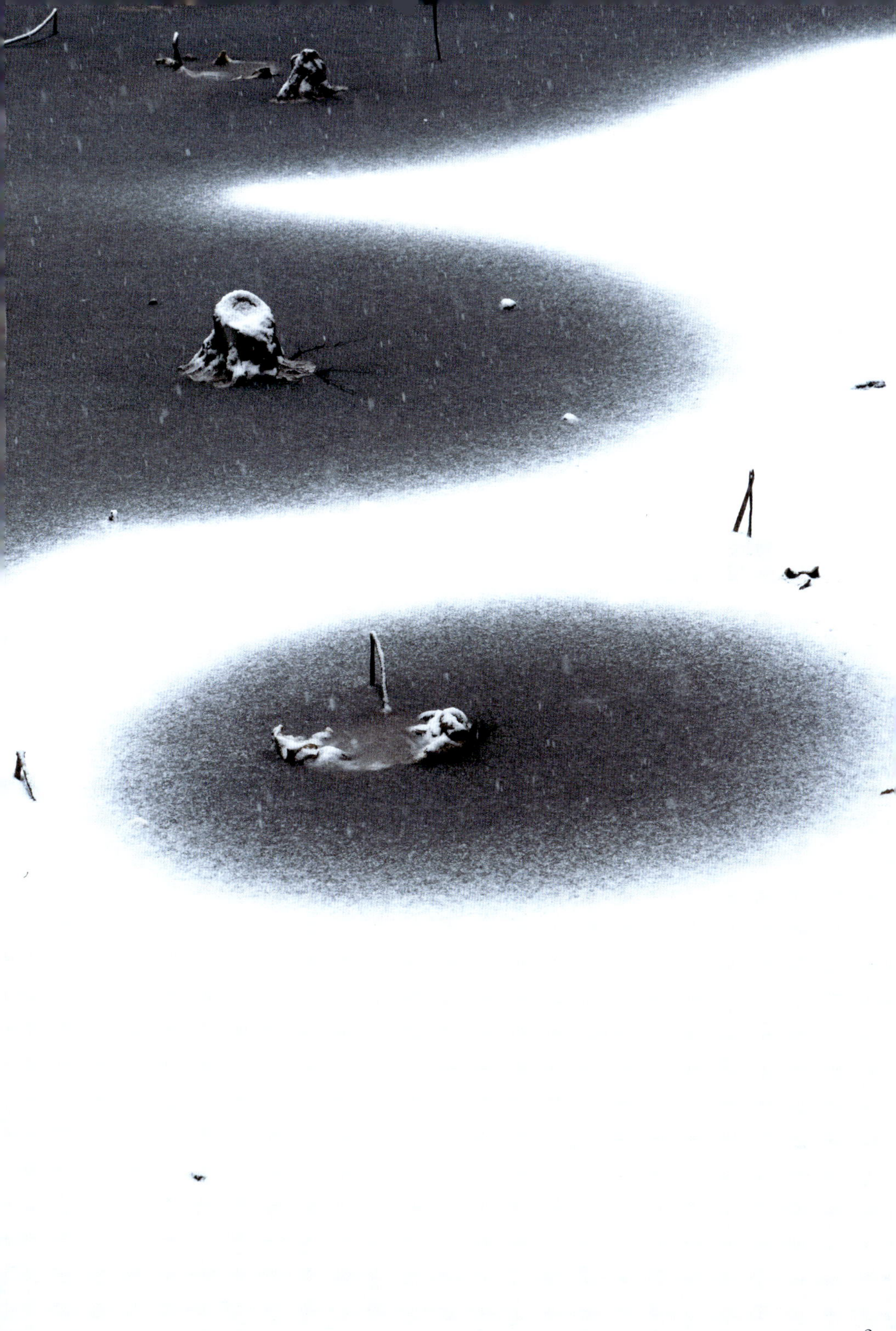

Introduction

Ink wash painting was born during China's Tang Dynasty (618-907). When this East Asian painting tradition was introduced to Japan together with Zen Buddhism during the mid-Kamakura period (1185-1333), ink wash paintings had already achieved maturity during the Song period (960-1279). This art thrived during the Muromachi period, with enormous impact on Japan's spiritual culture and art world, with ink wash paintings becoming a major component in the development of painting from Japan's Middle Ages on.

Ink wash painting is not technique for realistic depiction. It is regarded as a coherent format that integrates subject, composition, technique, and ways of appreciating paintings. It does not use colors but renders forms through light and dark tones of ink, shading, and blurring. This radical change from earlier line-based painting styles created a world quite different from paintings in colors.

Early ink wash painting in Japan was modeled on Southern Song painting. In Japan's Northern and Southern Courts period (1336-92), high-ranking priests, e.g., the

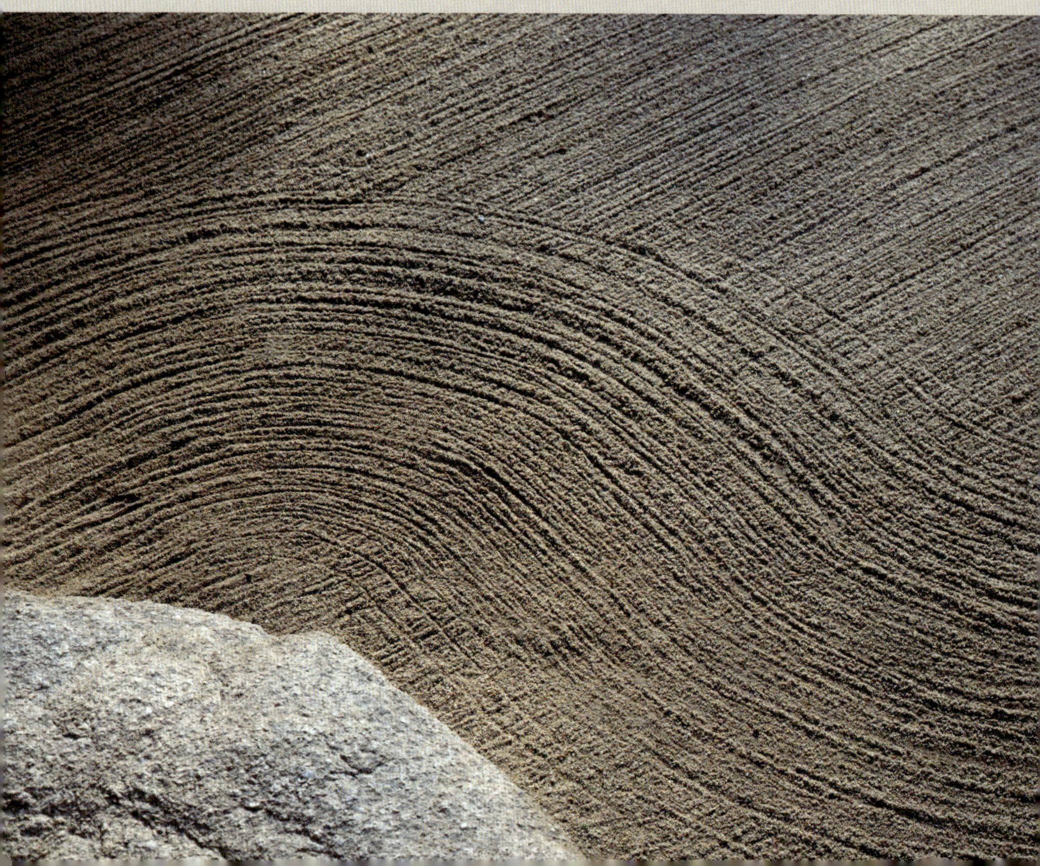

Zen priests Kaō Ninga and Mokuan Ryōen, were already creating mature Song style paintings. They were followed by Minchō, Josetsu, and Shūbun, whose achievements were carried on by Sesshū, who brought ink wash painting to great heights during the Muromachi period (1392-1573).

During Japan's Warring States period, the rise of Sesshū's students and samurai painters expanded the world of ink wash painting, which had been limited to Zen temples, to reach all parts of Japan. The preferences for painting subjects also changed from Zen-related themes to landscapes and bird-and-flower and other gorgeous topics. This period was the turning point when ink wash painting was integrated into Japanese culture. The exemplary work from this period was Hasegawa Tōhaku's Pine Trees. Ink wash paintings were created that rivaled Chinese paintings in both subject matter and skill.

The Kanō School carried on that evolution. As painters by appointment to the shogunate from the late Muromachi through the Momoyama and early Edo periods, they produced large-format folding screen and sliding door paintings for temples and shrines, Osaka Castle, the Jurakudai palace, and the imperial palace. There were periods, however, when their work descended into mannerism.

During that period, while unsurprisingly in a feudal society, people's freedoms were restricted, in the world of painting, artists known as the eccentrics emerged. Among them were Soga Shōhaku and Nagasawa Rosetsu, whose work portrayed surrealistic worlds.

Despite those oppressive circumstances, it was the Nanga painters, notably Buson and Taiga, who breathed new life into ink wash painting. They depicted, based on their imaginations, Chinese landscapes they had yet to see, brilliantly creating a romantic earthly paradise.

This book introduces five centuries of ink wash painting through these works, exploring the distinctive qualities of Japanese ink wash painting and considering the role it has played in the history of art in Japan and its significance in the history of Japanese culture.

「日本の水墨画雑感」 畠中光享

　水墨は現在でも、描いている人数や団体、教室が大変多い。それは墨と筆、紙だけで描けるからである。ただしその多くには写生や写意がなく、写真をもとに墨の白黒で描かれているだけで、何の感興もわかない。

　それは明治以降の日本画にもいえる。本来絵画は二次元の平面芸術であるのに、今や線や色の美しい絵は消えてしまった。西洋では写真の発明と共に、平面にそこにあるがごとく三次元のものを描くという絵画は、一気に崩れてしまった。絵画はもともと二次元芸術である。平面に三次元を追求するということは、一神教であるキリスト教において、人が神にどれだけ近づけるかということへの挑戦であり、レオナルド・ダ・ヴィンチ（1452〜1519）が活躍したルネサンス期までは、絵画は平面的、象徴的、装飾的に描かれていた。建築においても、ルネサンス前のゴシックの時代には高い尖塔の教会が建てられたが、それも天に届くように高く、人間がどこまで神に近づけるかという思想であった。

　絵を見るにも宗教と歴史、自然から学ばねばならない。日本画は戦後に大きく変わり、日本画第二芸術論という言葉ができた。第一は油絵で堅牢なマチエールの油絵の方が上であり、戦後の日本画はいまだにそのコンプレックスから脱することができず、今でもほとんどすべての日本画は後期印象派から抜け出していない。

　再び水墨画に戻る。戦前までの絵を描く基底材の多くは絹であり、それは西洋から入って来た空気遠近法を見事に表現するのに最適のものであった。菱田春草の名作「落葉」も琳派の没骨法に西洋の写生的空気遠近法を用いている。横山大観も絹に墨を用いているからあれほどの効果的な墨によるぼかしが出来た。上村松園の神技的な髪の生え際のぼかしも、絹と微粒子の顔料である墨だからこそできる賜物である。紙であれば絹のようなぼかしはとてもできない。明治期は江戸時代までの中国絵画（狩野派など漢画や幕末からの文人画）と西欧絵画の葛藤の時代であった。そのため墨を主にした絵では、西洋画に伝統的な中国絵画の影響を受けた中途半端なもの多く描かれた。

　基底材は重要で、絹は微粒子の墨には適している。紙は植物性繊維であるから発色が悪いが絹は動物性繊維であるために発色が良い。しかし絹は膨張、収縮が激しいため絵具を厚く塗ることができない。戦後の日本画は紙一辺倒になったため、本格的な水墨画はなくなり、意味もない厚塗りの日本画が溢れてしまった。基底材と墨を一考する必要がある。

　昔から水墨画は紙に描かれるが、墨の発色が悪いため多くは発墨のために紙に泥を漉き込んだ紙を使用している。このことも見落とされがちであるが水墨画の重要な点である。水墨画は勿論中国で発展し、名品の模写がずっと続けられてきた。唐代の残存する絵画は古墳壁画などが多いが、ほとんどは酸化第二鉄の黄土や代赭に墨で描かれている。敦煌壁画は漢民族の絵でなく極彩色の絵は別格である。唐代に描かれたといわれる「女史箴図」もその後の写しである可能性が高い。

　一般に宋元画といわれるが、宋、元の時代に格調の高い水墨画が描かれた。北宋の時代は郭煕（北宋の水墨画か）など、より豪壮で気高い山水画が描かれた。そのような神品の絵画は日本人には近寄りがたく、女真族の金に華北を奪われて南遷し首都を臨安に移した南宋の絵画は日本で好まれた。とくに南宋の花鳥画は

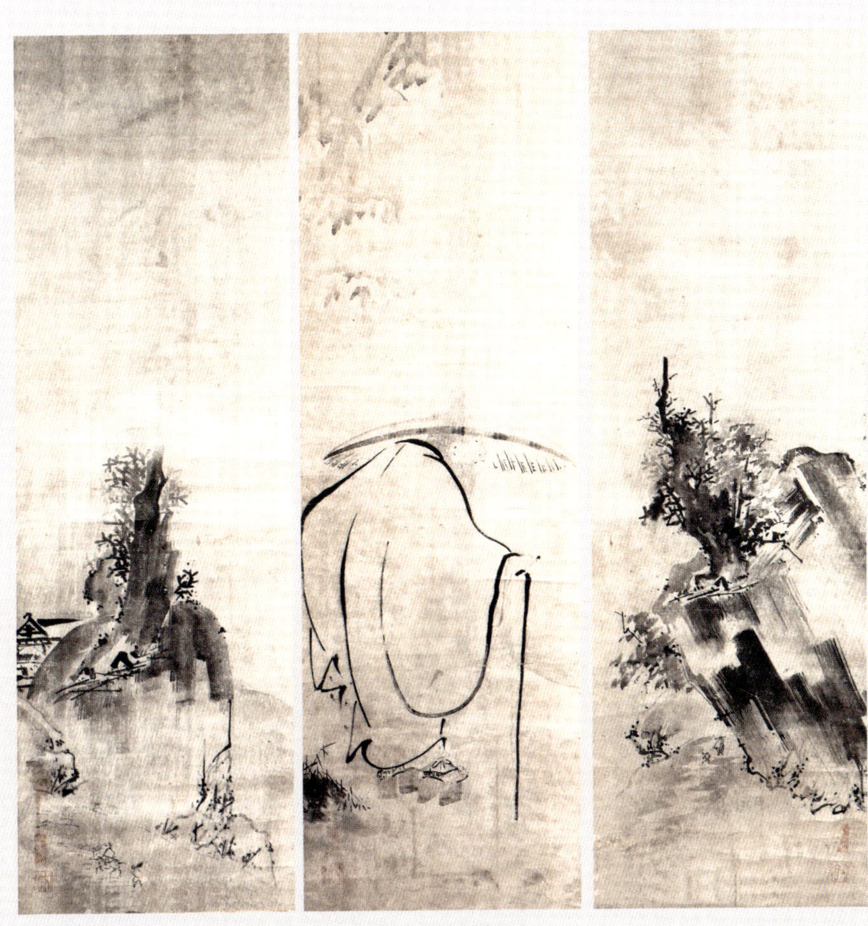

「雪中人物図」海北友松（筆者蔵）
薄墨で雪の様子がよく出ている。衣服は飄々とした墨線で描かれているが手は密な線で
的確な表現である。顔は細い線で繊細に描かれている。左右は破墨山水図である。

足利時代には莫大な値で取引された。その頃は有名な「桃鳩図」や「芙蓉図」などの彩色された絵も描かれていたが、次の元時代に入るとほとんどが水墨で描かれている。墨だけで描かれている絵も多いが、墨を主に使用し僅かな彩色を施している絵も多く、それも含めて水墨画といわれている。明時代まではなんとかすぐれた水墨画が描かれているが、それ以降の中国の水墨画は私の目に留まらない。その後も中国では水墨画が描かれ続けたが、墨に五彩ありの思想からか色彩に乏しい。

　室町時代、雪舟等揚が遣明船に同乗して中国に渡ったが、彼は当時の明の絵画を学ばずに南宋絵画に傾倒した。雪舟の審美眼である。同じように藤原時代に和様の仏像彫刻が完成したが、それを引き継がずに鎌倉の慶派の仏師は天平回帰からの新表現を追求した。すぐれた作家達はその時代や近い時代の真似はしない。雪舟は画聖とまでいわれ、日本の水墨画の頂点を極め、国宝だけで６点もある。

　雪舟伝といわれている作品が多くあるがどこまでが雪舟かはわからない。かなりの数の絵が描かれ、それなりに伝わっていると私は思っている。江戸中期の円山応挙にしても学者は伝世している真筆（しんぴつ）は少ないというが、弟子が五千人もいて需要に応じて描いていた応挙作品は、最低でも五千点はあるはずで、三百年余り前の絵は少なくともその十分の一は残存していると思っている。歴史に残っている画家は数多く制作している。もったいぶって現在の学者は残存が少ないということをいって貴重性を高めているように思えてならない。

　先に述べたように室町時代は雪舟の輩出を見る。鎌倉・南北朝時代からは武士の禅宗への庇護と共に中国から禅画僧の牧谿（もっけい）を呼んだ。日本人からは如拙や雪舟の弟子系統や、彼に私淑した画家が次々と現れる。長谷川等伯や海北友松などは、安土桃山時代から江戸時代初期にかけて活躍し、優れた水墨画を多く残している。東京国立博物館で必ず正月に展示される有名な長谷川等伯の「松林図屏風」は素晴らしい空気感を宿し、日本水墨画の頂点といわれているが、あくまでも本画ではなく下絵だということに気づいて欲しい。

　また伊豆の狩野川辺り出身といわれる狩野派の画師が、信長や秀吉と深い関りを持ち、徳川幕府の時代になると狩野探幽が御用絵師となる。狩野派は全国の藩城や寺院の壁画や襖絵を独占して制作し、江戸時代が終焉するまでその権勢は続いた。探幽はまた深く雪舟に私淑し、雪舟の絵の極め書きも数多く行っている。

　京都にある二条城は天皇を招くための城としてつくられたが、江戸時代を通じて徳川将軍の上洛は三度しかない。一度目は家康の時でその折に築城され、二度目は三代家光の時で増築された。将軍上洛の度に二千面を越す障壁画が新たに描かれるのが習わしであった。家康上洛の折の障壁画は焼かれ一点も残っていない。

　現存するのは三代家光の時のものである。三度目の上洛は慶喜の大政奉還の折であったが、その頃には既に幕府の力は失墜し、障壁画や襖絵の新調などは出来る余裕は無かったのである。多くは金箔極彩色のように思われているが、将軍の寝所などの重要な私的空間は、探幽が自ら水墨画を描いている。

　松と鷹を止まらせたような広間は、にらみを利かせるための外様大名用のもので、親藩、譜代用には穏やかな四季大和絵調のものが描かれている。狩野派は漢画であり、主題も中国山水や楼閣、人物は唐人、唐子で、憧れであった中国画にいかに追随していたかがわかる。

　江戸時代の元禄頃までには商人の力が強くなる。将軍の膝元である江戸においては町人の文化は浮世絵くらいであったが、江戸から遠く離れた京・大坂では町人文化の絵師が出現する。それまでは絵師は僧や一部の武士でしかなかったが、富裕商人の台頭で京都では俵屋宗達、尾形光琳といった、後に琳派と呼ばれる絵師が出現し、漢画に飽きた町衆に求められるようになった。一方で円山応挙や伊藤若冲といった町絵師も人気を博す。

　当時の画家番付には第一は応挙、第二は若冲と記されている。若冲は錦市場の八百屋の出身といわれているが、今でいえば京都青果商組合の理事長の家と思ってよい。応挙も若冲も最初は狩野派を学んでいるが、漢画に飽きたりず自然から独自の絵を極めていった。

　幕末近くになると大坂や京都で、抹茶道に対抗して煎茶道が急速に発展する。中国の明時代ごろから始まったと思われるが、煎茶会には中国で流行の文人画の展覧があり、池大雅や与謝蕪村、田能村竹田など文人水墨画との交流で大いに気を吐いた。煎茶と文人画は深い関係にあったのである。そして最後の文人画家は富岡鉄斎といってよいだろう。

　水墨画は中国の伝統であり、そこから日本水墨画が発展した。その後は西洋近代絵画にとって代わり、芸術といわれる水墨画は衰退する。戦後では小松均の「最上川シリーズ」や横山操の「越後路十景」が秀逸と思うが、墨を絵具として使用している画家は多くいる。墨ほど粒子が細かく線描がぼかしに適した顔料はないからである。

（はたなか こうきょう・日本画家）

Random Reflections About Japan's Ink Wash Paintings

Hatanaka Kōkyō

Even today, many people and groups produce ink wash paintings, and many classes teach this art. Why? Ink was painting requires only ink, a brush, and paper. Most of these paintings are, however, not based on sketching from life or the artists' imagination. They are merely black and white paintings in ink based on photographs. They do not interest me at all.

Something similar can be said of *Nihonga* (modern Japanese-style painting) from the Meiji period on. Painting is by nature a two-dimensional, planar art, but today paintings with beautiful lines and colors have vanished. Following the invention of photography in the West, painting that depicts three-dimensional objects as they are, on a two-dimensional surface, suddenly collapsed. Painting is essentially a two-dimensional art. Pursuing three dimensionality on a plane is a challenge like trying to see, in Christianity, a monotheistic religion, how close a human can get to God. During the Renaissance, Leonardo da Vinci (1452-1519)'s paintings were flat, symbolic, and decorative. In architecture, during the Gothic period, before the Renaissance, churches were built with tall steeples; the concept was that they were tall enough to reach heaven, suggesting how close humans could get to their god.

When we look at a painting, we must consider religion, history, and nature. *Nihonga* changed greatly after World War II. The phrase "*Nihonga* is a second class art" appeared. First class art was oil painting, with its robust matière. *Nihonga* has yet to shed that inferiority complex. Even now, almost all contemporary *Nihonga* still have not broken free from Post-Impressionism.

Returning, however, to ink wash painting: Until the 1930s, the usual support material for painting was silk. Silk was best for working splendidly using the aerial perspective introduced from the West. Hishida Shunsō's masterpiece, Fallen Leaves, used both the *mokkotsu* ("boneless"), outline-free, technique of the Rimpa School and Western-style, realistic aerial perspective. Yokoyama Taikan also used ink on silk to achieve effective blurring of the ink. Uemura Shōen's blurring of hair at the hairline, rendered with consummate skill, is a result possible only with silk and sumi ink, a pigment made of fine particles. It is utterly impossible, when painting on paper, to produce the blurred effects achieved with silk. The Meiji period (1868-1912) was the age of conflict between Chinese-style painting (Kanō School and other Chinese-influenced traditions and the literati painting that had emerged and flourished from the 1840s on) and Western-style painting. The result was that paintings using mainly ink became a half-baked combination of Western painting influenced by traditional Chinese painting.

The support is critical. Silk works well with ink's fine particles. Paper, made of plant fibers, has poor color development; the color development of silk, an animal fiber, is better. But because silk expands and contracts intensely, it is not suitable for applying pigments thickly. Because *Nihonga* shifted exclusively to paper after the war, true ink wash painting disappeared. *Nihonga* with thickly applied pigment—a meaningless approach—surged. It is imperative to think about sumi ink and its support together.

While ink wash paintings have long been created on paper, that paper usually had fine mineral particles embedded in it, to improved the expression of the sumi ink. That is a critical, but easily overlooked, point about ink wash paintings. They originated and developed, of course, in China, and countless copies of famous Chinese works have been made over the centuries. Paintings surviving from the Tang period are mainly murals in tombs, and almost all are painted in yellow loess (iron oxide), red ochre, and ink. The Dunhuang cave murals are not folk paintings; their extraordinarily vibrant colors are remarkable. The colorful *Admonitions Scroll* is also said to date from the Tang but is likely to be a copy.

Elegant ink wash paintings were produced in the Song and Yuan periods. During the Northern Song, Guo Xi and others created grand, noble landscape paintings. Those masterpieces were inaccessible to Japanese, but Southern Song paintings, created in the period after the Song lost northern China to the Jurchen Jin and moved its capital to Lin'an, were admired in Japan. Southern Song bird-and-flower paintings commanded huge prices during the Ashikaga (Muromachi, 1336-1573) period. Polychrome paintings such as the famous *Pigeon on a Beach Branch* and *Peonies* were produced, but in the following Yuan period, ink wash painting dominated. Many were painting in ink alone, but paintings that primarily used ink but had subtle colors added were also common and are included in the ink wash painting category. Superb ink wash paintings were created until the Ming period, but later examples from China are not memorable. Ink wash paintings continued to be produced in China but lacked color, perhaps because of the "ink has five colors" concept.

During the Muromachi period, Sesshū Tōyō was able to travel to Ming Dynasty China on a trading mission. There he did not study Ming painting but became an ardent admirer of Southern Song works. That was Sesshū's aesthetic sense, his eye for beauty, in action. Similarly, a Japanese style of Buddhist sculptures developed during the Heian period but fell out of use in the Kamakura period, when Kei School Buddhist sculptors introduced a new style based on the Tenpyō revival. Outstanding artists do not imitate works of their own period or recent periods. Sesshū is called "the saint of painting" and was the pinnacle of ink wash painting, with six works that are designated National Treasures.

There are many paintings attributed to Sesshū, but how many are actually his is unknown. He was a prolific painter, and a good number likely to have his own work been handed down. Scholars also believe that few of the works attributed to Maruyama Ōkyo, a mid Edo period artist, are actually by his own hand. He had, however, five thousand students, and there must have been at least five thousand "Ōkyo" paintings produced on demand. At least a tenth of those paintings may have survived from over three centuries ago. Historic painters produced many works. It seems to me that scholars today are pretentiously asserting that extant works are rare to boost their value.

Hatanaka Kōkyō, Nihonga artist

[**目次**]

雪舟等楊
Sesshū Tōyō

日本の山水画を完成させた室町時代の巨匠

せっしゅう とうよう　応永27年〜永正3年（1420〜1506）

　室町・戦国時代の画家。備中国（岡山県）赤浜に生まれる。出家して京都相国寺に入り入り、画技は周文に学んだとされる。春林周藤（しゅうりんしゅうとう）に禅の教えを受けるが、禅僧としては終生知客（しか）の位にとどまり、もっぱら絵画をもって名をなした。40歳すぎ、守護大名大内氏の庇護を受け周防山口にうつり雲谷庵（うんこくあん）をひらく。独自の山水画を追究し、日本の水墨画を大成した。

The Muromachi master who perfected landscape painting in Japan

Sesshū Tōyō (1420-1506) was a painter active in the Muromachi and Japan's Warring States periods born in Akahama, Bitchū province (now Okayama prefecture). He left home to become a Buddhist priest, entering Shōkokuji temple in Kyoto and studying painting with Shūbun. He studied Zen under Shūrin Shūtō but never advanced, as a Zen priest, beyond the position of "greeter of guests." Painting, however, made him famous. After turning forty, he moved to Suō Yamaguchi, under the patronage of the Ōuchi clan, and established the Unkokuan temple. Seeking his own approach to landscape painting, he made great advances in Japanese ink wash painting.

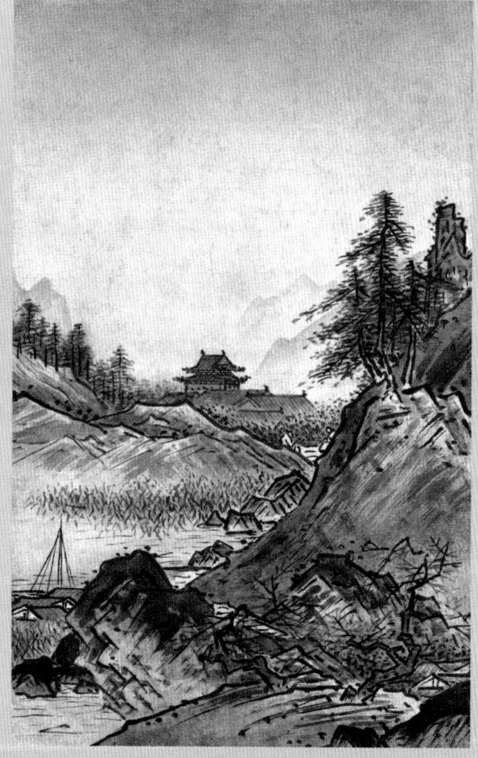

「秋冬山水図」国宝　雪舟等楊
室町時代（15世紀末〜16世紀初）
東京国立博物館蔵
Landscape of Autumn and Winter, National treasure, Sesshū Tōyō, Late 15th century-early 16th century, Tōkyō National Museum / ColBase (https://colbase.nich.go.jp)

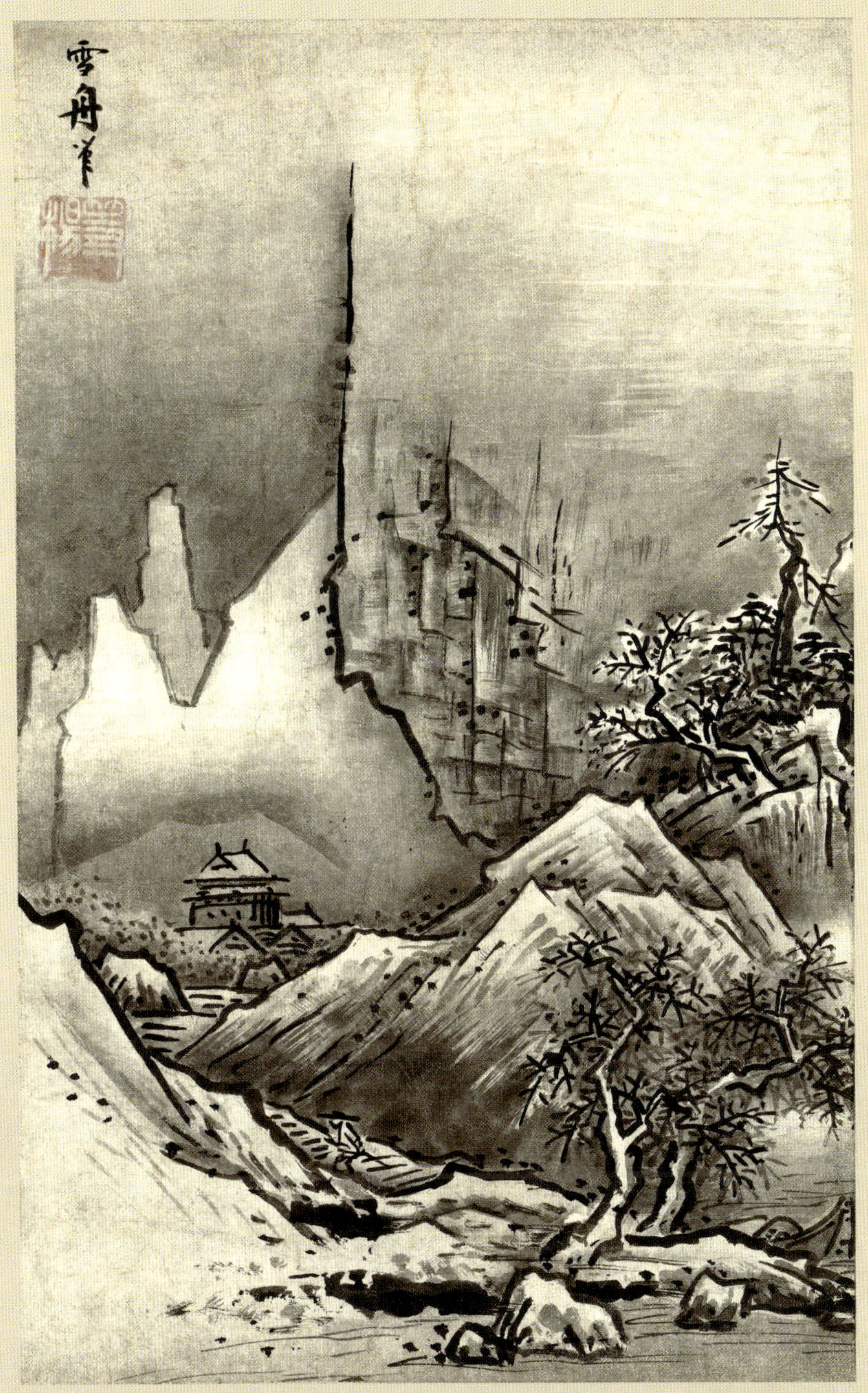

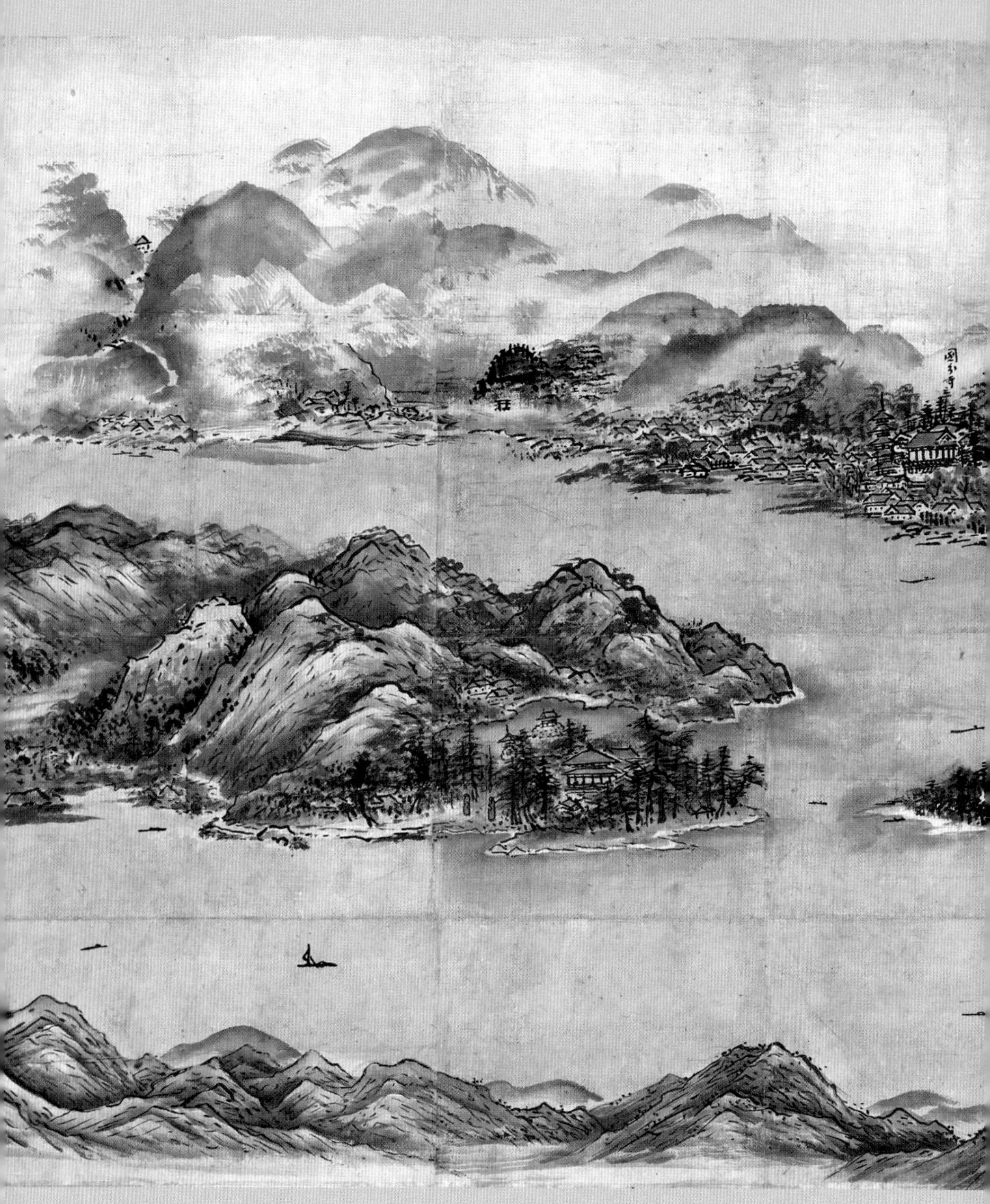

「天橋立図」国宝　雪舟等楊　室町時代（15～16 世紀）京都国立博物館蔵
Scene at *Ama no Hashidate*, National Treasure, Sesshū Tōyō, Late 15th century-early 16th century,
Kyoto National Museum / ColBase (https://colbase.nich.go.jp)

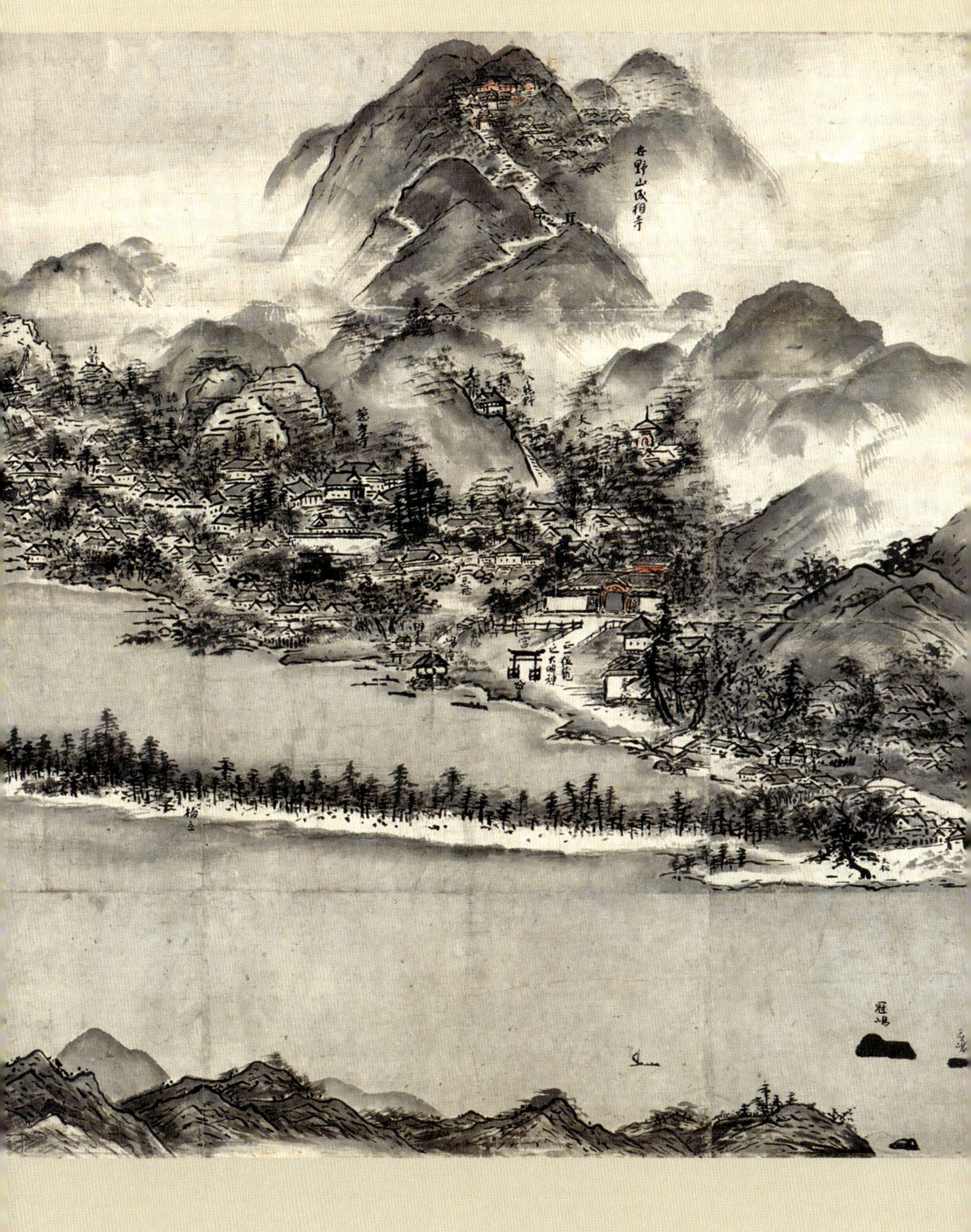

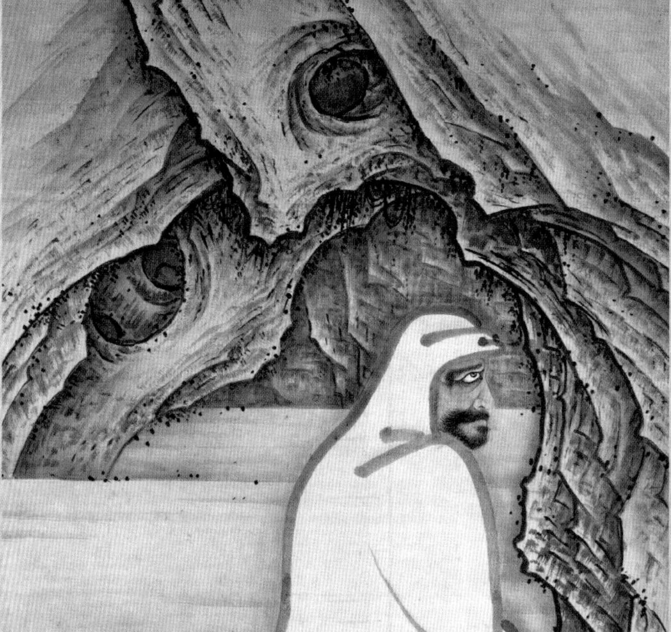

「恵可断臂図」国宝　雪舟等楊　明応 5 年（1496）齋年寺蔵
Hui-ke and Bodhidharma, National Treasure, Sesshū Tōyō, 1496, Sainen-ji

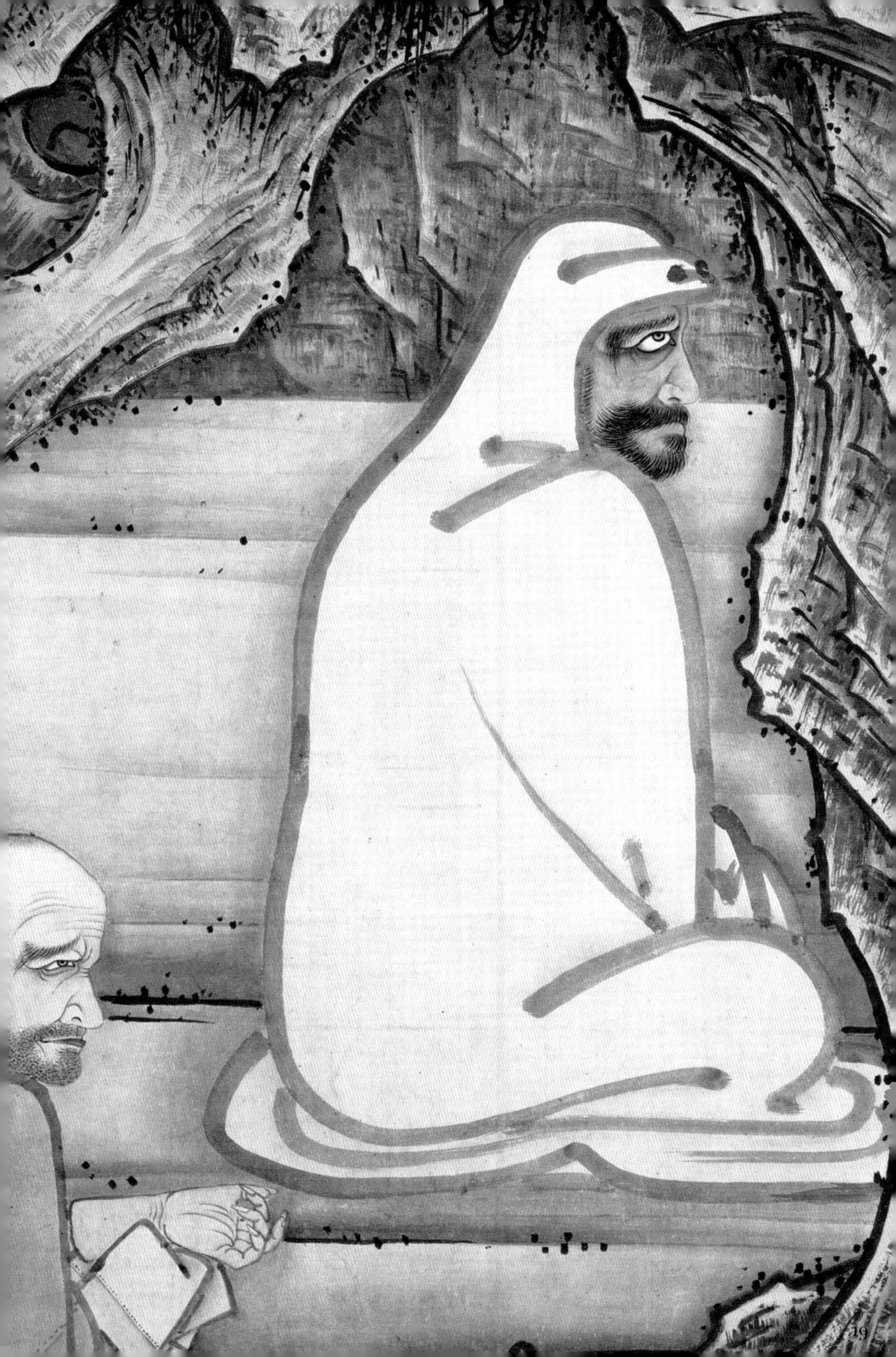

水と墨の無限の階調
Water and Ink: Infinite Gradations

　古くから「墨に五彩あり」と語り継がれてきましたが、これは墨の色には五彩、即ち青・黄・赤・白・黒の色があり、表現して得られるという意味ではなく、墨の色を抽象的に表現して言った言葉です。水墨画における墨の黒は西洋画における黒以上の色をあらわし、黒とは異なった意味を持つ豊かな色彩が含まれているということです。

　墨に水を加えると無限の階調が作り出せ、この微妙な階調の変化から色を感じることができます。つまりすべての色を超越するという意味で、眼に映る自然界の色は仮象にすぎず、墨はすべての色を凌駕しているのです。

　「破墨山水図」は雪舟の76歳のときの作品。墨一色の濃淡で風景をあらわした水墨画ですが、とても大雑把な絵なので何が描かれているかよくわかりません。薄く描かれているのが遠くにそびえる岩山、真ん中の少し濃い墨がその手前の小高い山で、いちばん下が、近くの山と穏やかな水面です。画面の上にいくほど遠い景色を描くというのが山水とよばれる風景画を描くときの基本なのです。

　破墨は溌墨とともに水墨画の技法で、溌墨が先淡後濃といわれるのに対し、破墨は先濃後淡といわれる用墨法です。まず濃墨によってだいたいのかたちを描き、そののち淡墨を重ねて濃淡をつけ、岩石の皴などを描き加えて立体感や生動感をあらわします。

It has long been said that "Ink has five colors," but that does not mean that ink actually comes in the five colors of blue, yellow, red, white, and black. The reference is to ink colors is an abstraction. The black of the *sumi* ink used in ink wash painting can, however, express more hues than the black found in Western paintings. It contains a rich array of tones with meanings beyond merely black.

Adding water to ink creates infinite gradations, whose subtle changes can be perceived as colors. That is, it transcends all colors; instead of a mere semblance of the colors of the natural world as our eyes see it, ink surpasses all colors.

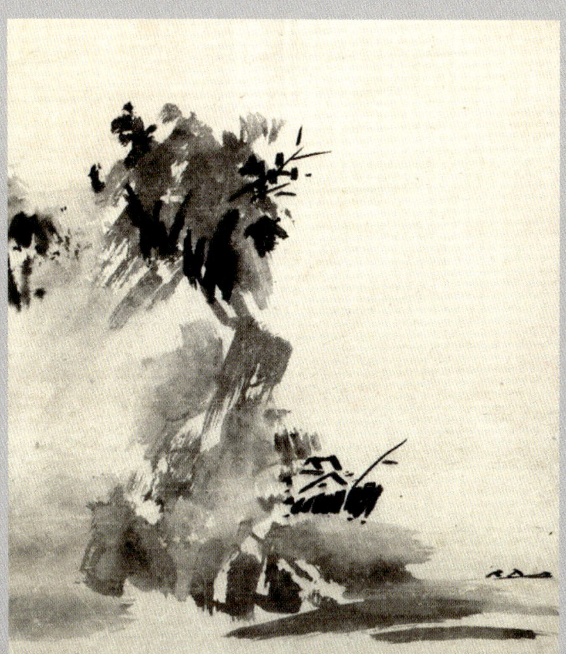

「破墨山水図」国宝　雪舟等楊筆　雪舟自序・月翁周鏡ら六僧賛
明応 4 年（1495）東京国立博物館蔵
Haboku Landscape, National Treasure, Sesshū Tōyō, Inscriptions by Sesshū, Getto Shukyo, 1495, Tōkyō National Museum / ColBase (https://colbase.nich.go.jp)

よく見ると手前の山に一軒の家が建っている。軒先から枝のようなものが出ているが、これは食事を出す店のしるしの旗です。水面には小舟も見えます。

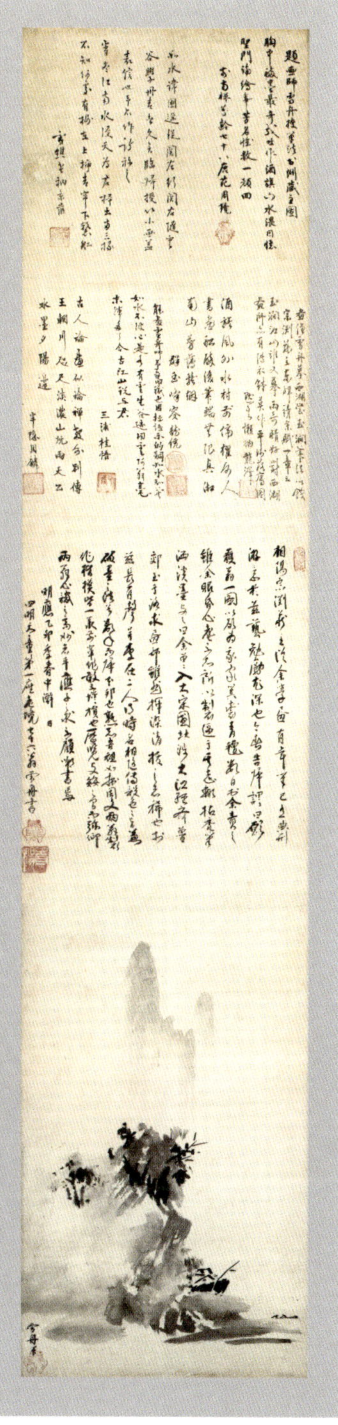

雪村周継

Sesson Shūkei

雪舟に私淑し、独自の画風を創造した禅画僧

せっそん しゅうけい　生没年不詳

　戦国・織豊時代の画僧。常陸国太田（福島県）に生まれる。戦国武将佐竹氏の一族の長男として生まれたが、家督争いのわずらわしさを避けて禅僧となる。晩年70歳の頃から会津の芦名盛氏の知遇を得て、会津に近い三春（福島県）に雪村庵を結び隠棲した。広く宋元画、ことに牧谿や玉澗などを学び、独自の様式を創造したと推定される。

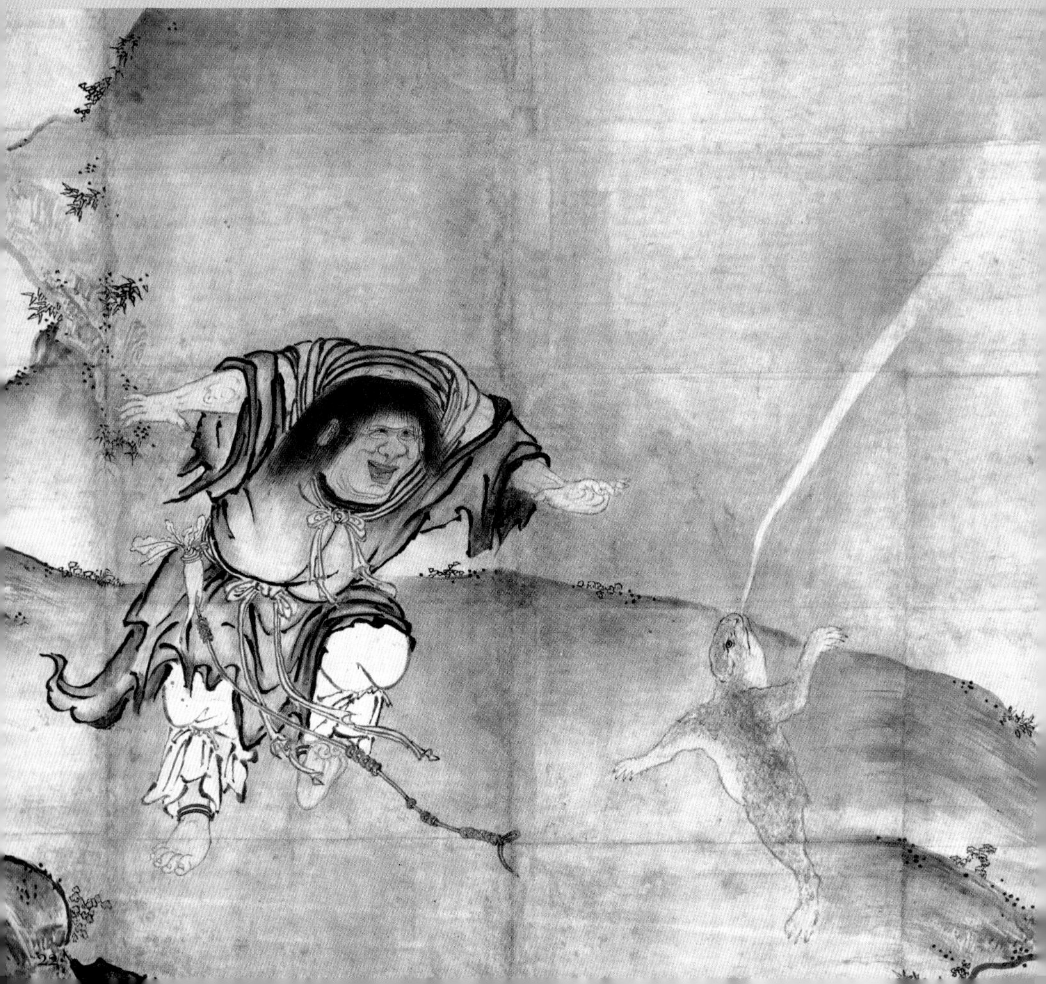

The Zen priest painter who admired Sesshu but created his own style

Sesson Shūkei was a painter priest who lived during Japan's Warring States period and the reigns of Oda Nobunaga and Hideyoshi Toyotomi. He was born in Ōta, Hitachi province (now Fukushima prefecture). He was born to the Satake clan as the eldest son of a Warring States military commander, but to avoid complex conflicts over succession, became a Zen priest. In old age, about 70, he won the favor of Ashina Moriuji of the Aizu domain and was able to build the Sesson'an hermitage, where he lived in seclusion. He is thought to have studied a wide range of Song and Yuan paintings from China, particularly Muqi and Yujian while creating his own style.

「蝦蟇鉄拐図」雪村周継　室町時代（16 世紀）東京国立博物館蔵
Immortais Tieguai and Xiama, Sesson Shūkei, 16th century, Tōkyō National Museum / ColBase (https://colbase.nich.go.jp)

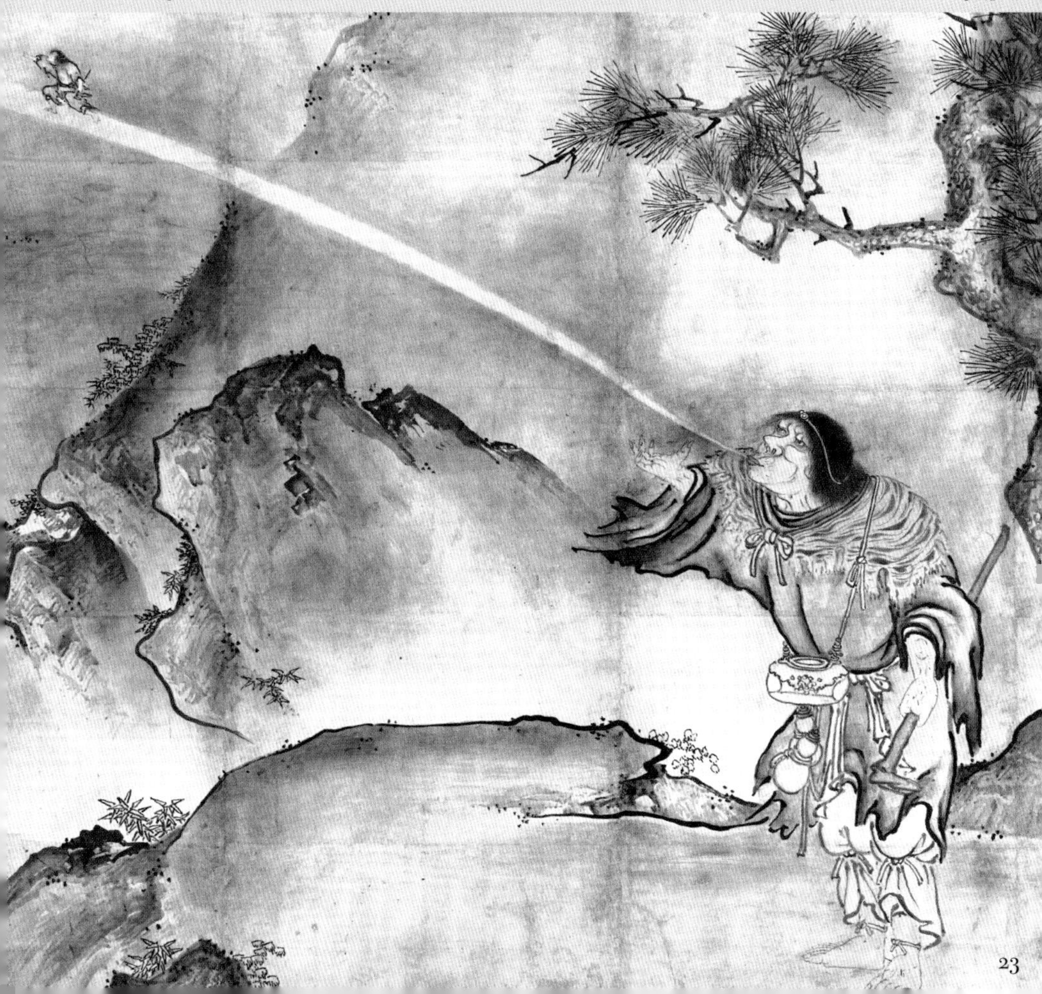

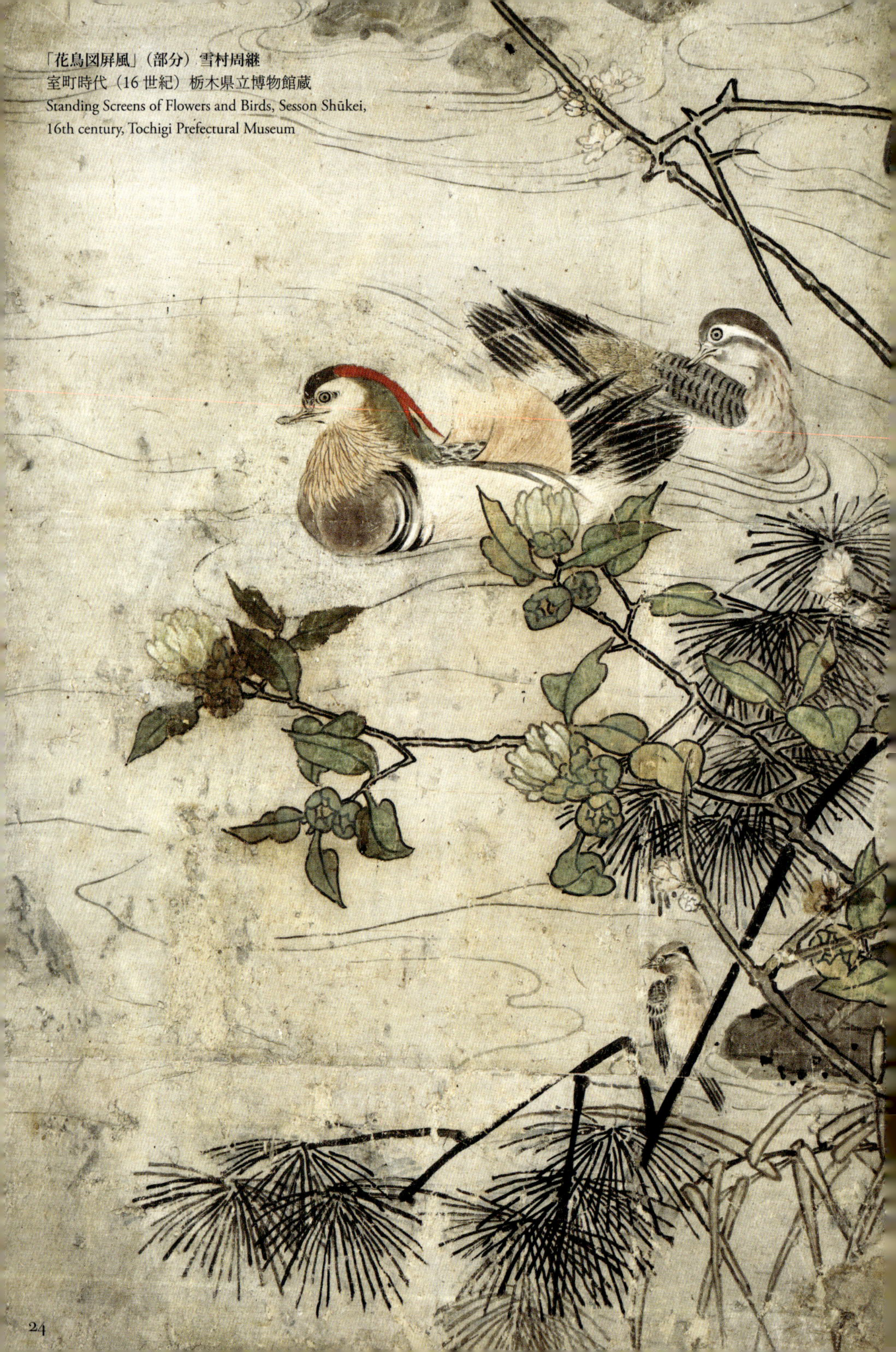

「花鳥図屏風」（部分）雪村周継
室町時代（16世紀）栃木県立博物館蔵
Standing Screens of Flowers and Birds, Sesson Shūkei,
16th century, Tochigi Prefectural Museum

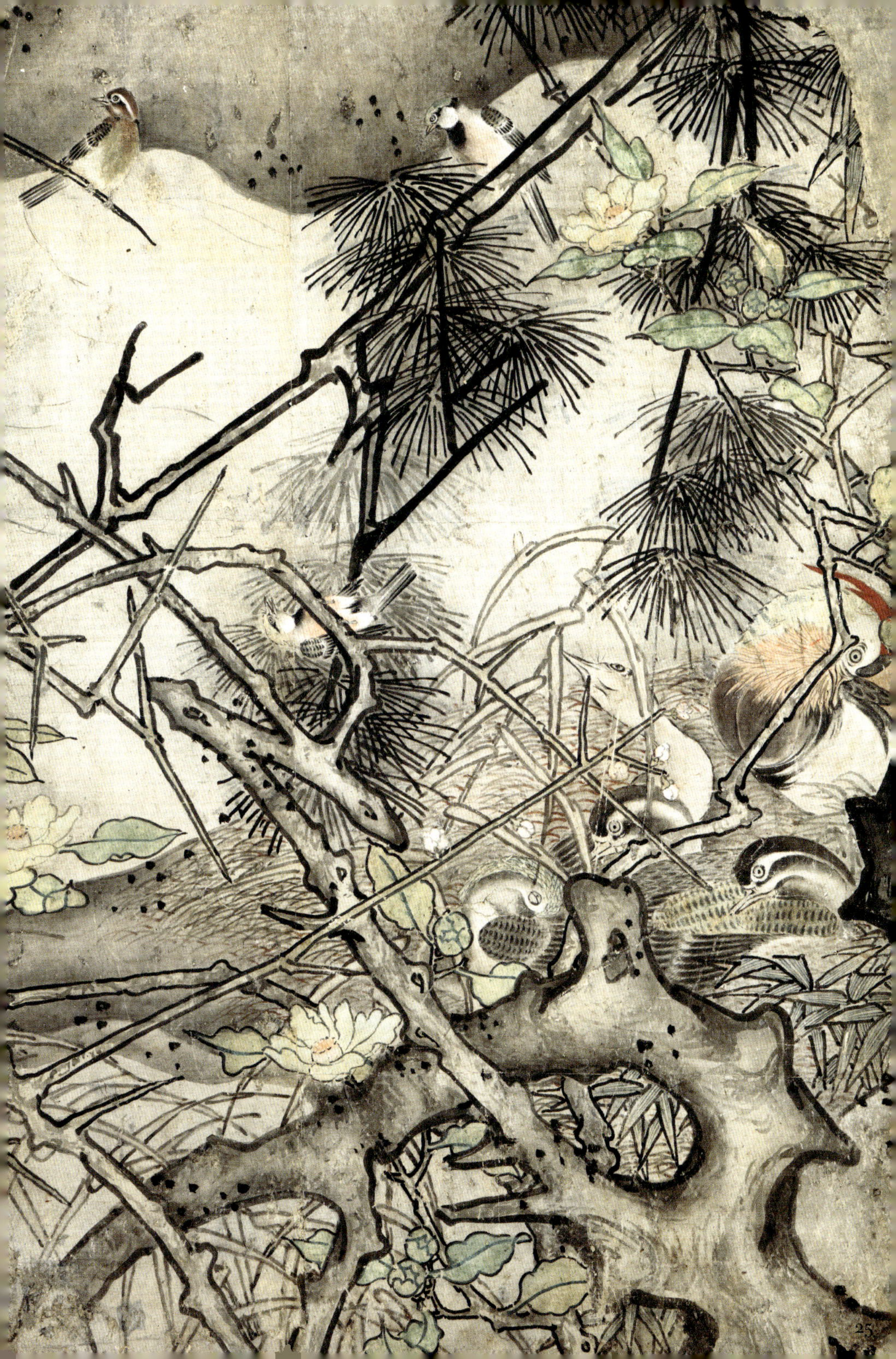

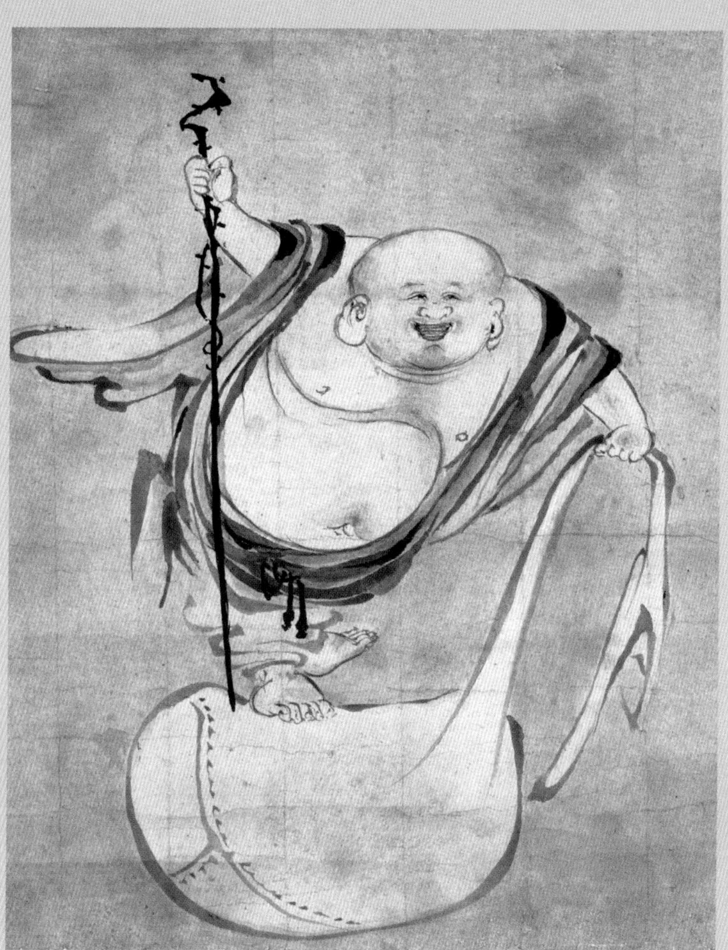

「布袋図」（部分）雪村周継
室町時代（16世紀）板橋区立美術館蔵
Budai, Sesson Shūkei, 16th century, Itabashi
Art Museum

「松鷹図」重文　雪村周継
室町時代（16世紀）東京国立博物館蔵
Hawks and Pines, Important Cultural Property,
Sesson Shūkei, 16th century, Tōkyō National
Museum / ColBase (https://colbase.nich.go.jp)

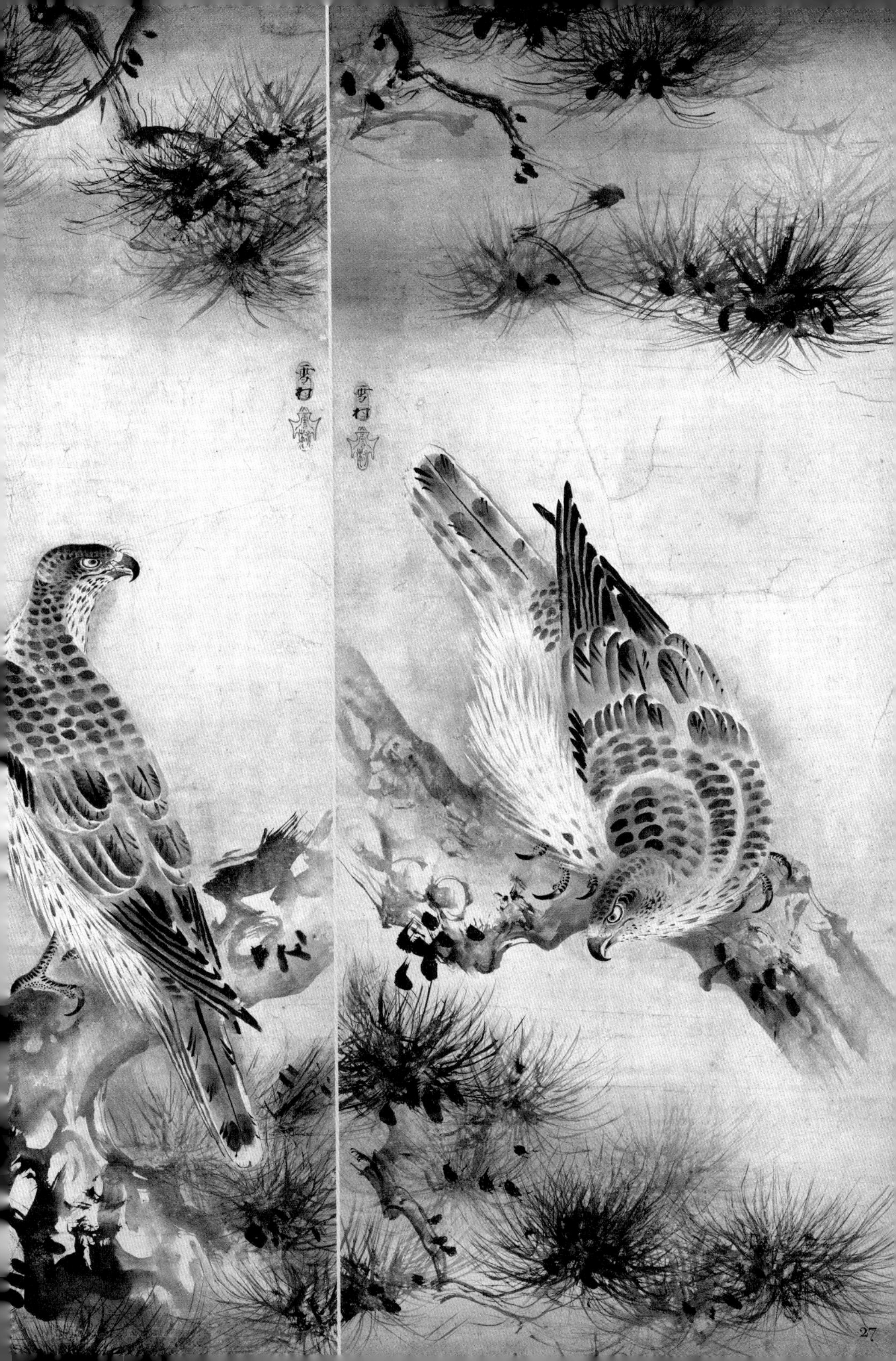

長谷川等伯

日本の心を水墨画に込めた、桃山時代の代表的画家

はせがわ とうはく　天文8~慶長15年（1539~1610）

　織豊時代の画家。能登（石川県）七尾の城主畠山氏の家臣奥村文之丞宗道の子、染色家長谷川宗清の養子。能登ではじめ信春の号で法華宗関係の仏画や肖像画を制作。のち京都で狩野派の画風や雪舟の水墨画などを学び、金碧障壁画と水墨画に独自の画風を創造した。代表作には水墨画史上最大の傑作「松林図屏風」がある。

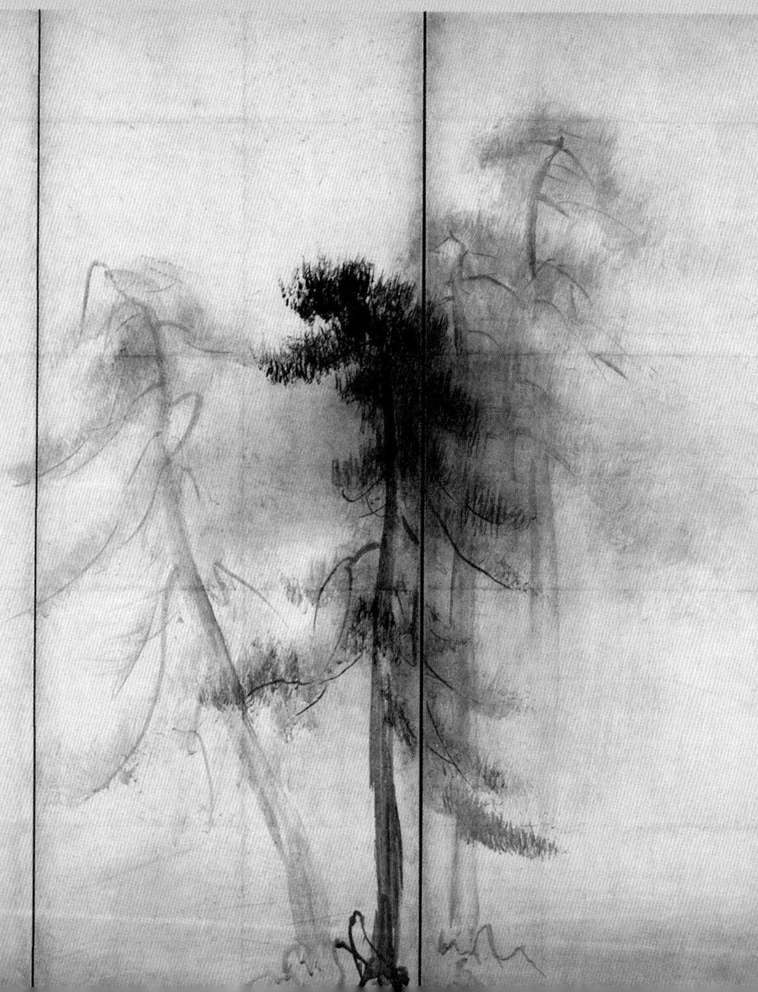

「松林図屏風」国宝　長谷川等伯　安土桃山時代（16世紀）東京国立博物館蔵
Standing Screens of Pine Grove, National Treasure, Hasegawa Tōhaku, 16th century, Tōkyō National Museum/ ColBase (https://colbase.nich.go.jp)

The leading Momoyama-period painter whose ink wash paintings captured the spirit of Japan

Hasegawa Tōhaku (1539-1610) lived during the reigns of Oda Nobunaga and then Hideyoshi Toyotomi. He was the son of Okumura Bunnosuke Sōdō, a retainer of the Hatakeyama clan, lords of the Noto Nanao Castle (Ishikawa prefecture), and was adopted by Hasegawa Munekiyo into a family of dyers. While on the Noto Peninsula, he initially used the art name Shinshun and produced Buddhist paintings related to the Lotus Sutra school as well as portraits. Later in Kyoto he studied the Kanō school painting style and Sesshū's ink wash paintings. He then created his own style of *sumi* ink painting and *kinpeki shōhekiga*, large-format paintings on screens, sliding doors, or walls using ultramarine and other bright colors on gold backgrounds. His signature work is the *Pine Trees* folding screens, the ultimate masterpiece in the history of ink wash painting.

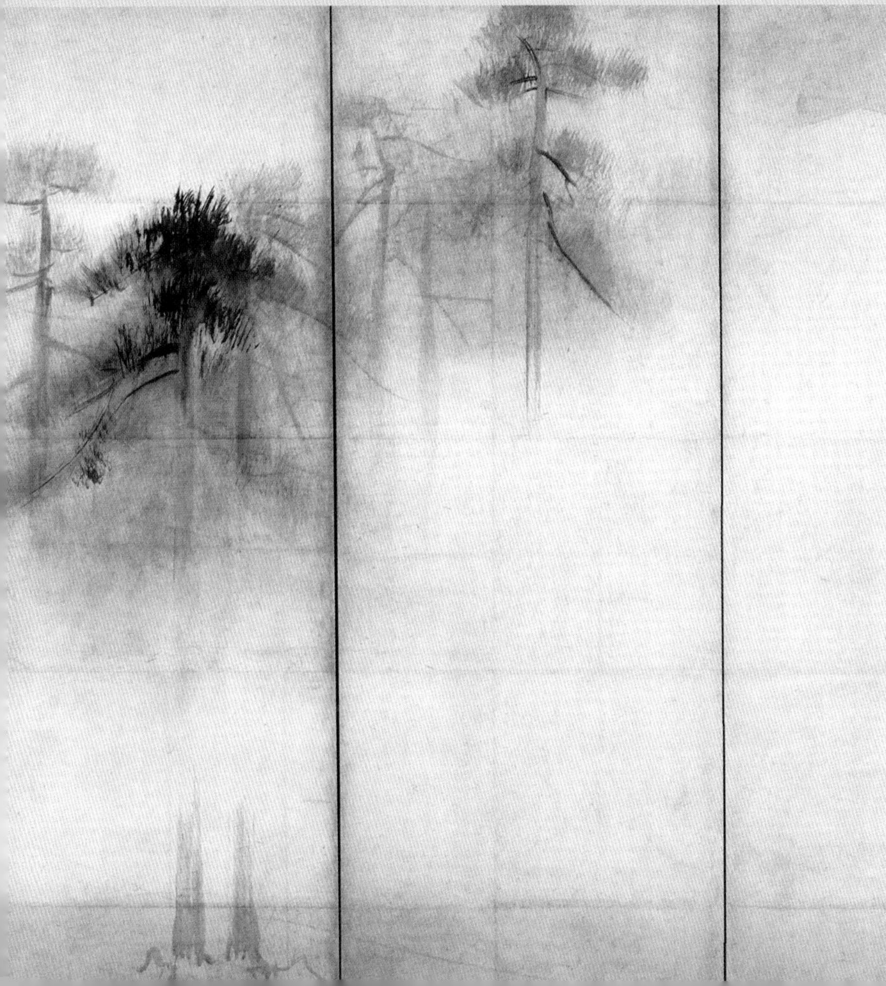

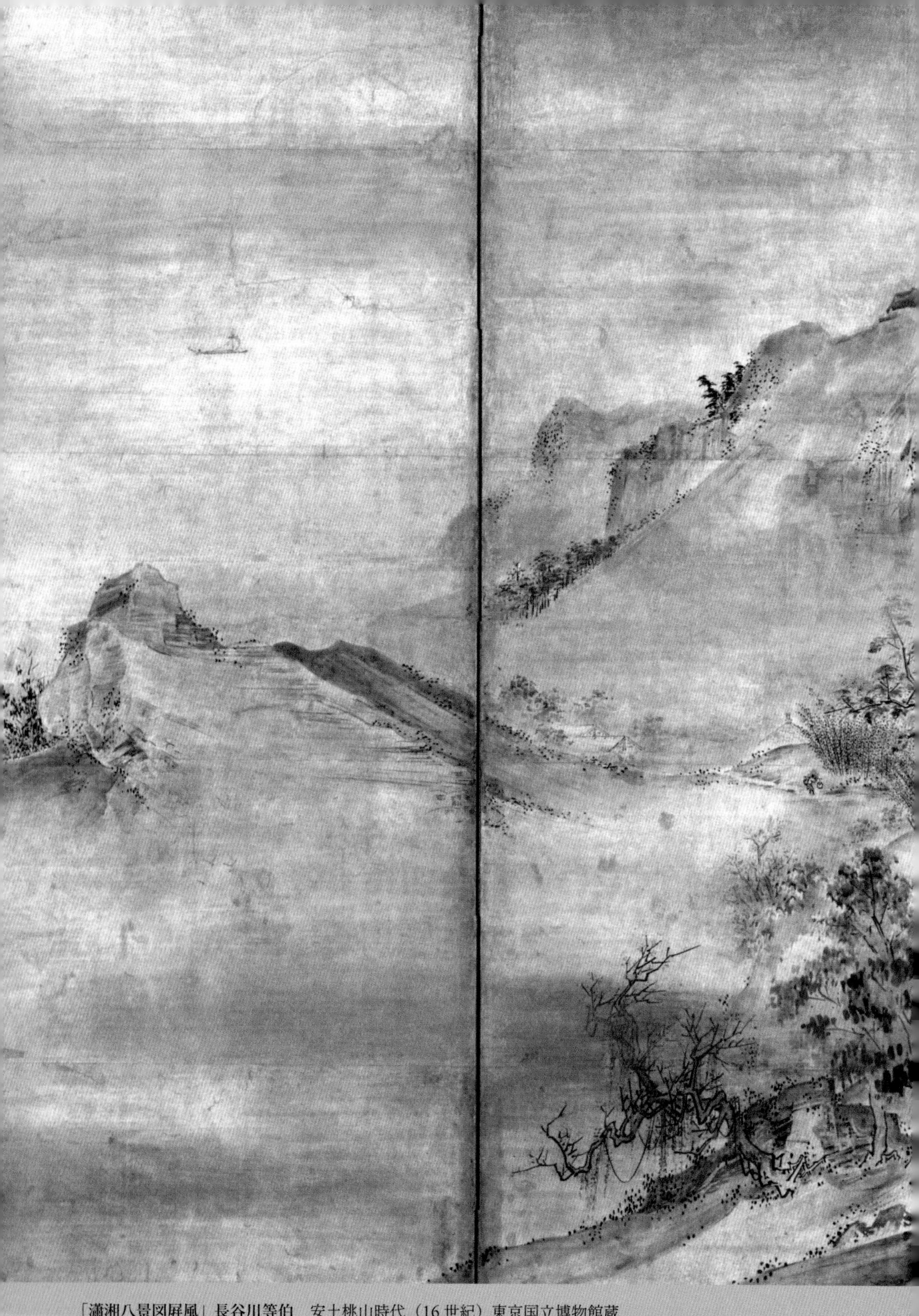

「瀟湘八景図屏風」長谷川等伯　安土桃山時代（16世紀）東京国立博物館蔵

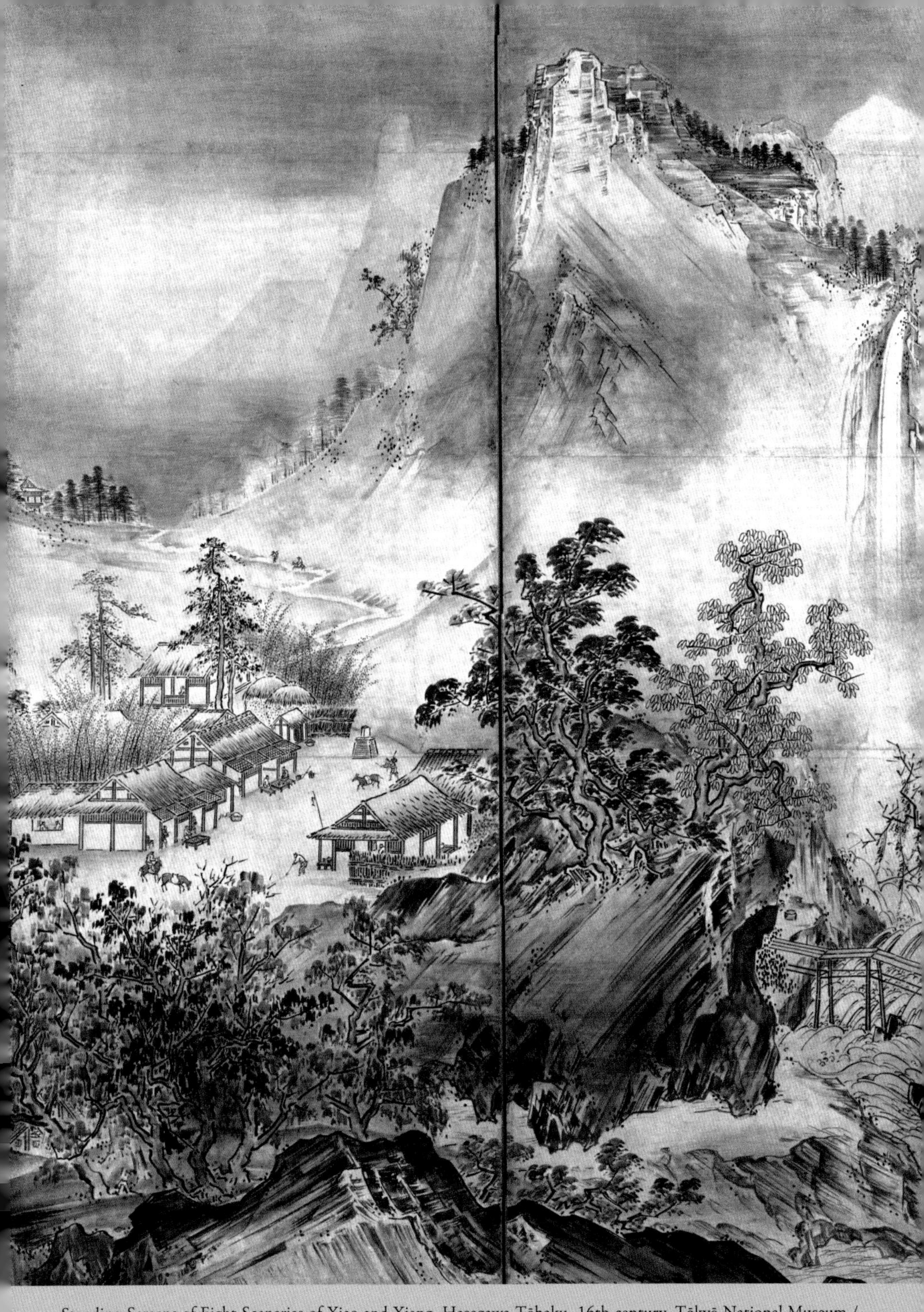

Standing Screens of Eight Sceneries of Xiao and Xiang, Hasegawa Tōhaku, 16th century, Tōkyō National Museum / ColBase (https://colbase.nich.go.jp)

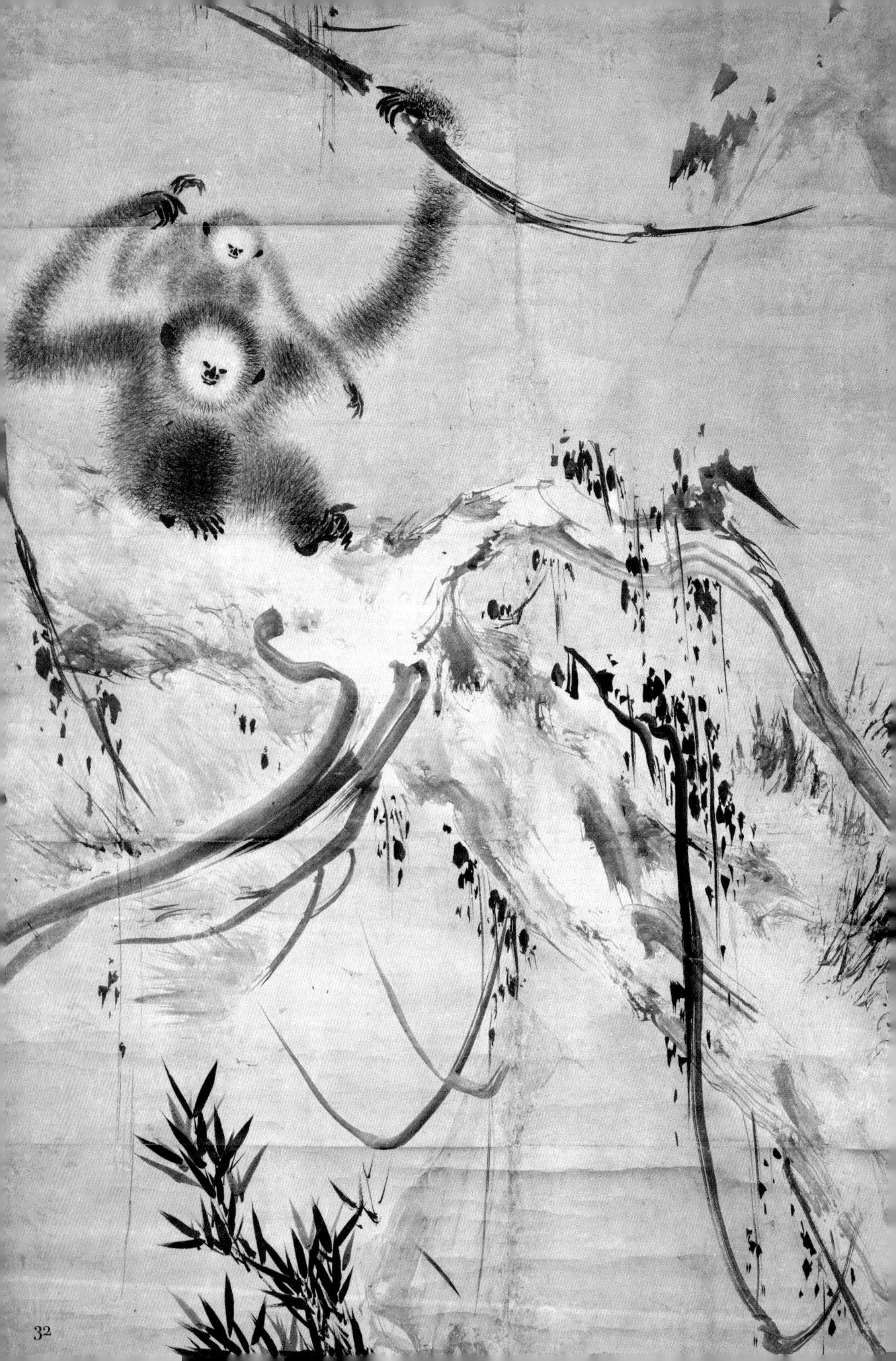

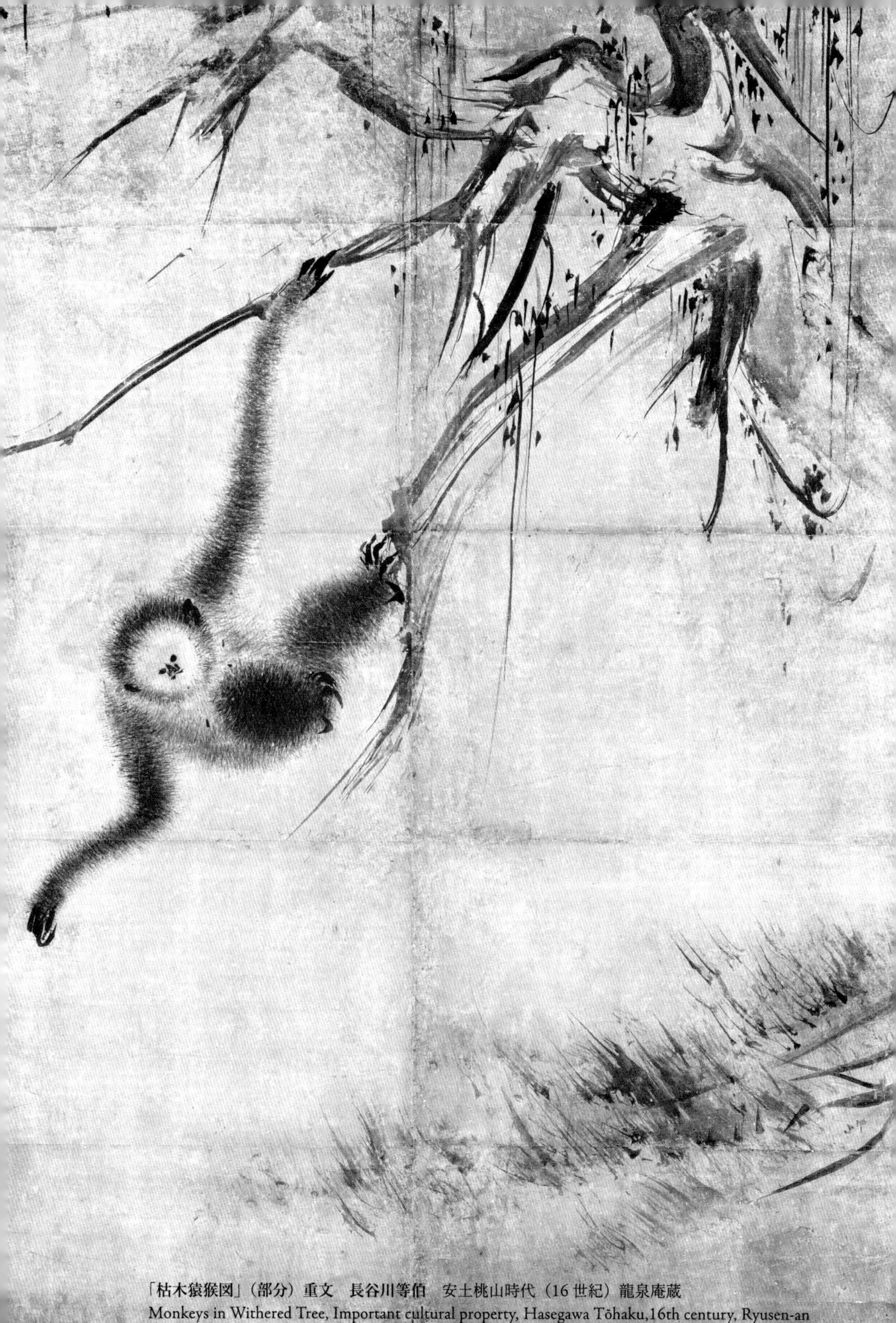

「枯木猿猴図」（部分）重文　長谷川等伯　安土桃山時代（16世紀）龍泉庵蔵
Monkeys in Withered Tree, Important cultural property, Hasegawa Tōhaku,16th century, Ryusen-an

33

海北友松

戦国の世を生きた武人画家で、海北派の開祖

かいほう ゆうしょう　天文2〜元和元年（1533〜1615）

　織豊時代の画家。近江国（滋賀県）坂田郡に生まれる。浅井長政の重臣海北綱親の三男。京都東福寺で出家したが、主家浅井家滅亡ののち還俗。絵の師は狩野元信、あるいは永徳と伝えられるが、中国南宋の梁楷の画法などを学び、独自の画風を形成した。余白のなかに豊かな情感を漂わせる作風の水墨画を得意とした。

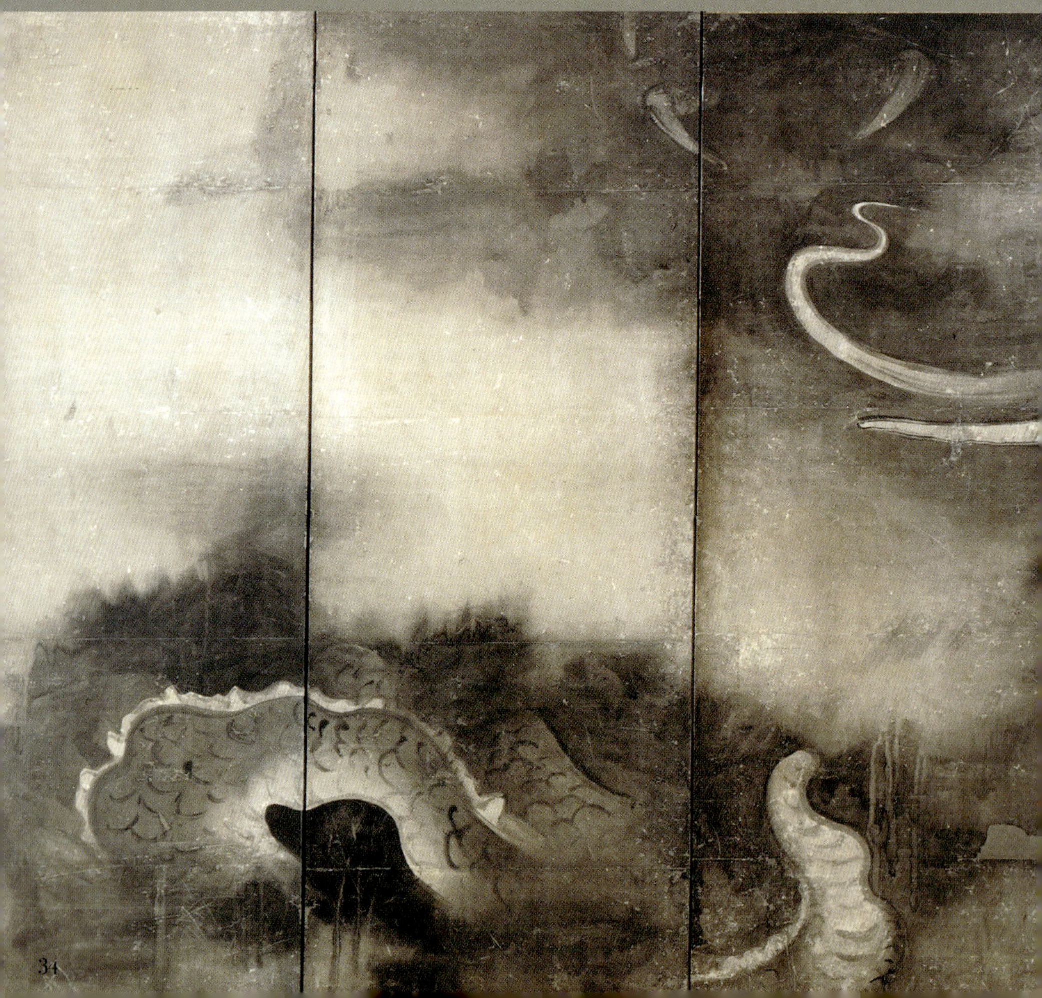

A warrior painter who lived through Japan's Warring States period
Kaihō Yūshō

Kaihō Yūshō (1533-1615) lived during the reigns of Oda Nobunaga and then Hideyoshi Toyotomi. He was born in Sakata-gun, Ōmi province (now Shiga prefecture), the third son of Kaihō Tsunachika, a senior retainer of Asai Nagamasa. He left home to become a priest at Tōfukuji temple in Kyoto, but returned to secular life after the downfall of his sponsoring family, the Asai clan. He is said to have studied painting with Kanō Motonobu or Eitoku but also incorporated the techniques of the Southern Song painter Liang Kai and other artists into his own style. He excelled at ink wash painting filled with rich feelings in its reserved space.

「雲龍図屏風」重文　海北友松　桃山時代（17 世紀）北野天満宮蔵
Standing Screens of a Dragon and Tigers, Important Cultural property, Kaihō Yūshō, 17th century, Kitano Tenmangu Shrine

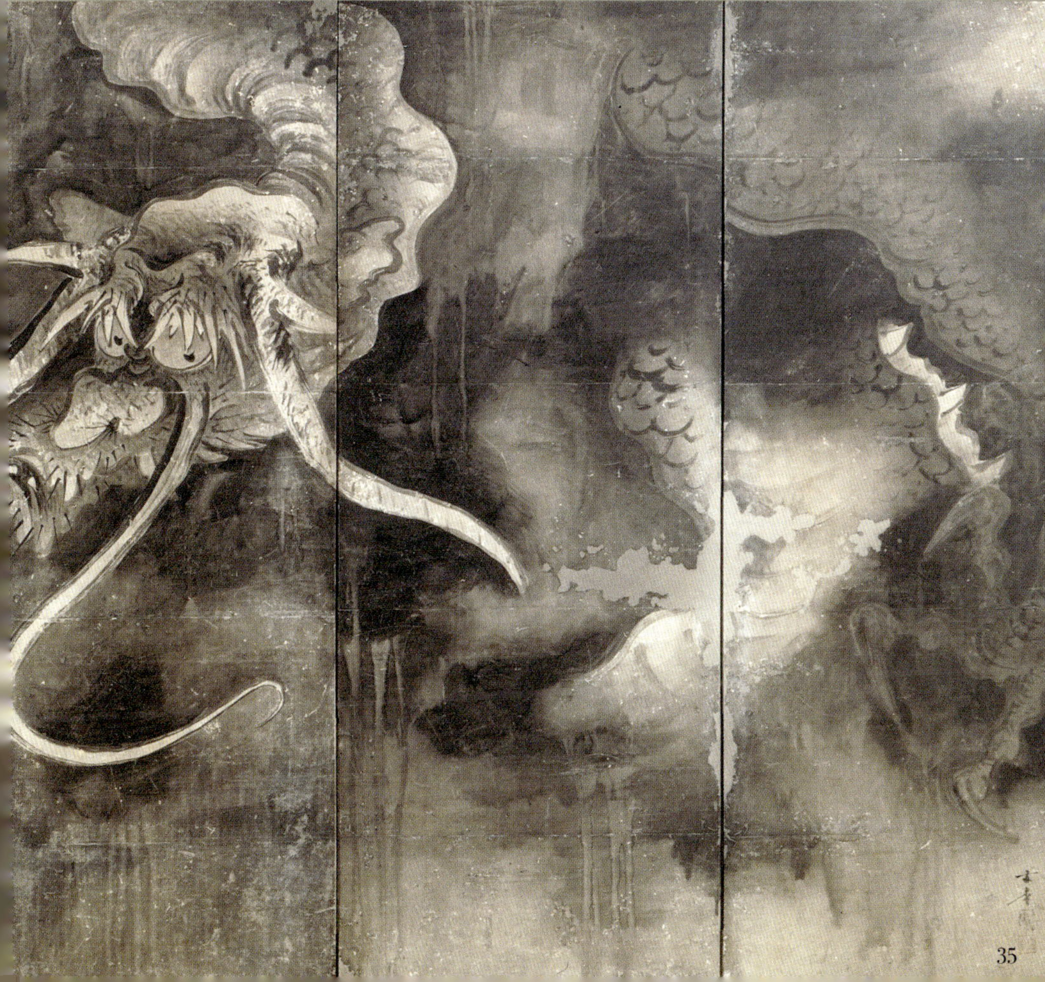

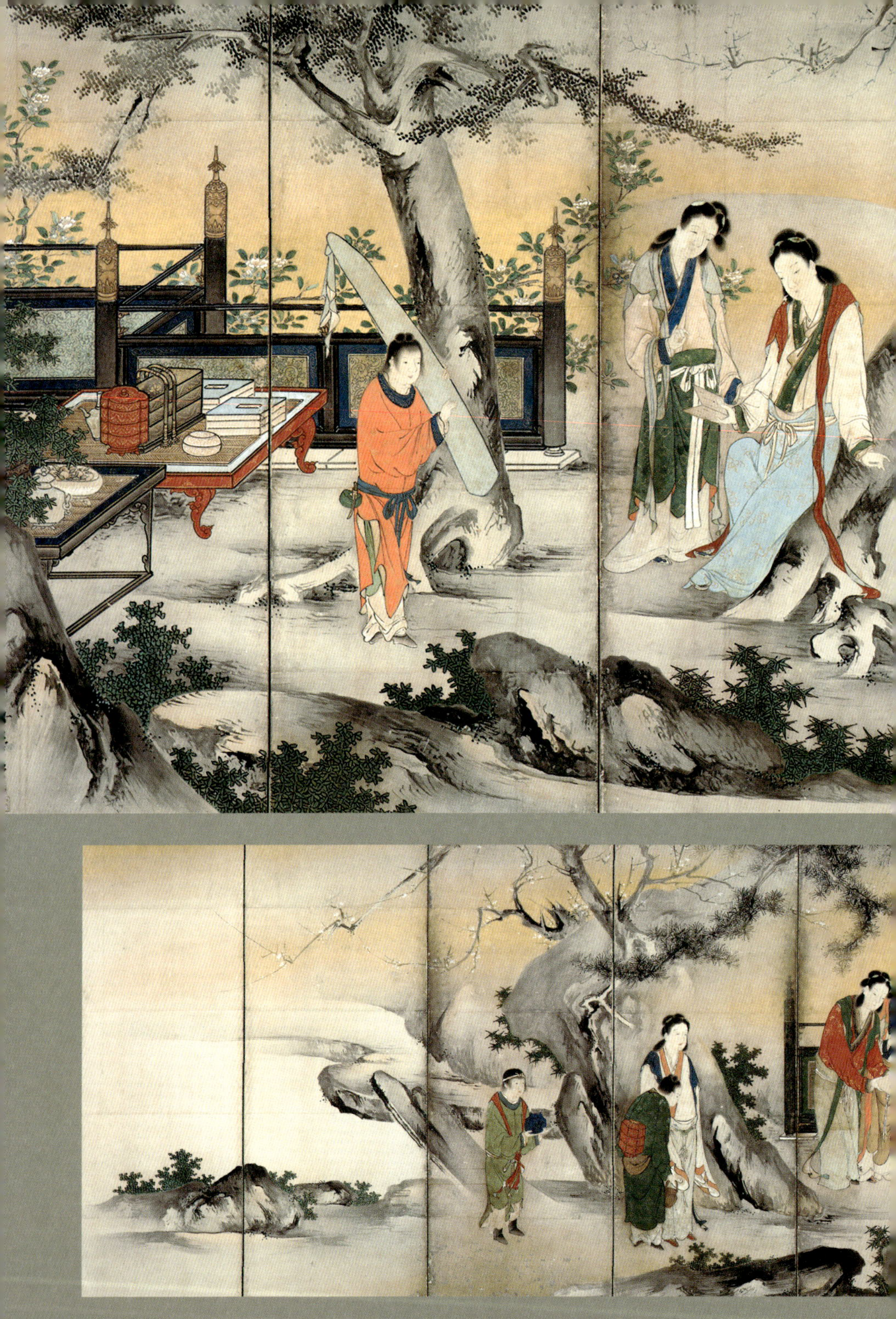

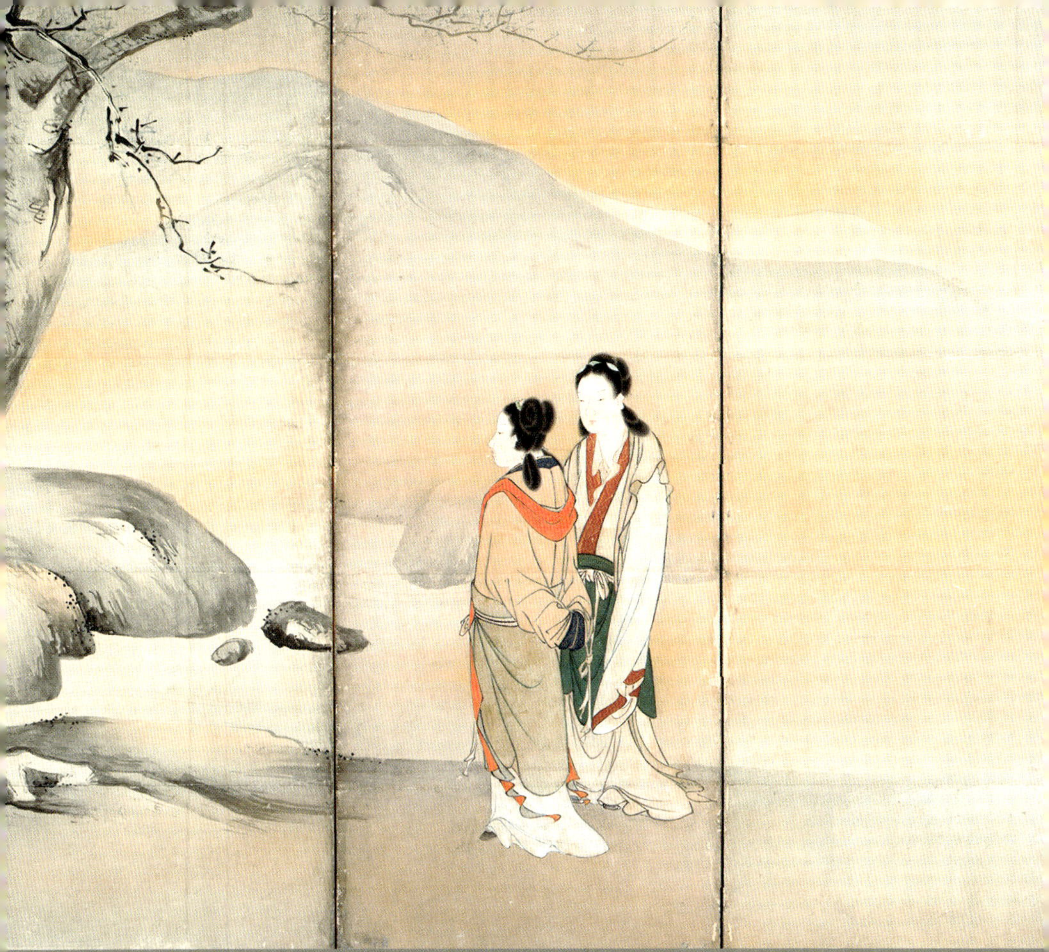

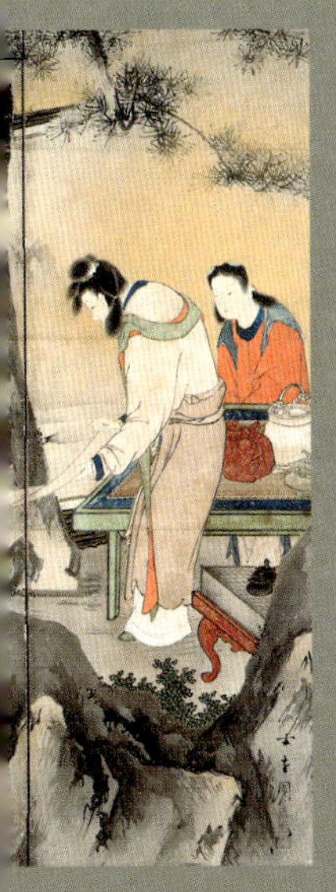

「宮女琴棋書画図屏風」重文　海北友松
安土桃山〜江戸時代（16 〜 17 世紀）
東京国立博物館蔵
Kyujyo Standing Screens of Four Elegant
Pastimes, Important Cultural property,
Kaihō Yūshō, 16th to 17th century, Tōkyō
National Museum / ColBase (https://col-
base.nich.go.jp)

禅問答と禅画の世界
The Zen Kōan and the World of Zen Painting

　禅画のモティーフは「禅宗祖師図」といって祖師の行状や悟りの場面を描いたもので、公案（坐禅をする者に考えさせる問題）の内容や、歴史上の故事人物を描いたものなどがあります。

　この「南泉斬猫」は、「この猫の首を斬らずにすむ方法や如何」という公案のひとつで、中国の唐時代の禅僧南泉普願に関する故事です。ある時、東堂西堂の両堂で猫に仏性（すべての生き物が本来持っている仏になれる性質）があるかどうかを争っていた僧たちに、南泉和尚はその猫をとらえ、どのように会得したかを説くことができるなら斬らないが、できなければ斬るといって返答を求めましたが、誰も答えられないので猫の首は切られたということです。

　日暮れになって高弟の趙州が帰ってきたので、和尚はことの次第を話し、「お前ならどう答える」ときいたところ、趙州は草履を頭に乗せてスタスタと出て行きました。これを見て南泉は膝をうち、「お前がもう少し早く帰ってきたら、猫の命は助かったものを」と言ったとのことです。

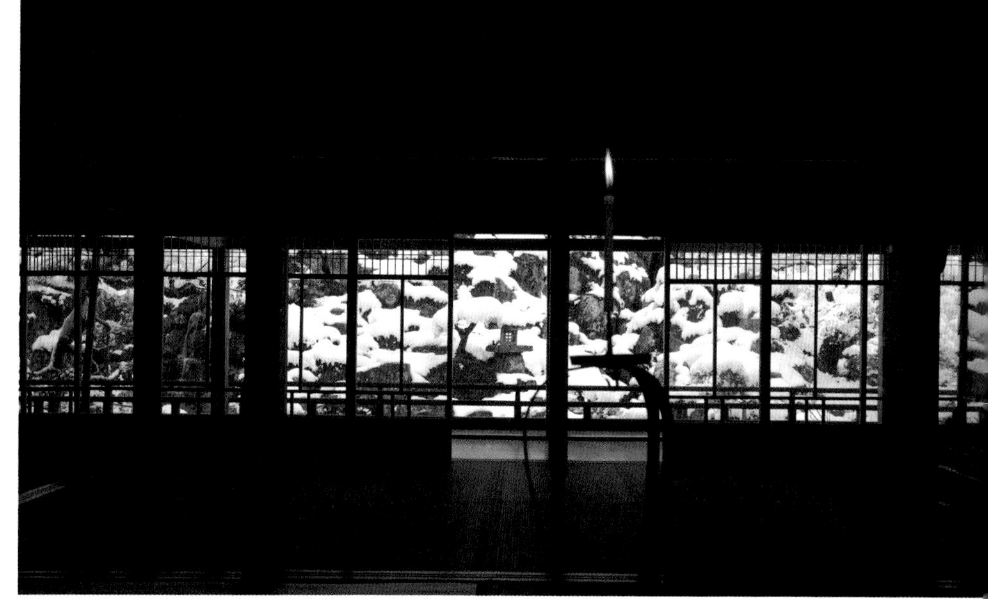

Zen painting motifs included the actions of the founder of the Zen sect and scenes of attaining enlightenment. These paintings also depict the contents of *kōan*, questions posed to make those undergoing Zen training think, and historic personages. One *kōan*, "Nansen kills the cat," is about "a way to end up not decapitating this cat." It is a tale about the Tang-period Zen monk Nansen Fugan (Chinese: Nanguan Puyuan). One day the priests in the east and west halls of the temple were arguing over whether a cat has the Buddha nature. Nansen Fugan picked up the cat and said, "If you can explain what you have learned, I will not hurt the cat, but if you have nothing to say, I will take a sword to it." When no one responded, he cut the cat's head off.

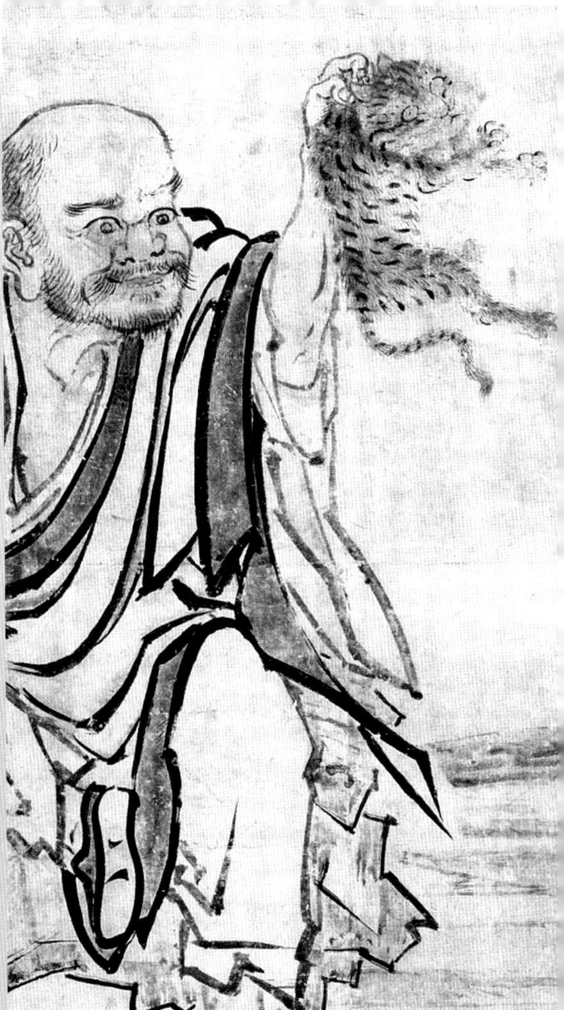

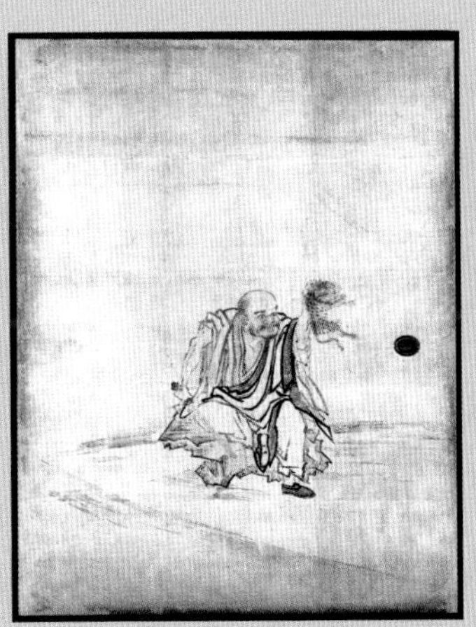

猫の首をぶら下げて、剣を片手に、「皆の者、何とでも言ってみろ、言えればよし、言えなければこの首をぶった切るぞ」と問答しているのは南泉和尚。

「南泉斬猫」（「禅宗祖師図」襖十六面の内　部分）重文　伝長谷川等伯
慶長 7 年（1602）天授庵蔵
Nansen Cuts the Cat in Two, Important cultural property, Attributed to Hasegawa Tōhaku, 1602, Tenju-an

狩野元信

Kanō Motonobu

中国の水墨画と大和絵を融合した画家

かのう もとのぶ　文明8～永禄2年（1476～1559）

　戦国時代の画家。山城国（京都府）に生まれる。狩野家二代目、狩野正信の長男。足利家の御用絵師となり、法眼に叙せられる。中国画の諸様式に大和絵の色彩や装飾性を合わせ、平明で装飾的な障壁画様式を打ち出した。多数の門人を率いて障壁画のほか扇面画なども手がける。その作品は宮廷や公家、武家、町衆など幅ひろい層の需要に応えた。

A painter who integrated Chinese ink wash painting and Yamato-e

Kanō Motonobu (1476 -1559) was a Warring States period painter born in Yamajiro province (now Kyoto prefecture). The eldest son of Kanō Masanobu, he was the second generation of the Kanō school artists. He served the Ashikaga clan and was given the rank of hōgen. Motonobu developed a lucid style of screen and wall painting combining various styles of Chinese painting with the colors and decorativeness of Yamato-e, a Japanese style of painting that was secular, decorative, and colorful. While training many students, he produced not only screen and wall paintings but also fan paintings and other formats. Those works were popular in a wide range of segments of society, from members of the imperial family and nobles to warriors and townsmen.

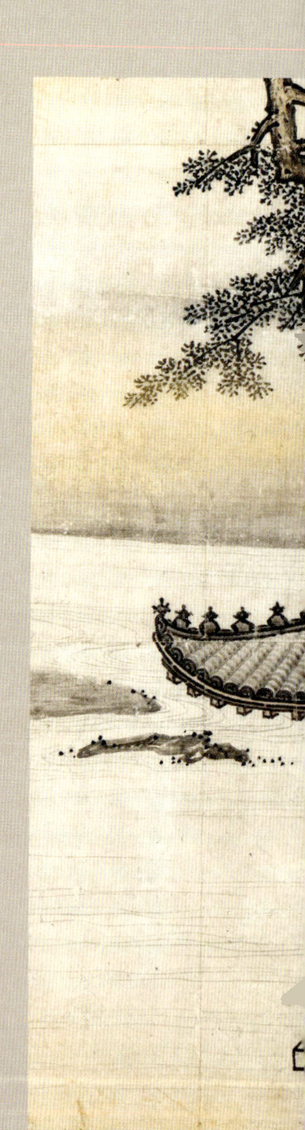

「楼閣山水図屏風」伝狩野元信
室町時代（16世紀）東京国立博物館蔵
Standing Screens of Landscape with Pavilion and Figures, Attributed to Kanō Motonobu, 16th century, Tōkyō National Museum / ColBase (https://colbase.nich.go.jp)

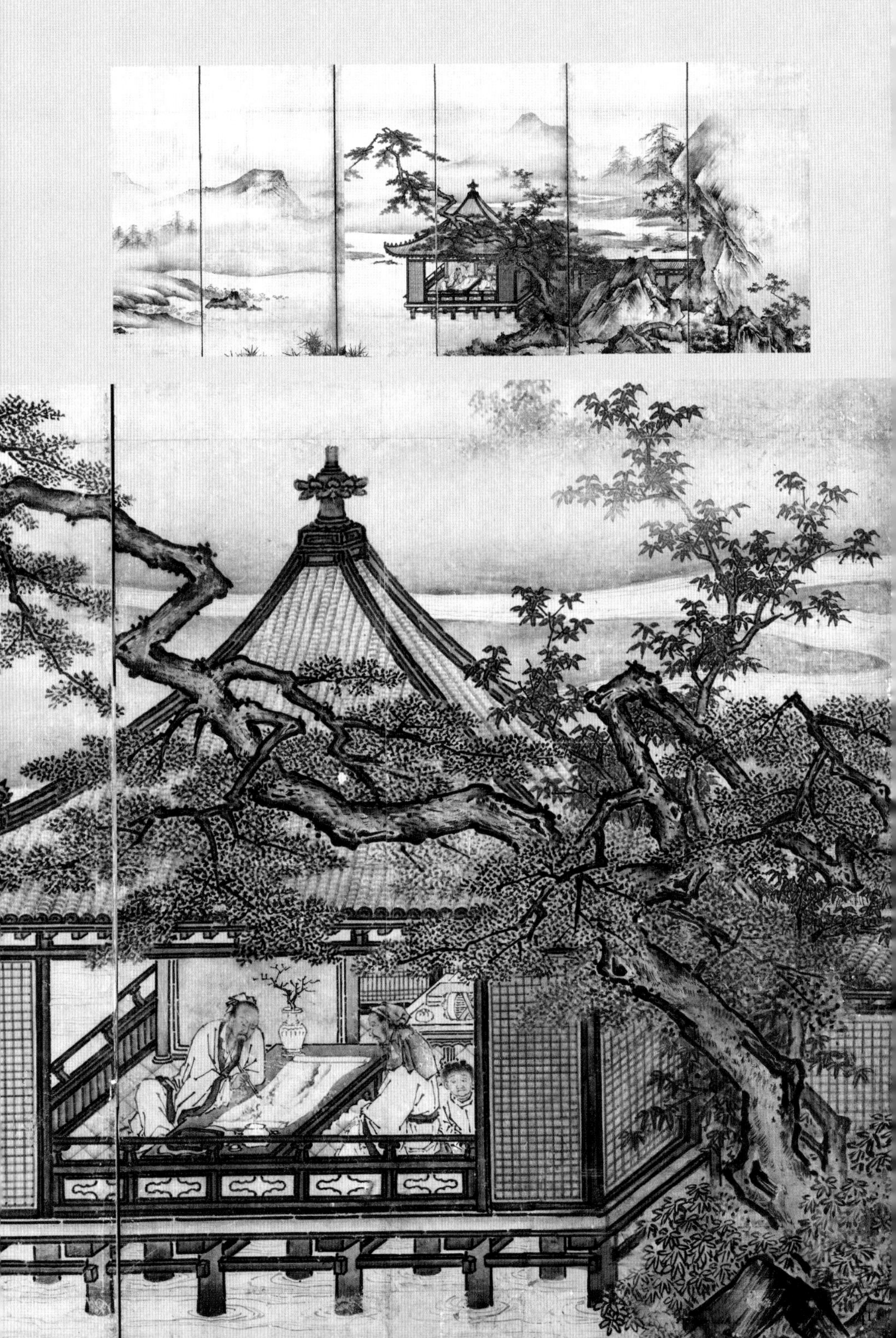

「囲碁観瀑図屏風」（部分）伝狩野元信　室町時代（16 世紀）東京国立博物館蔵
Standing Screens of Igo and Kanbaku, Attributed to Kanō Motonobu, 16th century,
Tōkyō National Museum/ ColBase (https://colbase.nich.go.jp)

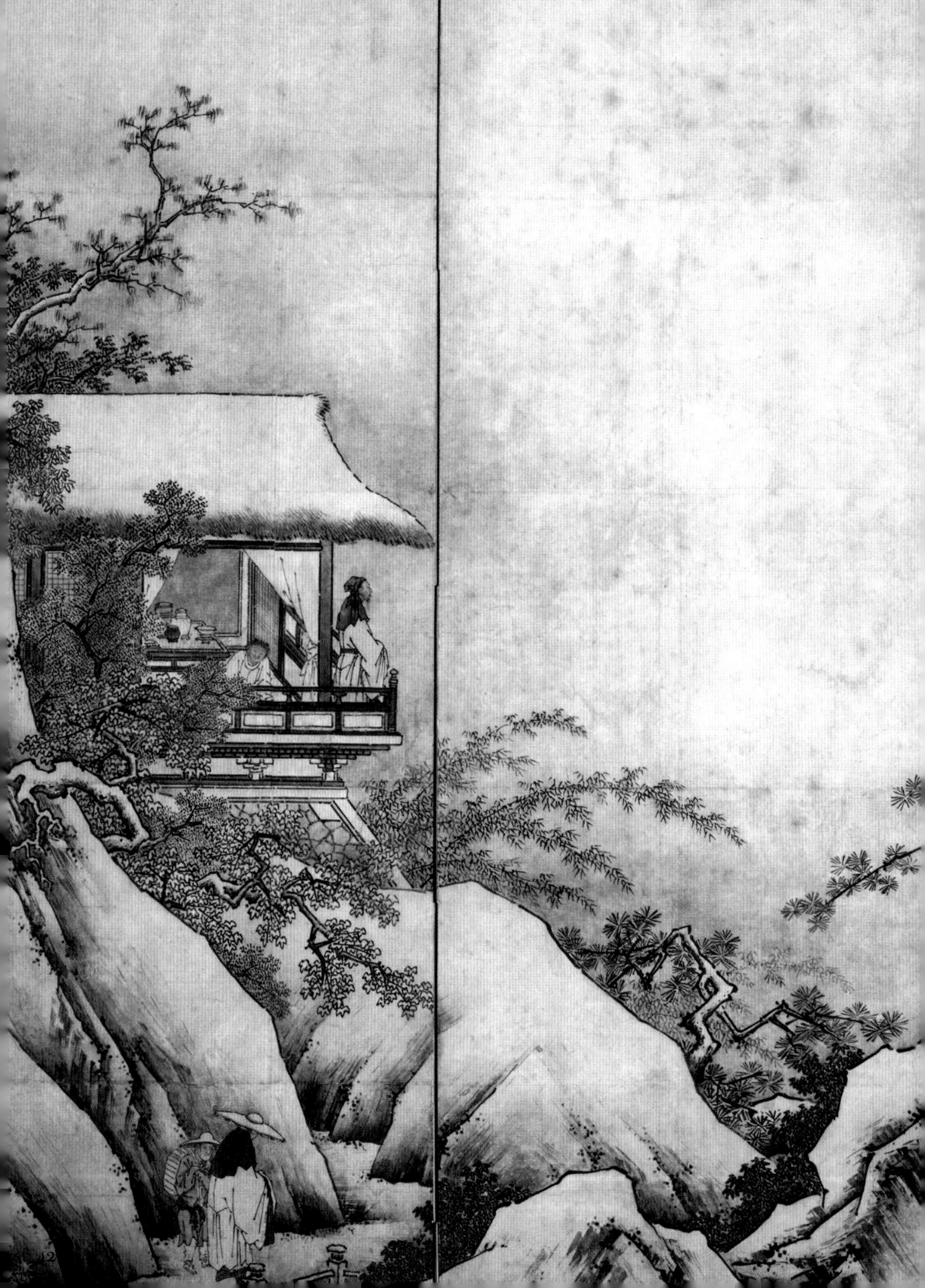

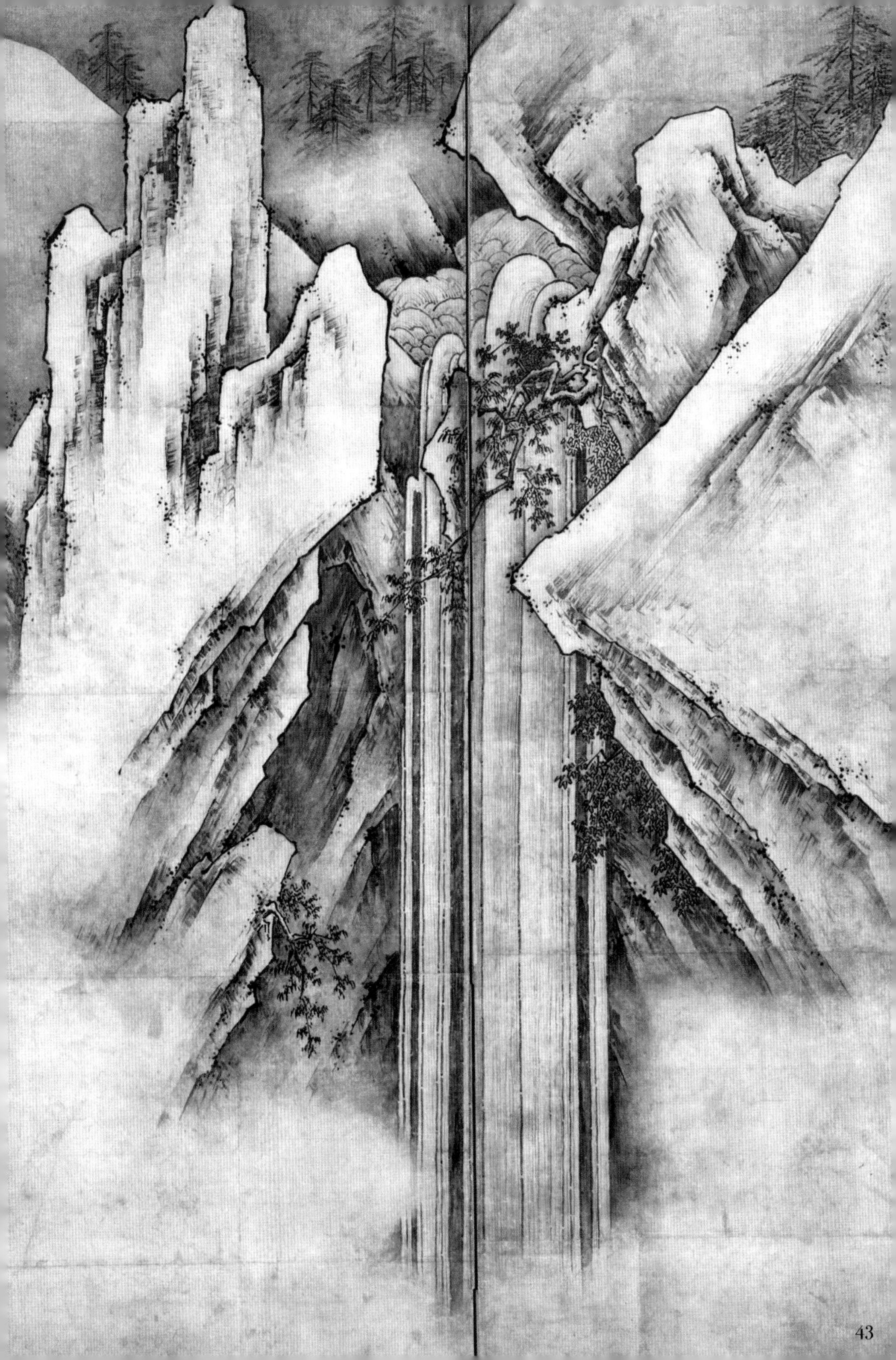

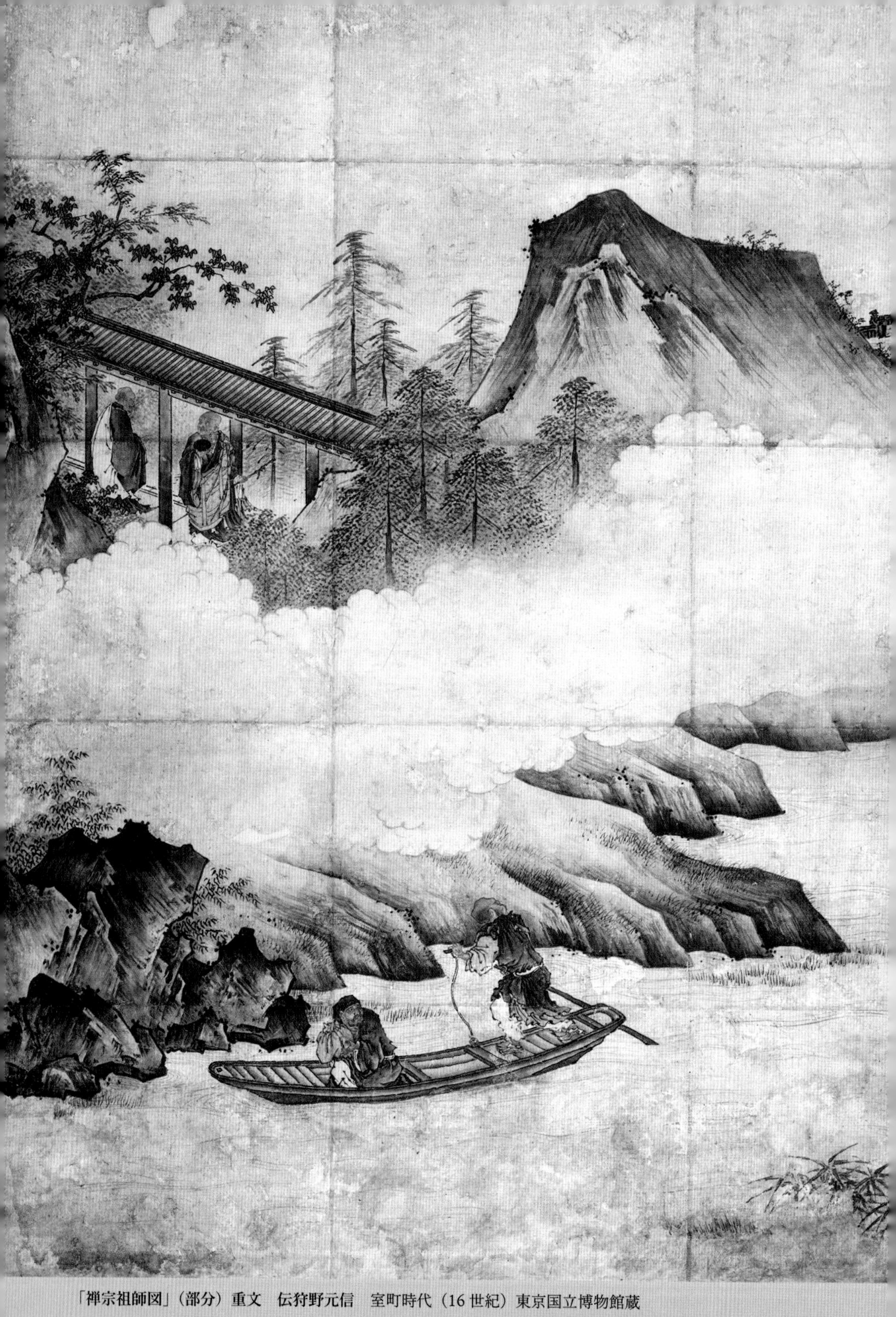

「禅宗祖師図」（部分）重文　伝狩野元信　室町時代（16世紀）東京国立博物館蔵

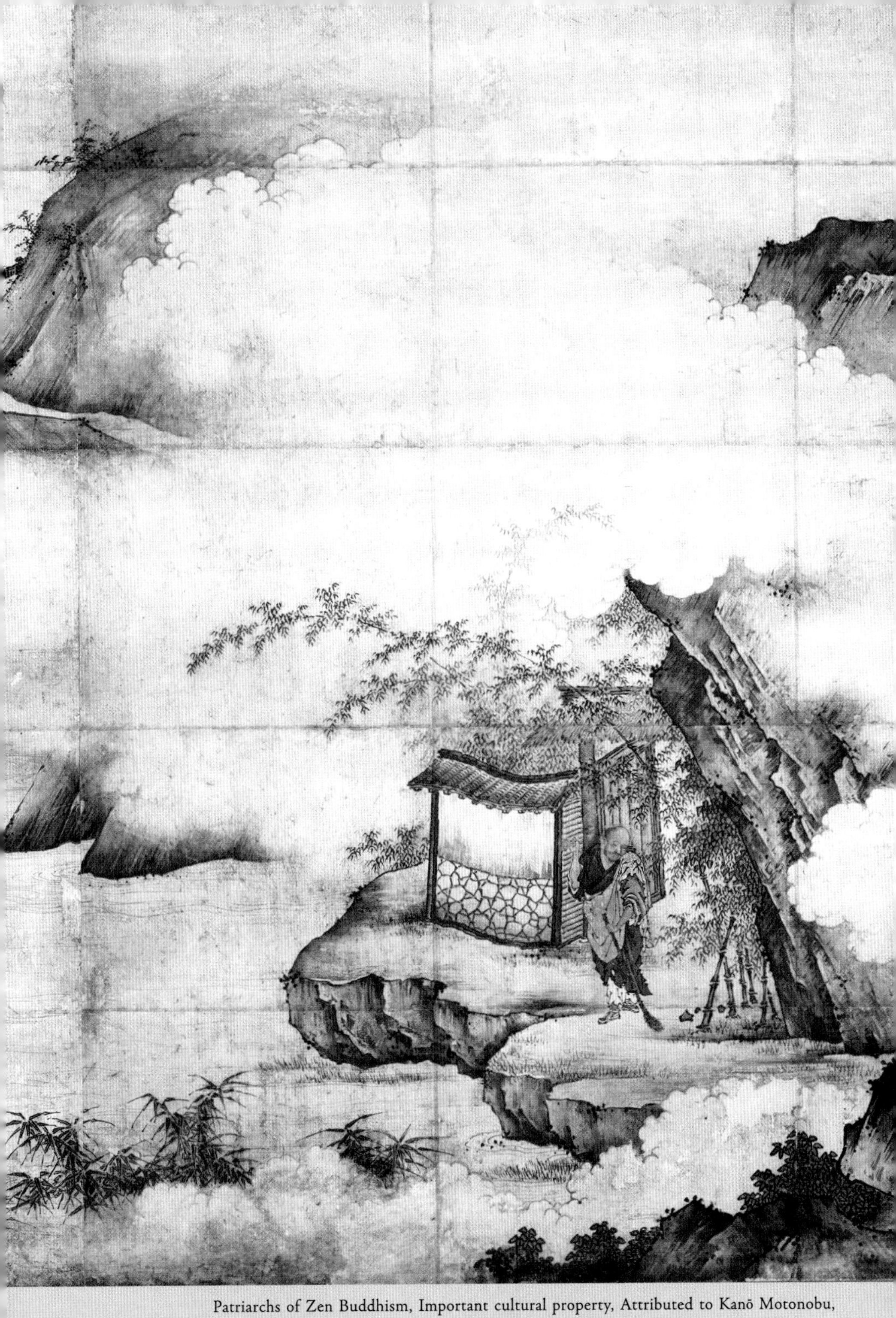

Patriarchs of Zen Buddhism, Important cultural property, Attributed to Kanō Motonobu, 16th century, Tōkyō National Museum/ ColBase (https://colbase.nich.go.jp)

45

狩野永徳

Kanō Eitoku

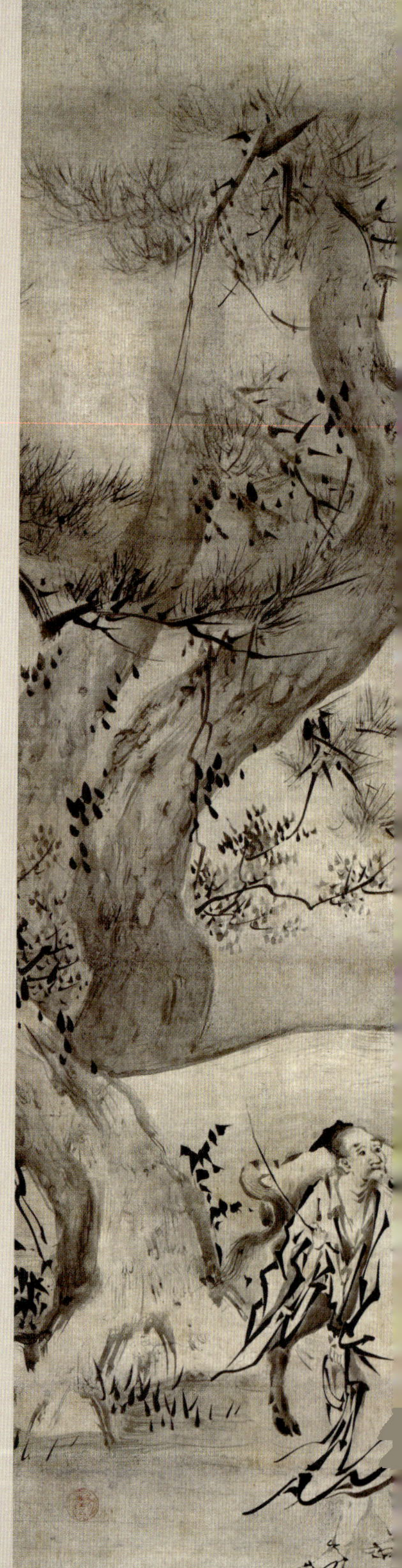

「許由巣父図」（部分）重文　狩野永徳
安土桃山時代（16世紀）
東京国立博物館蔵
Xuyou Washing His Ears and Chaofa with His Ox, Important cultural property, Kanō Eitoku, 16th century, Tōkyō National Museum / ColBase (https://colbase.nich.go.jp)

狩野派の黄金期をもたらした画家

かのう えいとく　天文12～天正18年（1543～90）

　織豊時代の画家。山城に生まれる。狩野松栄の長男。祖父元信に学ぶ。大徳寺聚光院の襖絵を制作。永徳の大画面様式は、織田信長や豊臣秀吉の注目するところとなり、安土城や豊臣秀吉の大坂城、聚楽第などの障壁画を手がける。華麗でダイナミックな表現様式により、狩野派の黄金期をもたらした。

The artist who brought the Kanō School to its golden age

Kanō Eitoku (1543-90) lived during the reigns of Oda Nobunaga and then Hideyoshi Toyotomi. The eldest son of Kanō Shōei, he studied with his grandfather, Motonobu. He created the sliding door paintings for the Jukōin subtemple at Daitokuji temple. Eitoku's large-format style attracted the attention of the hegemons Oda Nobunaga and Hideyoshi Toyotomi, and he then produced sliding door and wall paintings for Azuchi Castle as well as Hideyoshi's Osaka Castle and Jurakudai palace. His gorgeously dynamic style epitomizes the Kanō School's golden age.

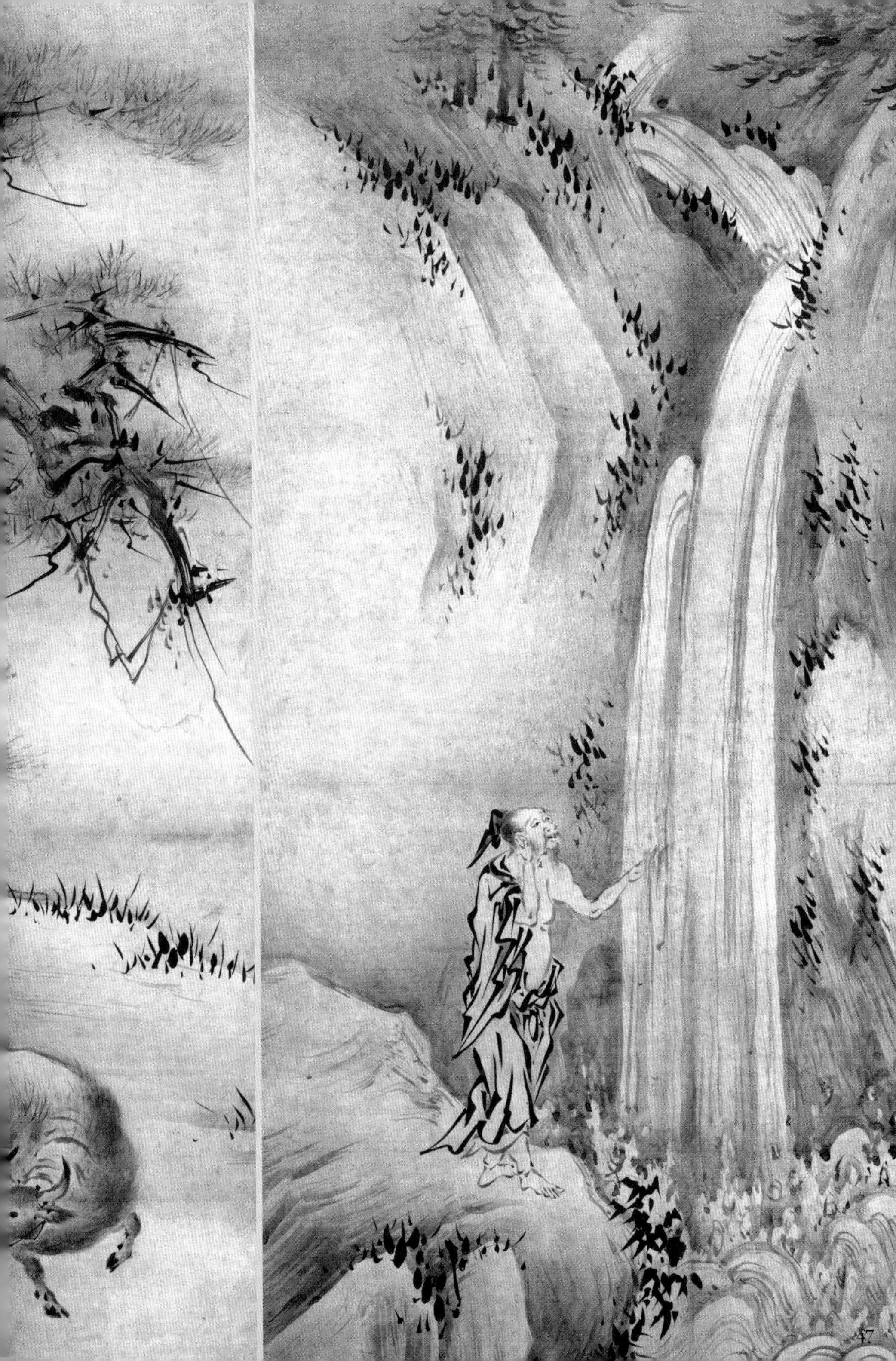

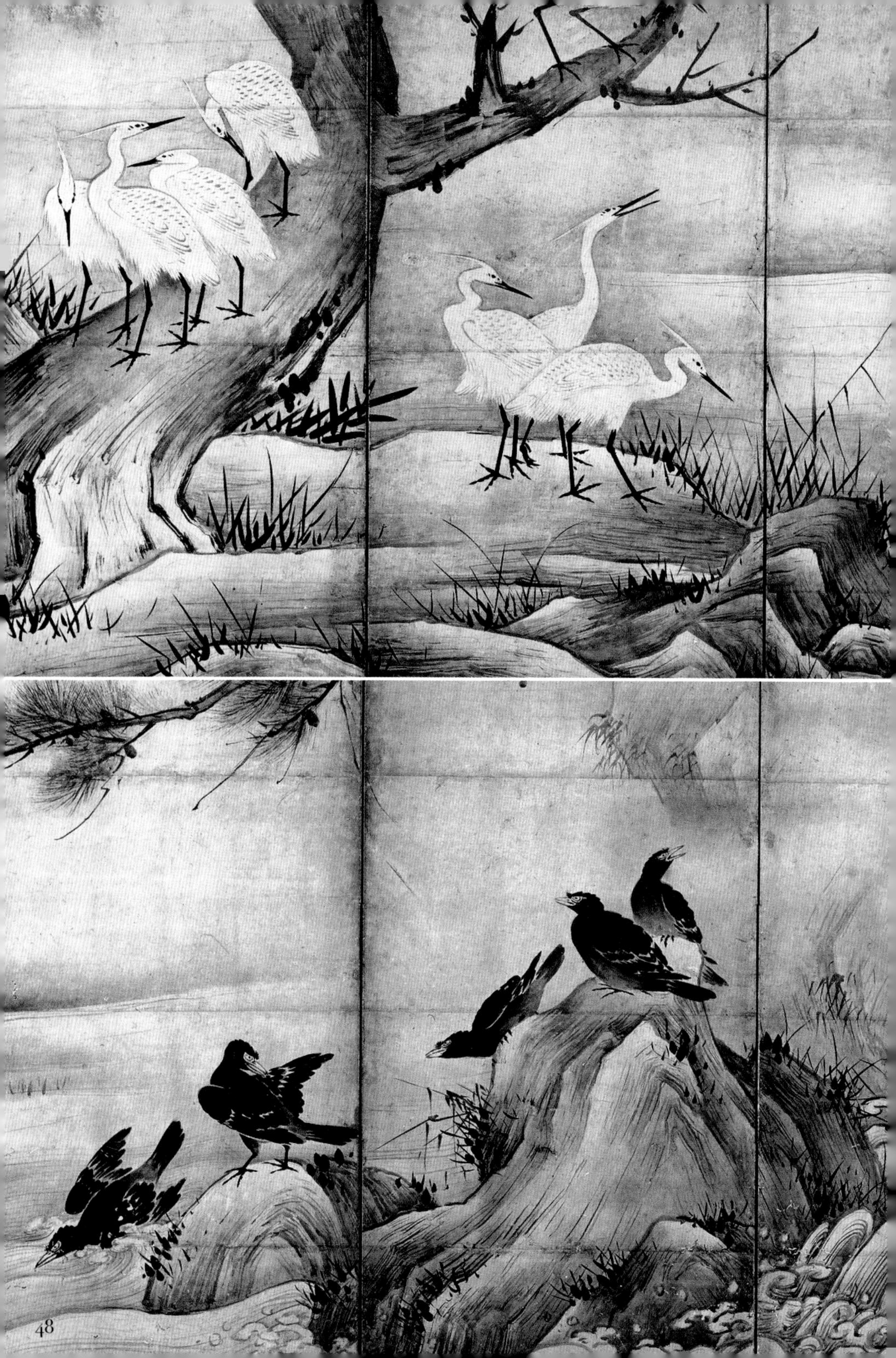

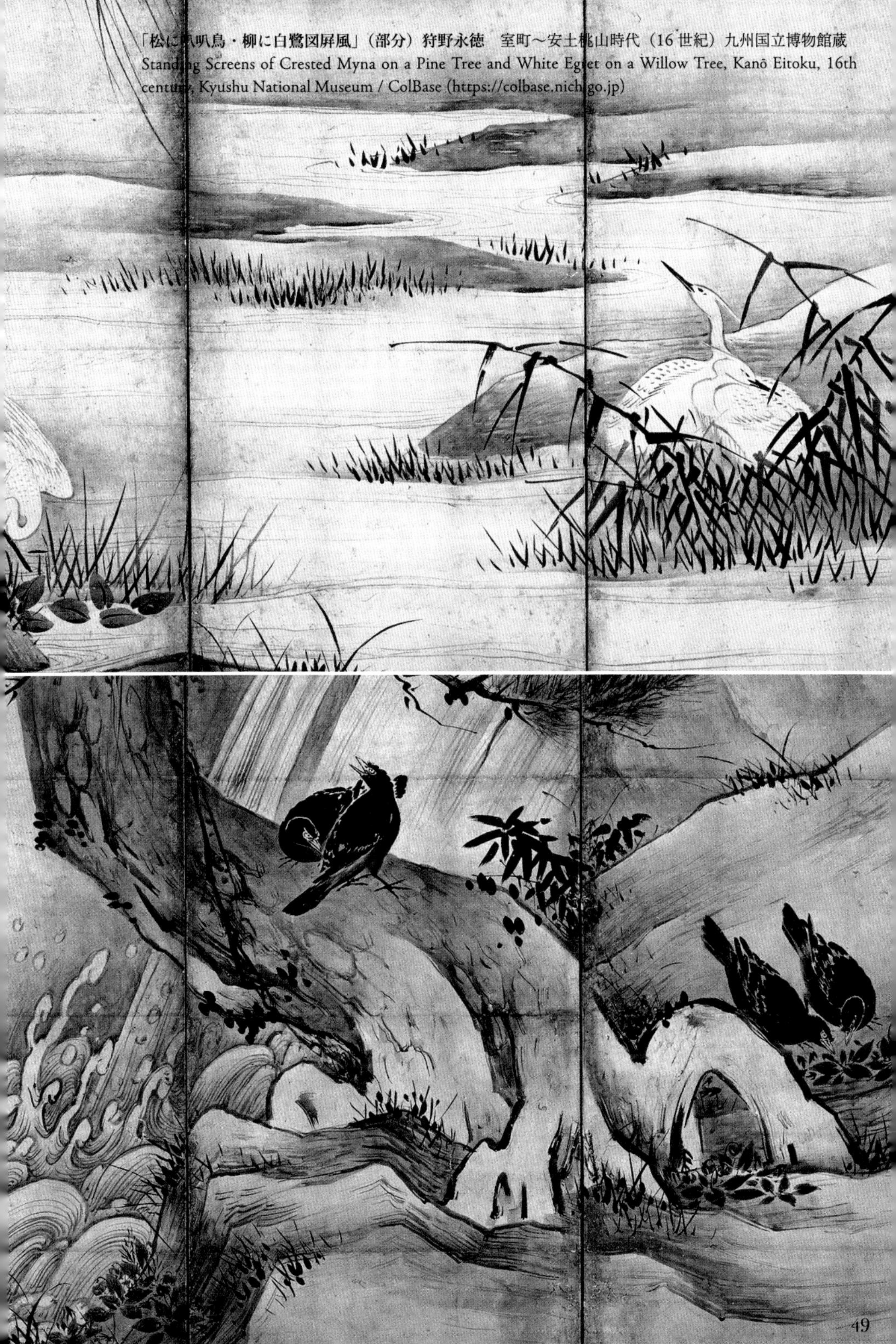

「松に叭叭鳥・柳に白鷺図屏風」（部分）狩野永徳　室町〜安土桃山時代（16世紀）九州国立博物館蔵
Standing Screens of Crested Myna on a Pine Tree and White Egret on a Willow Tree, Kanō Eitoku, 16th century, Kyushu National Museum / ColBase (https://colbase.nich.go.jp)

桃山文化の装飾豊かな作風を確立した画家

うんこく とうがん　天文16〜元和4年（1547〜1618）

　織豊・江戸時代前期の画家。肥前能古見（佐賀県）の城主原直家の次男と伝えられる。一族の滅亡後、またはその少し前に画家へ転向し、京都で狩野派に学ぶ。その後再び西国に戻り、安芸広島城主毛利輝元につかえる。この頃から雪舟に私淑し、輝元の命で雪舟筆「山水長巻」を模写。輝元から雪舟の旧跡雲谷庵をあたえられて雲谷と名のった。

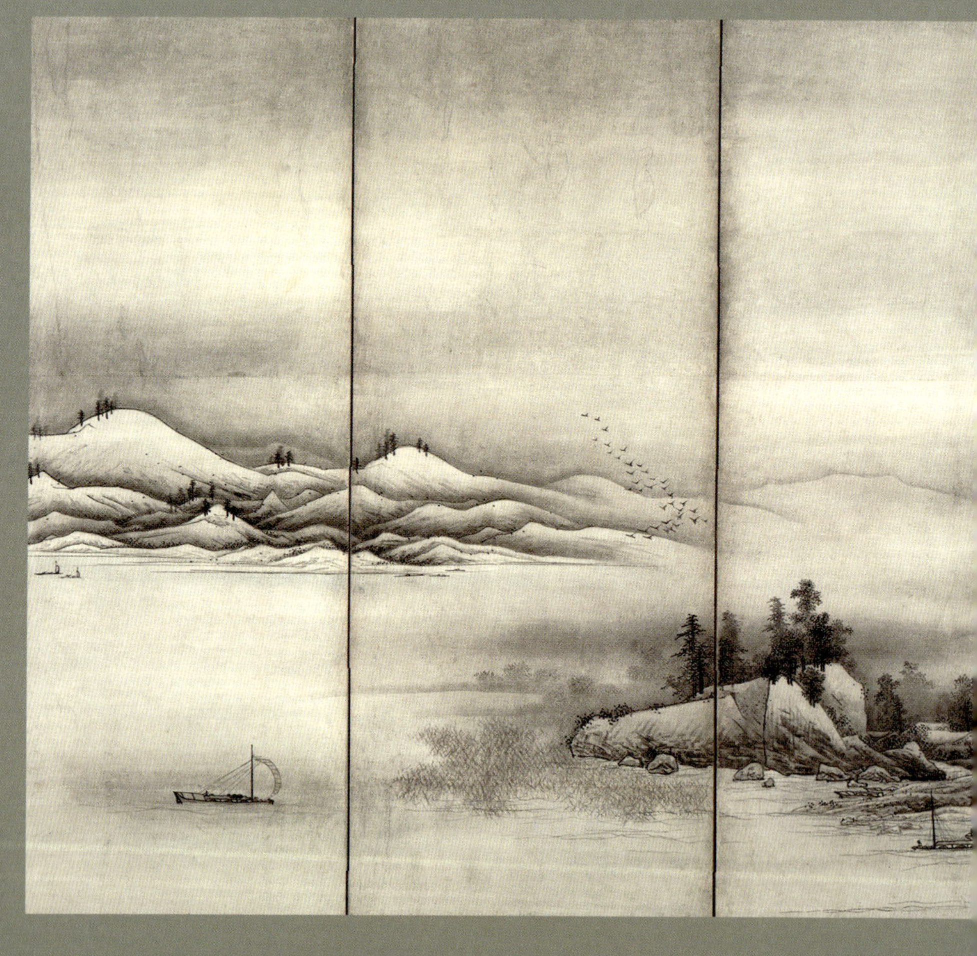

The painter who established the richly decorative Momoyama style

Unkoku Tōgan (1547–1618) was a painter active during the reigns of Oda Nobunaga and Hideyoshi Toyotomi and then the early Edo period. His is said to have
been the second son of Hara Naoie, lord of Nokomi castle in Bizen province (now
Saga prefecture). After or slightly before his family's downfall, he chose to become a
painter and studied Kanō School painting in Kyoto. He later moved back to western
Japan, serving Mōri Terumoto, lord of Hiroshima Castle in Aki province. From that
period on, he admired Sesshū and was ordered by Terumoto to copy Sesshū's Long
Landscape Scroll. Terumoto gave him Sesshū's historic Unkokuan, and the artist
took the name Unkoku.

「山水図屏風」重文　雲谷等顔　安土桃山〜江戸時代（16 〜 17 世紀）東京国立博物館蔵
Standing Screens of Landscape, Important cultural property, Unkoku Tōgan, 16th to 17th century,
Tōkyō National Museum / ColBase (https://colbase.nich.go.jp)

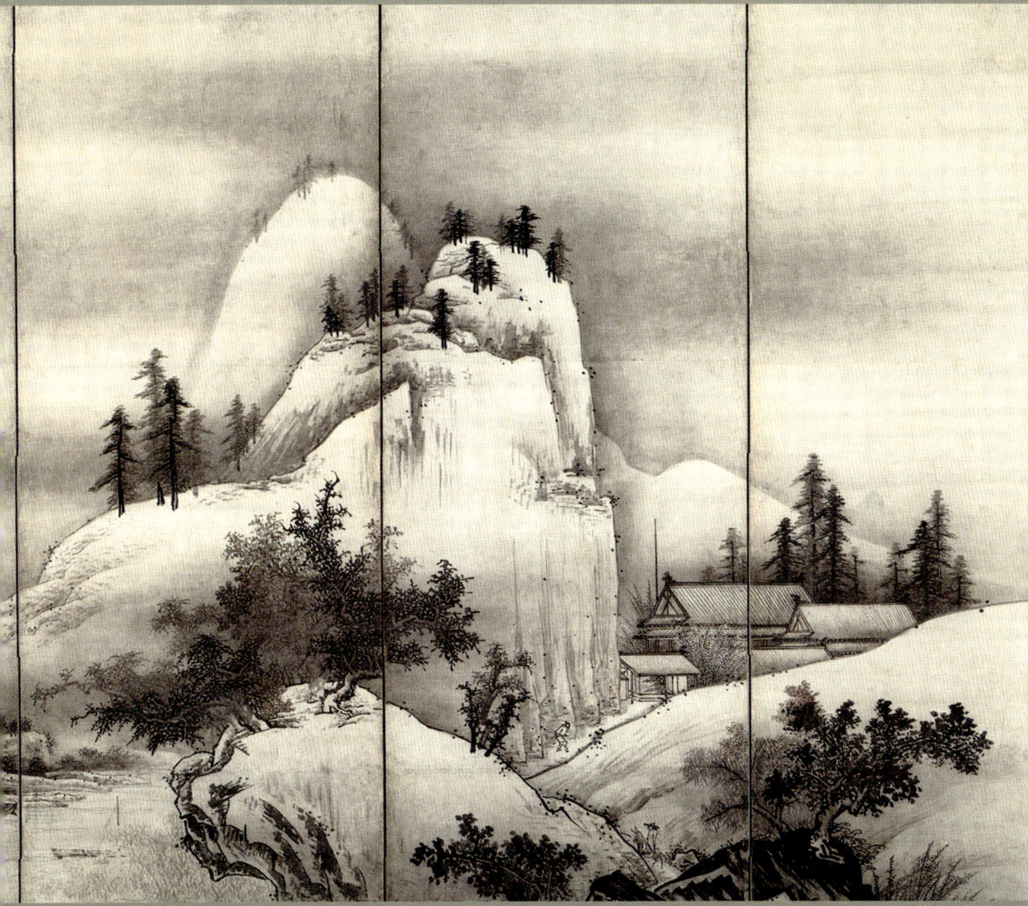

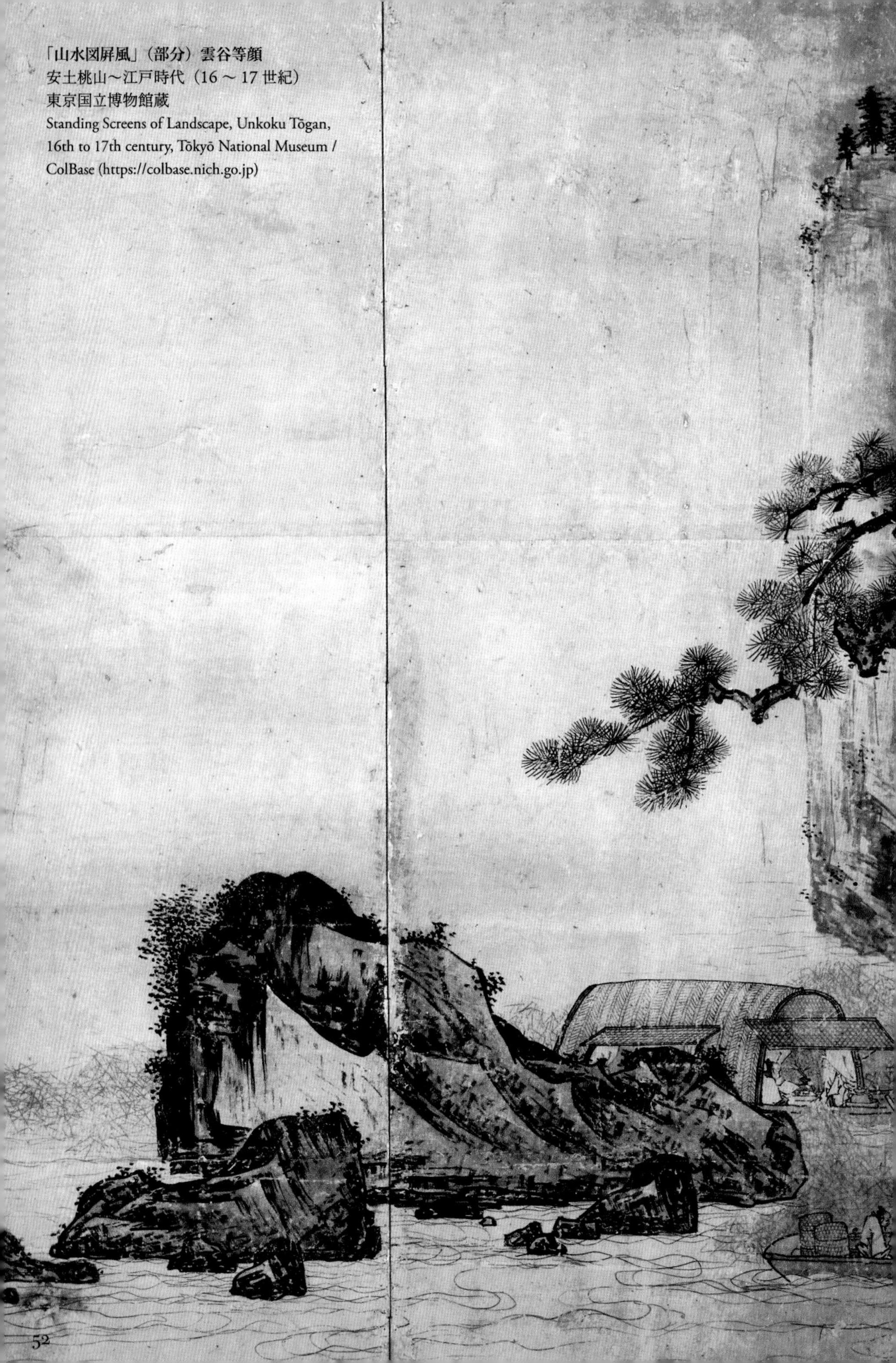

「山水図屏風」（部分）雲谷等顔
安土桃山〜江戸時代（16 〜 17 世紀）
東京国立博物館蔵
Standing Screens of Landscape, Unkoku Tōgan,
16th to 17th century, Tōkyō National Museum /
ColBase (https://colbase.nich.go.jp)

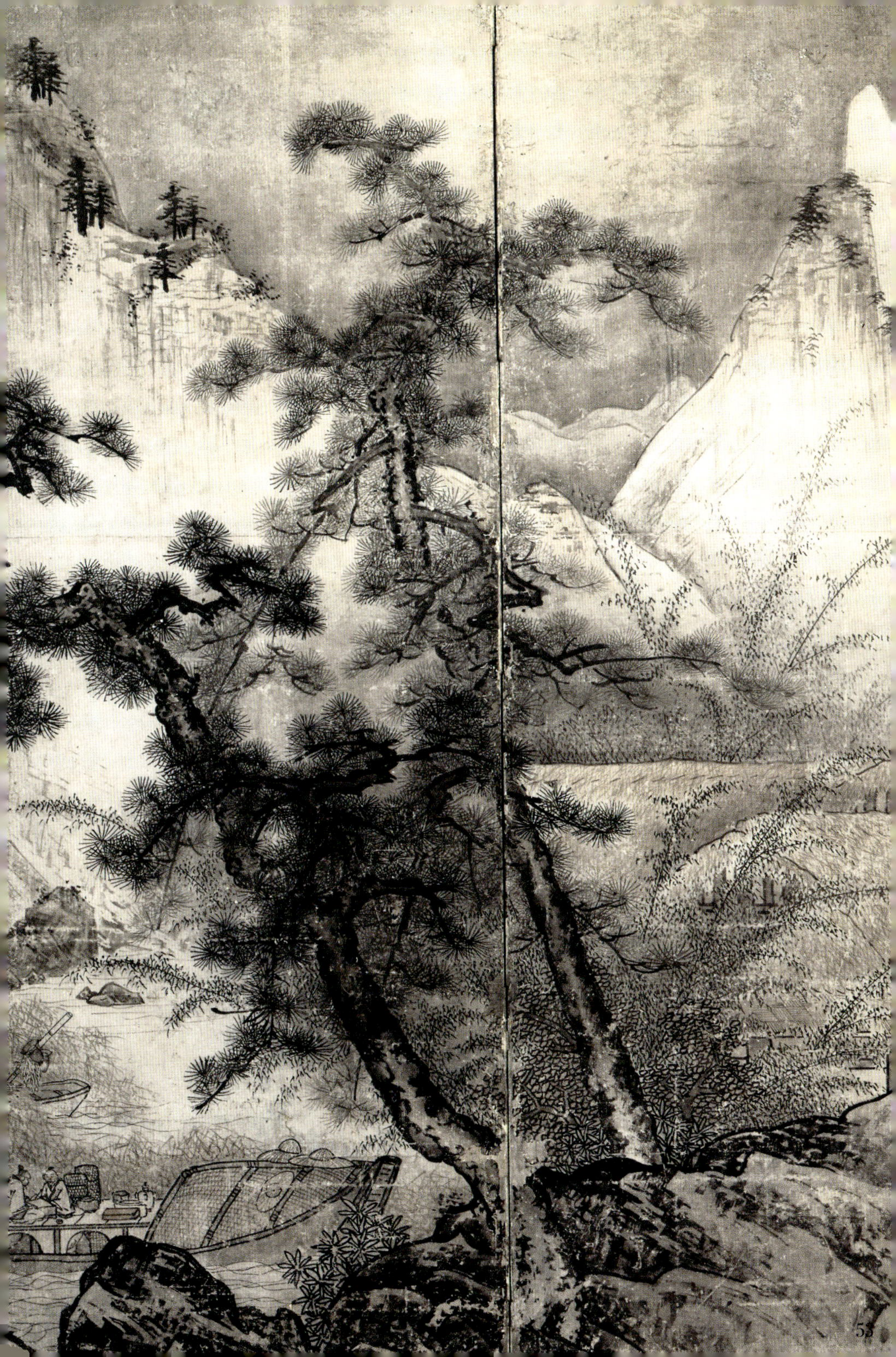

本阿弥光悦

Hon'ami Kōetsu

書や陶芸で新しい芸術を切り開いた指導者

ほんあみ こうえつ　永禄元~寛永14年（1558~1637）

　織豊・江戸時代前期の芸術家。京都の人。本阿弥家の分家に生まれ、家職である刀剣の鑑定や浄拭（ぬぐい）のほかに、書画、蒔絵、陶芸などにすぐれ、茶道、築庭にも長じた。晩年徳川家康からあたえられた洛北鷹峯（たかがみね）に芸術村をつくった。古典を研究して独自の書風を開き、近衛信尹（このえのぶただ）、松花堂昭乗（しょうかどうしょうじょう）とともに寛永の三筆にかぞえられた。

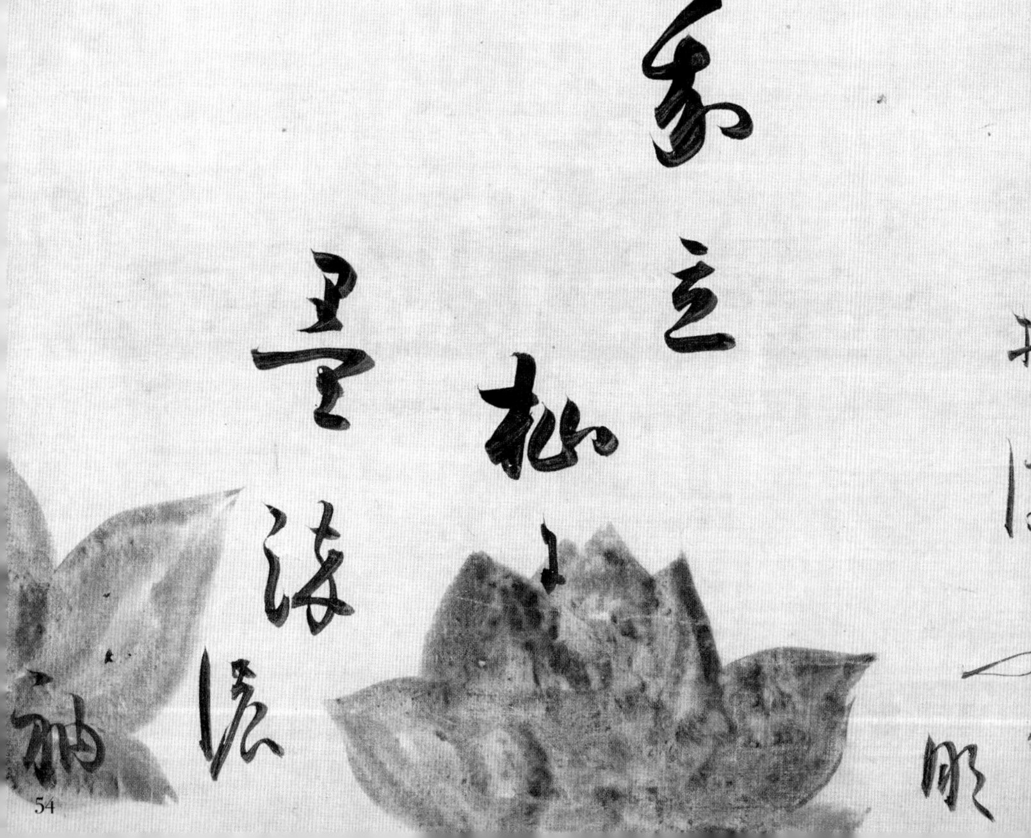

A pioneer who opened up new artistic terrain in calligraphy and ceramics

Hon'ami Kōetsu (1558–1637) lived during the reigns of Oda Nobunaga and Hideyoshi Toyotomi and then the early Edo period. Born into a branch of the Hon'ami family, he was active as an appraiser of swords and interpreter of writing on them, his family business, excelled at calligraphy, painting, *maki-e* decoration on lacquerware, and ceramics, and also the way of tea and garden design. In his later years, he established an artists village in Takagamine, north of Kyoto, on land granted him by Tokugawa Ieyasu. Studying the classics, he developed his own style of calligraphy and was known, with Konoe Nobutada and Shōkadō Shōjō, as one of the three great calligraphers of the Kan'ei era (1624-44).

「蓮下絵和歌巻断簡」本阿弥光悦　江戸時代（17 世紀）東京国立博物館蔵
Fragment of a Lotus-illustrated *Waka* Scroll, Hon'ami Kōetsu, 17th century, Tōkyō
National Museum / ColBase (https://colbase.nich.go.jp)

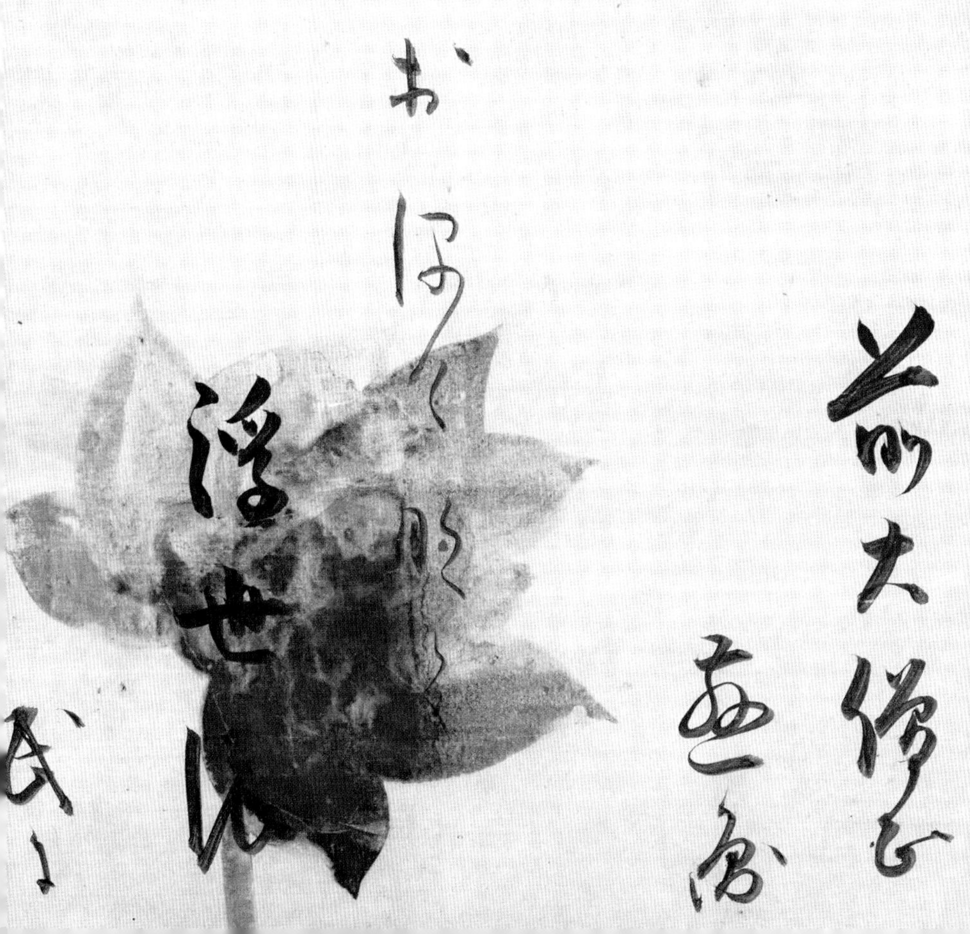

「摺下絵和歌巻」本阿弥光悦
江戸時代（17世紀）
東京国立博物館蔵
Poem Anthology *Waka* Scroll Over
Printed Design, Hon'ami Kōetsu, 17th
century, Tōkyō National Museum /
ColBase (https://colbase.nich.go.jp)

「歌仙　凡河内躬恒」本阿弥光悦
江戸時代（17世紀）
黎明教会資料研修館蔵
Kasen: Ōshikōchi no Mitsune,
Hon'ami Kōetsu. 17th century, Reimei
Art Gallery

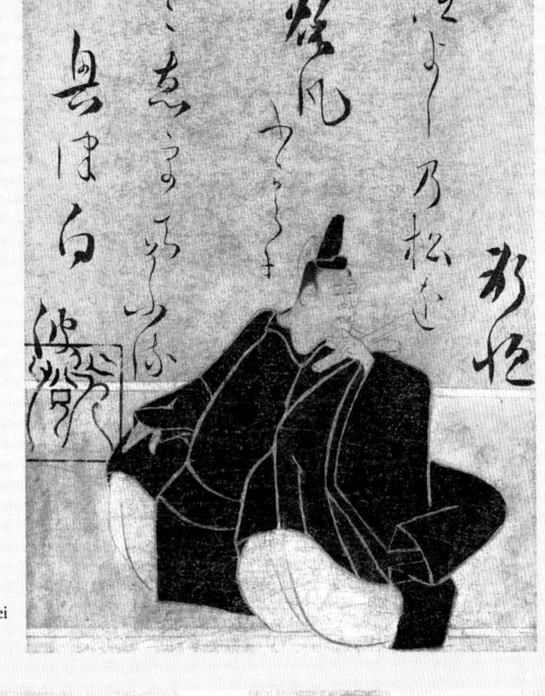

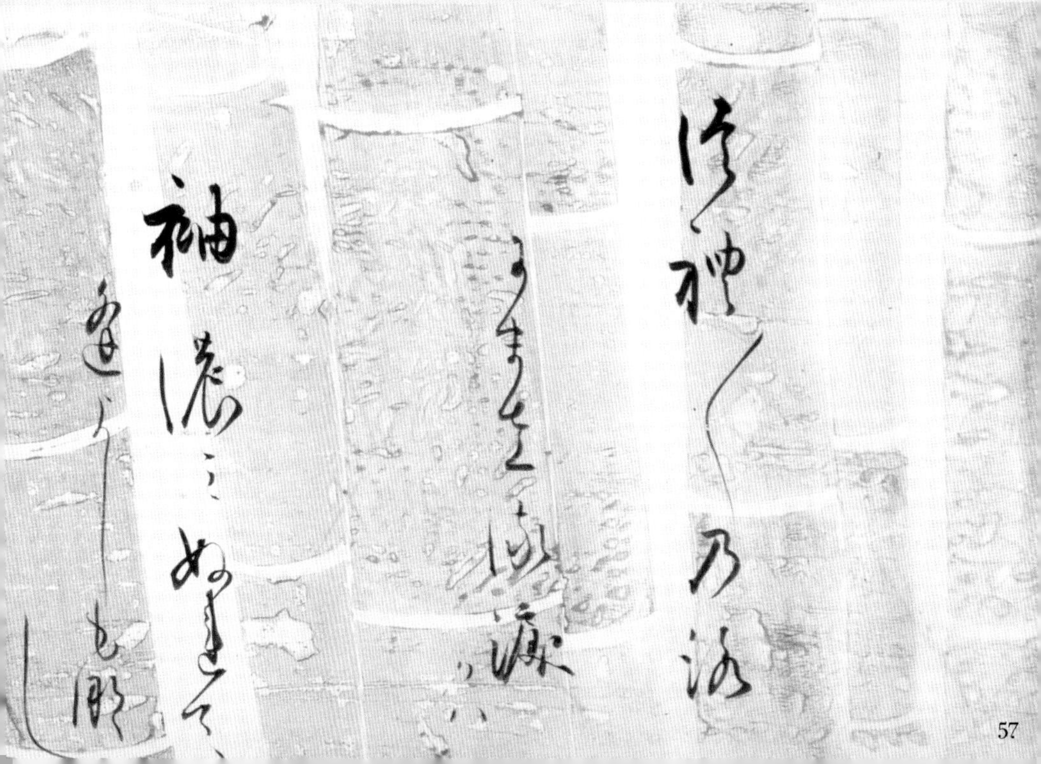

宮本武蔵

Miyamoto Musashi

気魄のこもった
鋭い表現の武人画家

みやもと むさし
天正12〜正保2年（1584〜1645）

　江戸時代前期の剣術家。二刀流剣法の祖。美作（岡山県）宮本村に生まれる。実歴は不明な部分が多く、生涯60余度の試合に不敗をほこり、吉岡一門の佐々木小次郎との決闘が知られる。晩年は熊本藩主細川忠利の客分となった。余技ながら書画にもすぐれ、南宋の梁楷や桃山時代の海北友松の影響をうかがわせる減筆体で、武人らしい簡潔で、しかも気魄を感じさせる作品が多い。

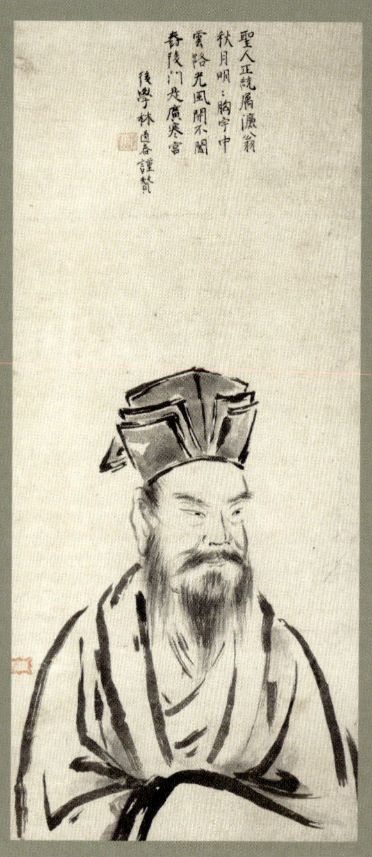

「周茂叔図」宮本武蔵
江戸時代（17 世紀前期）
岡山県立美術館蔵
Zhou Maoshu, Miyamoto Musashi,
Early 17th century, Okayama
Prefectural Museum of Art

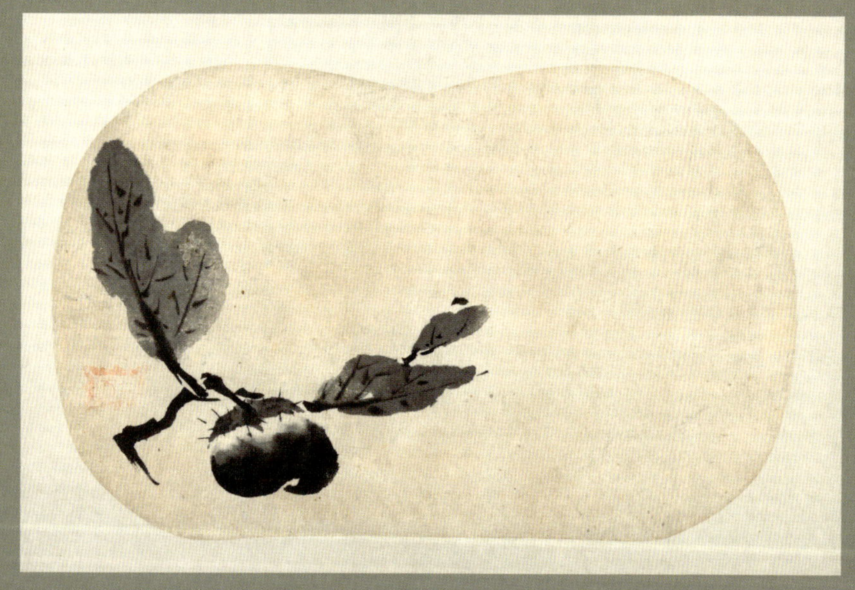

A samurai painter with a sharply honed style

Miyamoto Musashi, an early Edo-period swordsman (1584–1645), was the founder of the Nitō school of swordsmanship. He was born in Miyamoto village, in Mimasaka (now Okayama prefecture). Many details of his life are uncertain, but he is known for being undefeated in over 60 duels, including his bout with Sasaki Kojirō, in which Sasaki was killed. In his later years, he was treated as a guest by Hosokawa Tadatoshi, lord of the Kumamoto domain. He excelled at calligraphy and painting and created many works that make us sense his spirit, what is known as the *genpitsu* style of abbreviated brush painting, a concise style that seems very appropriate for a samurai. In his works we can see the influence of the Southern Song painter Liang Kai and the Momoyama-period painter Kaihō Yūshō.

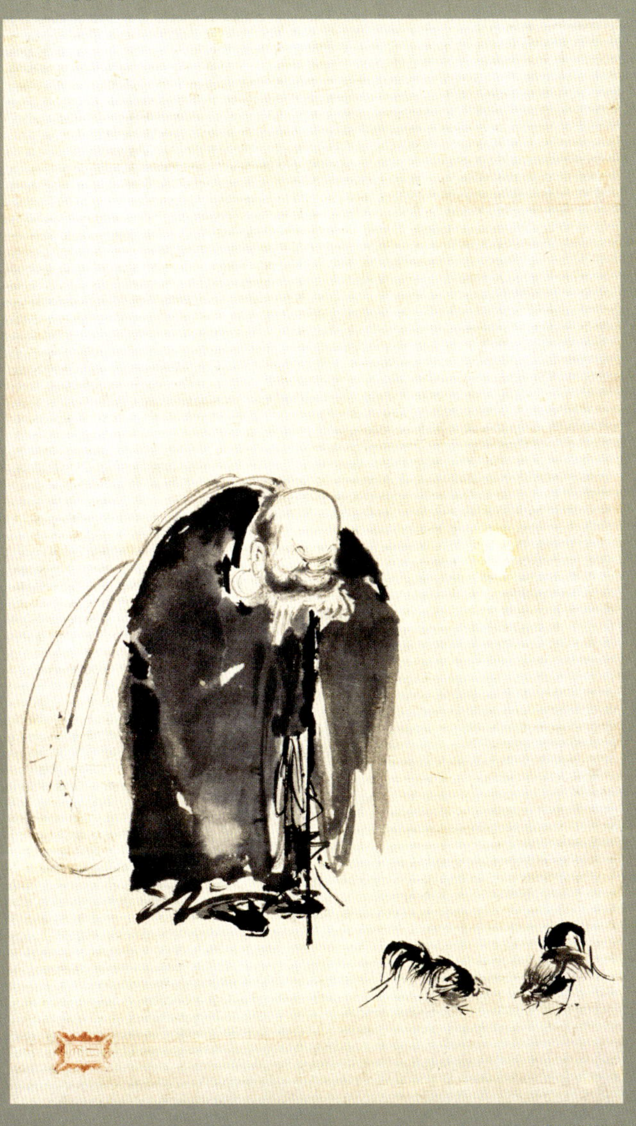

前頁下：
「茄子図」宮本武蔵
江戸時代（17 世紀）
岡山県立美術館蔵
Eggplant, Miyamoto Musashi,
17th century, Okayama Prefectural Museum of Art

「布袋観闘鶏図」宮本武蔵
江戸時代（17 世紀前期）
福岡市美術館蔵
（松永コレクション）
画像提供：福岡市美術館
／ DNPartcom ／撮影：山﨑信一
Priest Budai watching Cockfight, Miyamoto Musashi, Early 17th century,
Fukuoka Art Museum/ Matsunaga
Collection

武士が描いた水墨画
Ink Wash Paintings by a Warrior

　宮本武蔵の水墨画は武者修行のなかで訪れた神社や仏閣の襖絵や杉戸を見て学んだといわれ、南宋の梁楷や桃山時代の海北友松の影響がうかがえます。対象を省略して描く減筆体の画法で、武人らしい簡潔でしかも気魄が感じられます。

　武蔵は晩年の寛永17年（1640）、肥後の熊本藩に客分として招かれ、座禅三昧の生活を送りました。また細川家の菩提寺である泰勝寺の春山和尚と親交を結んだとも伝えられ、禅に対する関心の深さがうかがわれます。

　自由奔放な筆致を駆使した武蔵の絵は、剣禅一如の境地を描き出しています。武蔵の禅と結びついた絵は高い精神性と深い情趣により、観るものにかぎりない静寂をあたえてくれるのです。

　鎌倉時代中期、当時中国で盛んになっていた禅宗が日本に伝えられると、この禅的心境をあらわす手段として描かれた絵画は、しだいに従来の華やかな色彩や克明な描写から遠ざかり、むしろ墨一色によって万象を捉えるといった、何事にも制約されない自由な筆使いによる水墨画に変わっていきました。

　光と影、陰と陽という対照的な要因によって生まれるあらゆるもの姿を、水と墨、白と黒、明と暗、線と面といった対照的要素におきかえることによって表現する水墨画の世界は、いわば天から授かった究極の画法ということができるでしょう。

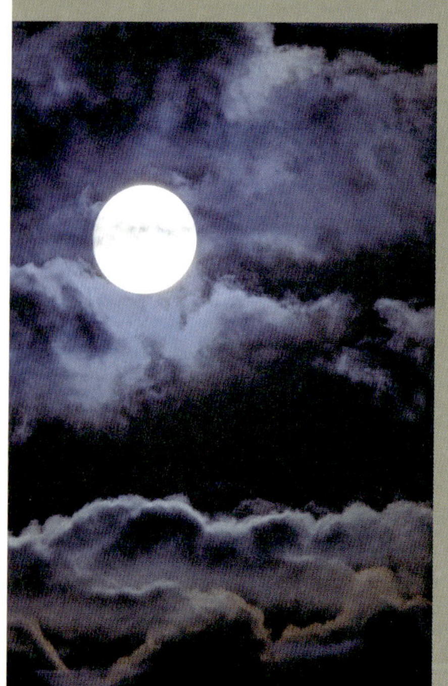

「布袋竹雀枯木翡翠図」宮本武蔵　江戸時代（17世紀）岡山県立美術館蔵
Hotei, Sparrow on Bamboo and Kingfisher on Withered Branch, Miyamoto Musashi, 17th century, Okayama Prefectural Museum

Miyamoto Musashi is said to have learned ink wash painting by looking at sliding door paintings and paintings on cypress wood doors in the temples and shrines he visited while training as a warrior. His works show the influence of the Southern Song painter Liang Kai and the Momoyama-period painter Kaihō Yūshō. His abbreviated *genpitsu* style seems very appropriate for a samurai.

Near the end of his life, in 1640, Musashi was invited as a guest to the Kumamoto domain in Higo province. There he engaged in seated Zen meditation (*Zazenzanmai*). He is also said to have become friends with Haruyama Oshō of the Taishōji Temple, the Hosokawa clan's mortuary temple, a connection suggesting the depth of Musashi's interest in Zen.

Musashi's paintings, with his skillful use of uninhibited brushwork, depict the state in which Zen and the way of the sword are one. His Zen-associated paintings, with their elevated spirit and profound feeling, bring the viewer endless tranquility.

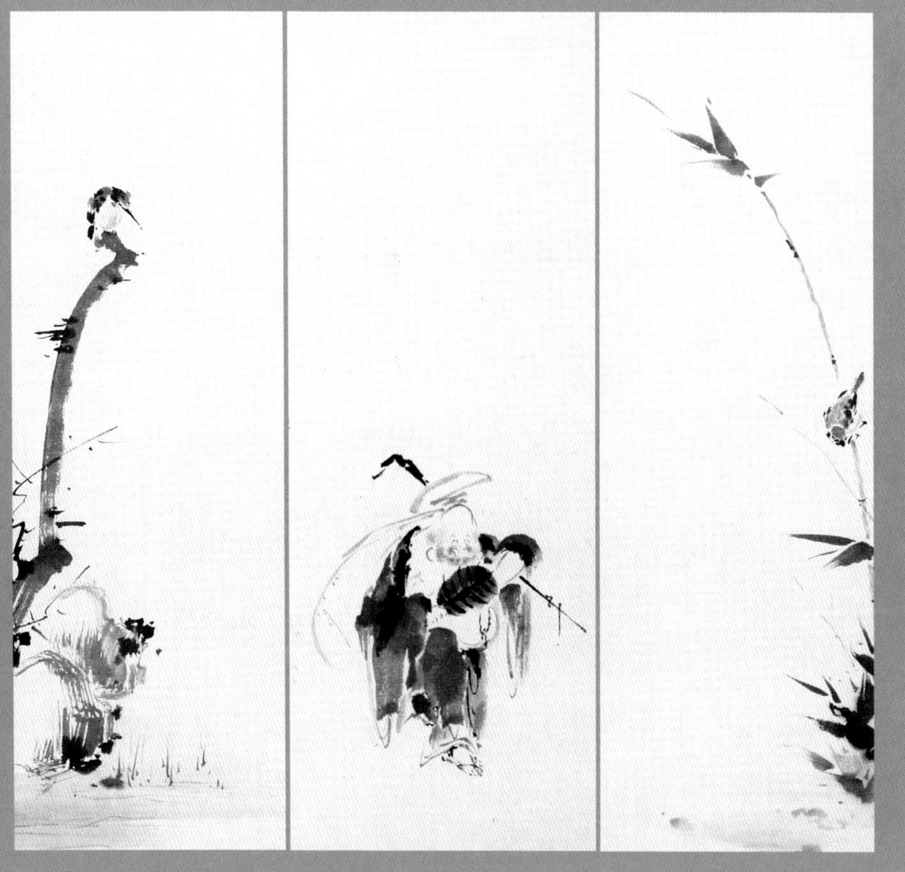

狩野山雪
Kanō Sansetsu

若冲や蕭白などの個性的画家の先駆者

かのう さんせつ

天正17/18～慶安4年 （1589/90～1651）

　江戸時代前期の画家。和歌山藩執政千賀道元の子として九州肥前国に生れる。狩野山楽の門人。のち婿養子となり京狩野家を継ぐ。山楽の指導を受けながら制作した妙心寺天球院の金碧障壁画はとくに有名である。山楽の装飾的画風を受け継ぎつつも、理知的で明快な画面構成に独自の造形性を示した。

A forerunner to eccentrics such as Jakuchū and Shōhaku

Kanō Sansetsu (1589/90–1651), a painter active in the first half of the Edo period, was born in Hizen province, on Kyushu, as the son of Senga Dōgen, administrator of the Wakayama domain. He studied under Kanō Sanraku, later becoming his adopted son-in-law and carrying on the Kyoto Kanō line. The sliding door paintings on gold ground that he created for the Tenkyūin in Myōshinji Temple under Sanraku's direction are particularly famous. While carrying on Sanraku's decorative style, Sansetsu displayed his own aesthetic in the logical, coherent compositions of his paintings.

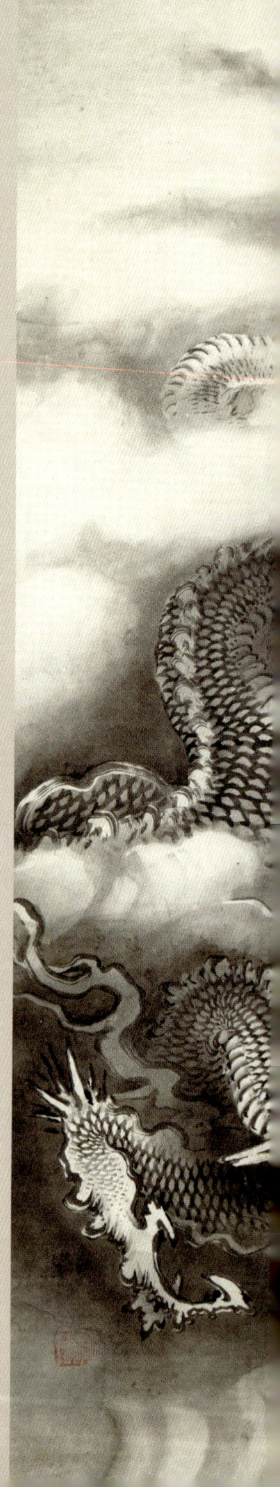

「双龍図」狩野山雪
江戸時代 （17 世紀） 東京国立博物館蔵
Twin Dragons, Kanō Sansetsu, 17th century, Tōkyō National Museum / ColBase (https://colbase.nich.go.jp)

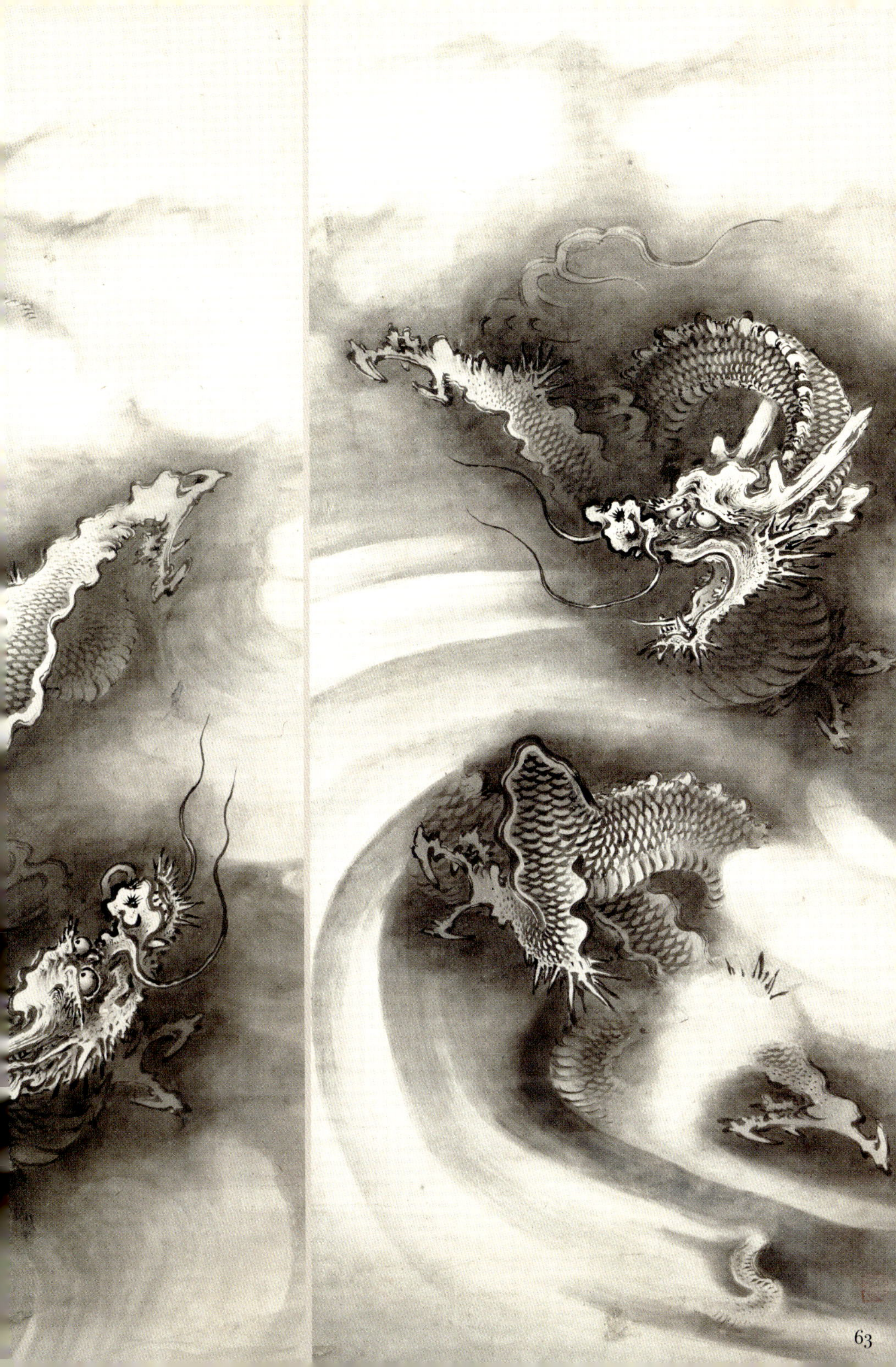

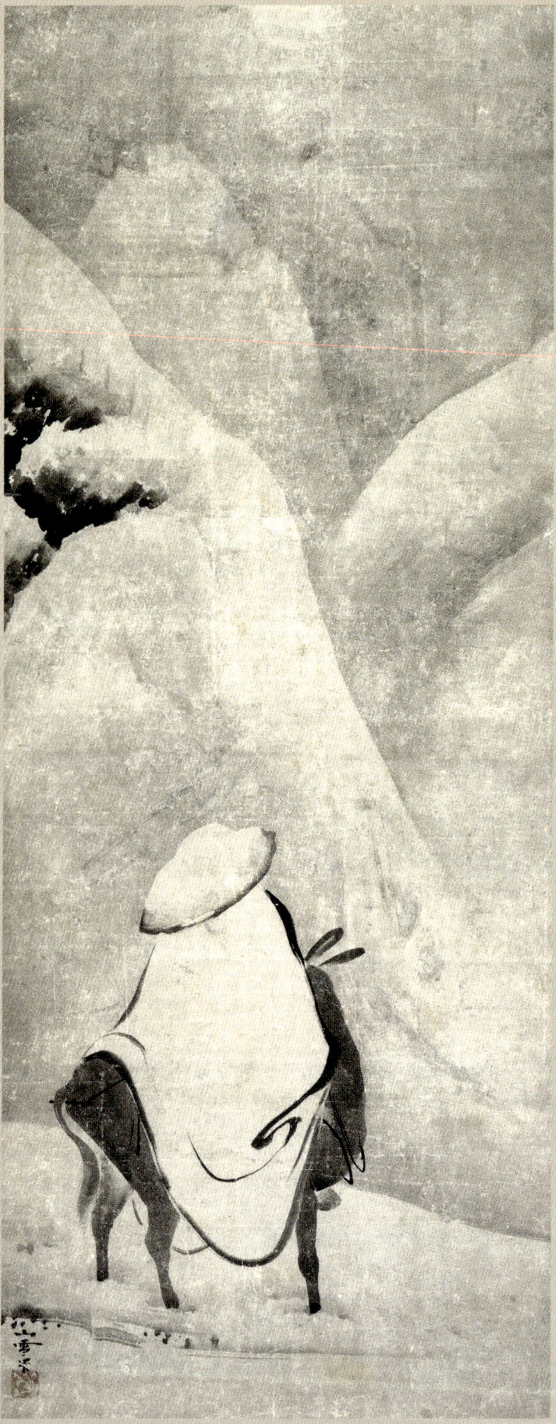

「雪中騎驢図」狩野山雪
寛永（1624 〜 43）後期〜正保期
（1644 〜 47）頃　千葉市美術館蔵
Riding on Donkey's Back in Snow, Kanō
Sansetsu, ca.1624-47, Chiba City Museum of Art

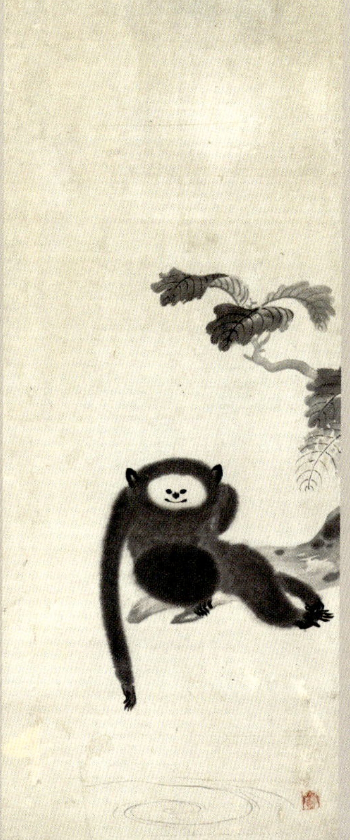

「猿猴図」狩野山雪
江戸時代（17 世紀）東京国立博物館蔵
Monkey, Kanō Sansetsu, 17th century, Tōkyō
National Museum / ColBase (https://colbase.
nich.go.jp)

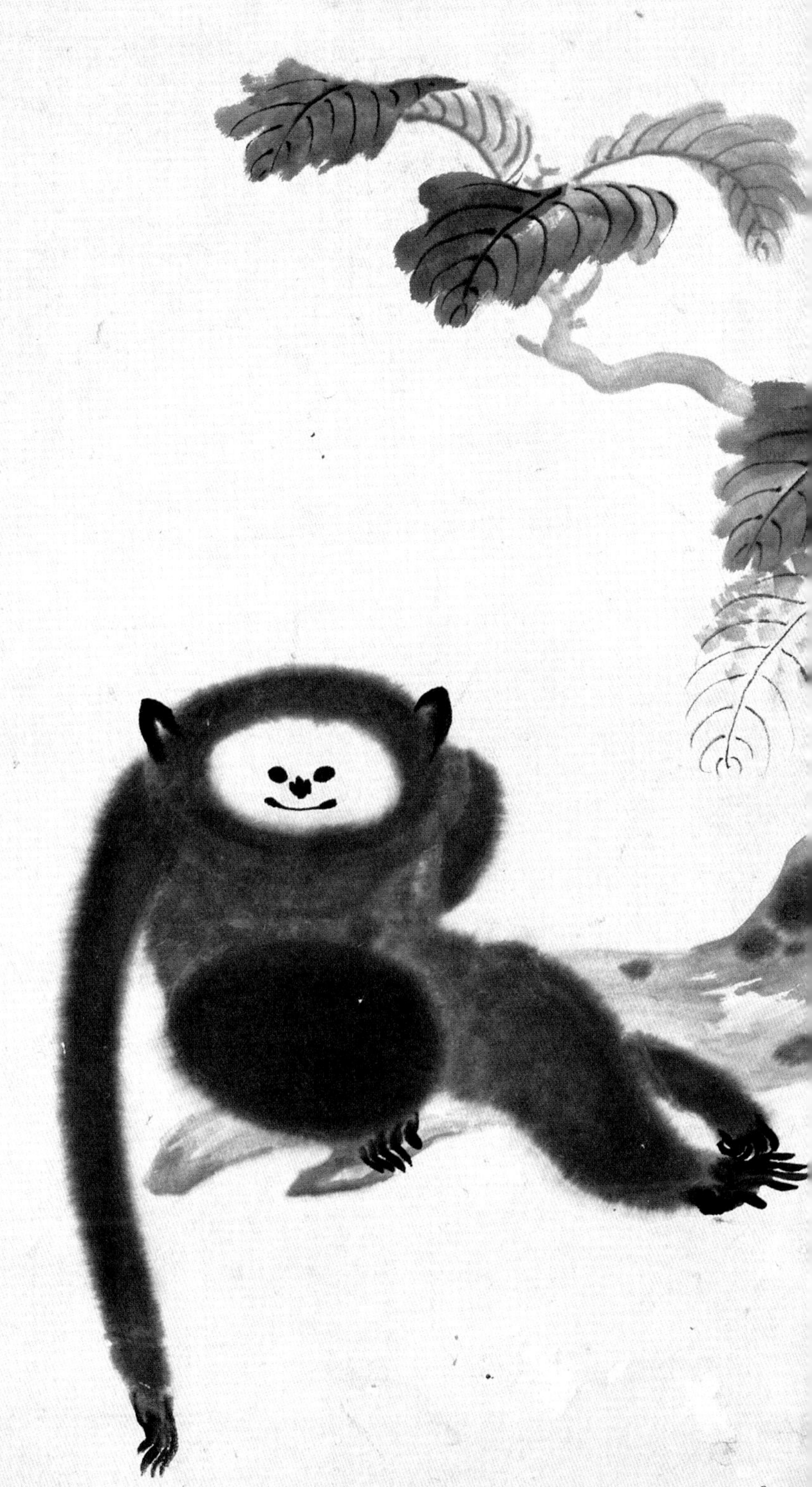

狩野探幽

Kanō Tan'yū

**江戸時代最大の巨匠であり、
狩野派の画風を和様化させた画家**

かのう たんゆう　慶長7~延宝2年（1602~74）

　江戸時代前期の画家。狩野孝信の長男として京都に生まれる。幼くして才能を発揮して、11歳の時に駿府で徳川家康に謁見する。江戸に移住後、16歳で徳川幕府の御用絵師となり、江戸城鍛冶橋門外に屋敷をもらい鍛冶橋狩野家をおこした。二条城などの障壁画制作では一門を率いて活躍。その後、名古屋城、江戸城、京都御所、日光東照宮など、障壁画の制作では指導的な役割を果たした。その組織や社会的地位の確立におおきな影響をあたえた。

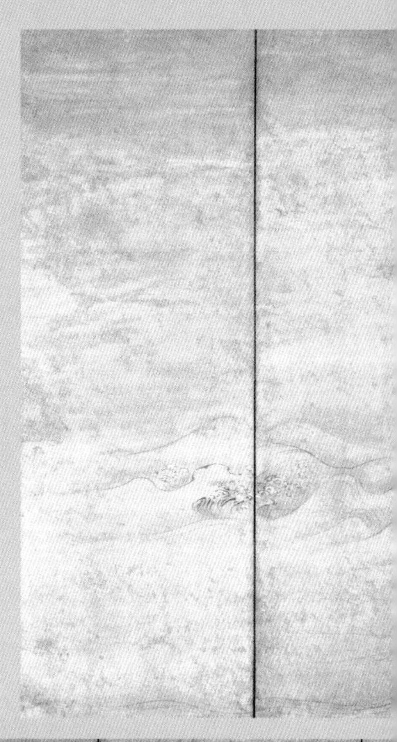

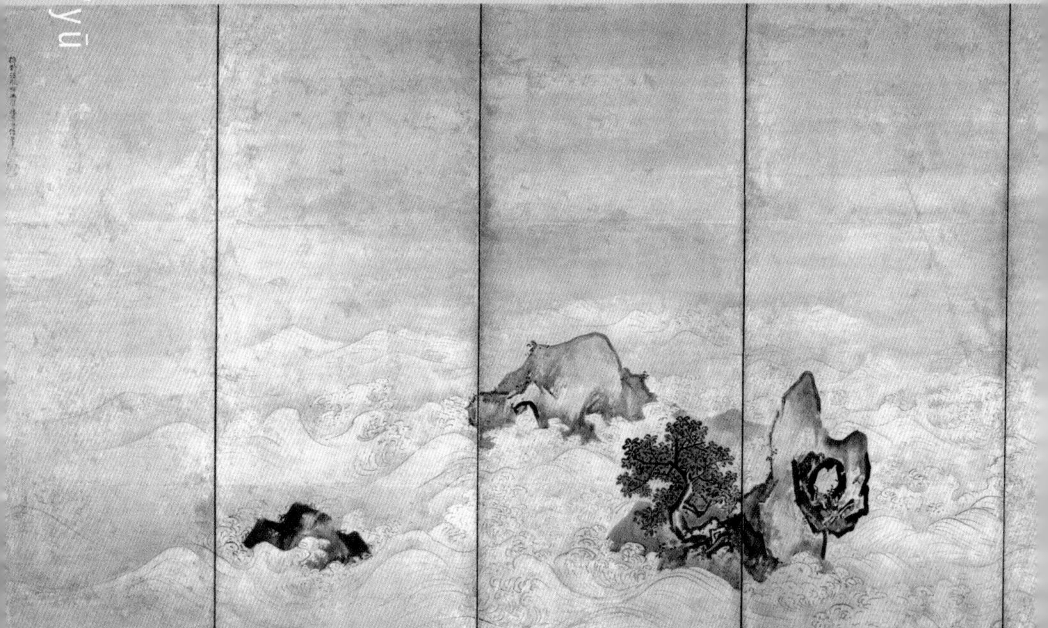

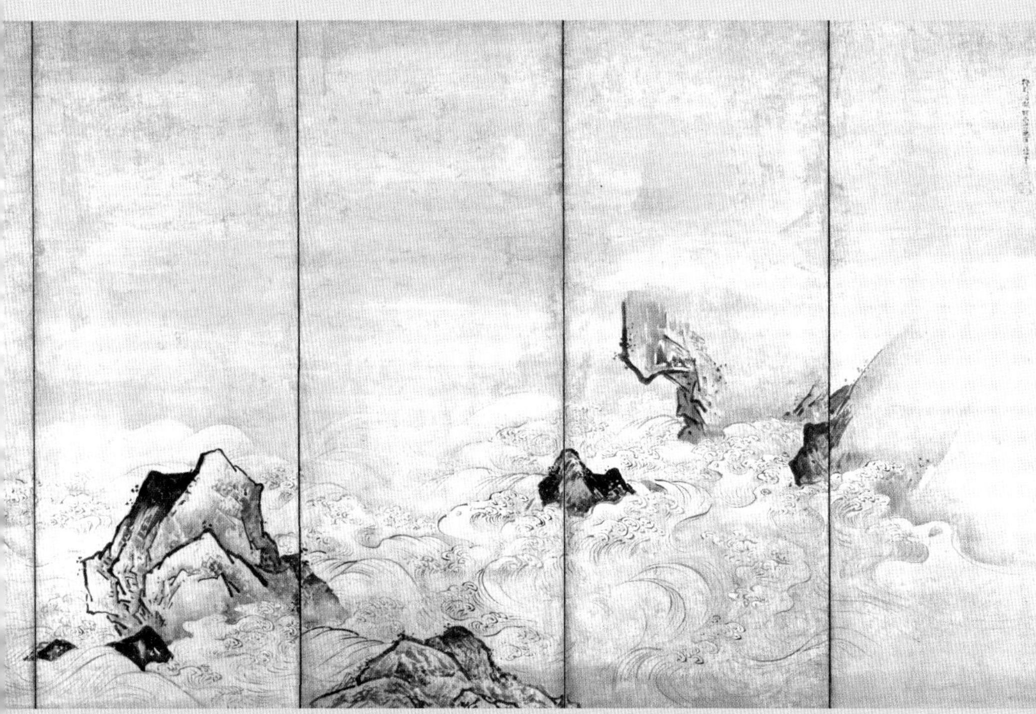

The ultimate Edo-period maestro who domesticated the Kanō School style

Kanō Tan'yū (1602-74), the eldest son of Kanō Takano-bu, was active in the first half of the Edo period. This extraordinary artist was granted an audience with Tokugawa Ieyasu, then in retirement in Sumpu, when only eleven. After moving to Edo, he became an artist by appointment to the Tokugawa shogunate at the age of sixteen. Having received a residence outside Edo Castle's Kajibashi Gate, he founded the Kajibashi Kanō line. His work included leading his students in creating large-scale works (sliding door or folding screen paintings) for Nijō Castle, in Kyoto. He then played the director's role in creating large-scale works for Nagoya Castle, Edo Castle, the Imperial Palace in Kyoto, and the Tōshōgū Shrine in Nikko and had a huge influence on the Kanō School's organization and social position.

「波濤図」狩野探幽
寛永末期（1642 〜 44）島根県立美術館蔵
Waves, Kanō Tan'yū, ca.1642-44, Shimane Art Museum

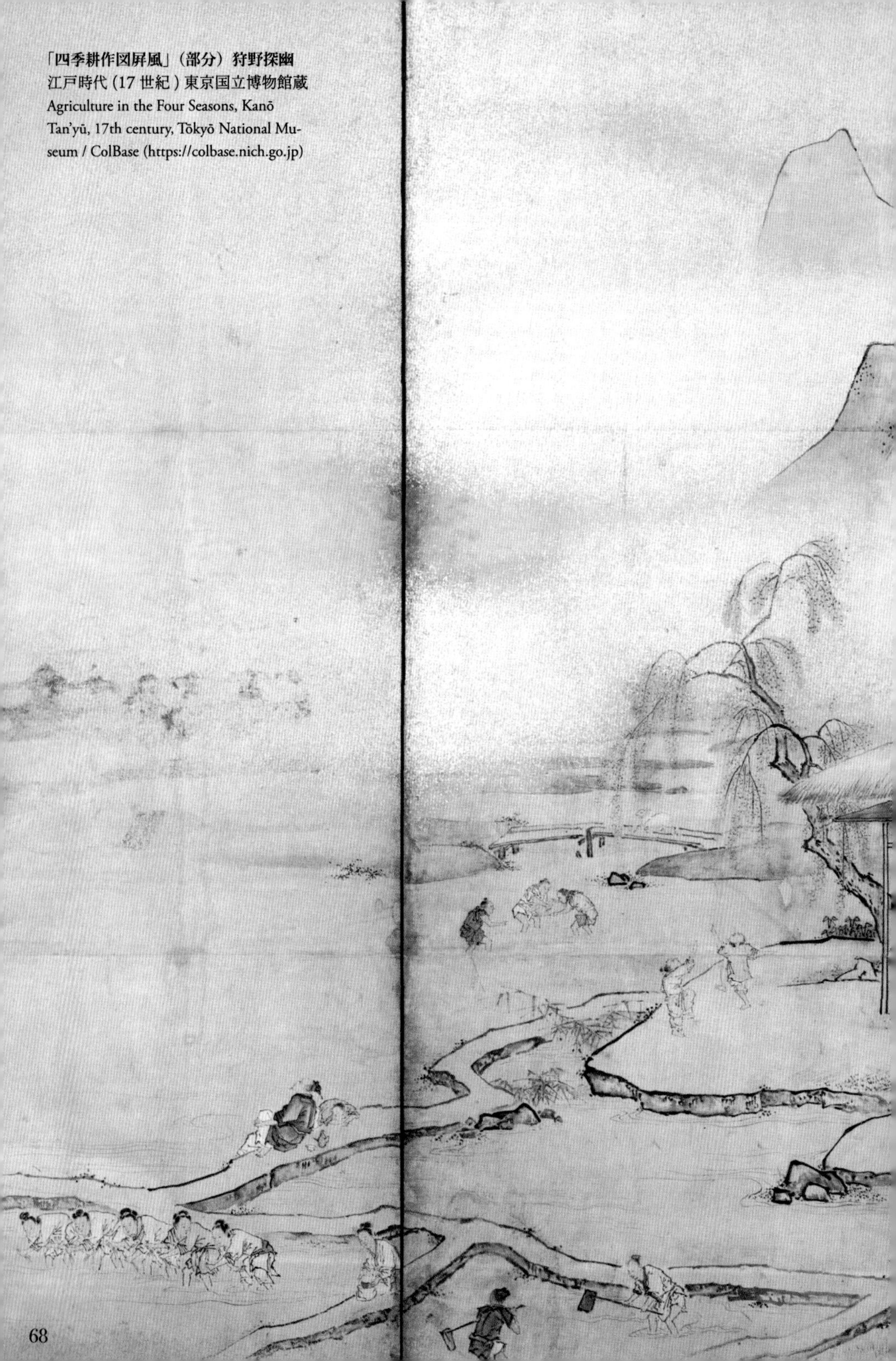

「四季耕作図屏風」（部分）狩野探幽
江戸時代（17世紀）東京国立博物館蔵
Agriculture in the Four Seasons, Kanō
Tan'yū, 17th century, Tōkyō National Museum / ColBase (https://colbase.nich.go.jp)

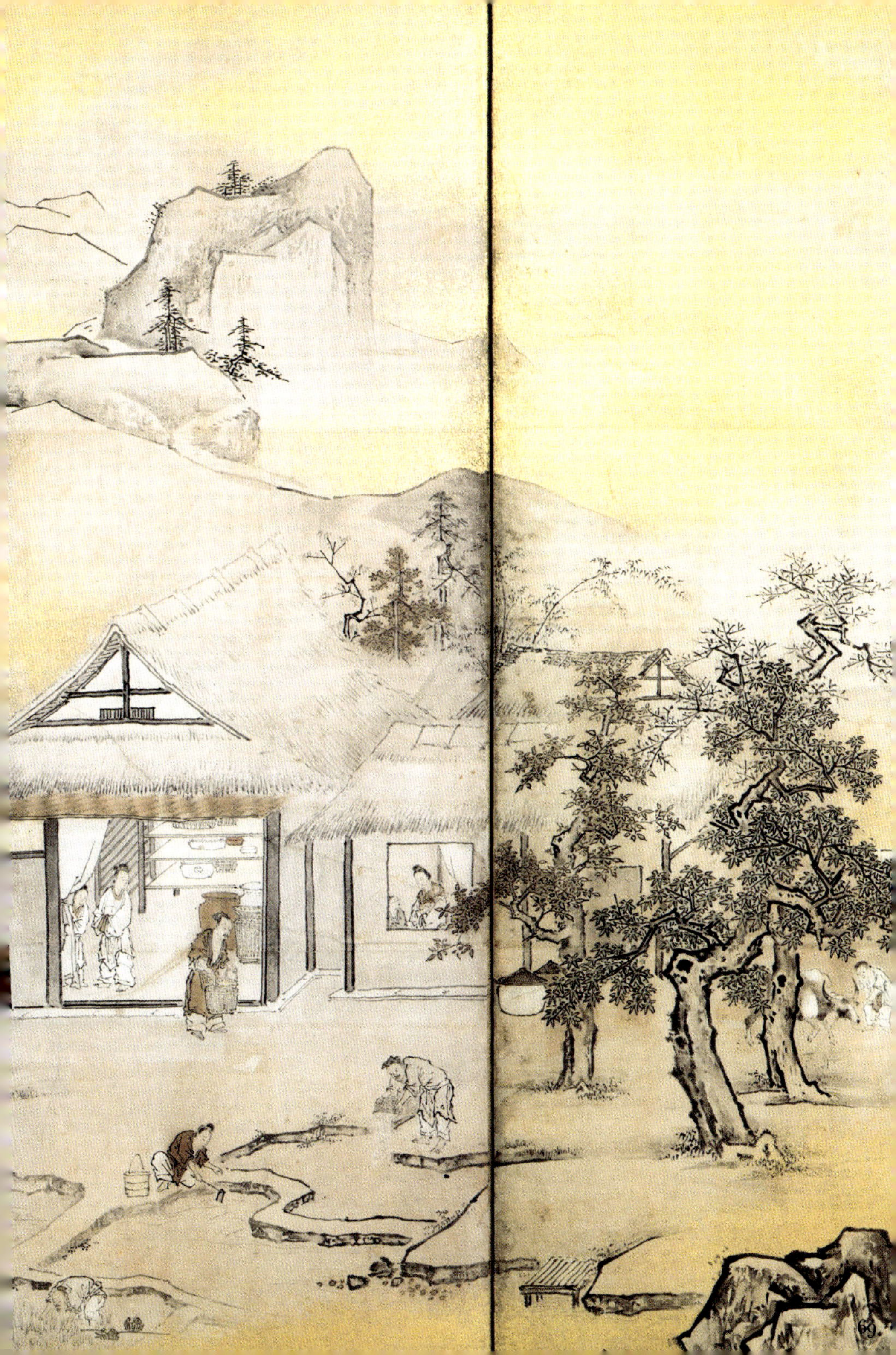

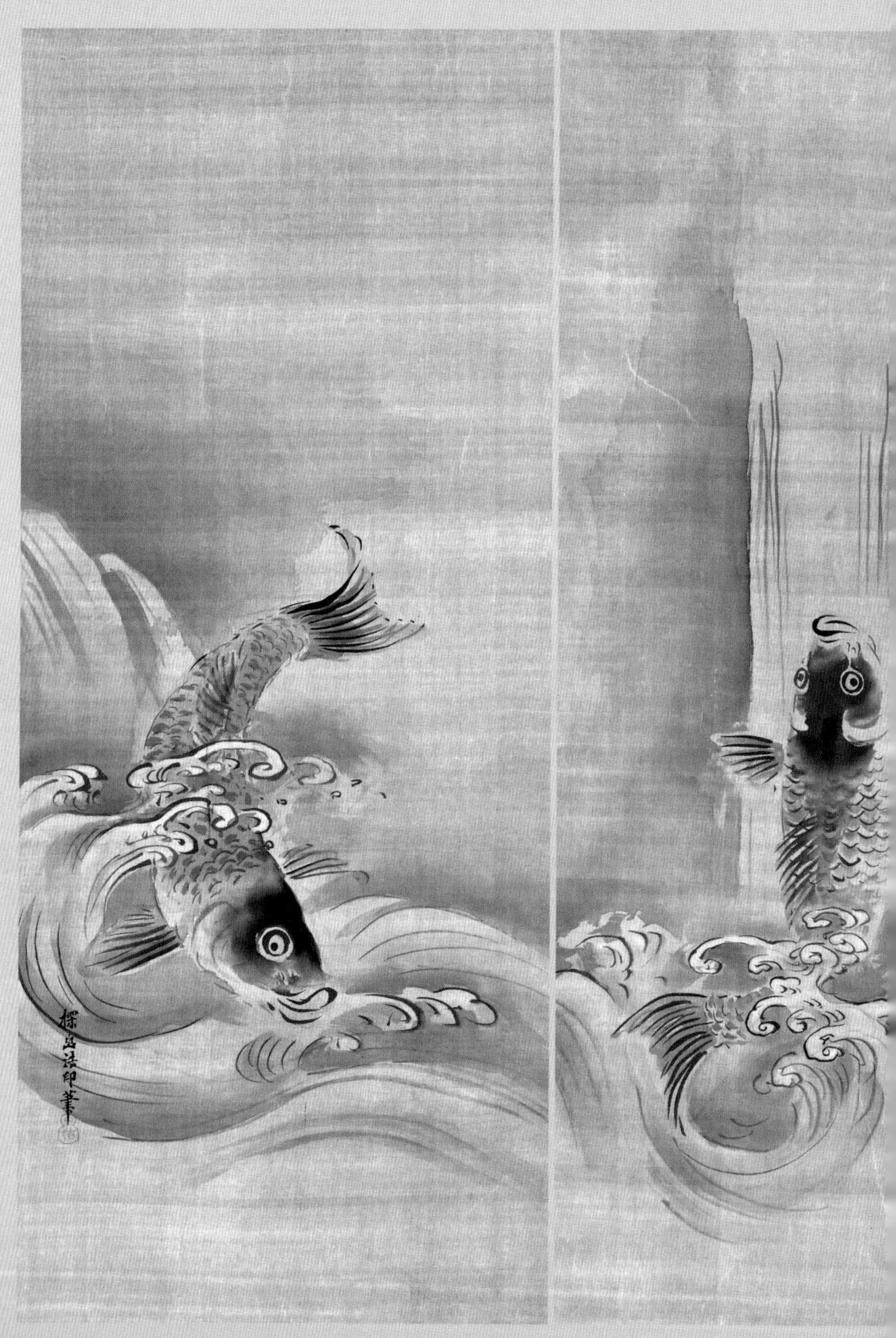

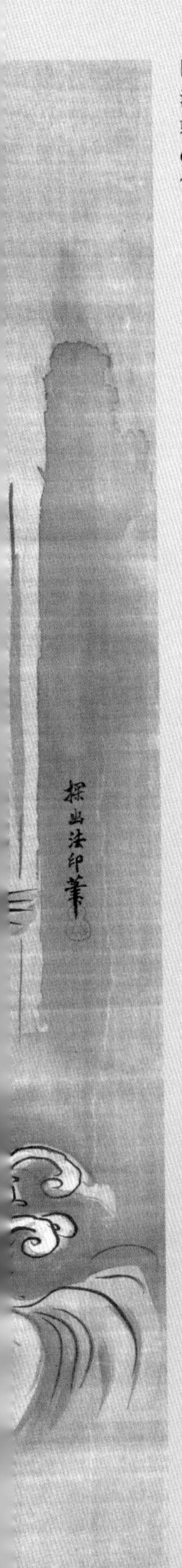

「鯉図」狩野探幽
江戸時代 (17 世紀)
敦賀市博物館蔵
Carp, Kanō Tan'yū, 17th century,
Tsuruga City Museum

「鸕鶿草葺不合尊降誕図」
狩野探幽
江戸時代 (17 世紀)
東京国立博物館蔵
The Birth of *Ugayafukiaezu no Mikoto*, Kanō Tan'yū, 17th century, Tōkyō National Museum / ColBase (https://colbase.nich.go.jp)

久隅守景

Kusumi Morikage

移ろう時を永遠に描き留めた画家

くすみ もりかげ　生没年不詳

　江戸時代前期の画家。狩野派の女流画家として知られた清原雪信（きよはらゆきのぶ）の父。狩野探幽門下の四天王の一人と称され、近江（滋賀県）大津の聖衆来迎寺の障壁画の制作に参加する。明暦のころ加賀金沢藩主前田家につかえ、粉本主義から創造性を失いつつあった江戸狩野派を離れ、農民の生活に取材した田園風俗の作品に本領を発揮し、独自の画風をうちたてた。

A painter who captured forever fleeting time

An early Edo-period painter, Kusumi Morikage was the father of Kiyohara Yukinobu, famed as a rare example of a female painter in the Kanō School. Called one of Kanō Tan'yū four best pupils, he took part in creating large-format pointings for the Shōju Raigōji Temple in Ōtsu, Ōmi province (now Shiga prefecture). In the mid 1650s, he served the Maeda clan, rulers of the Kaga Kanazawa domain and left the Edo Kanō School, which was losing creativity through its commitment to copying model paintings, again and again. Morikage developed his abilities through works with rural landscapes as their subject, establishing his own style.

「納涼図屛風」国宝　久隅守景
江戸時代（17世紀）東京国立博物館蔵
Nōryōzu (A Peasant Family Beneath a Hanging Gourd Trellis), National Treasure, Kusumi Morikage, 17th century, Tōkyō National Museum / ColBase (https://colbase.nich.go.jp)

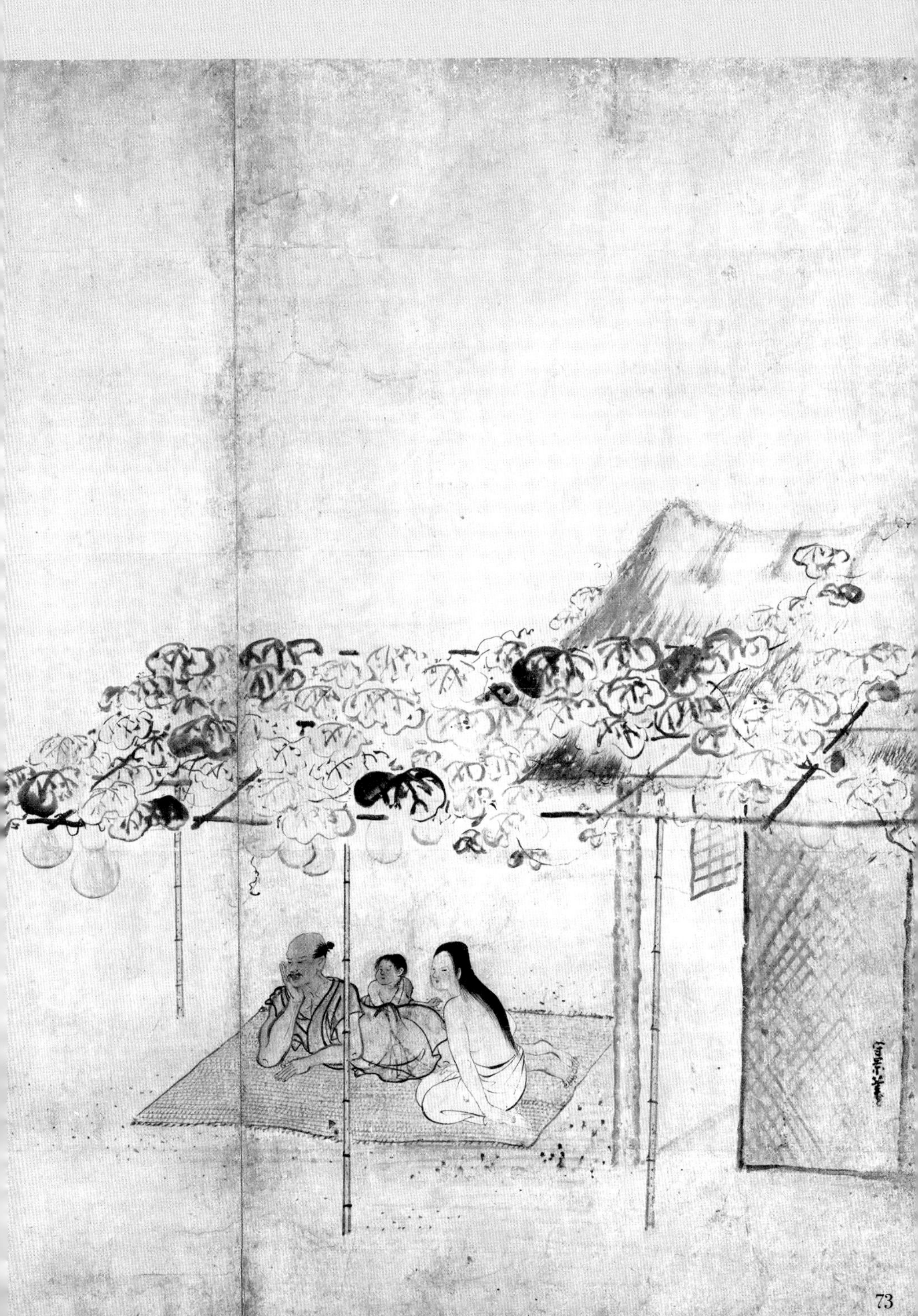

「許由巣父図屛風」久隅守景
江戸時代（17 世紀）東京国立博物館蔵
Xuyou Washing His Ears and Chaofa with His
Ox, Kusumi Morikage, 17th century, Tōkyō
National Museum/ ColBase (https://colbase.
nich.go.jp)

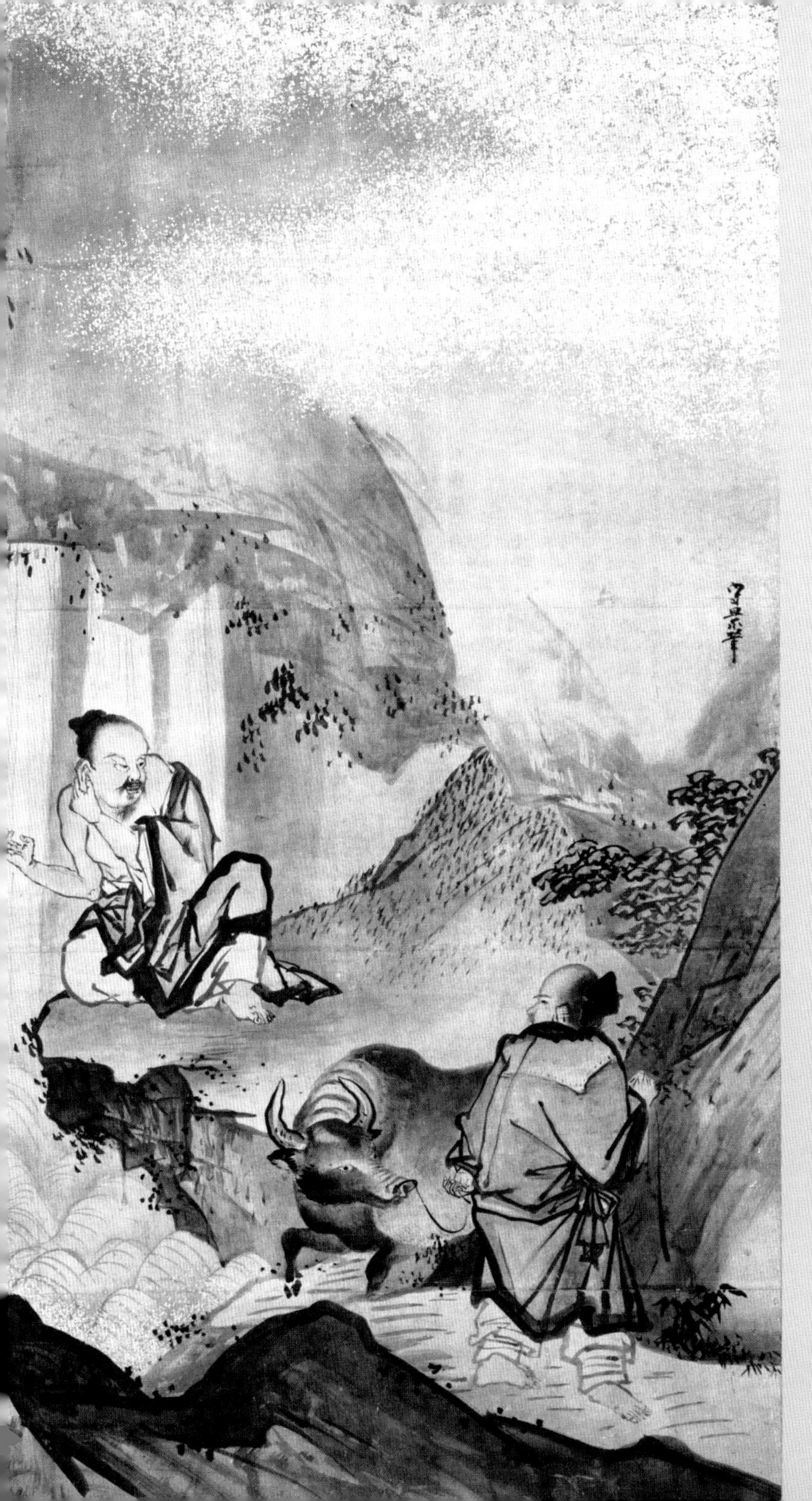

俵屋宗達

王朝美を新しい感性で復興させた琳派の画家

たわらや そうたつ　生没年不詳

　桃山から江戸時代初期の画家。琳派の様式を創始した。京都で活躍した町絵師で「俵屋」はその屋号。宗達の伝記や出身の詳細は不明であるが、絵師として活躍する一方、烏丸光広、千少庵ら当時の公卿や文化人との広い交際があり、京都の裕福な町衆階層に属していたものと思われる。扇面や色紙など様々な料紙装飾を手掛ける工房を主宰。金銀泥を駆使した雅で大胆な構図の金地屏風や華麗な料紙装飾に新しい画境を獲得した。

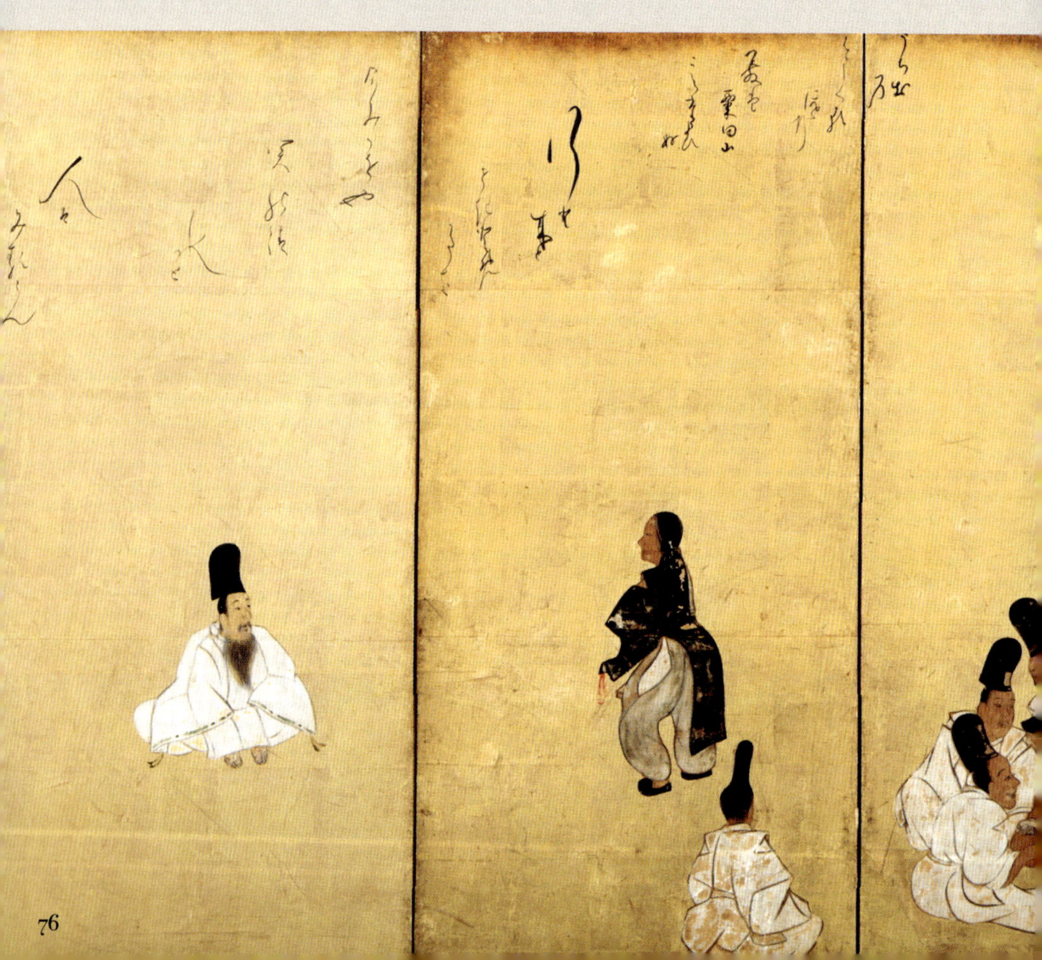

The Rimpa painter who revived the court style with a new sensibility

Tawaraya Sōtatsu was a painter active in the Momoyama and early Edo periods who originated what became the Rimpa style. He was active in Kyoto as a *machi-eshi*, a painter with no official assignment who sold his work to townspeople; his studio and shop was called the Tawaraya. Details about his life are unclear, but it is believed that, while working as a painter, he formed ties with a broad range of aristocrats and literati, including Karasumaru Mitsuhiro and Senshōan. He is thus thought to have been part of Kyoto's affluent townsman class. His elegant screen paintings on gold ground, combining skillful use of gold pigment and bold compositions, and his gorgeous decorated papers opened up new terrain.

「関屋図屏風」（部分）重文　俵屋宗達・烏丸光弘　江戸時代・17 世紀　東京国立博物館蔵
Standing Screens of the Tale of Genji: *Sekiya*, Important Cultural Property, Tawaraya Sōtatsu, praised by Karasuma Mitsuhiro, 17th century, Tōkyō National Museum / ColBase (https://colbase.nich.go.jp)

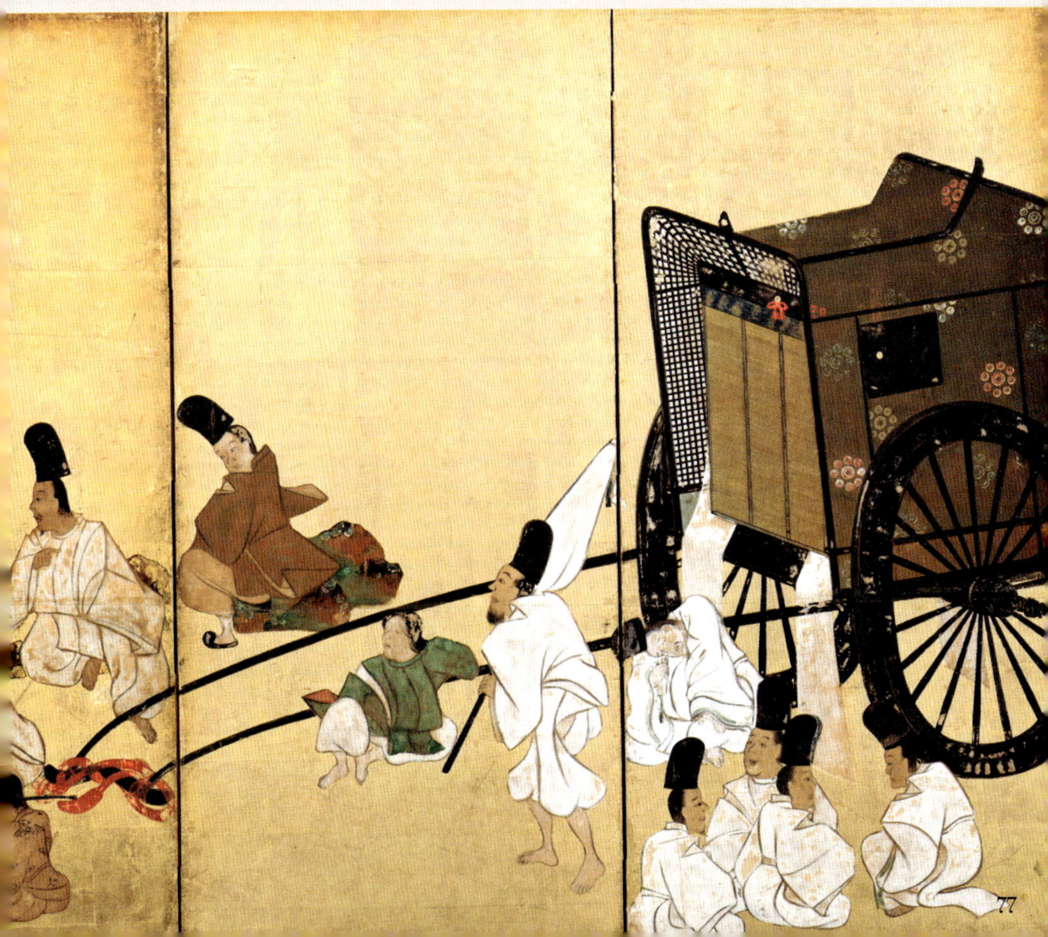

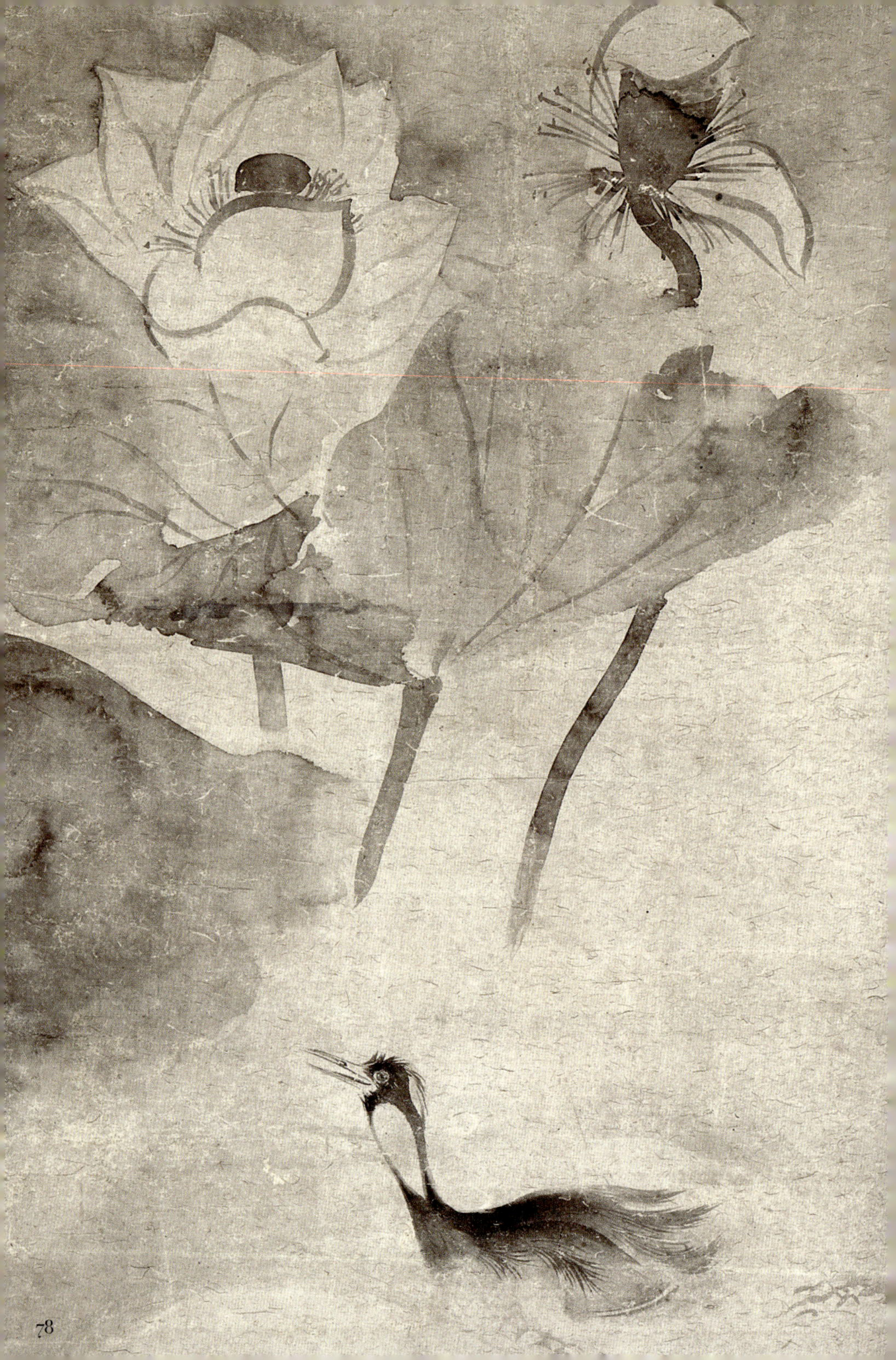

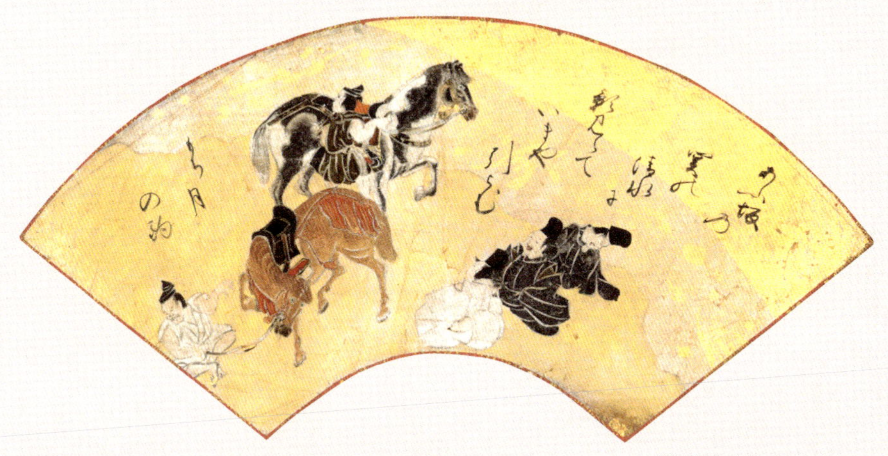

「駒引図扇面」俵屋宗達
江戸時代（17 世紀）
黎明教会資料研修館蔵
Fan painting of a Horse pulling,
Tawaraya Sōtatsu, 17th century,
Reimei Art Gallery

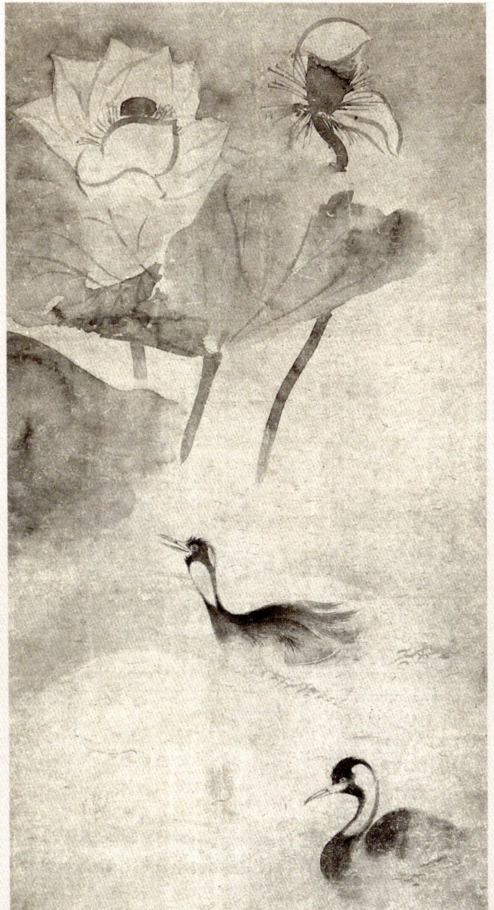

「蓮池水禽図」国宝
俵屋宗達　江戸時代（17 世紀）
京都国立博物館蔵
Water Birds in Lotus Pond, National
Treasure, Tawaraya Sōtatsu, 17th century,
Kyoto National Museum/ ColBase
(https://colbase.nich.go.jp)

尾形光琳

Ogata Kōrin

光悦や宗達の絵画に魅了され、琳派の装飾様式を成し遂げた

おがた こうりん　万治元~享保元年（1658~1716）

　江戸時代前期の画家。工芸意匠家であり琳派の大成者。生家は桃山時代以来の高級呉服商雁金屋。初め山本素軒から狩野派の画法を学び、のちに生家の所蔵品から光悦蒔絵や宗達の絵にふれ、その作風の復興を志した。金と銀、明と暗、写実とデザイン的要素を強引に統一した装飾性に富む光琳模様ともいえる新たな大和絵画風を確立した。

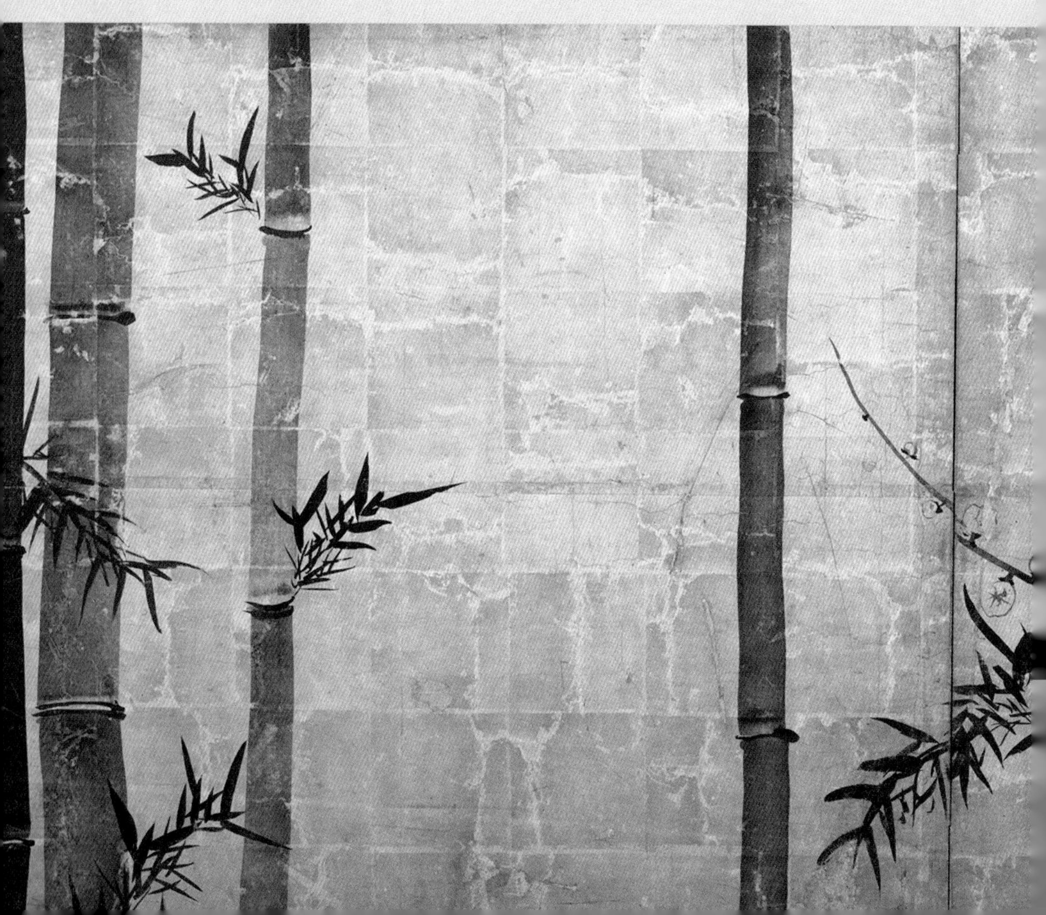

Fascinated by the paintings of Kōetsu and Sōtatsu, he developed the decorative Rimpa style

Ogata Kōrin (1658-1716), who was active in the first half of the Edo period, was a designer of craft objects as well as the artist who brought the Rimpa School to perfection. At first he studied Kanō-style painting techniques under Yamamoto Soken, then, encountering works in *maki-e* by Kōetsu and paintings by Sōtatsu from his family collection, set his heart on reviving their style. Gold and silver, light and dark, realistic and stylized—he drew out those elements and integrated them to establish a new Yamato-e painting style. The result was his richly decorative, characteristically Kōrin motifs.

「竹梅図屏風」重文　尾形光琳　江戸時代（18 世紀）東京国立博物館蔵
Standing Screens of Bamboo plums, Important Cultural Property, Ogata Kōrin, 18th century, Tōkyō National Museum / ColBase (https://colbase.nich.go.jp)

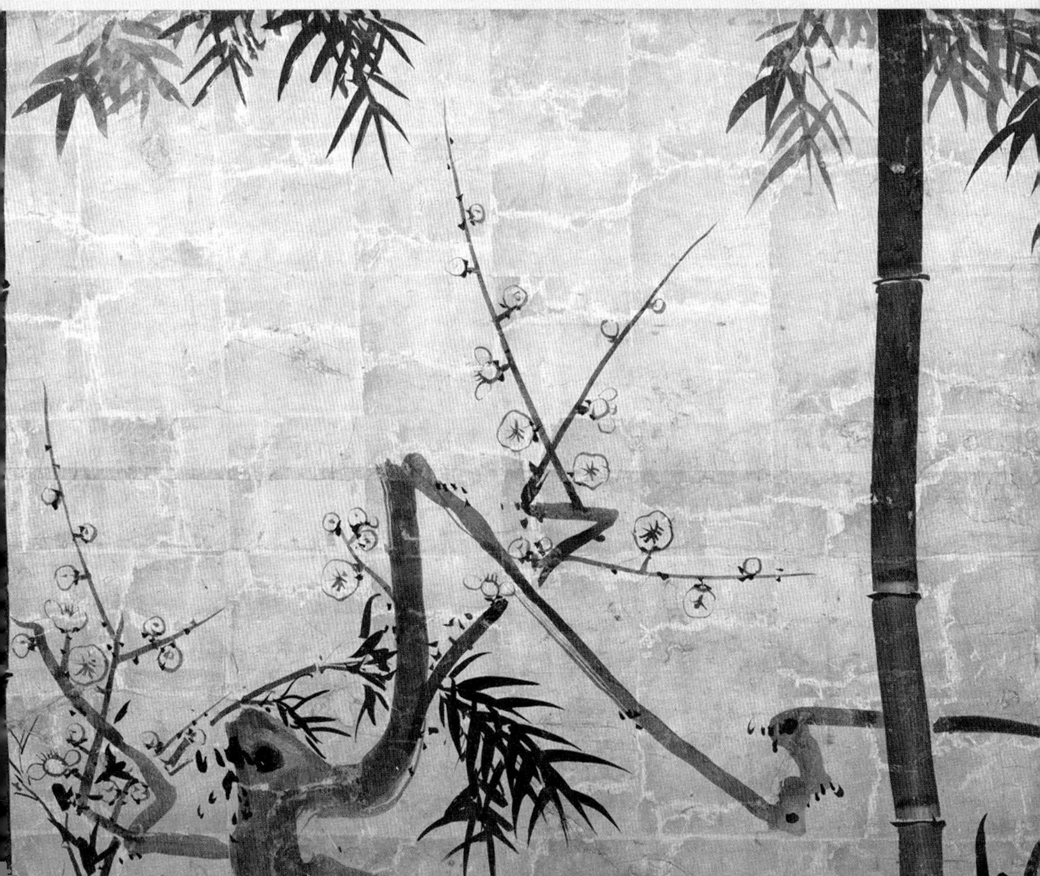

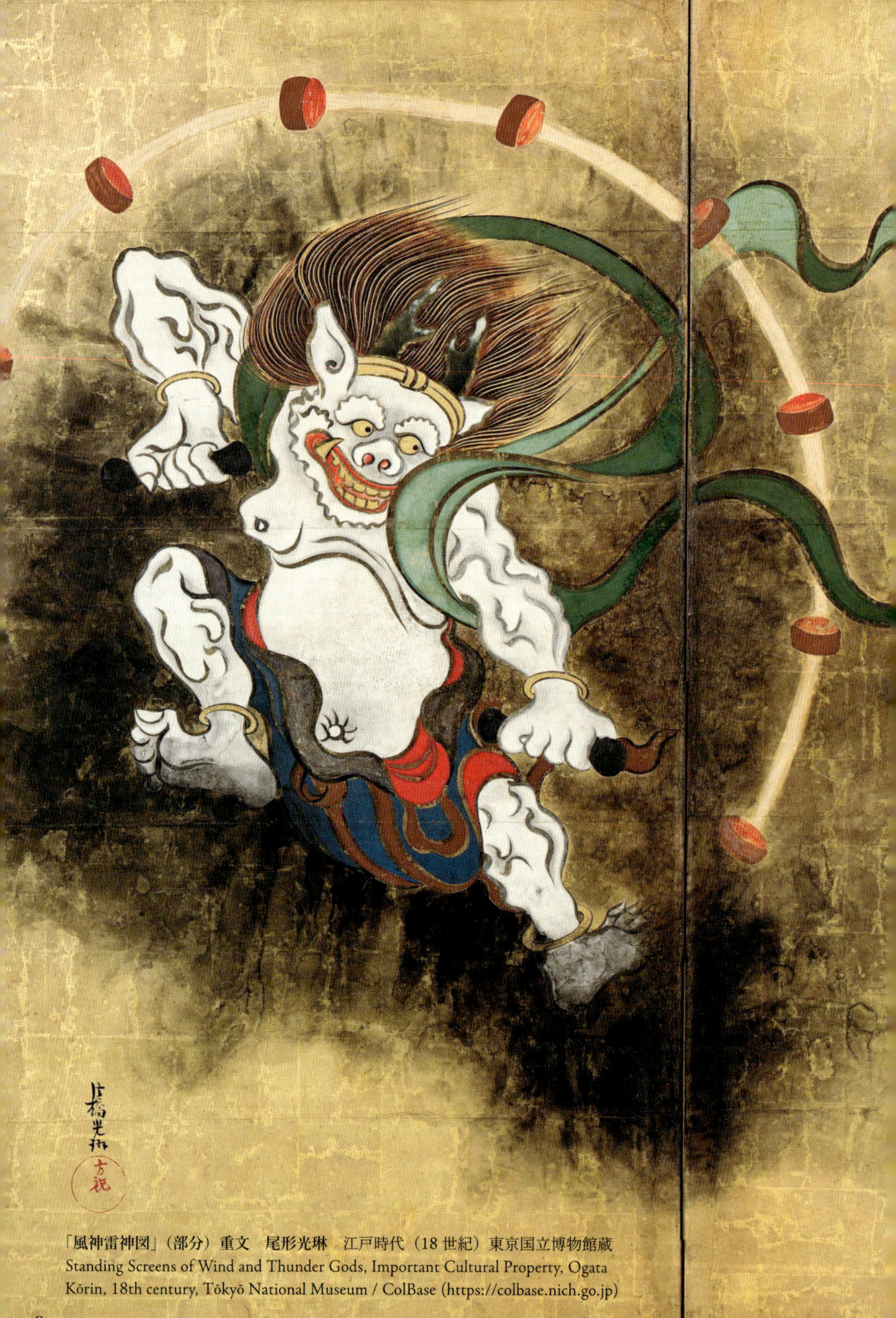

「風神雷神図」（部分）重文　尾形光琳　江戸時代（18 世紀）東京国立博物館蔵
Standing Screens of Wind and Thunder Gods, Important Cultural Property, Ogata Kōrin, 18th century, Tōkyō National Museum / ColBase (https://colbase.nich.go.jp)

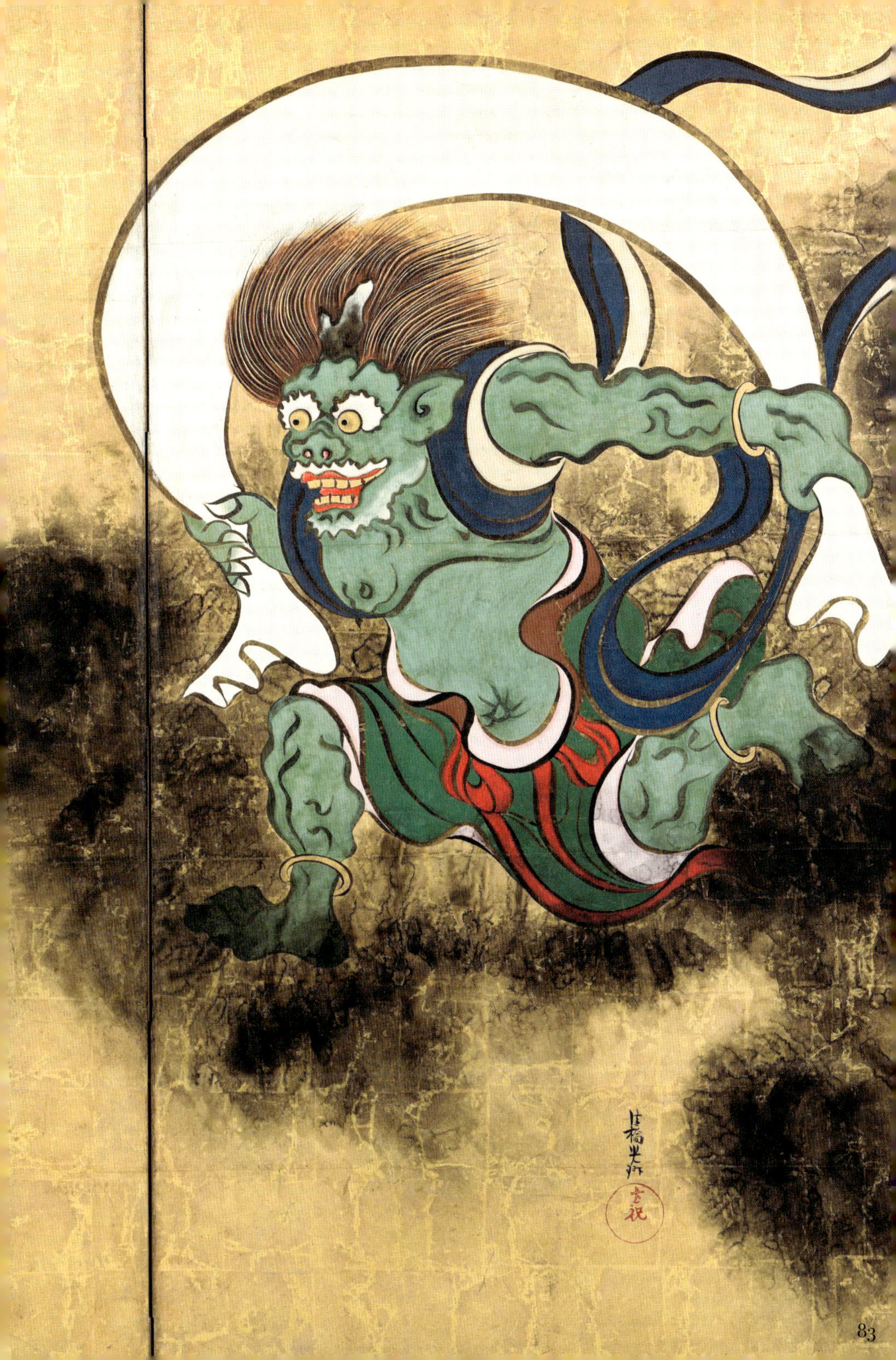

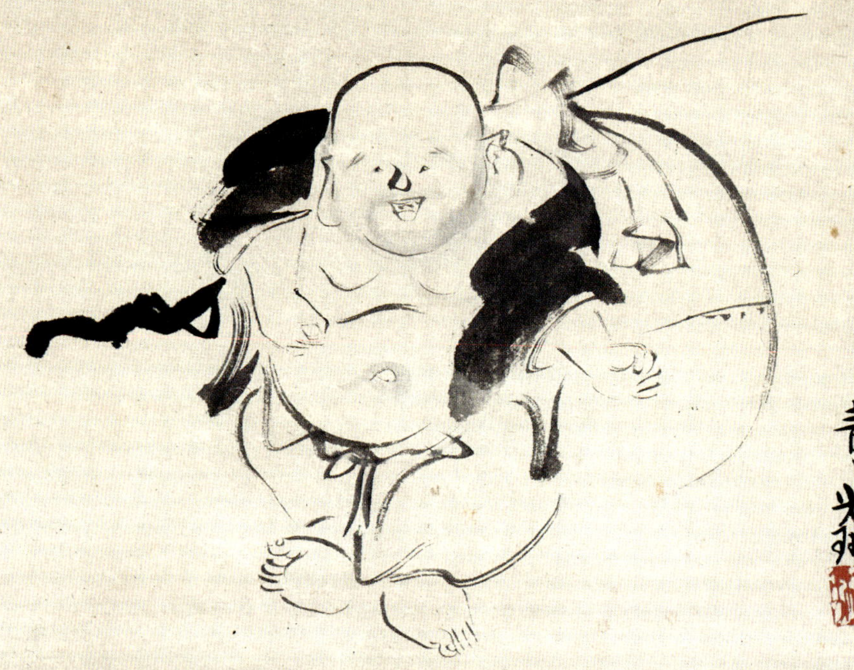

「布袋図」尾形光琳　江戸時代（18世紀）黎明教会資料研修館蔵
Budai, Ogata Kōrin, 18th century, Reimei Art Gallery

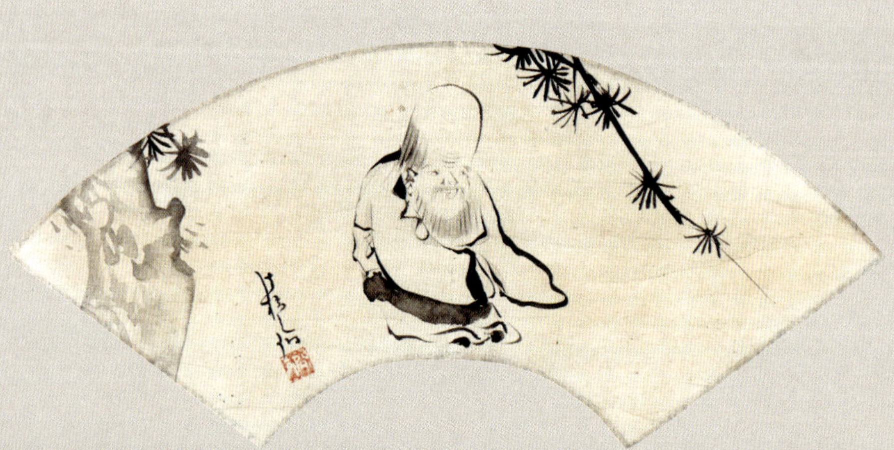

「寿老人図扇面」尾形光琳　江戸時代（18世紀）黎明教会資料研修館蔵
Fan-shaped paintings of Shou Laoren, Ogata Kōrin, 18th century, Reimei Art Gallery

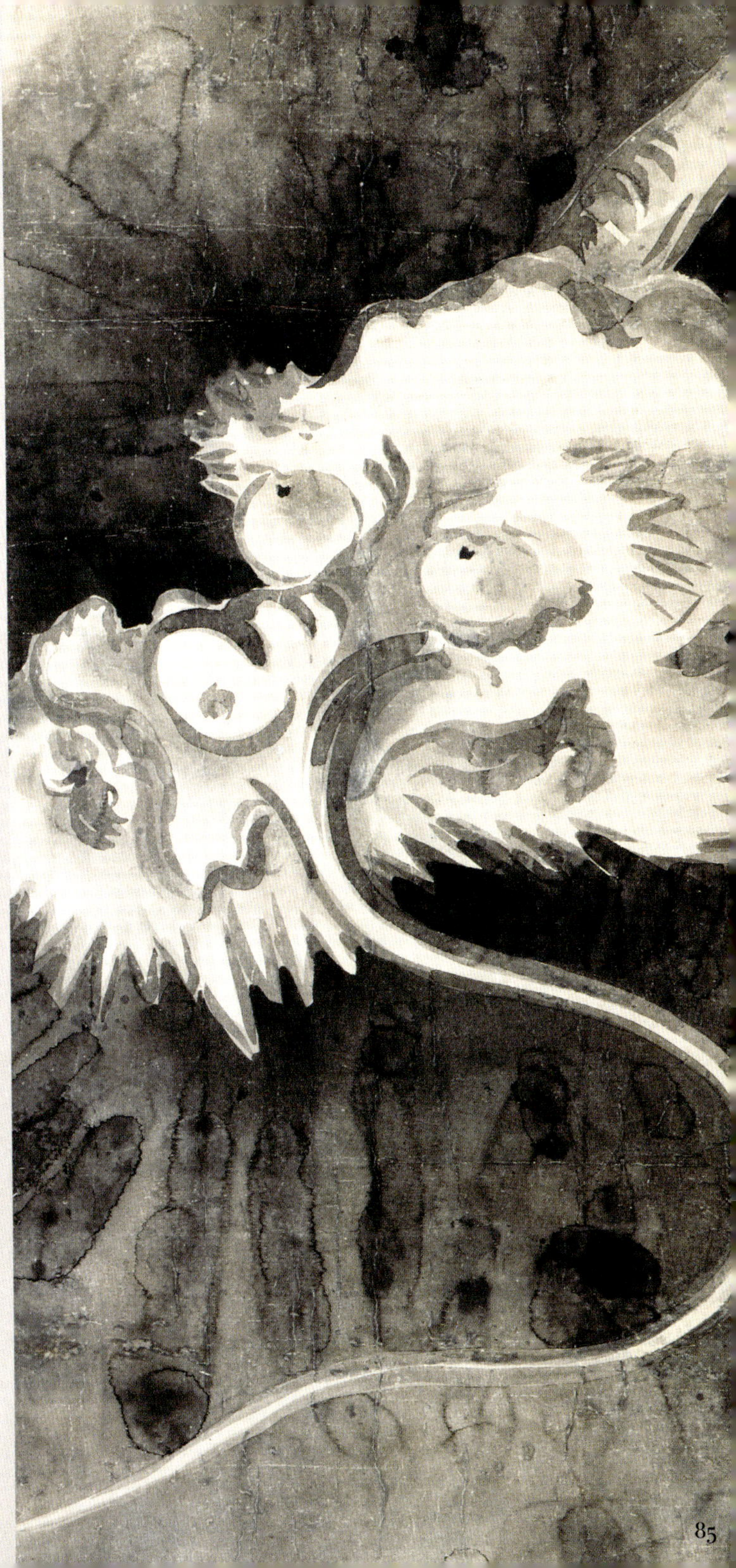

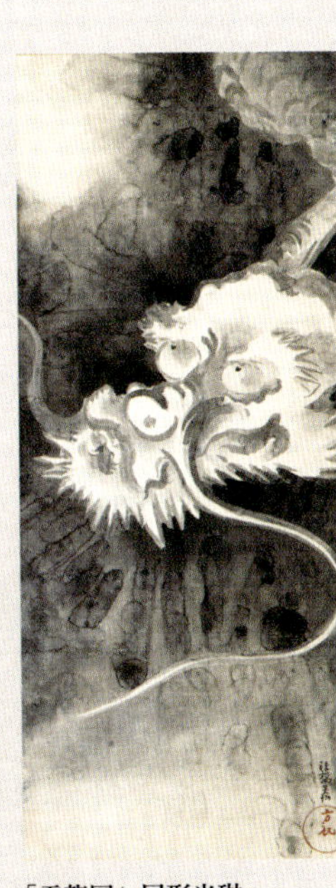

「雲龍図」尾形光琳
江戸時代（18世紀）
黎明教会資料研修館蔵
Dragon and Clouds, Ogata
Kōrin, 18th century, Reimei
Art Gallery

禅の民衆化につくした近世禅画の巨匠

はくいん えかく　貞享2~明和5年（1685~1768）

　江戸時代中期の臨済宗の僧。15歳で郷里駿河（静岡県）の松蔭寺で得度。信濃飯山の道鏡慧端（正受老人）の法をつぐ。のち松蔭寺に戻って禅の民衆化につくし、臨済宗中興の祖と称せられた。還暦を過ぎた頃から禅画墨跡を描くようになり、達磨や観音、布袋などの祖師や、神仏や寓意画などを個性的な筆致で描いた。

A master of early-modern Zen painting who devoted himself to popularizing Zen

Hakuin Ekaku (1685-1768), a Rinzai sect priest active in the mid-Edo period, entered the Buddhist priesthood at Shōinji Temple in Suruga province (now Shizuoka prefecture) at the age of fifteen. He received the dharma from Dōkyō Etan of Shinshū Iiyama, and later returned to Shōinji, where he worked hard to make Zen accessible to ordinary people, for which he is known as a founder of the Rinzai revival. After turning sixty, he painted zen paintings with inscriptions, producing paintings of the Bodhidharma, Kannon, Hotei, and other canonical figures and divinities as well as allegorical paintings in his distinctive brushwork.

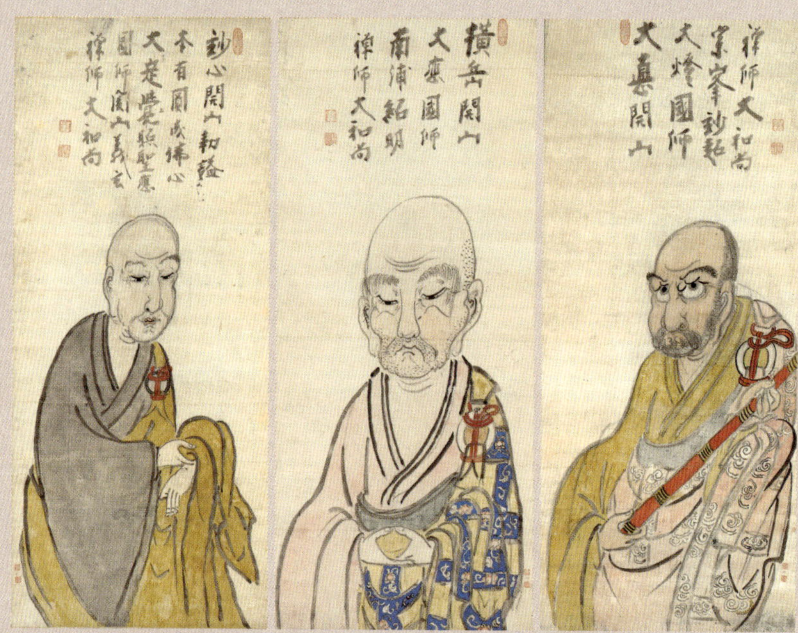

「大応・大燈・関山像」白隠慧鶴　江戸時代（18世紀）九州国立博物館蔵
Statue of Daio, Daito, Sekizan, Hakuin Ekaku, 18th century,
Kyushu National Museum/ ColBase (https://colbase.nich.go.jp)

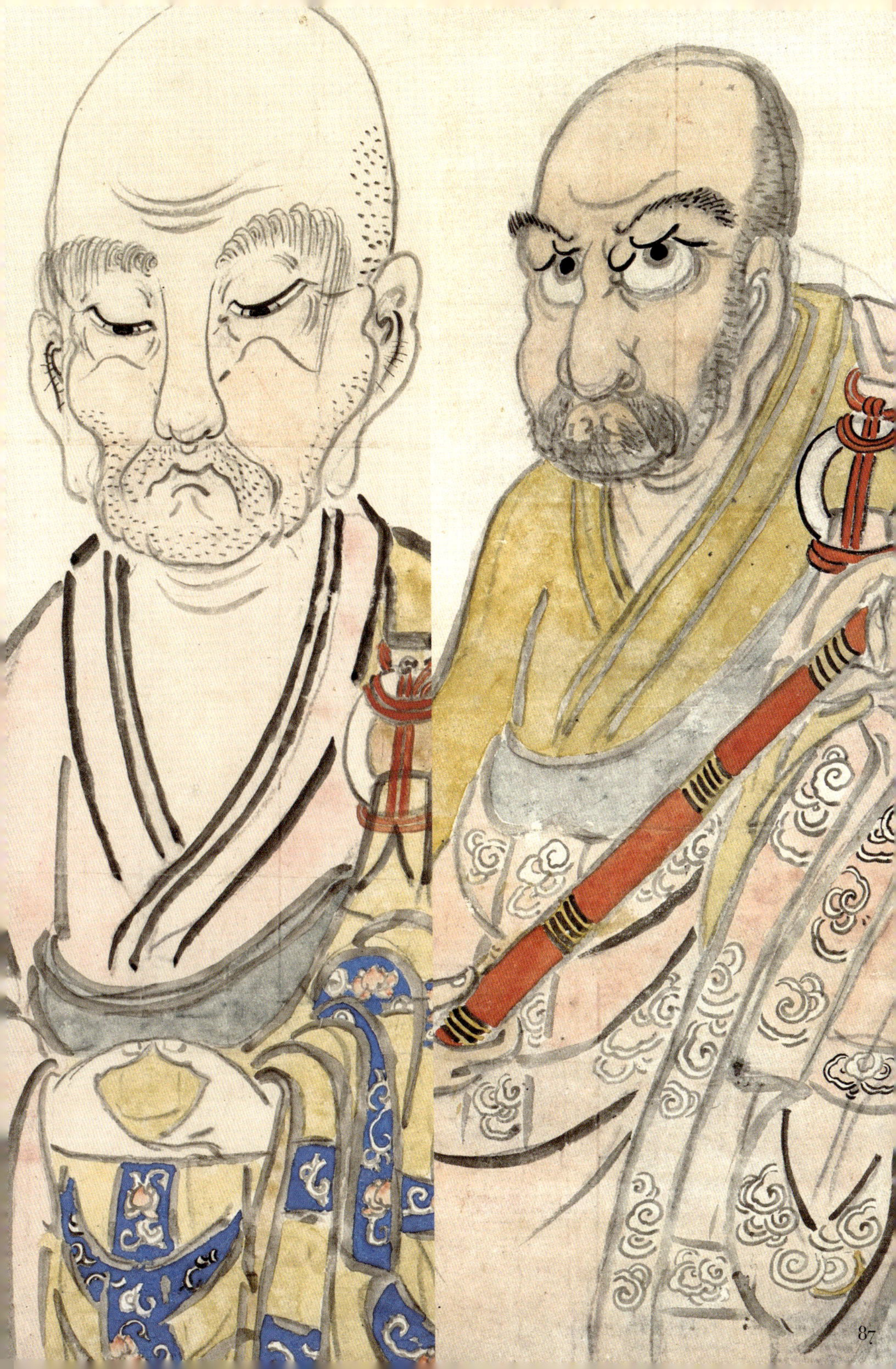

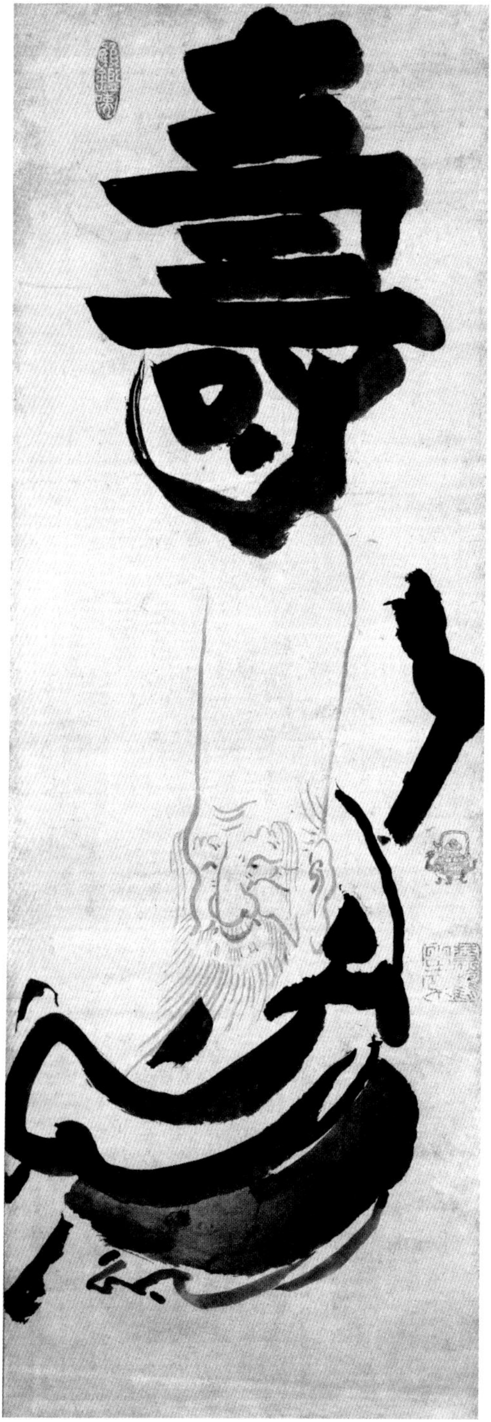

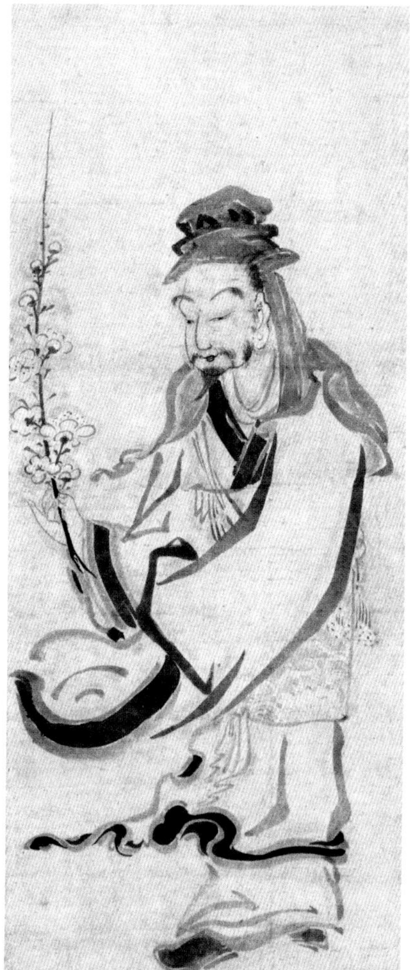

「渡唐天神図」白隠慧鶴
江戸時代（18 世紀）
愛知県美術館蔵（木村定三コレクション）
Tenjin Visiting China, Hakuin Ekaku, 18th century, Aichi Prefectural Museum of Art/ Kimura Teizo Collection

「寿老人図」自賛　白隠慧鶴
江戸時代（18 世紀）
愛知県美術館蔵（木村定三コレクション）
Shou Laoren, Hakuin Ekaku, 18th century, Aichi Prefectural Museum of Art/ Kimura Teizo Collection

仙厓義梵
Sengai Gibon

飄 逸な画風で、悟りの境地を機知に
富んだ筆墨で描いた画僧

せんがい ぎぼん　寛延3～天保8年（1750～1837）

　江戸時代後期の臨済宗の禅僧。美濃（岐阜県）に生まれる。はじめ臨済宗の月船禅慧より学問を受け、その後、39歳で博多に赴き、栄西が開いた聖福寺住持となり同寺の復興に努力した。50歳ごろから書画の才をあらわし、あらゆる階層の人々の求めに応じて筆を振るった。技巧にとらわれず自己流に徹した絵は、白隠の絵とともに近世禅画を代表する。

A priest painter who depicted the state of enlightenment in a witty, free style

Sengai Gibon (1750-1837) was a Rinzai sect Zen priest in the latter half of the Edo period. Born in Mino (now Gifu prefecture), he was first educated by Gessen Zenne of the Rinzai sect, then, at the age of 39, he moved to Hakata and became the head priest at Shūfukuji Temple, which Eisai had founded. He began expressing his talent for calligraphy and painting in his fifties and wielded his brush in response to requests from people far and wide. His paintings are consistently in his own style, unbound by technique, and are regarded, with Hakuin's work, as the finest early modern Zen paintings.

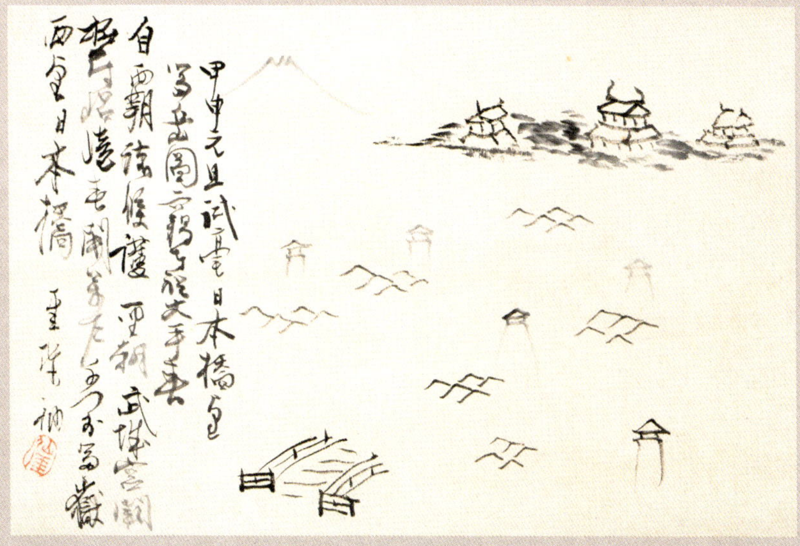

「富嶽図」仙厓義梵　文政7年（1824）東京国立博物館蔵
Mt. *Fuji*, Sengai Gibon, 1824, Tōkyō National Museum / ColBase (https://colbase.nich.go.jp)

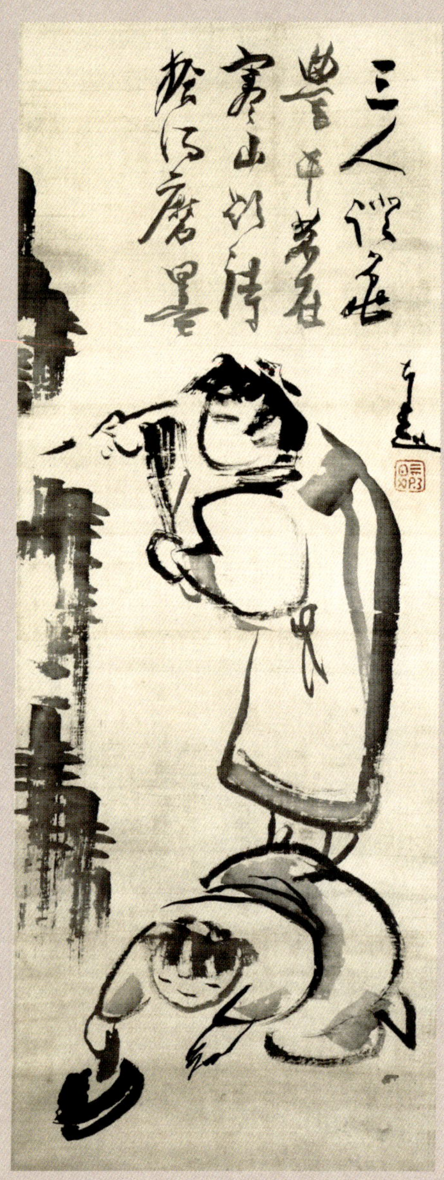

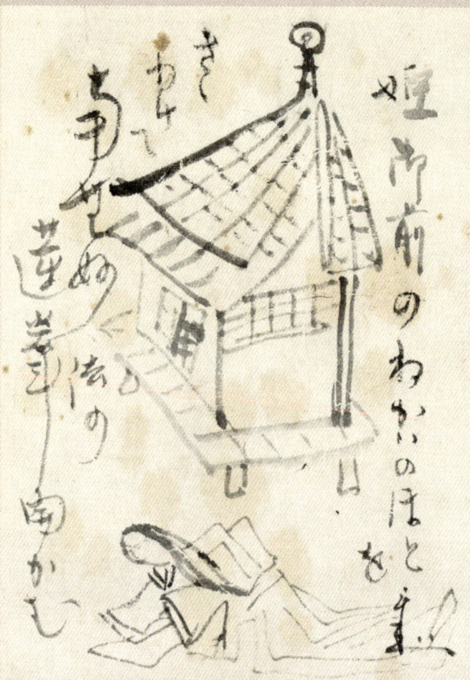

「姫御前図」仙厓義梵
江戸時代（18 世紀後半～ 19 世紀前半）
愛知県美術館蔵（木村定三コレクション）
Princess, Sengai Gibon, Latter half of the 18th century-first half of the 19th century, Aichi Prefectural Museum of Art/ Kimura Teizo Collection

「寒山拾得図」自賛　仙厓義梵
江戸時代（18 世紀後半～ 19 世紀前半）
愛知県美術館蔵（木村定三コレクション）
Hanshan and Shide, Sengai Gibon, Latter half of the 18th century-first half of the 19th century, Aichi Prefectural Museum of Art/ Kimura Teizo Collection

「滝図自画賛」仙厓義梵
文政 10 年 (1827) 東京国立博物館蔵 .
Waterfall, Sengai Gibon, 1827, Tōkyō National Museum / ColBase (https://colbase.nich.go.jp)

「趙州狗子図」（部分）仙厓義梵
江戸時代（18 世紀後半～ 19 世紀前半）
愛知県美術館蔵（木村定三コレクション）
Catechetical Question about Puppies, Sengai Gibon, Latter half of the 18th century-first half of the 19th century, Aichi Prefectural Museum of Art/ Kimura Teizo Collection

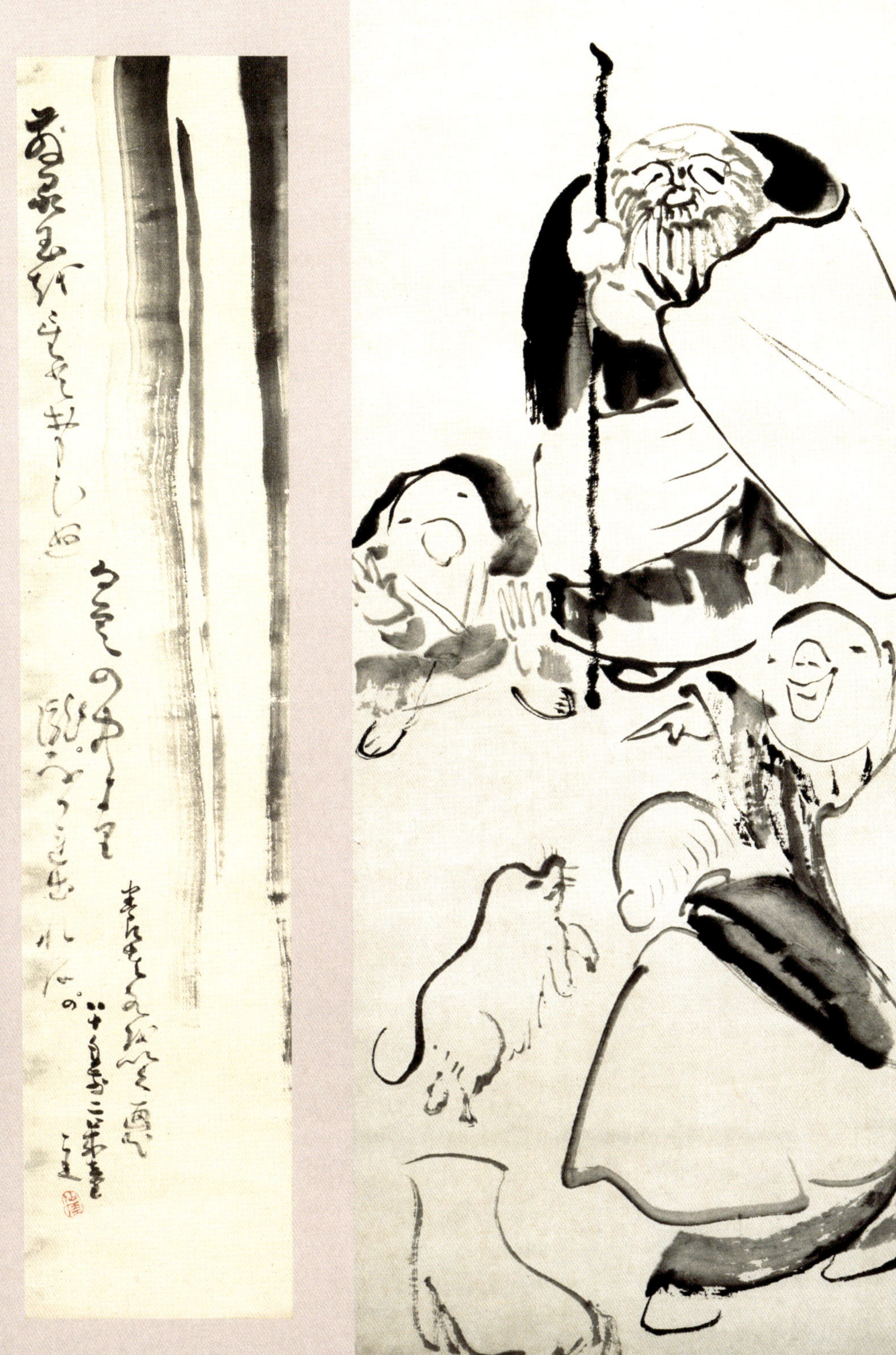

風外慧薫
Fūgai Ekun

墨戯を能くし、達磨や布袋の絵を得意とした画僧

ふうがい えくん　永禄11～没年不詳（1568～1654?）

　江戸時代前期の禅僧画家。上野国（群馬県）に生まれる。同国の乾窓寺や長源寺、双林寺などで修行の後、相模国小田原（神奈川県）の成願寺に住む。のち曾我山中の巌窟にすみ、遠江石岡に移る。承応3年（1654）ごろ人を雇って墓穴をほらせ、自らそこに投じて入寂したという。墨戯を能くし、達磨や布袋、自画像など多くの禅画を描いた。

A painter Priest who depicted the Bodhidharma and Hotei with witty brush strokes

Fūgai Ekun (1568- 1654?) was an early Edo period Zen priest paint-er born in Kōzuke province (now Gunma prefecture). After training at temples in his home province (including Kensōji, Chōgenji, and Sōrinji), he resided in Seiganji Temple in Odawara, Sagami province (now Kanagawa prefecture). He later lived in a cave on Mount Soga, then moved to Tōtsu Ishioka. It is said that at the end of his life, he hired someone to dig a grave, threw himself in it, and died. He produced many Zen paint-ings in his witty brushwork, including pictures of the Bodhidharma, Hotei, and self portraits.

「半身達磨図」自賛　風外慧薫
江戸時代（16世紀後期～ 17世紀）
愛知県美術館蔵（木村定三コレクション）
Bodhidharma, Fūgai Ekun, Latter half of the
16th century-17th century, Aichi Prefectural
Museum of Art/ Kimura Teizo Collection

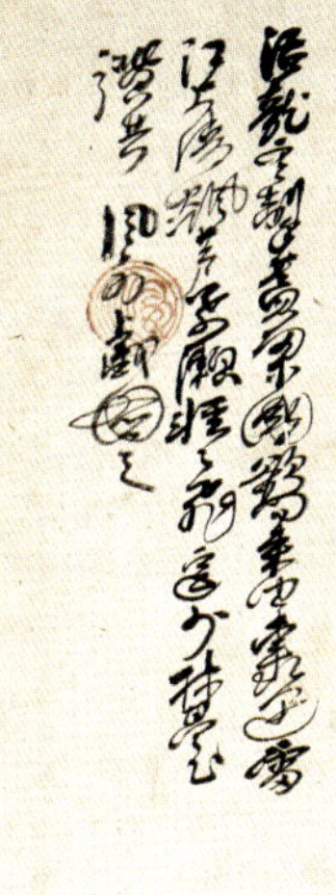

「芦葉達磨図」自賛　風外慧薫
江戸時代（16世紀後期〜 17世紀）
愛知県美術館蔵
（木村定三コレクション）
Bodhidharma on a Reed, Fūgai Ekun,
Latter half of the 16thcentury-17th
century, Aichi Prefectural Museum of
Art/ Kimura Teizo Collection

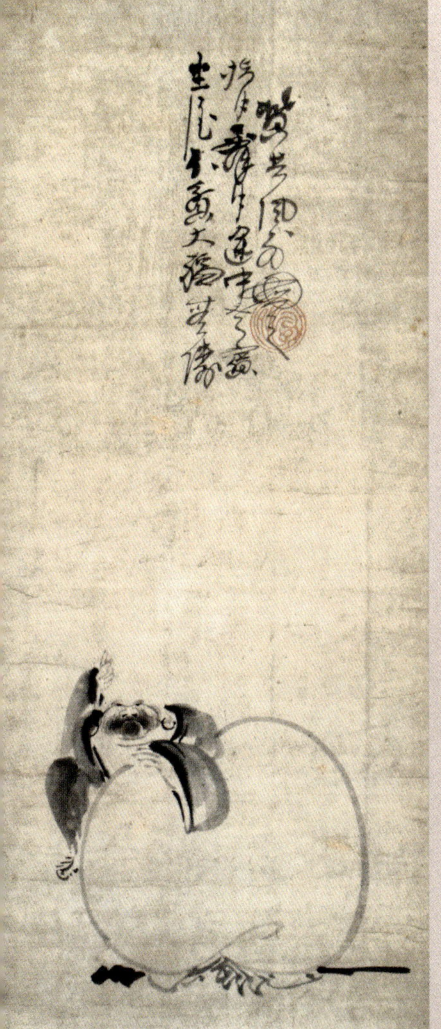

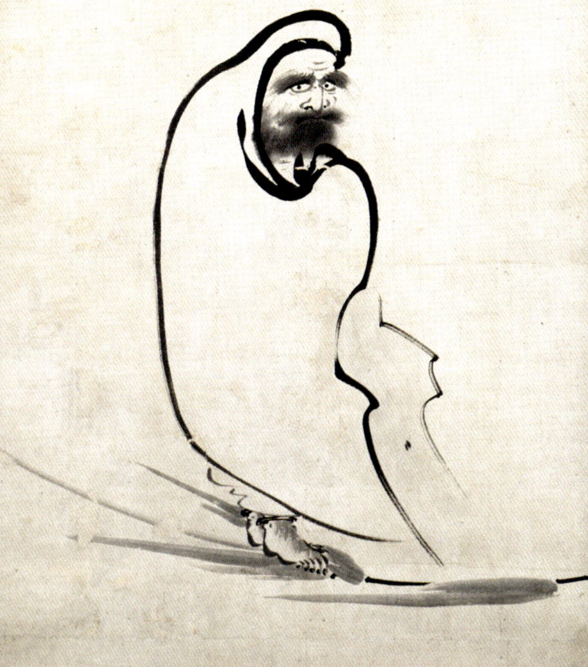

「指月布袋図」自賛　風外慧薫
江戸時代（16世紀後期〜 17世紀）
愛知県美術館蔵（木村定三コレクション）
Bodai Pointing at the Moon, Fūgai Ekun, Latter
half of the 16th century-17thcentury, Aichi Prefectural Museum of Art/ Kimura Teizo Collection

禅僧が描いた水墨画
Ink Wash Paintings by Zen Priests

　禅定は古代インドでは仏教以前から広く行われていた修行法の一つで、その思潮が中国に伝わり、雑念を払い絶対の境地に入る瞑想を経て日本に上陸しました。鎌倉時代に宋から伝わった禅は、皇室や幕府を渡来文化の知的好奇心として魅了し、一気に日本文化に影響をあたえたのです。こうして日本の水を得た禅の心は、数多くの禅者や文人の手を経て水墨禅の世界を完成させます。

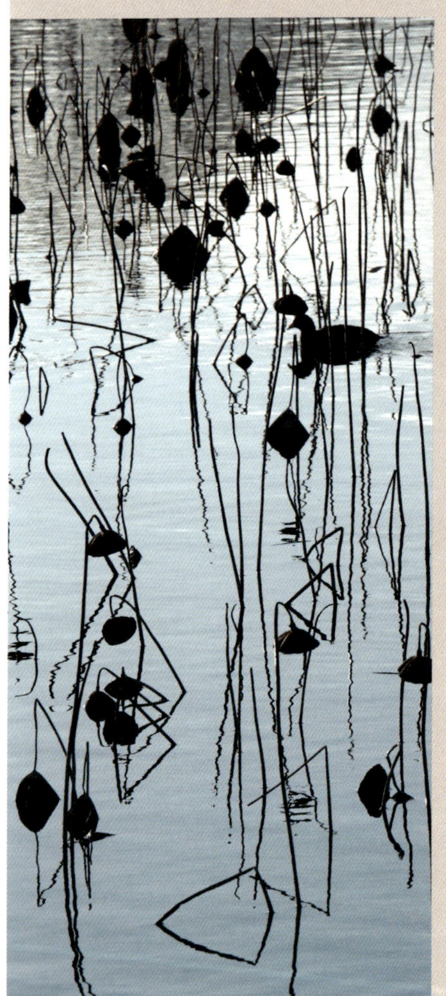

　それでは禅と水墨とは、いつ、どこで、なぜ結びついたのでしょう。禅宗の始源は釈迦にさかのぼるので、禅の生まれはインドです。一方の水墨は文字通り水と墨ですから、水はとにかく墨は中国生まれで、中国で誕生し発展した水墨画は東洋独自の絵画芸術です。こうして宗教のひとつである禅と人がつくりだした水墨とが出会い、たぐいまれな文化現象として日本の精神文化や美術の世界に大きな影響を及ぼし開花したのです。

　禅の水墨画は禅の心と出会い、心に吹く風を描き出します。偶像の神秘性を認めず、人間自身の内なる世界に目を向けたものです。そしてその画題のなかに精神表現の比喩としてあらわします。それは修道の人や大自然の断片をとらえ、そこに悟りにいたる禅機を読みとるためなのです。そしてここに水墨禅の画題が選ばれます。

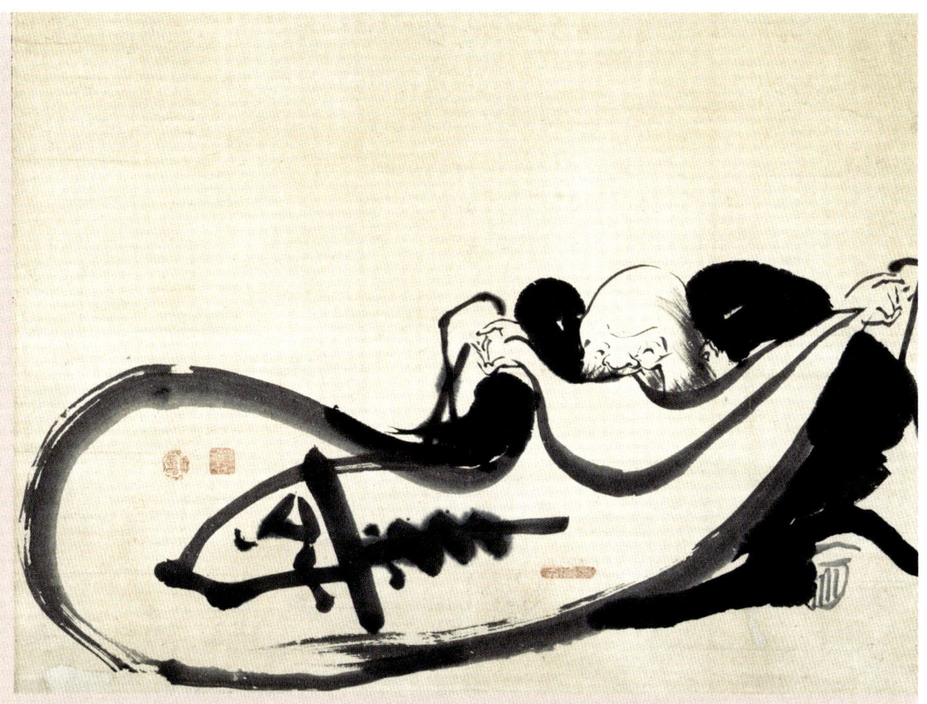

「布袋図」白隠慧鶴　江戸時代（18世紀）愛知県美術館蔵（木村定三コレクション）
Budai, Hakuin Ekaku, 18th century, Aichi Prefectural Museum of Art/ Kimura Teizo Collection

Zen meditation is derived from one of the training methods widely practiced in India before Buddhism developed. The concept of meditation that casts out worldly thoughts and enters an absolute state spread to China and then reached Japan. Zen reached Japan from Song-period China during the Kamakura period (1185-1333) and almost instantly influenced Japanese culture, having fascinated members of the imperial family and the shogunate who were intellectually curious about cultural contributions from abroad. The spirit of Zen, having found its element in Japan, passed through the hands of countless Zen practitioners and literati, resulting in the world of ink-wash Zen.

When were Zen and ink wash painting connected, where, and why? The Zen sect's origins date back to Sakyamuni, the historical Buddha, in India. Ink wash painting uses only ink and water. The *sumi* ink used was invented in China; water, of course, was not. Ink wash painting, born in China and developed there, is a uniquely East Asian painting technique. The encounter between Zen, a religion, and the ink wash technique created by human beings spurred a rare cultural phenomenon that flourished, greatly influencing both Japanese spiritual culture and its art world.

大津絵

Ōtsu-e

　近江国（滋賀県）大津の追分、三井寺の周辺で、参詣の人々や東海道中の旅人を相手に売られていた素朴な民芸絵画。手軽な土産物として求められた。寓意を込めたユーモラスな画題と奔放な筆致で、先に泥絵具で彩色し、最後に描線を施すのが特徴である。寛永年間（1624~44）頃から始まったといわれ、はじめは仏画が描かれていた。のちに藤娘や鬼の念仏、瓢簞鯰（ひょうたんなまず）などの戯画が描かれ、手法も肉筆から版画へと移っていった。

Ōtsu-e are rustic folk art pictures that were sold to people visiting Miidera temple in what is now Shiga Prefecture or travelers on the Tokaido Road. They were sought after as an inexpensive souvenir. With their humorous motifs that were loaded with hidden meaning and spirited brushwork, the pictures feature *Fujimusume* (Wisteria maiden), prayers to Amida Buddha and the Kabuki dance, *Hyōtan-namazu*.

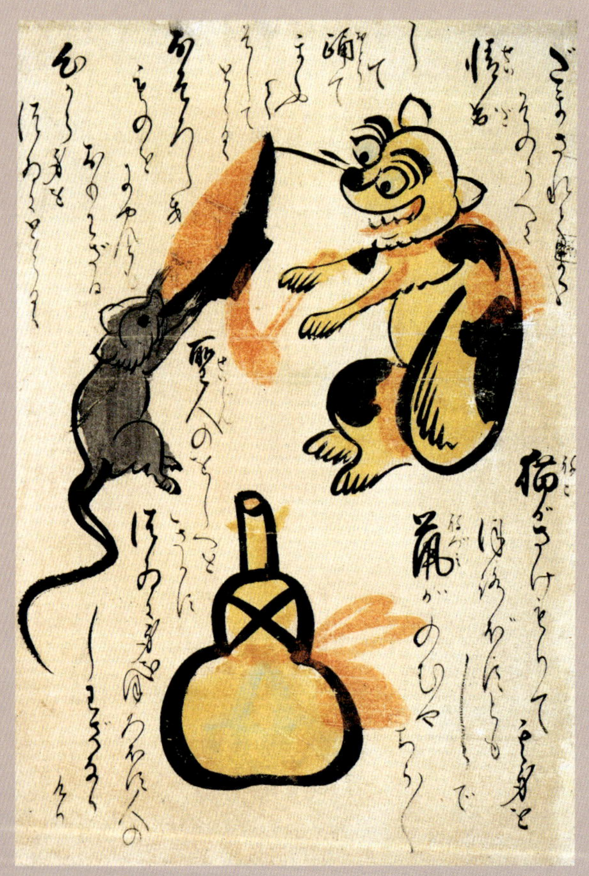

左：「大津絵 猫とねずみ図」
江戸時代　大津市歴史博物館蔵
Ōtsu-e: Cat Drinking with Mouse, Edo period, Otsu City Museum of History

右頁左：「大津絵　為朝」
江戸時代　大津市歴史博物館蔵
Ōtsu-e: Tametomo, Edo period, Otsu City Museum of History

右頁右：「大津絵　鬼の念仏」
江戸時代　大津市歴史博物館蔵
Ōtsu-e: Goblin praying to Buddha, Edo period, Otsu City Museum of History

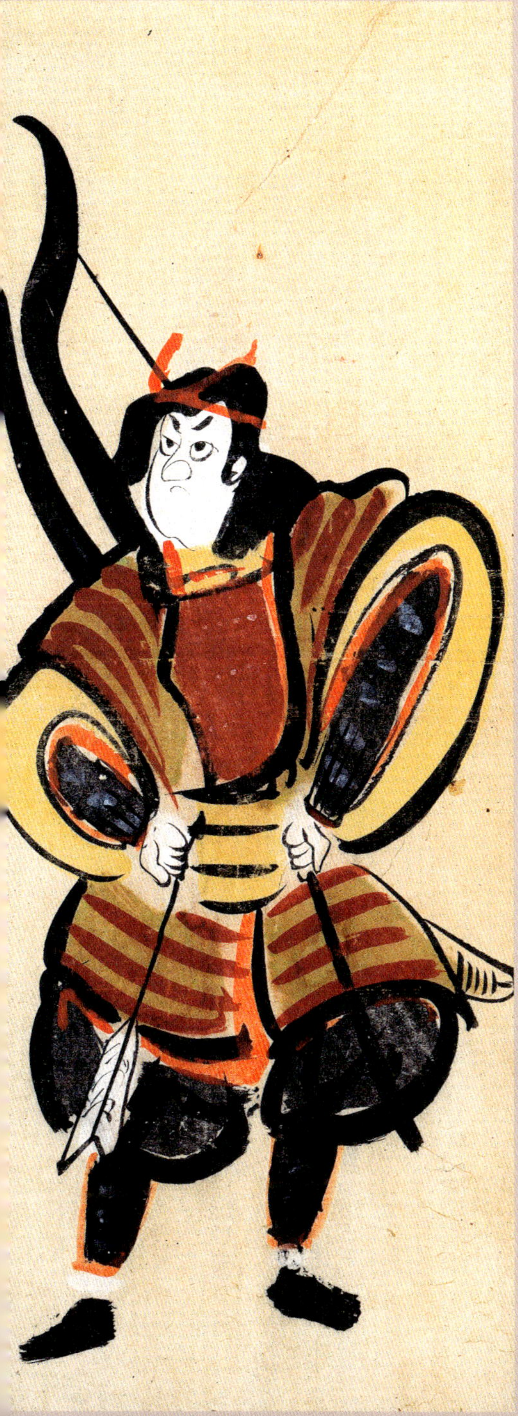

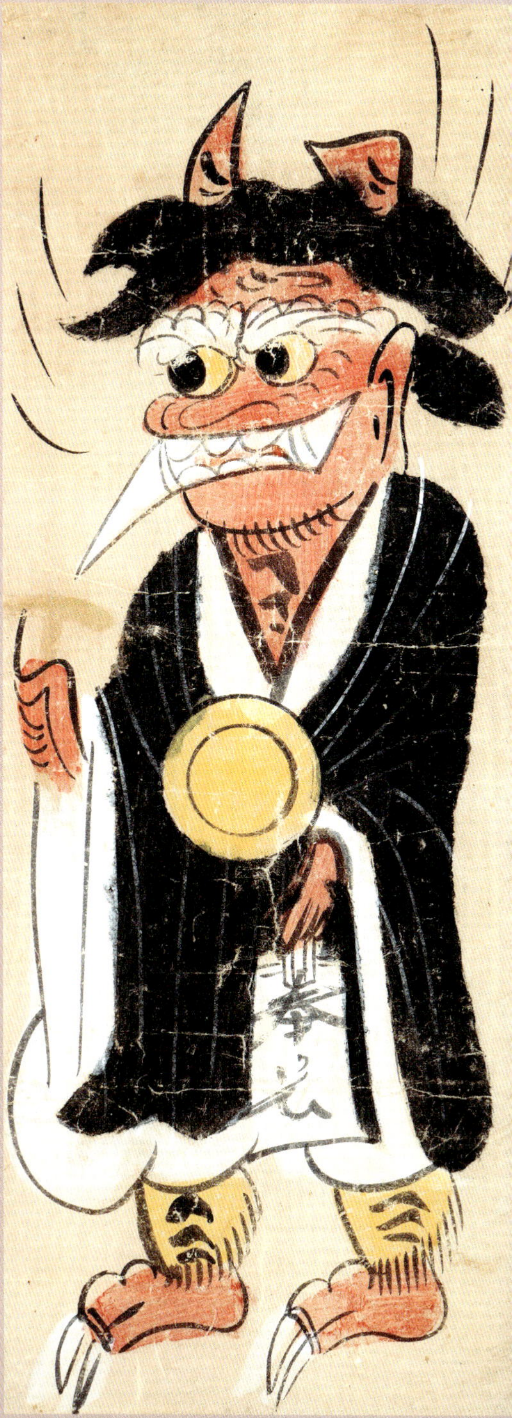

曾我蕭白

Soga Shōhaku

奇想の迫力を発揮した、江戸時代きっての異端画家

そが しょうはく　享保15～天明元年（1730～81）

　江戸時代中期の画家。京都の商家に生まれる。京狩野派の高田敬甫に師事し絵を学んだ。また、室町時代の曾我派に私淑し、独自に蛇足や直庵の画風を学ぶ。類い稀な想像力と力強い筆致、鮮烈な彩色があふれる画風により、型破りな独自の世界を確立した。

An iconoclastic Edo-period painter who demonstrated the power of his bizarre ideas

Soga Shōhaku (1730-81) was a mid Edo period painter born into a Kyoto merchant family. He studied painting with Takada Keiho, a member of the Kyoto Kanō School. He admired the Soga School of the Muromachi period and studied the styles of Jasoku and Chokuan on his own. With his extraordinary imagination, powerful brushwork, and vivid colors, he established an unconventional world of his own.

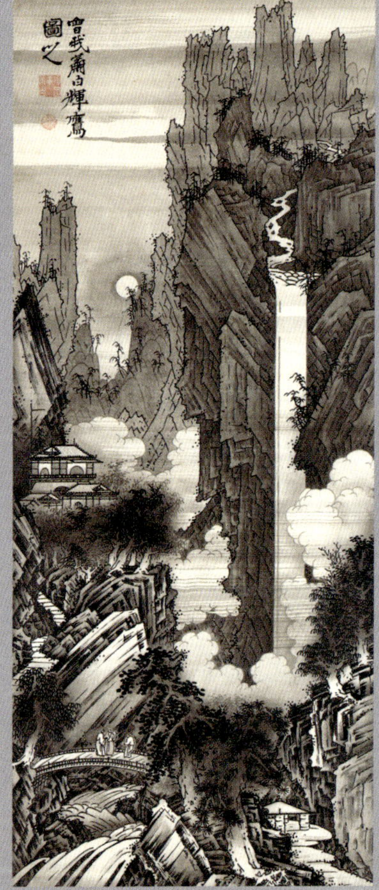

「虎渓三笑図」曾我蕭白
安永期（1772 ～ 81）頃
千葉市美術館蔵
The Three Laughters of Tiger Ravine,
Soga Shōhaku, ca.1772-81, Chiba
City Museum of Art

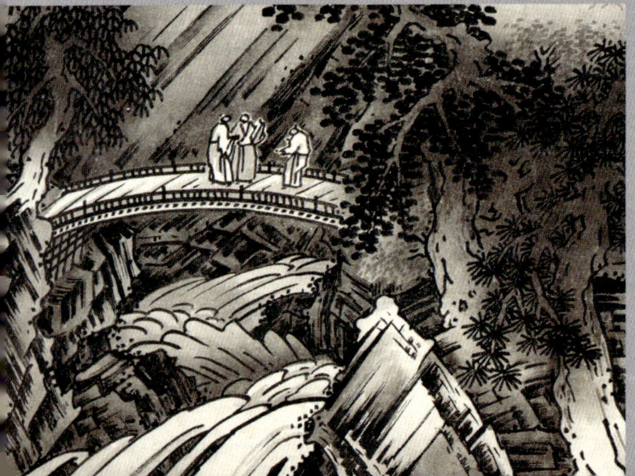

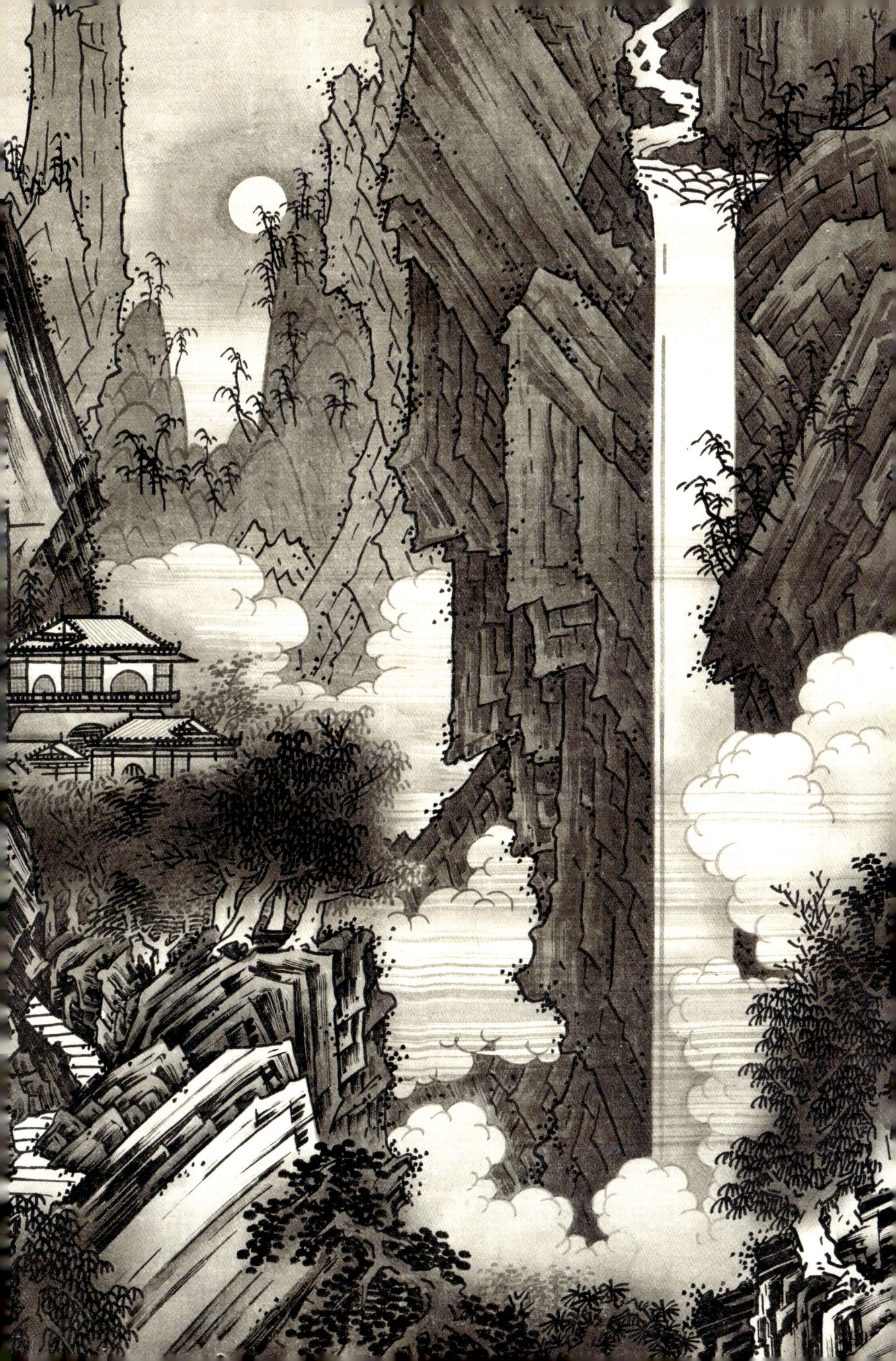

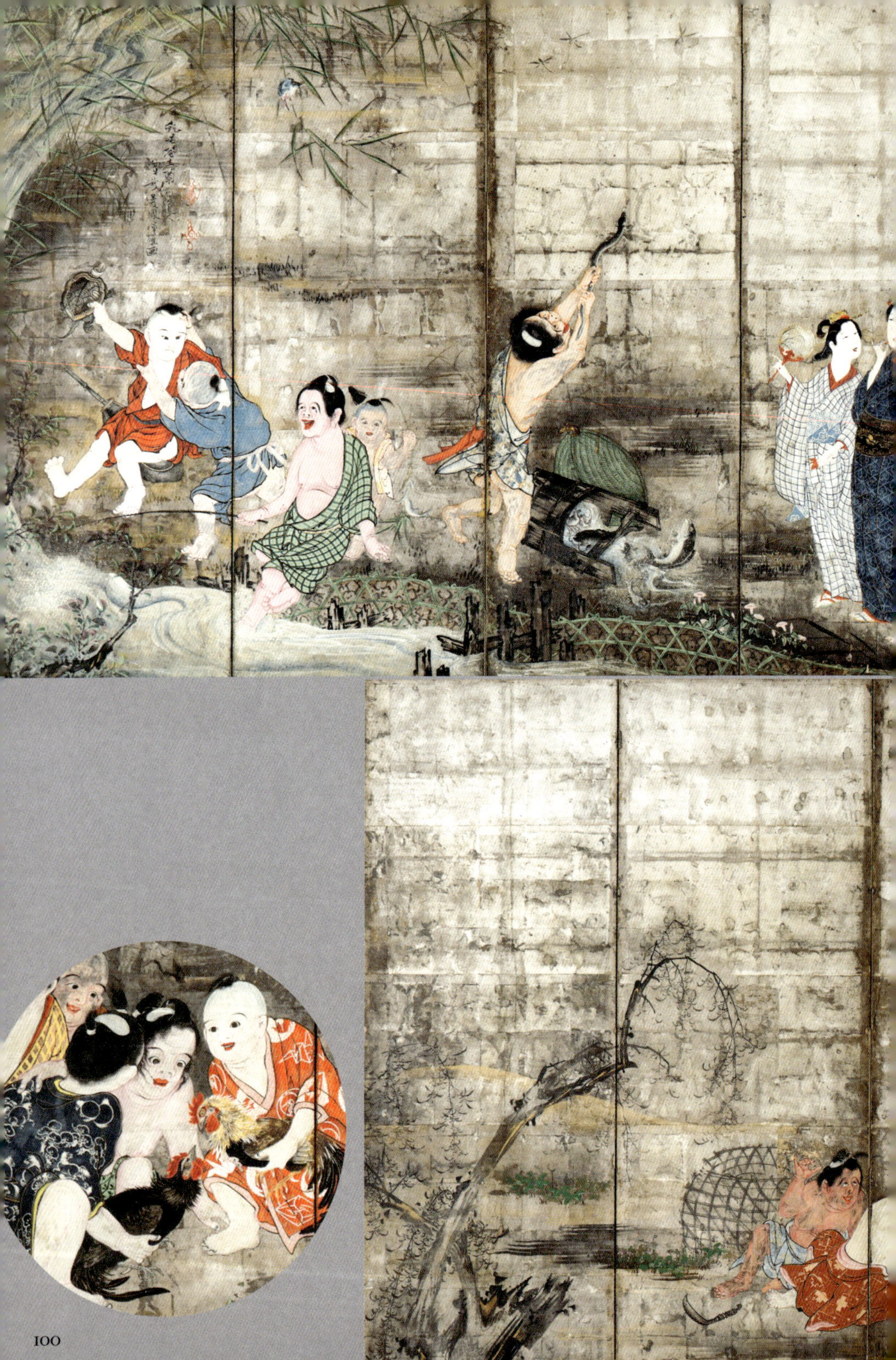

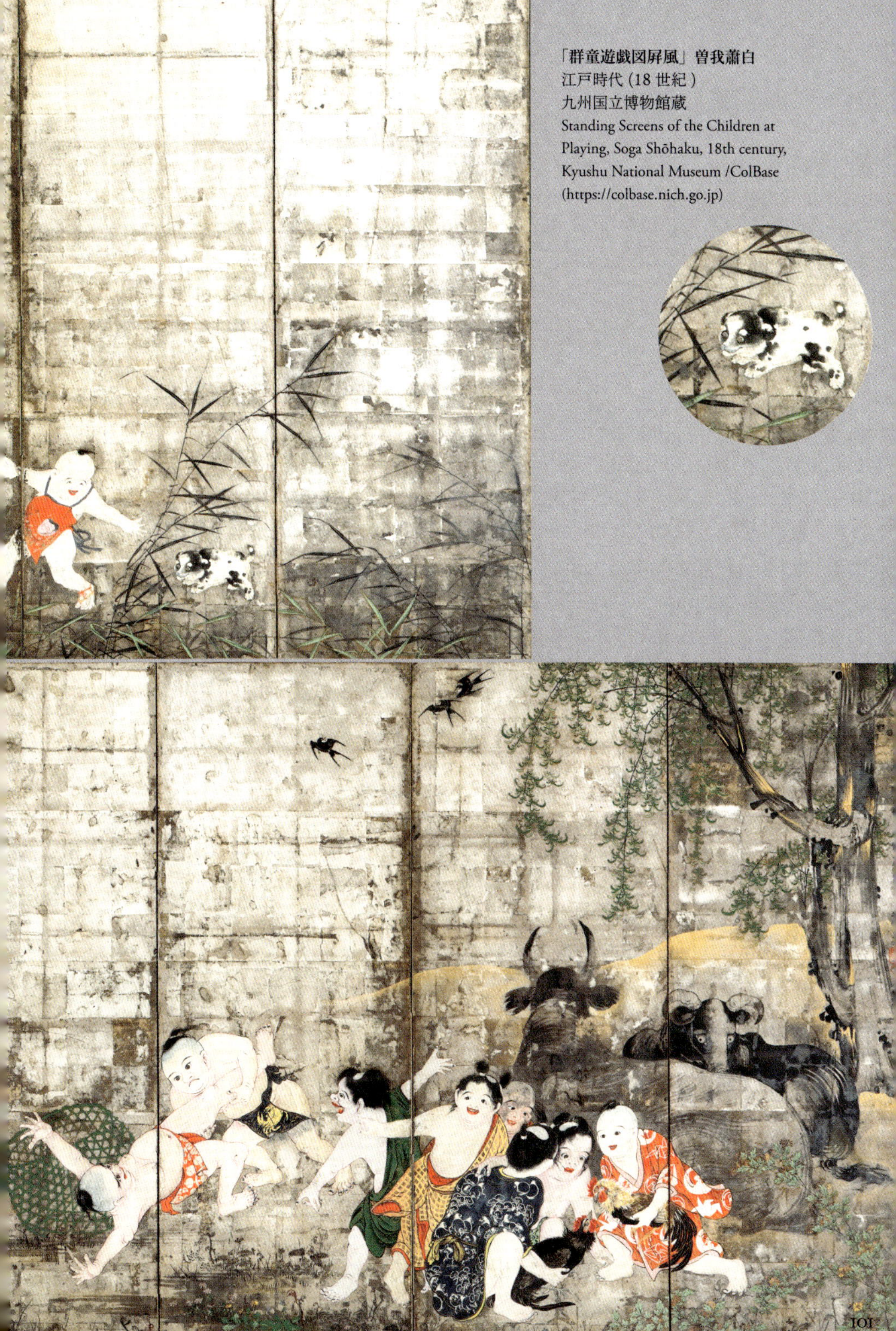

「群童遊戯図屏風」曽我蕭白
江戸時代（18 世紀）
九州国立博物館蔵
Standing Screens of the Children at
Playing, Soga Shōhaku, 18th century,
Kyushu National Museum /ColBase
(https://colbase.nich.go.jp)

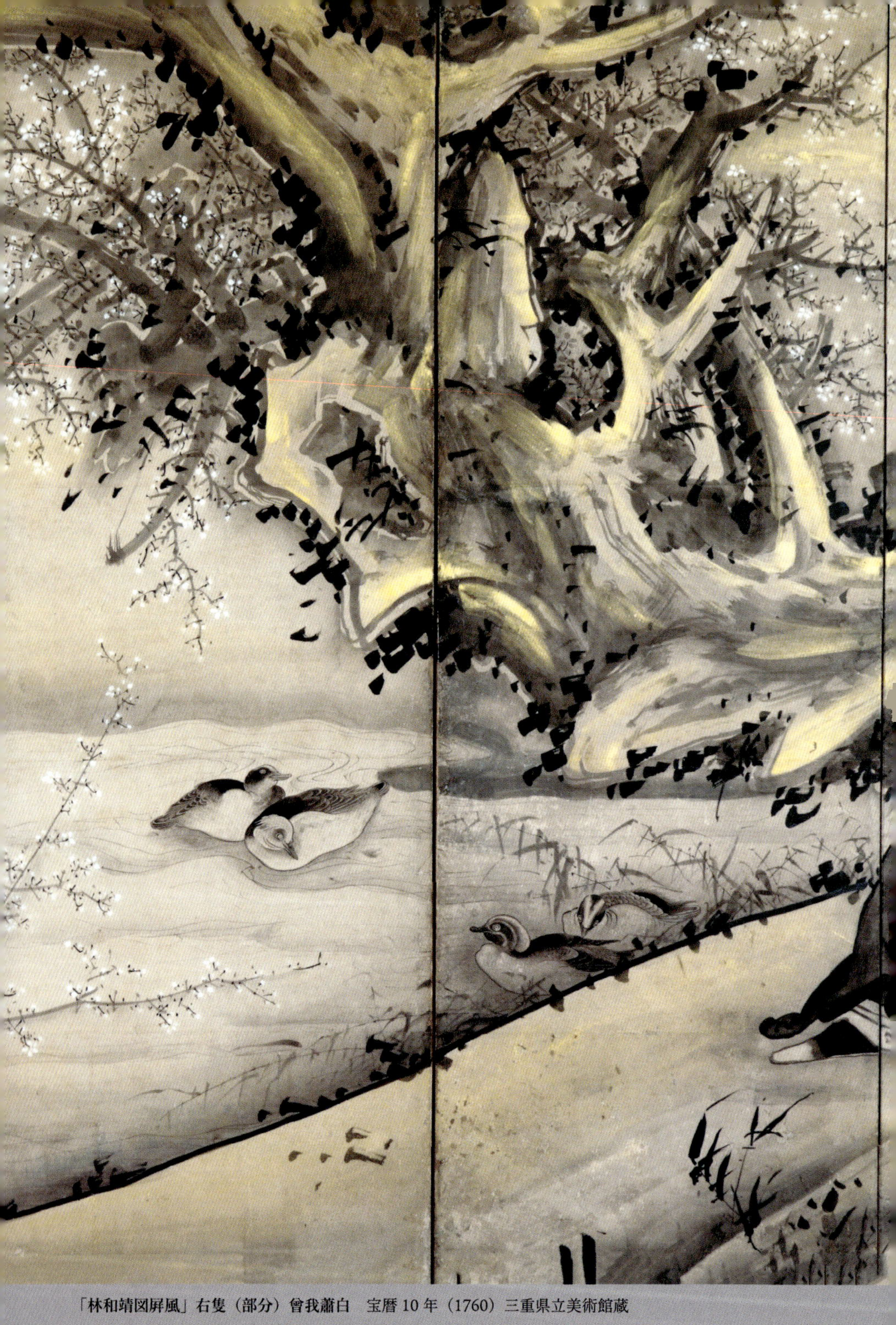

「林和靖図屏風」右隻（部分）曾我蕭白　宝暦 10 年（1760）三重県立美術館蔵

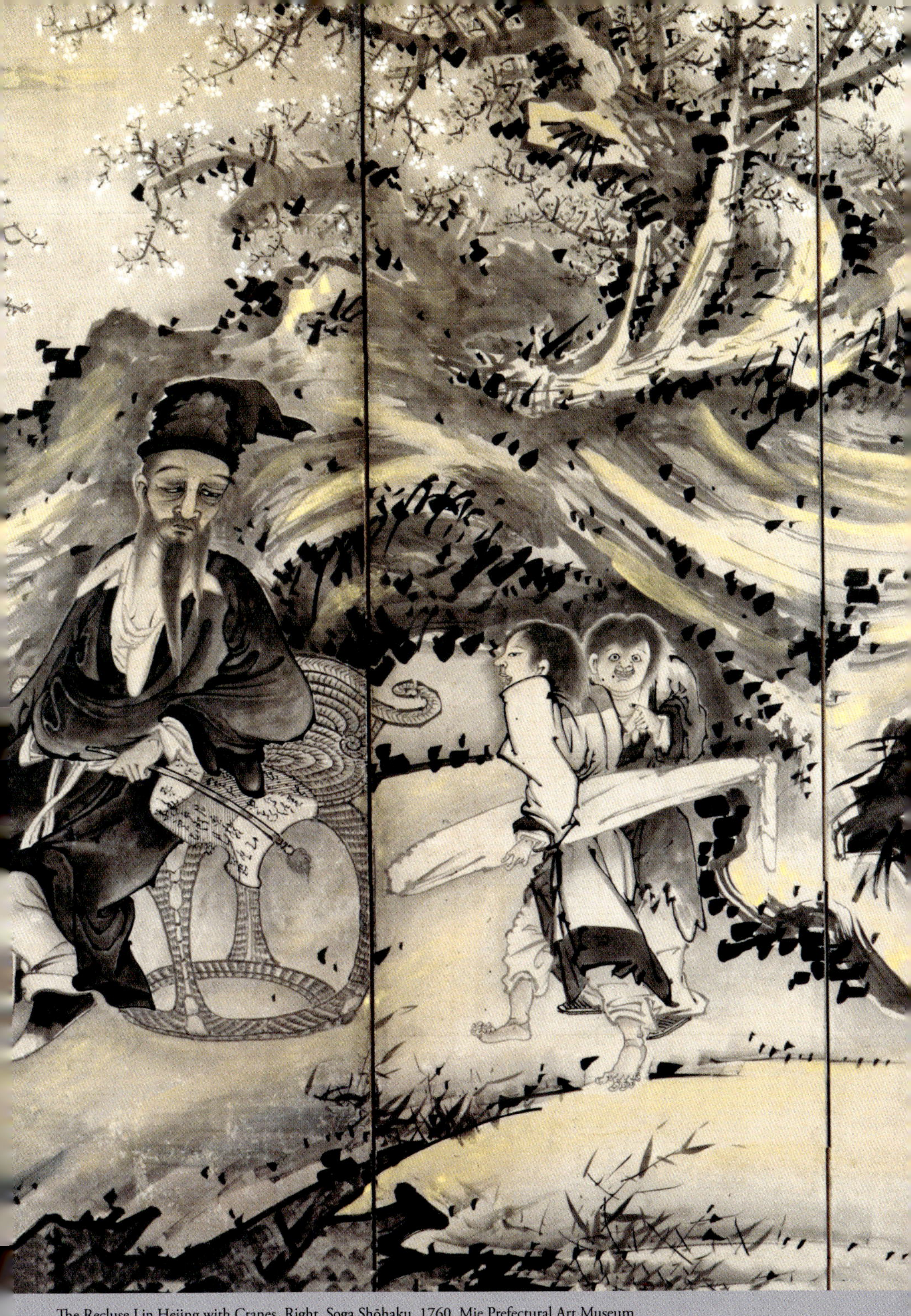

The Recluse Lin Hejing with Cranes, Right, Soga Shōhaku, 1760, Mie Prefectural Art Museum

曾我蕭白の水墨画
Soga Shōhaku's Ink Wash Paintings

　蕭白が活躍した宝暦年間（18世紀後半）の京都には、新しい漢画のスタイルである南画を描く池大雅や与謝蕪村がおり、眼鏡絵の制作で得た西洋画の透視図法をもとにした写生主義の円山応挙、そして鶏の観察や写生に余念のない伊藤若冲がいました。

　そのなかで一度見たら忘れられない、サイケデリックで幻覚世界に引き込まれるような蕭白の絵。そうかといえば繊細で洒脱な水墨画も描く技巧者でもある蕭白の絵の魅力は何なのか。それは描かれた画面から受ける力強い筆致と鮮烈な彩色が溢れんばかりに共鳴する世界であり、独特の超現実的要素で構成された摩訶不思議な世界を垣間見せてくれるエネルギーなのであろう。

　「群仙図屏風」の大画面を観ていると何を目的にこのような破天荒な絵が描かれたのか。悪い夢でも見たような気にさせられるこの絵を、我々はどう考えたらいいのだろうか。狂的な画面を支えるのは、蕭白の冷静な構成力だけである。

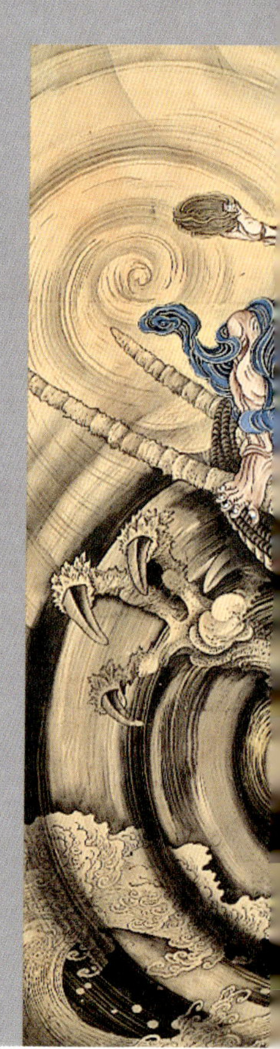

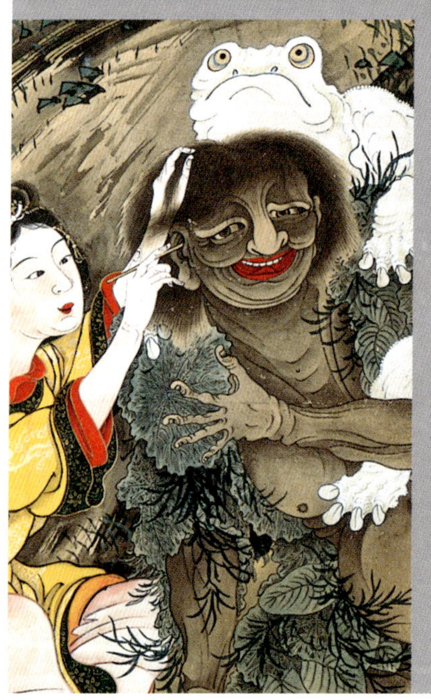

「群仙図屏風」（部分）重文　曾我蕭白
明和元年（1764）文化庁蔵
Standing Screens of the Immortals, Soga
Shōhaku,1764, Agency for Cultural Affairs

右隻には笙（しょう）を吹く蕭史（しょうし）と龍に乗る呂洞賓（りょどうひん）、左隻には鶴の前に立った林和靖（りんなせい）、耳掃除中の劉海蟾（りゅうかいせん）、西王母（せいおうぼ）たちで、奇怪な姿で登場している。

In Kyoto, where Shōhaku was active in the latter half of the eighteenth century, Ike no Taiga and Yosa Busan were painting Nanga in the new Chinese style, Maruyama Ōkyo was embracing realism, based on Western perspective methods he had learned to create perspective-view paintings, and Itō Jakuchū was engrossed in observing and sketching his chickens.

Another presence, once seen, never forgotten, were paintings by Shōhaku—psychedelic works that draw one into an almost hallucinatory world. What makes those paintings by Shōhaku, a highly skilled artist who also produced detailed, refined ink paintings, so fascinating? It is a world that resonates with the powerful brushwork and the vivid colors of the picture plane, a world filled with energy that offers us glimpses of a mysterious world composed of uniquely surreal elements.

When we look at the large picture plane of his Immortals folding screens, we wonder why he created this wild, uninhibited painting. Shōhaku's tranquil composition is the foundation of this mad painting.

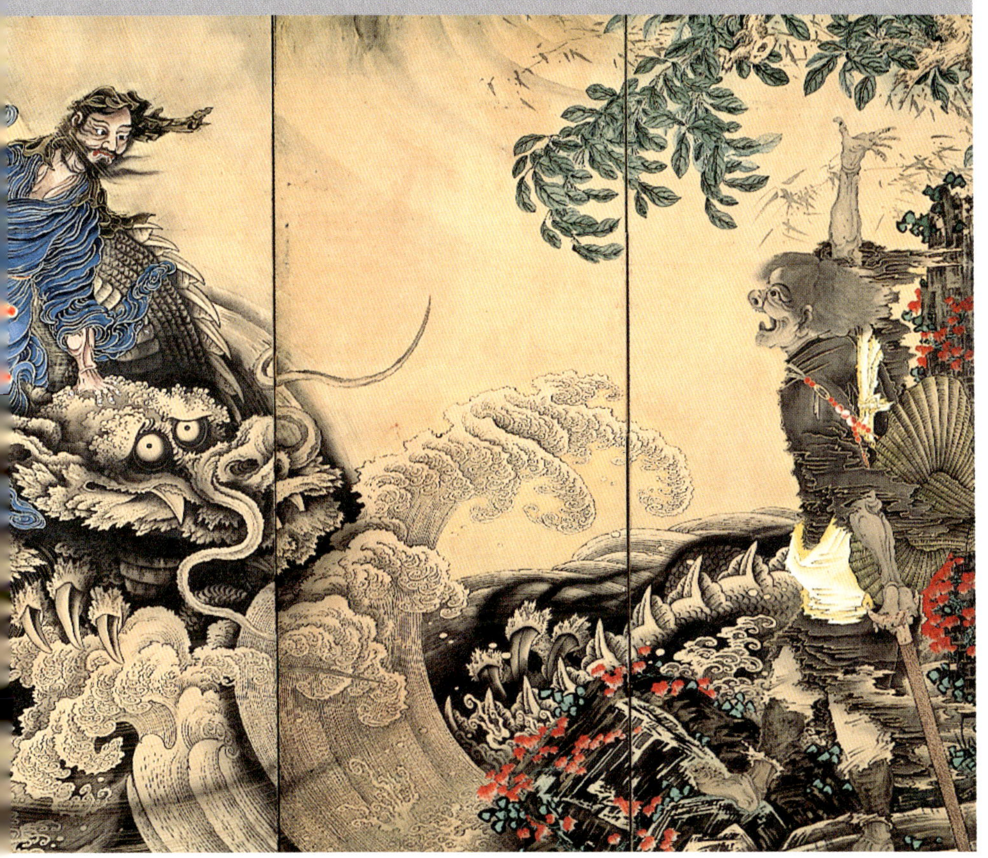

伊藤若冲

幻想的で独得の花鳥画の世界を創造した画家
いとう じゃくちゅう　享保元~寛政12年（1716~1800）

　江戸時代中期の画家。京都高倉錦小路の青物問屋「枡源」の長男として生まれる。はじめ狩野派を学び写生の重要性を認識、さらにその後、中国の宋や元、明の花鳥画を模写した。また尾形光琳の画風を研究し独自の画風を開き、他方では鋭く飄逸な水墨画を描いた。とくに鶏の絵を得意とし、写生を基礎にした装飾性のある作品を描いた。

The painter who created a imaginative and unique bird-and-flower painting world

Itō Jakuchū (1716-1800), a mid-Edo period painter, was born as the eldest son of the family operating the Masugen, a greengrocer in Takakura Nishikikōji, Kyoto. He began by studying Kanō School painting, recognized the importance of realism, and made copies of Chinese Song, Yuan, and Ming bird-and-flower paintings. He also studied Ogata Kōrin's style and produced sharp, free ink wash paintings. His forte was paintings of chickens, in decorative works based on sketching from life.

Itō Jakuchū

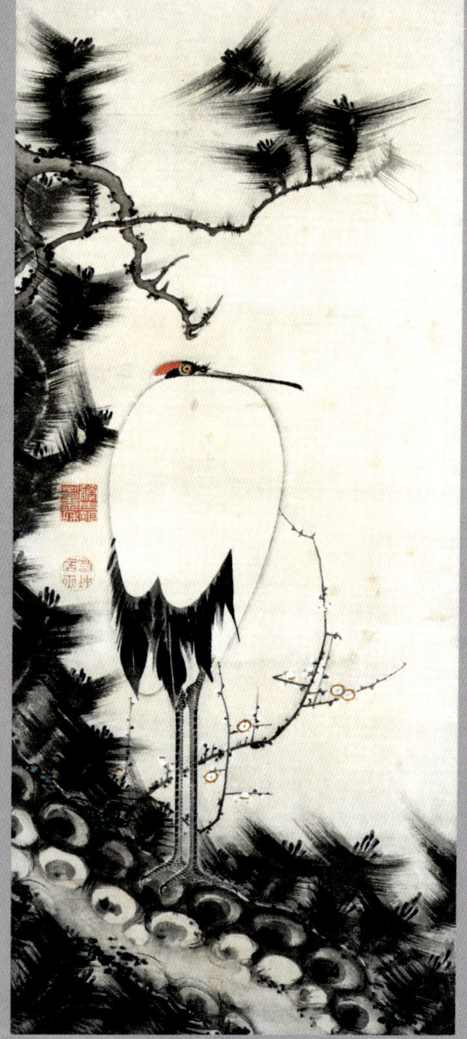

「松梅孤鶴図」伊藤若冲
江戸時代（18世紀）東京国立博物館蔵
Pine, Plum and Solitary Crane, Itō Jakuchū,
18th century, Tōkyō National Museum /
ColBase (https://colbase.nich.go.jp)

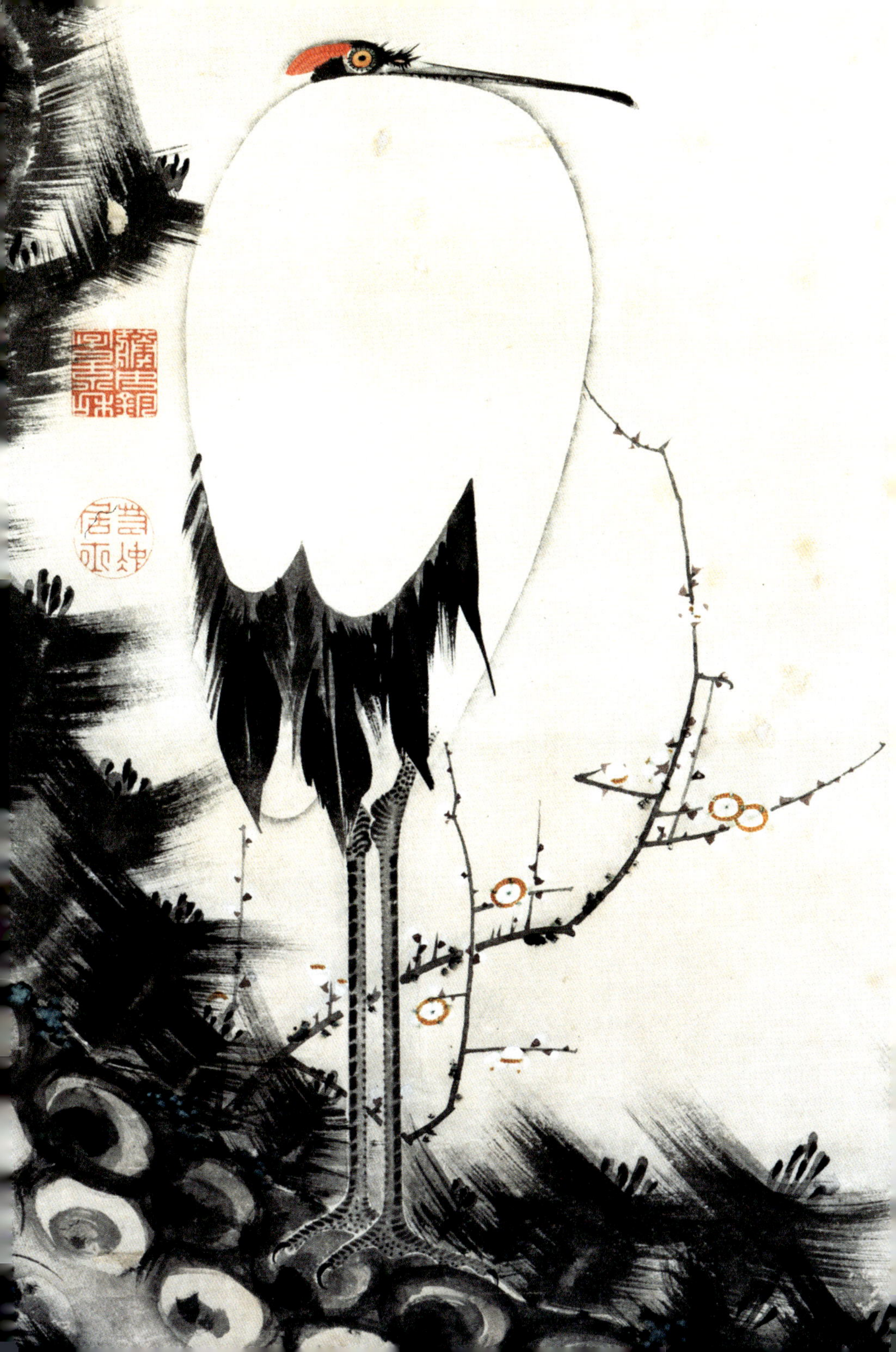

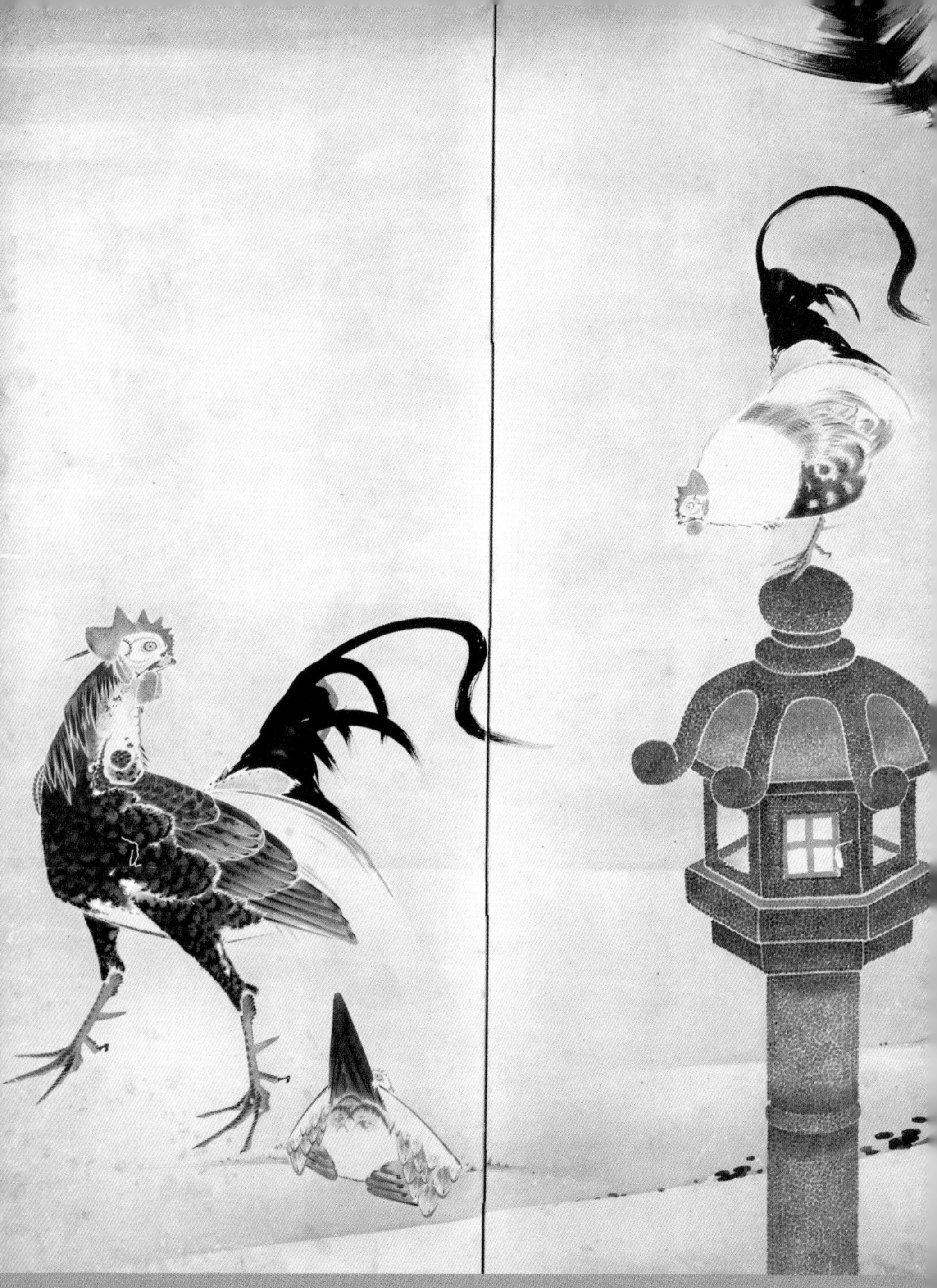

「松梅群鶏図屏風」（部分）伊藤若冲　江戸時代（18 世紀）東京国立博物館蔵
Standing Screens of the Pine, Plum Blossoms and Fowls, Itō Jakuchū, 18th century,
Tōkyō National Museum / ColBase (https://colbase.nich.go.jp)

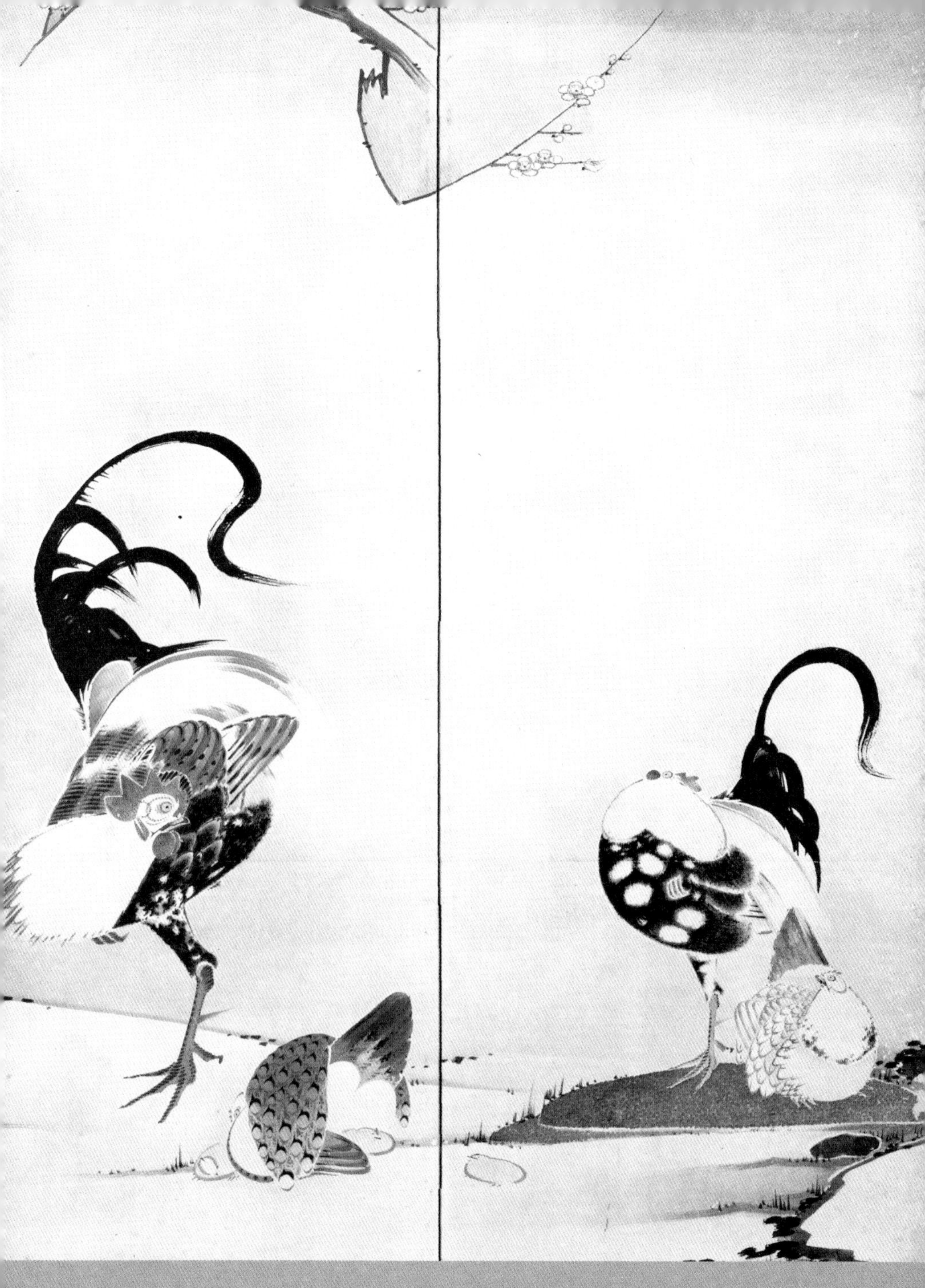

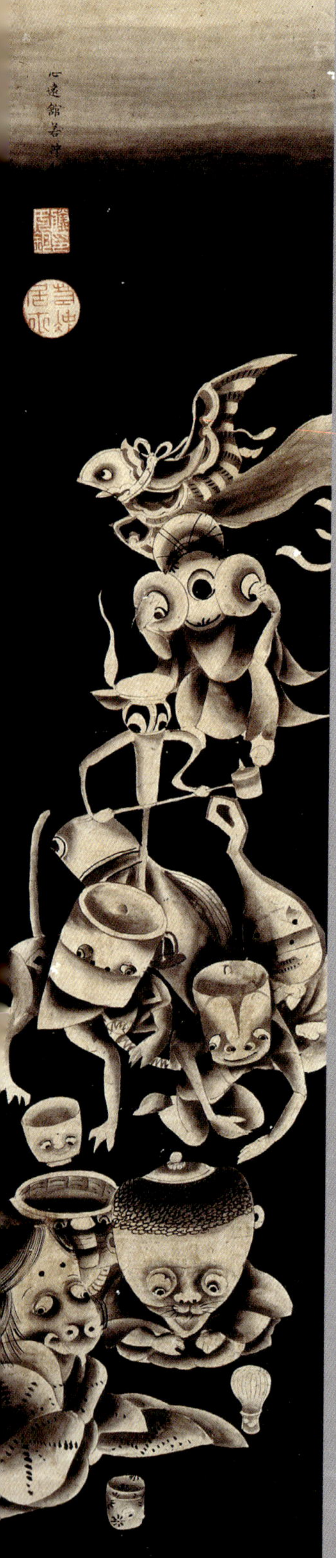

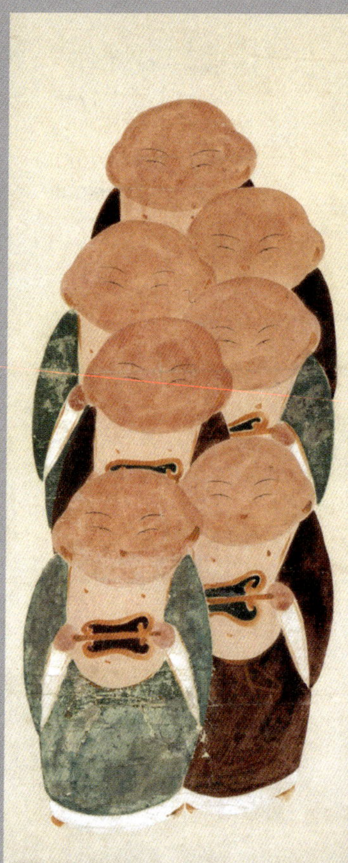

「伏見人形図」伊藤若冲
江戸時代（18世紀後半）
愛知県美術館蔵（木村定三コレクション）
Fushimi Dolls, Itō Jakuchū, Latter half of the
18th century, Aichi Prefectural Museum of
Art/ Kimura Teizo Collection

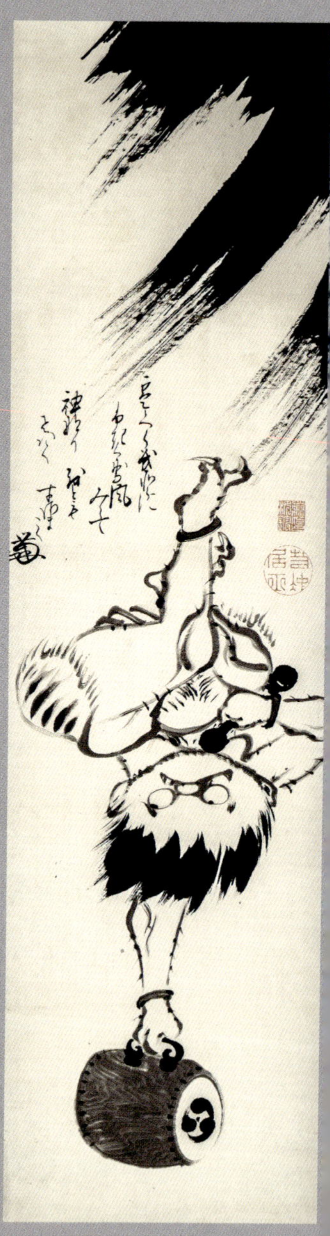

「付喪神図」伊藤若冲
江戸時代（18世紀）
福岡市博物館蔵　画像提供：福岡
市博物館 / DNPartcom
Tsukumo-gami (Spirits of Used Items),
Itō Jakuchū, 18th century, Fukuoka
Municipal Museum

「雷神図」伊藤若冲
宝暦〜明和期（1751〜72）頃
千葉市美術館蔵
God of Thunder, Itō Jakuchū, ca.1751-
72, Chiba City Museum of Art

「雨龍図」伊藤若冲
1760 年代前半
秋田市立千秋美術館蔵
Rain Dragon, Itō Jakuchū, Early
1760s, Akita Senshu Museum of Art

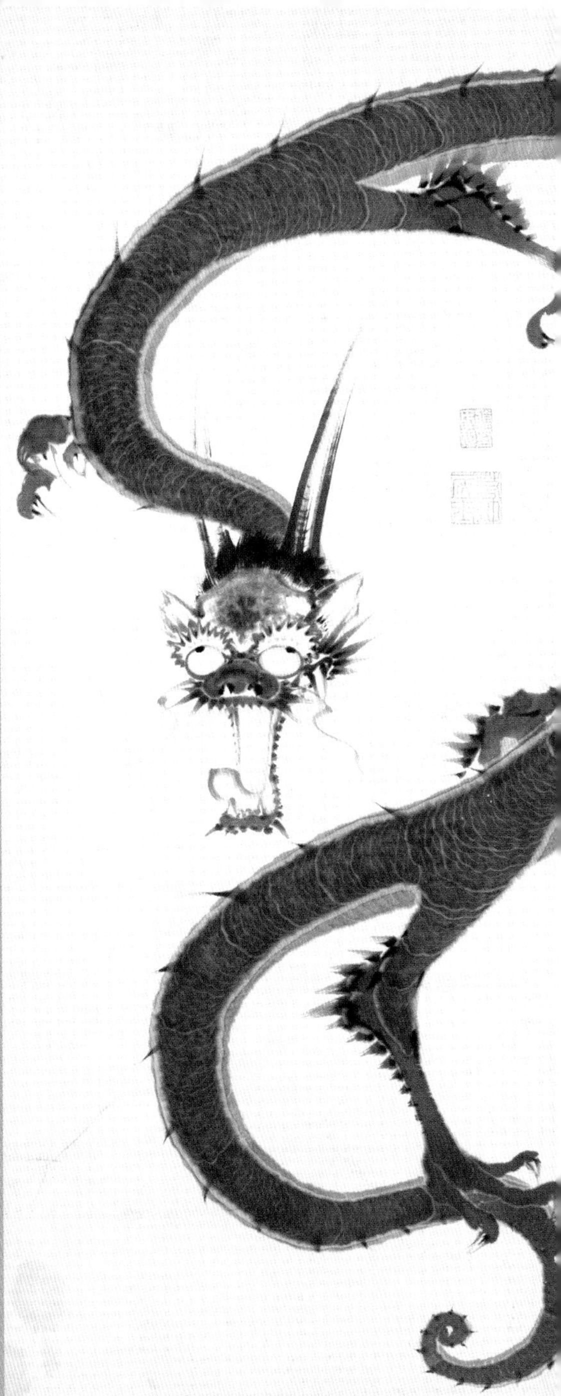

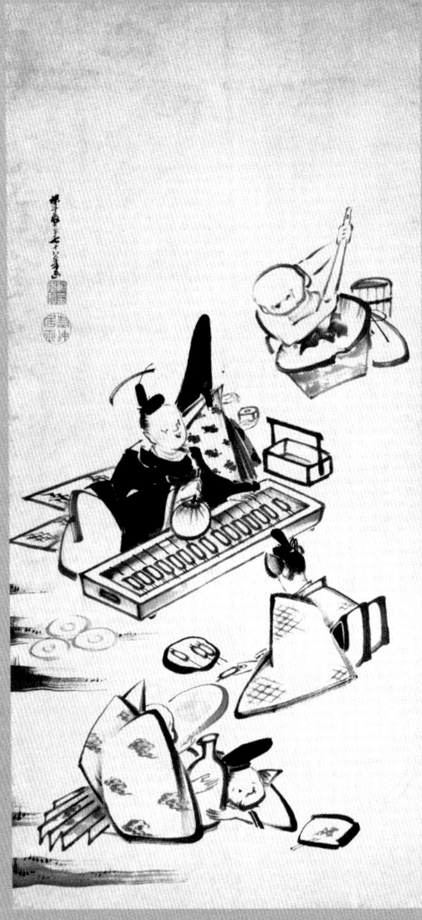

「六歌仙図」伊藤若冲
寛政 3 年（1791）
愛知県美術館蔵（木村定三コレクション）
Six Poetic Immortals, Itō Jakuchū, 1791, Aichi
Prefectural Museum of Art/ Kimura Teizo Collection

京都画壇の中心的存在で円山派の祖

まるやま おうきょ　享保18〜寛政7年（1733〜95）

　江戸時代中期の画家。丹波桑田郡（京都府）の農家に生まれる。石田幽亭に入門しだが、狩野派の形式化した画風に飽き足らず、眼鏡絵の制作を通じて西洋画法に親しみ、中国画の沈南蘋にも影響されて写生の重要性に開眼する。写生を基本とした写実的作風に独自の画風をひらいた。京都画壇の中心的存在として旺盛な制作活動を展開させた。

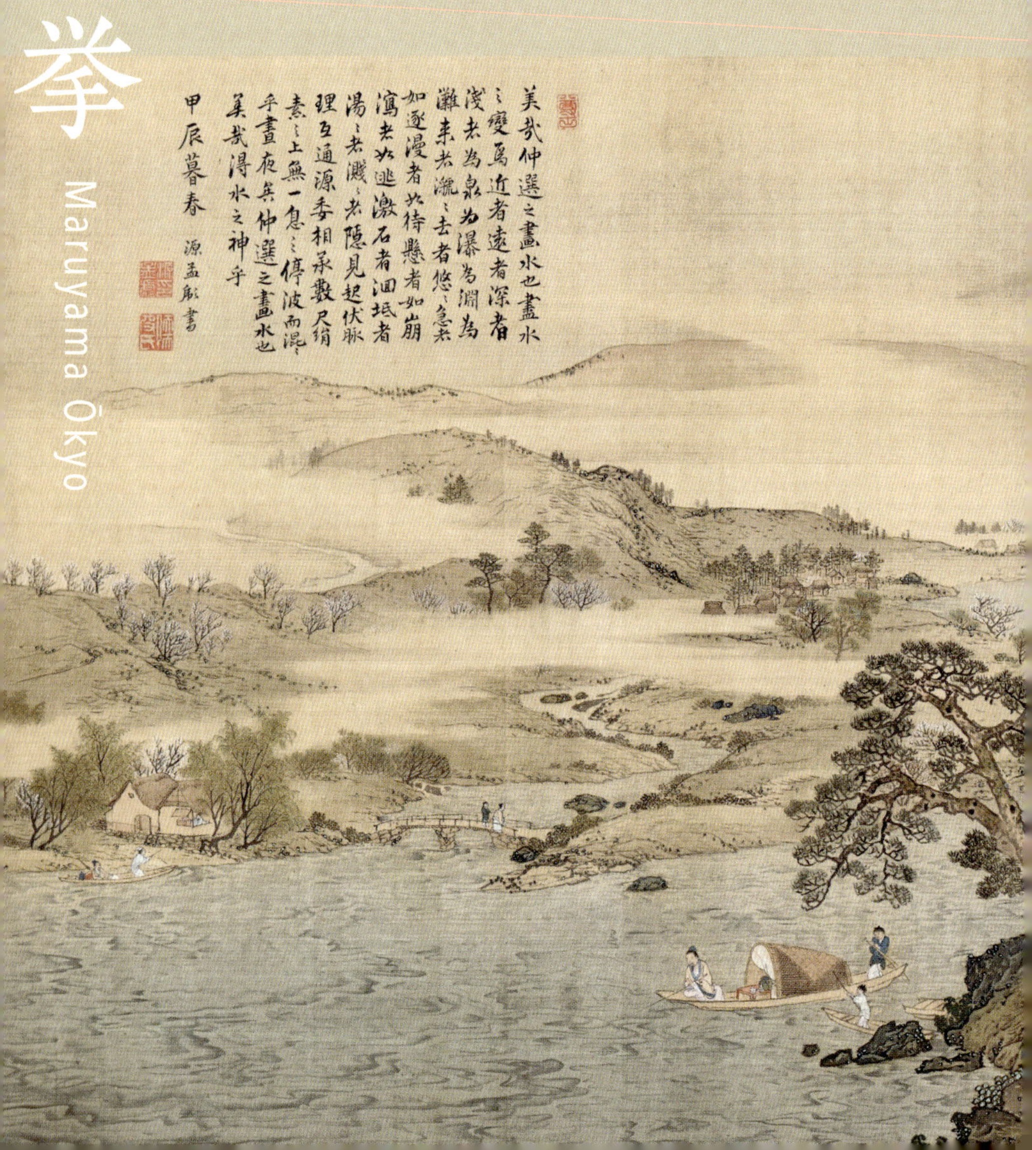

Founder of the Maruyama School, center of the Kyoto painting world

Maruyama Ōkyo (1733-95), a mid Edo period painter, was born to a farming
family in Kuwada-gun, Tanba (now Kyoto prefecture). He entered the studio of
Ishida Yūtei, but became dissatisfied with the stylized Kanō School style, and,
while creating perspective-view paintings, encountered Western painting techniques. He was also influenced by the Chinese painter Shen Nanpin. His eyes
opened to the importance of sketching from life, he created his own realistic style
of painting based on sketching.

「仙山観花図」円山応挙・高芙蓉賛　安永7年（1778）九州国立博物館蔵
Seeing the Flowers in Hermit Mountains, Maruyama Ōkyo, 1778, Kyushu National Museum / ColBase (https://colbase.nich.go.jp)

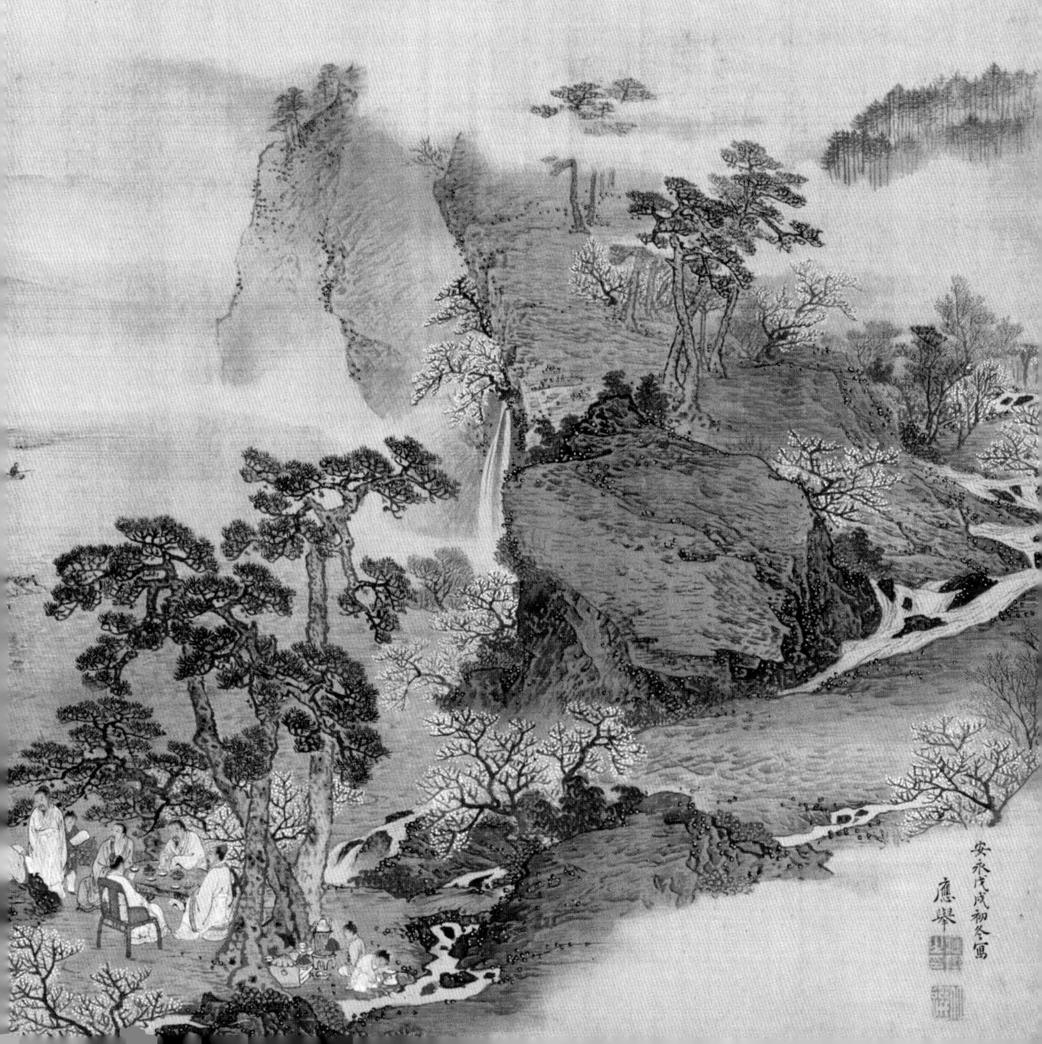

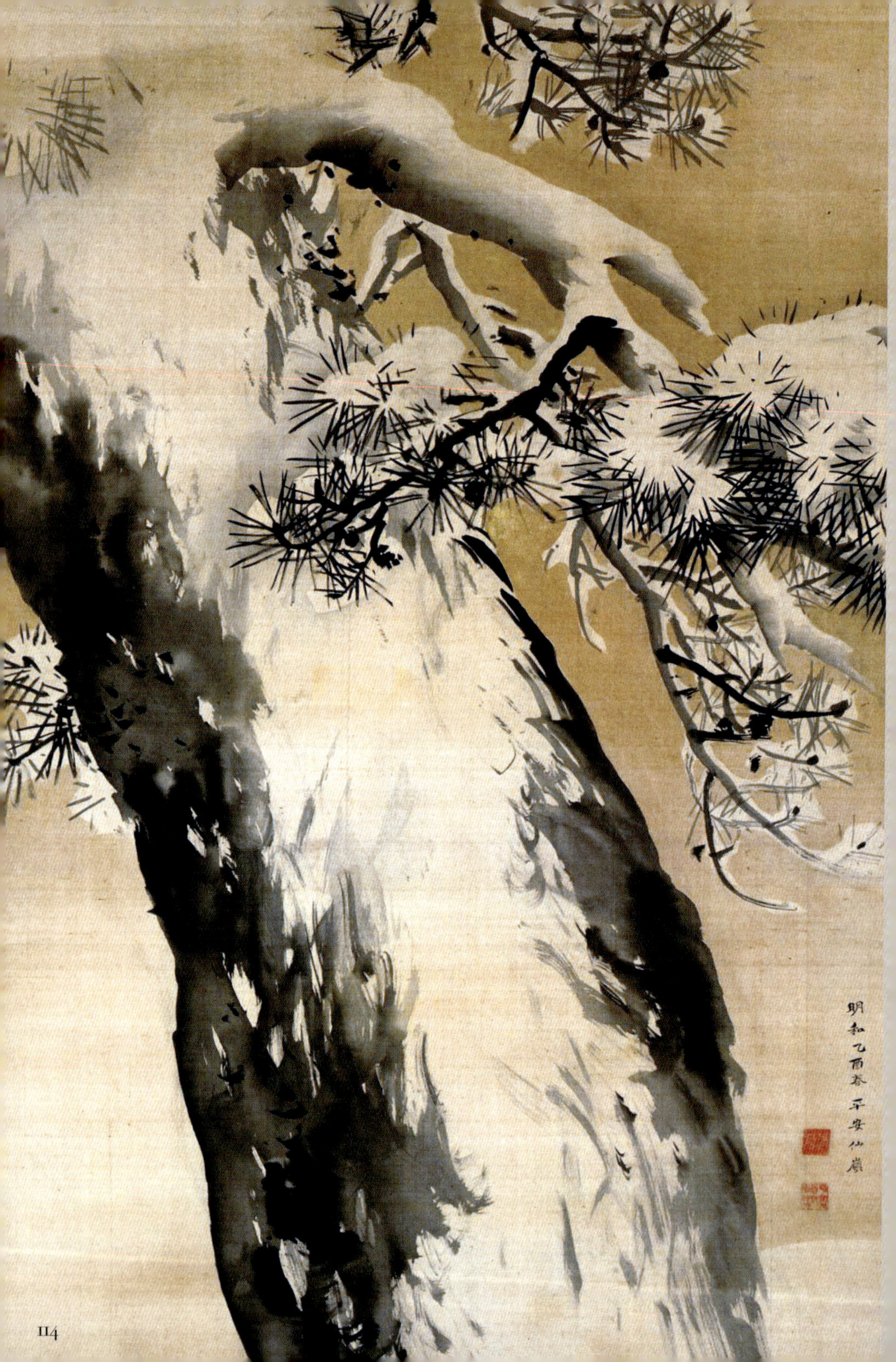

明和乙酉春
平安仙嶺

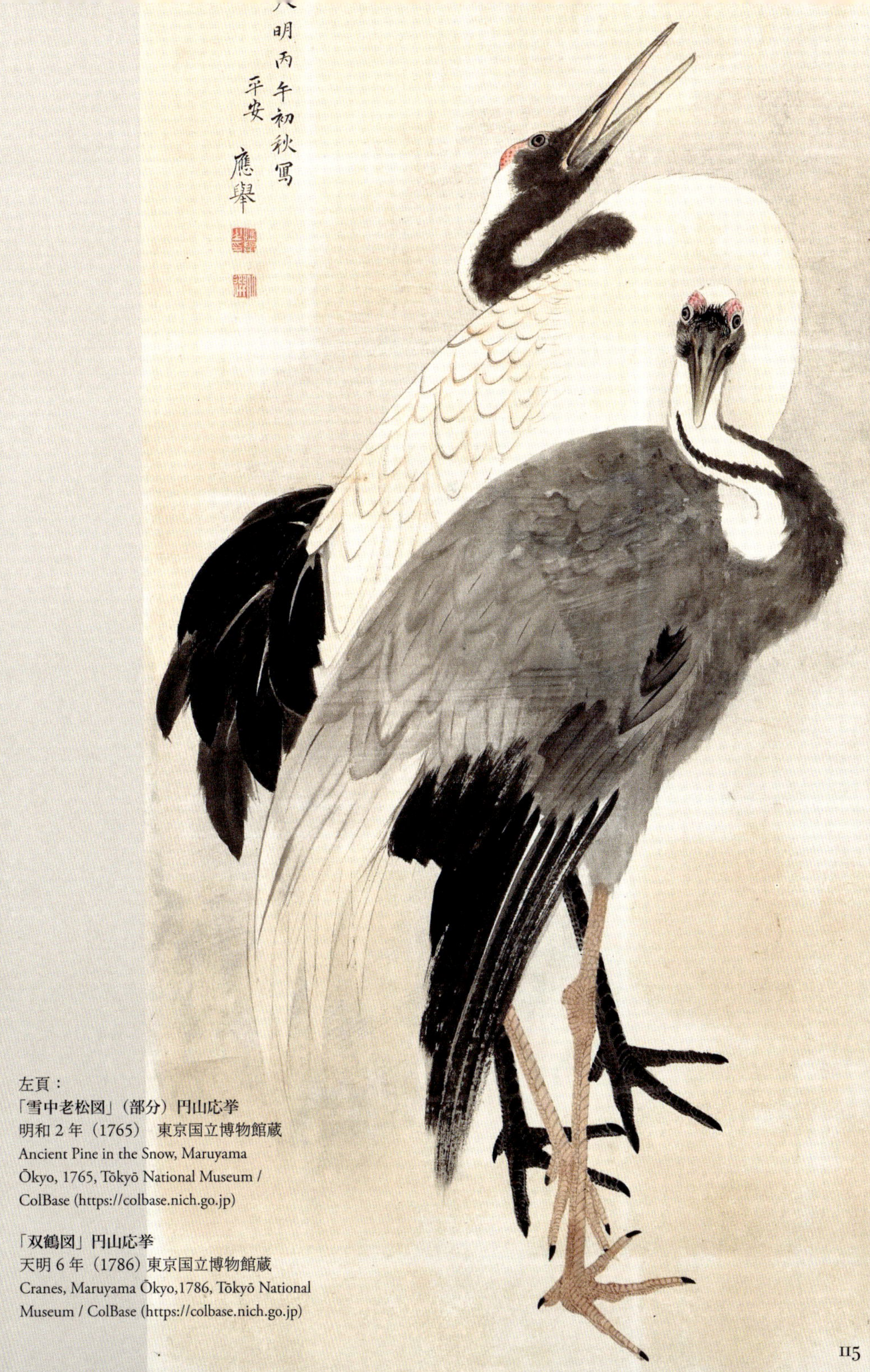

左頁：
「雪中老松図」（部分）円山応挙
明和 2 年（1765） 東京国立博物館蔵
Ancient Pine in the Snow, Maruyama
Ōkyo, 1765, Tōkyō National Museum /
ColBase (https://colbase.nich.go.jp)

「双鶴図」円山応挙
天明 6 年（1786） 東京国立博物館蔵
Cranes, Maruyama Ōkyo,1786, Tōkyō National
Museum / ColBase (https://colbase.nich.go.jp)

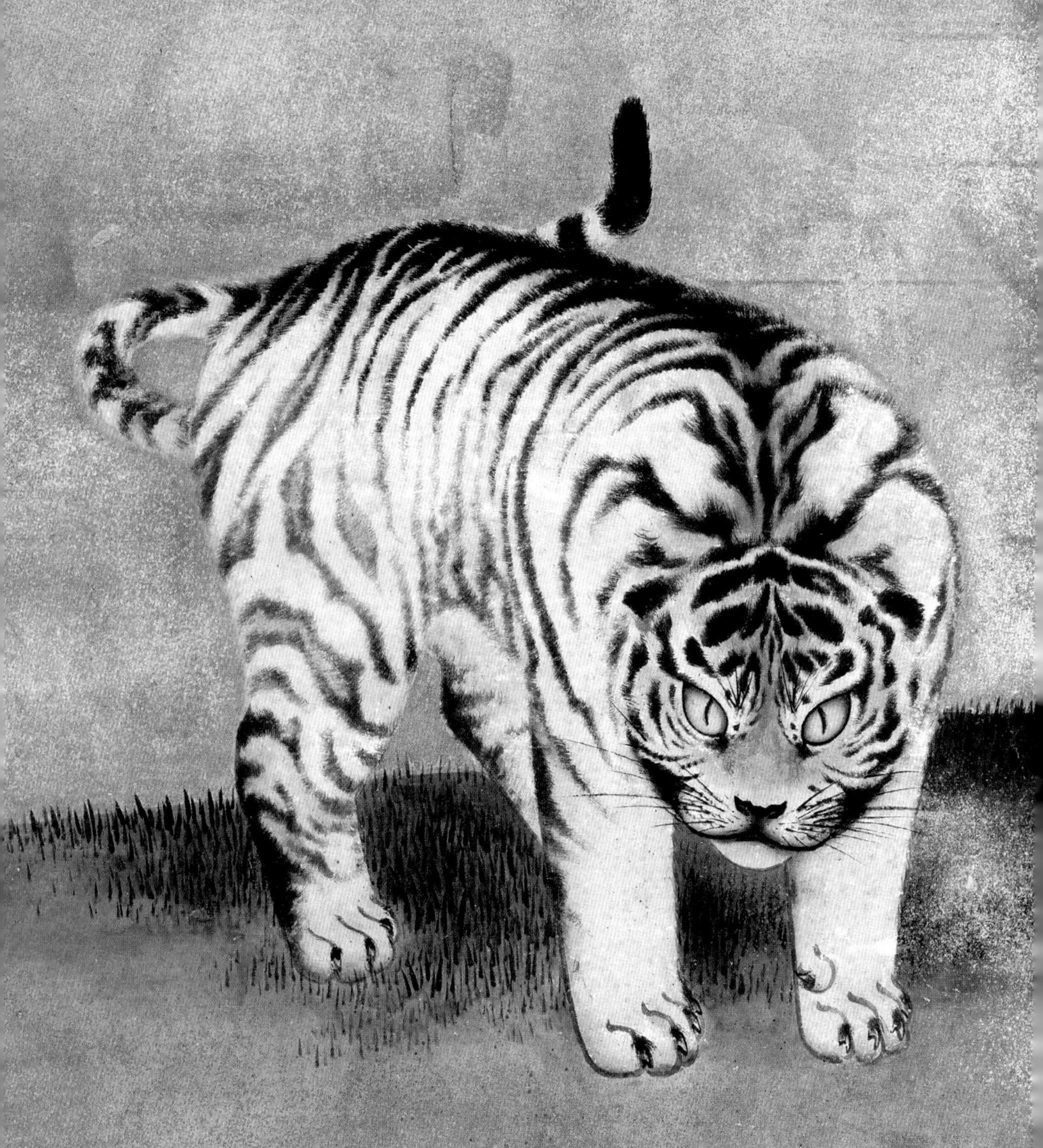

「遊虎図」（部分）重文　円山応挙　天明７年（1787）金刀比羅宮蔵
Leisurely Tiger, Important Cultural Property, Maruyama Ōkyo, 1787, Kotohira-Gu

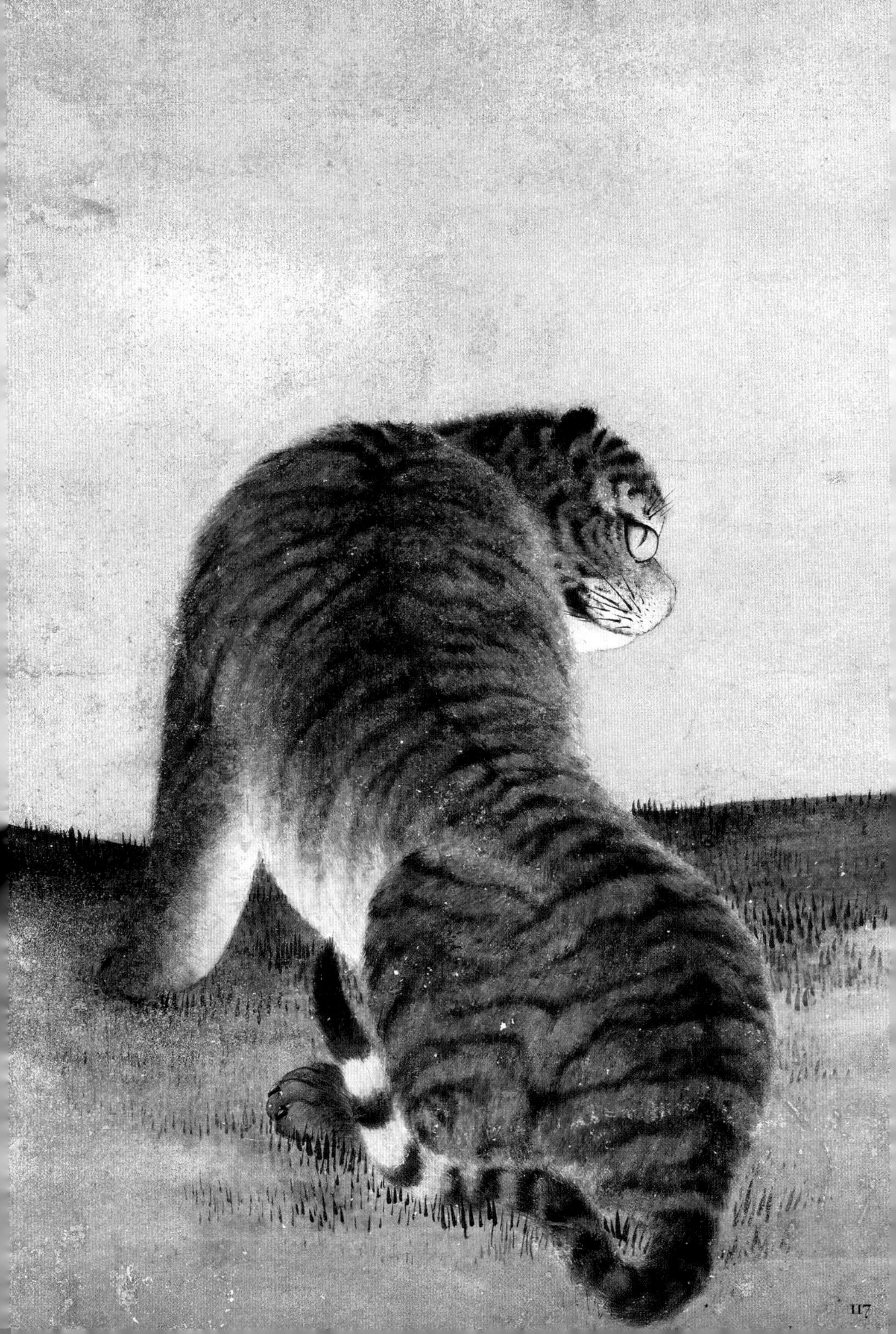

池大雅

日本的詩情を謳う文人画の大成者

いけの たいが　享保8〜安永5年（1723〜76）

　江戸時代中期の文人画家、書家。京都の町人として生まれる。15歳の頃には扇屋、篆刻を業とし、中国の南宗画を独学した。柳沢淇園や祇園南海の影響を受け、日本各地を旅しながら明るく新鮮な色彩で詩情豊かな作品を生み出した。妻の玉瀾に水墨を教え女流の文人画家に育て、おしどり夫婦として聞こえた。

Master of literati painting expressing Japanese sentiments

Ike no Taiga (1723-76), a mid Edo period literati painter and calligrapher, was born, a townsman, in Kyoto. He began making his living selling fans at his store, Tenkoku, when about fifteen, and taught himself the Southern Song style of painting. He was also influenced by Yanagisawa Kien and Gion Nankai. While traveling throughout Japan, he created richly lyrical works in bright, fresh colors. He taught ink wash painting to his wife, Gyoku-ran, who had been brought up to become a female literati painter. They were called an *oshidori fūfu*, a couple with a warm, loving relationship.

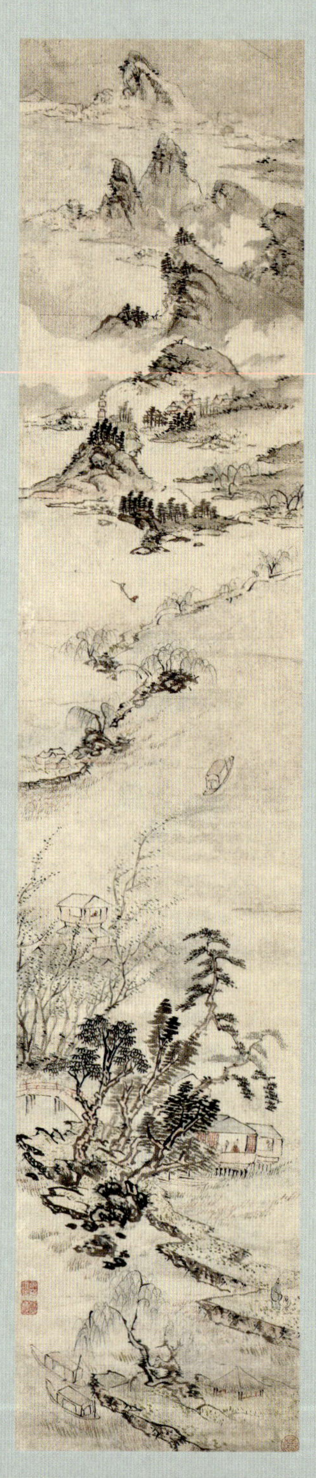

右：「西湖図」池大雅
江戸時代（18世紀）東京国立博物館蔵
Landscape in the Xī hú, Ike no Taiga, 18th century, Tōkyō National Museum / ColBase (https://colbase.nich.go.jp)

右頁左：「春景山水図」池大雅
江戸時代（18世紀）東京国立博物館蔵
Spring Landscape, Ike no Taiga, 18th century, Tōkyō National Museum / ColBase (https://colbase.nich.go.jp)

右頁右：「酔李白図」池大雅
江戸時代（18世紀）東京国立博物館蔵
Drunken Li Bai, Ike no Taiga, 18th century, Tōkyō National Museum / ColBase (https://colbase.nich.go.jp)

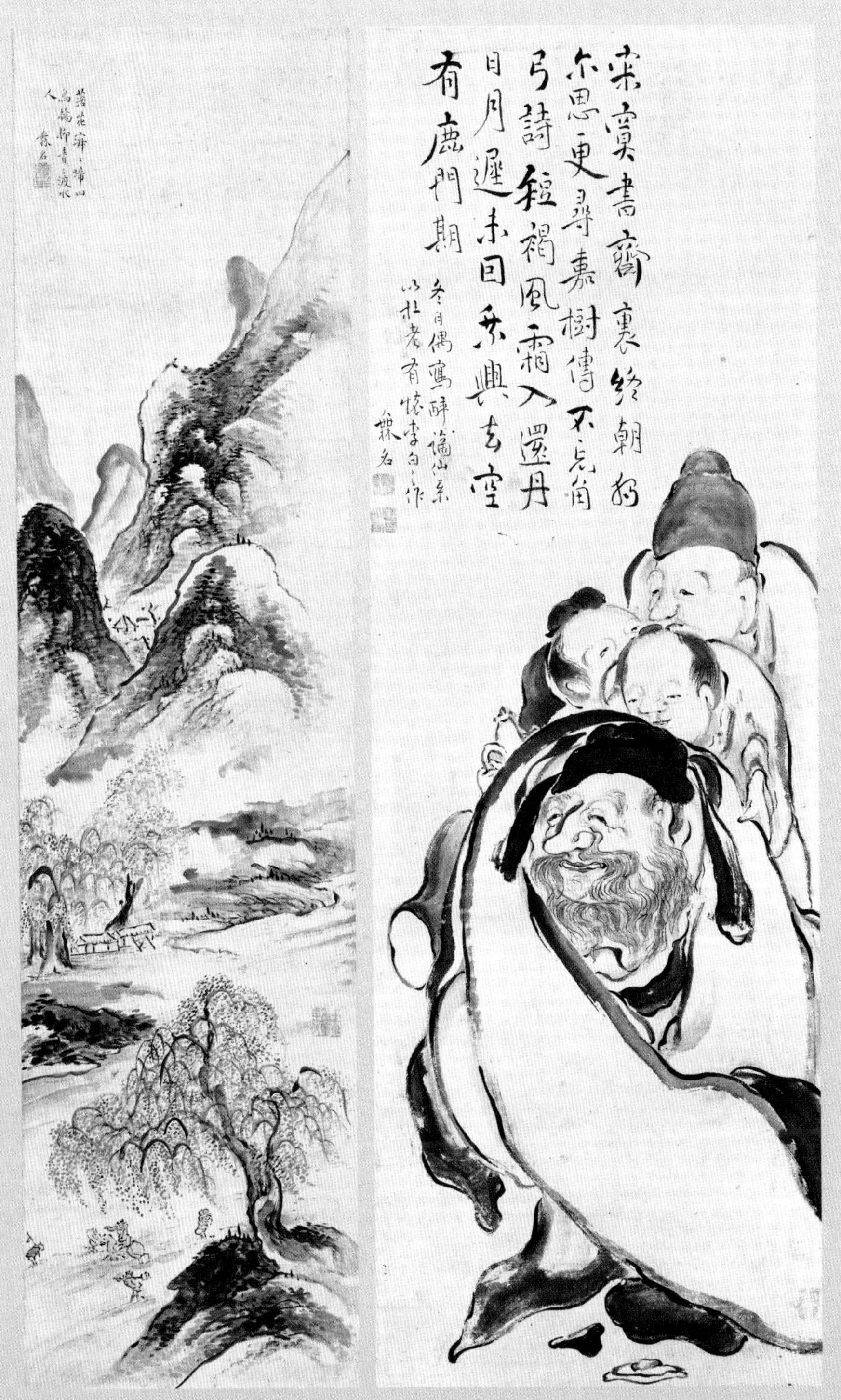

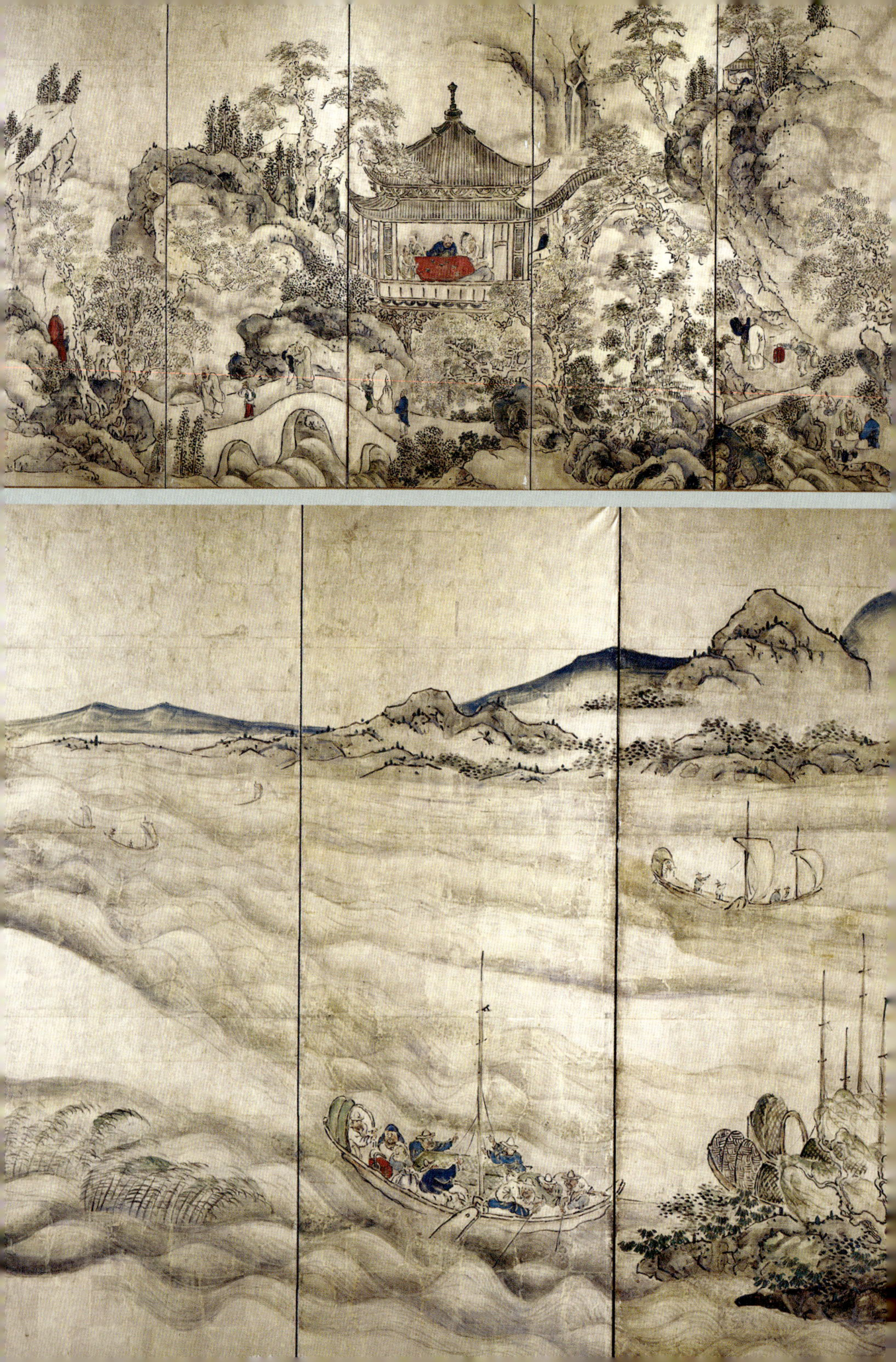

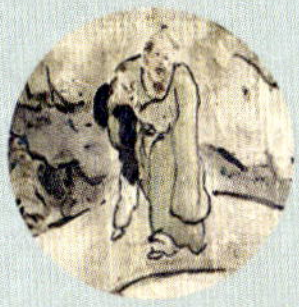

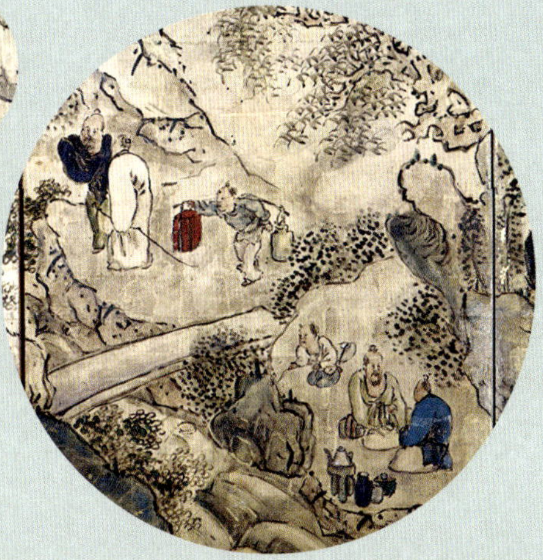

「楼閣山水図屏風」国宝　池大雅
江戸時代（18世紀）東京国立博物館蔵
Landscape with Pavilion, National Treasure,
Ike no Taiga, 18th century, Tōkyō National
Museum / ColBase (https://colbase.nich.go.jp)

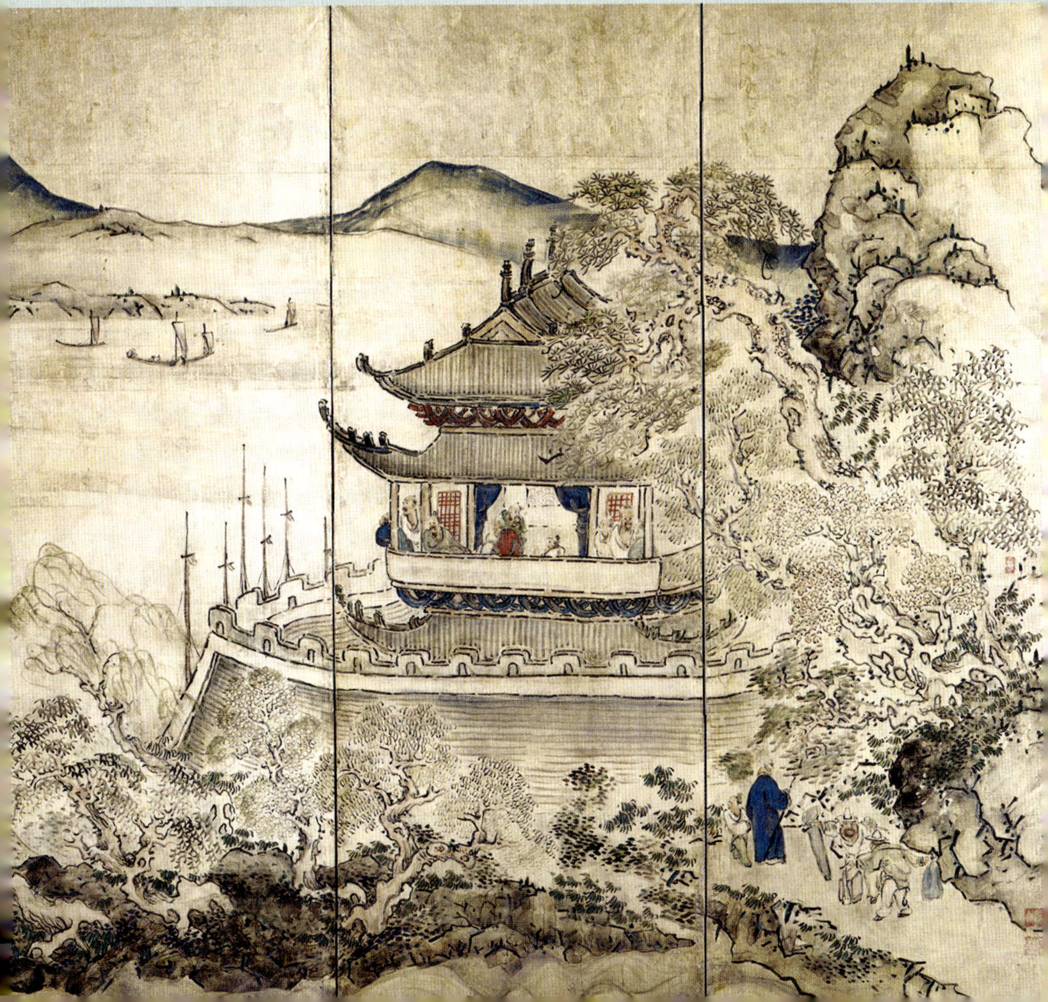

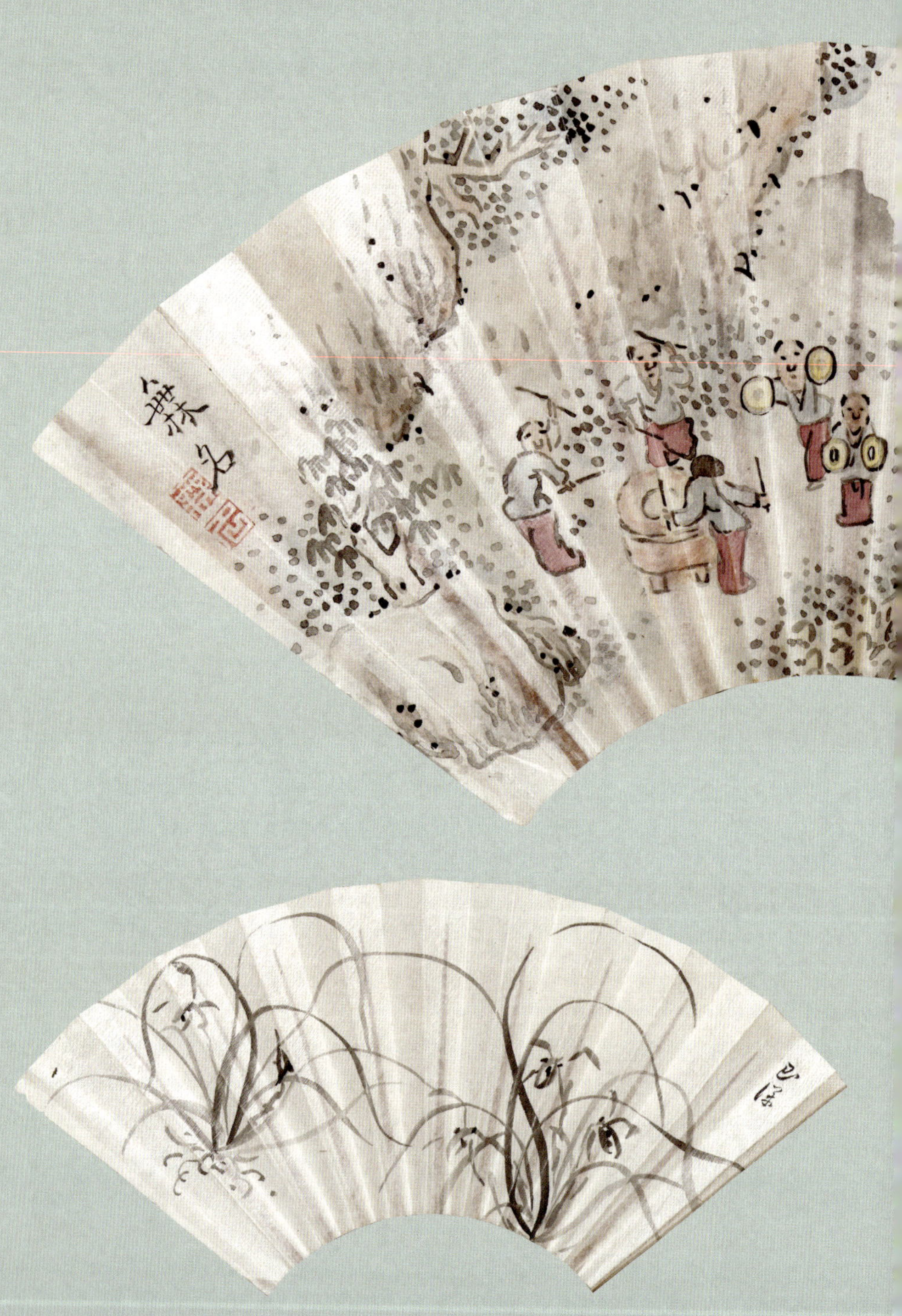

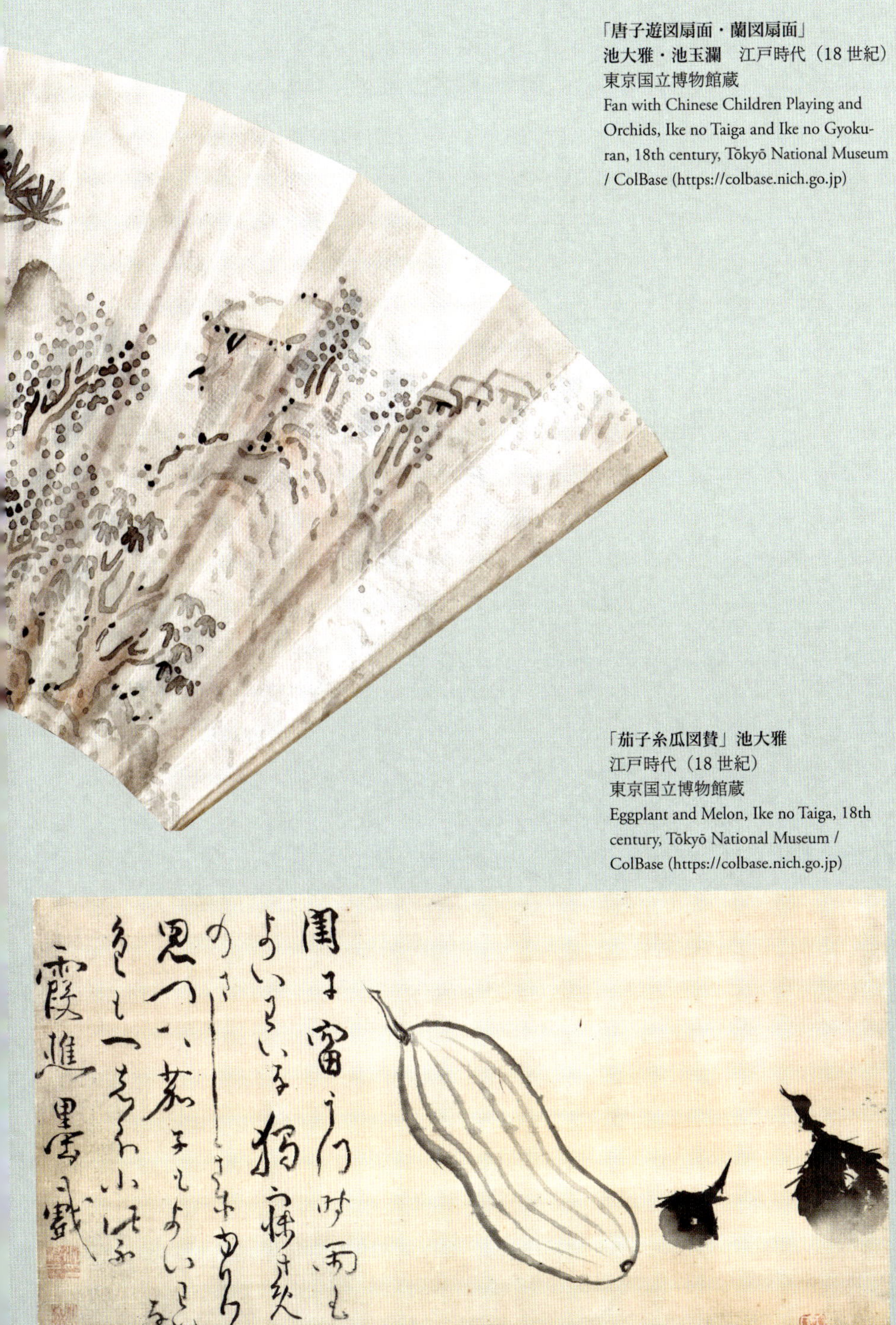

「唐子遊図扇面・蘭図扇面」
池大雅・池玉瀾　江戸時代（18世紀）
東京国立博物館蔵
Fan with Chinese Children Playing and
Orchids, Ike no Taiga and Ike no Gyoku-
ran, 18th century, Tōkyō National Museum
/ ColBase (https://colbase.nich.go.jp)

「茄子糸瓜図賛」池大雅
江戸時代（18世紀）
東京国立博物館蔵
Eggplant and Melon, Ike no Taiga, 18th
century, Tōkyō National Museum /
ColBase (https://colbase.nich.go.jp)

俳諧中興の祖にして、池大雅とならぶ文人画の巨匠

よさ ぶそん　享保元〜天明3年（1716〜83）

　江戸時代中期の俳人、文人で画家。摂津東成郡（大阪府）に生まれる。20歳のころ江戸に出て早野巴人（夜半亭宋阿）の門に入り俳諧を学ぶ。巴人没後、関東や奥州を遊歴して36歳のときに京都に移る。写実性や浪漫性、叙情性に富む俳風で中興期俳壇の中心的存在となる。晩年は蕉風復興を提唱し、画家としては池大雅とならんで文人画を大成する。

Leader of the Haikai revival and a literati painter to rival Ike no Taiga

Yosa Buson (1716-84) was a mid-Edo period haiku poet, literatus, and painter. Born in Kema-gun, Settsu province (now Osaka prefecture), he moved to Edo when about 20 and studied *haikai* poetry under Hayano Hajin (Yahantei Sōa). After Hajin's death, Buson traveled around the Kanto region and the Oshu region further north before moving to Kyoto at the age of 36. With his realistic, romantic, and lyrical style of haiku composition, he was a central figure in the world of haiku poetry during its revival. Late in life, he called for a revival of the Bashō style of haiku. He is also seen as ranking with Ike no Taiga as a great literati painter.

「富嶽列松図」（部分）重文　与謝蕪村
江戸時代（18 世紀後半）
愛知県美術館蔵（木村定三コレクション）
Mt.*Fuji* Seen beyond Pine Trees, Yosa Buson, Important Cultural Property, Latter half of the 18th century, Aichi Prefectural Museum of Art/ Kimura Teizo Collection

右頁：「薄に鹿図」与謝蕪村
江戸時代（18 世紀後半）
愛知県美術館蔵（木村定三コレクション）
Eulalias and Deer, Yosa Buson, Latter half of the 18th century, Aichi Prefectural Museum of Art/ Kimura Teizo Collection

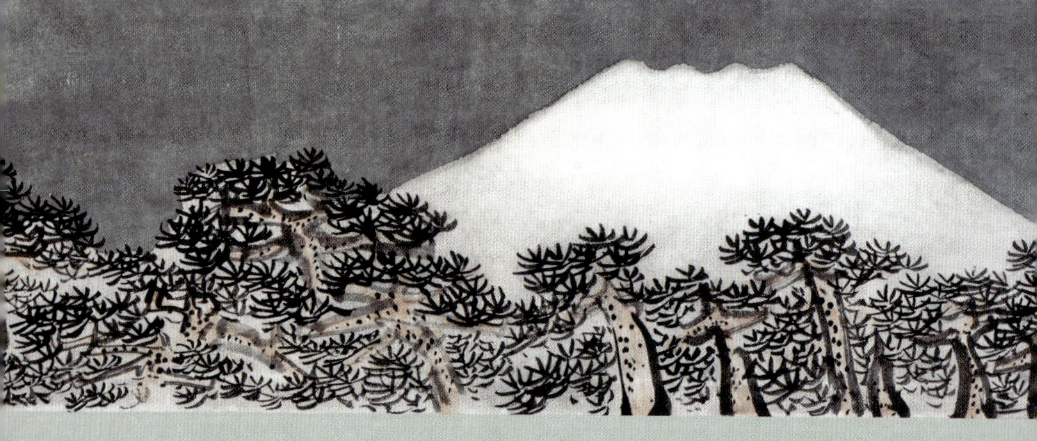

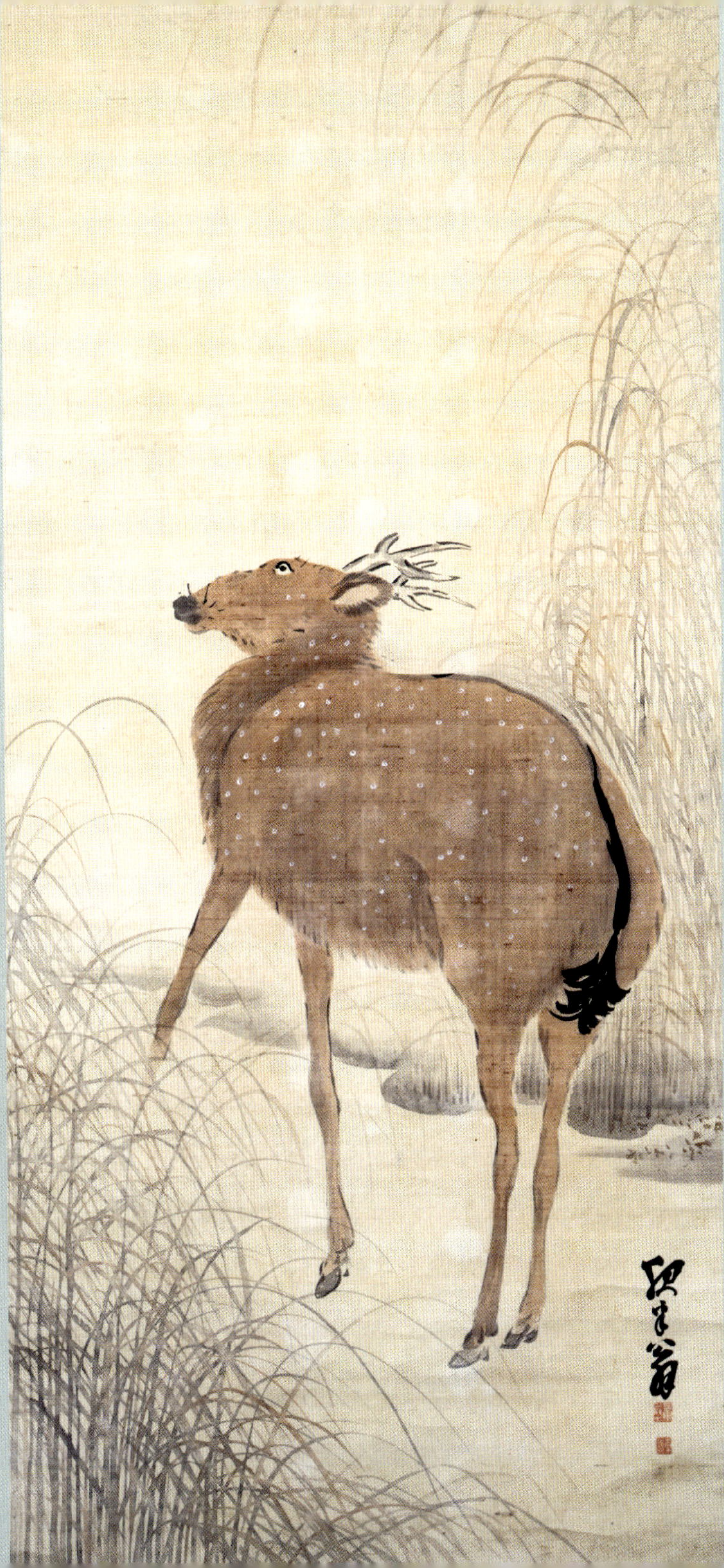

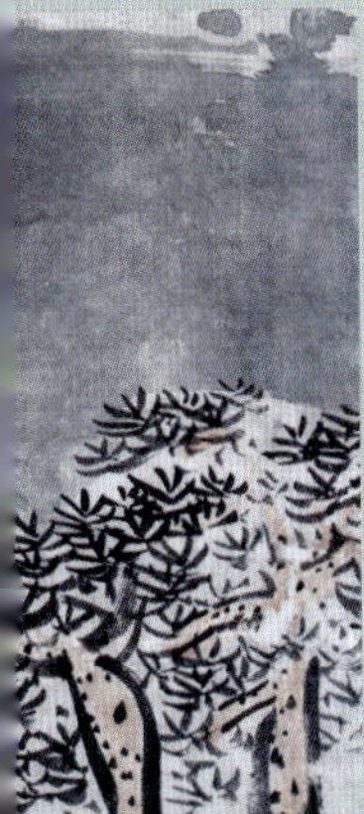

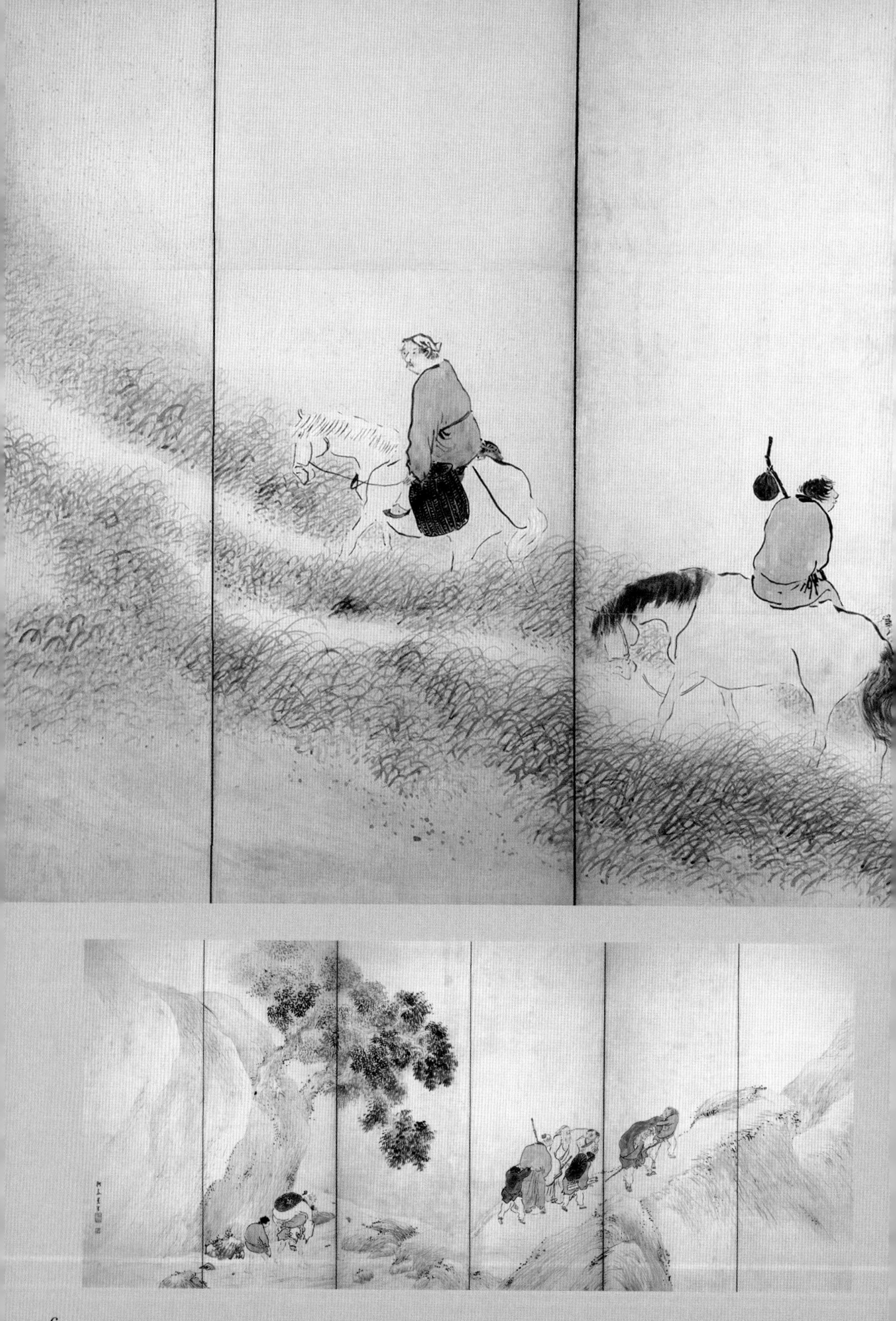

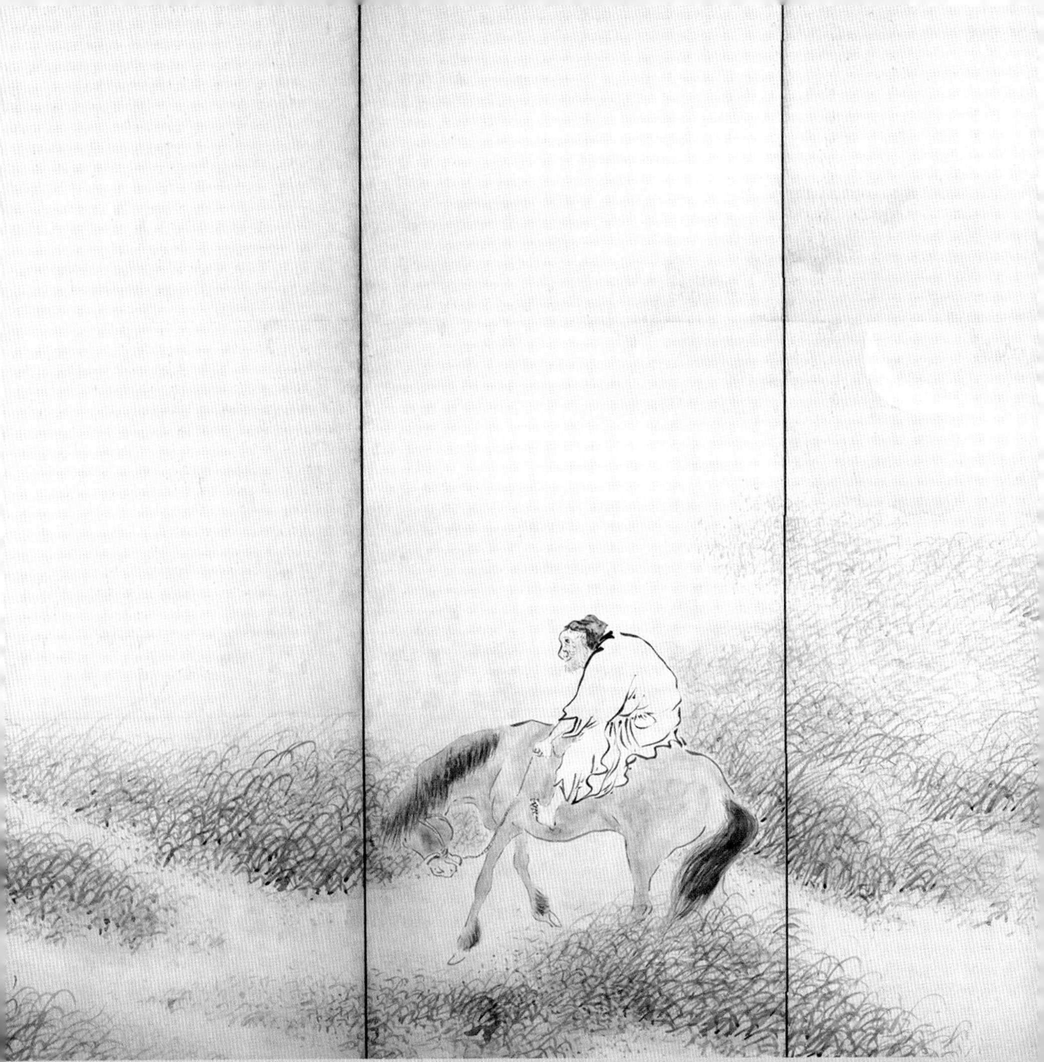

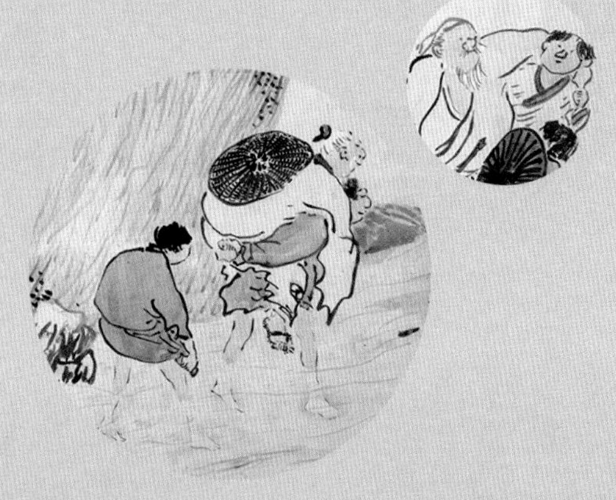

「山野行楽図屏風」重文　与謝蕪村
江戸時代（18 世紀）東京国立博物館蔵
Standing Screens of the Old Scholar's Travels,
Important Cultural Property, Yosa Buson,
18th century, Tōkyō National Museum /
ColBase (https://colbase.nich.go.jp)

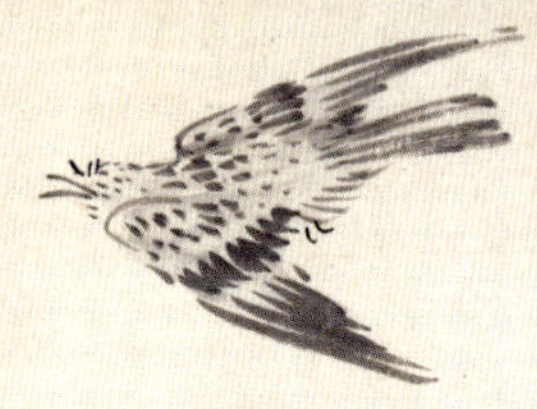

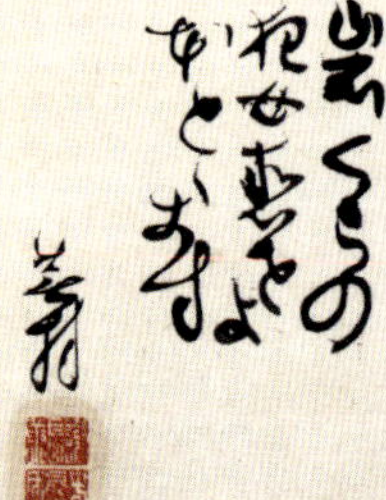

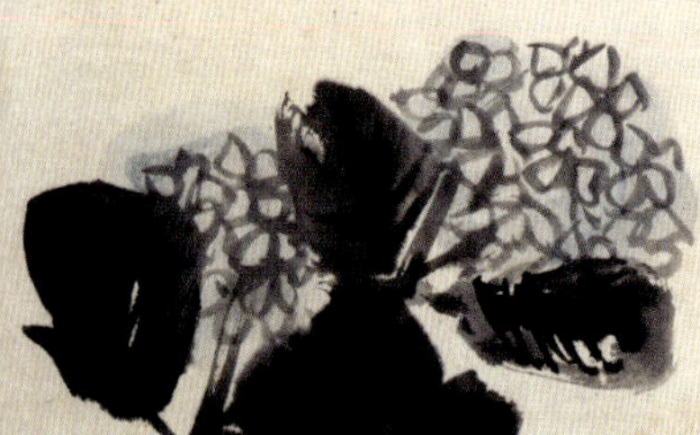

「紫陽花にほととぎす図」
与謝蕪村
江戸時代（18世紀後半）
愛知県美術館蔵
（木村定三コレクション）
Eulalias and Deer, Yosa Buson,
Latter half of the 18th century,
Aichi Prefectural Museum of Art/
Kimura Teizo Collection

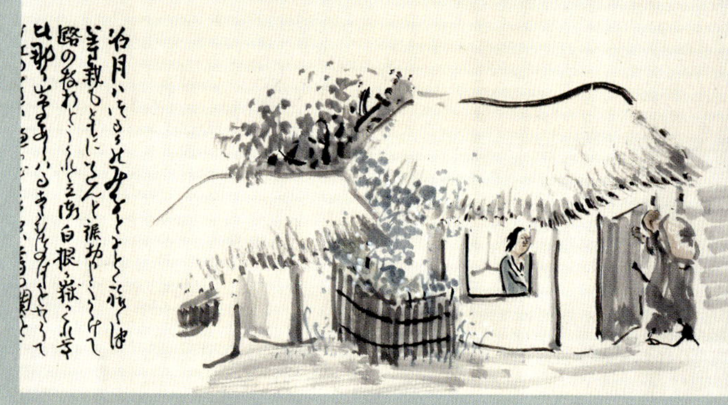

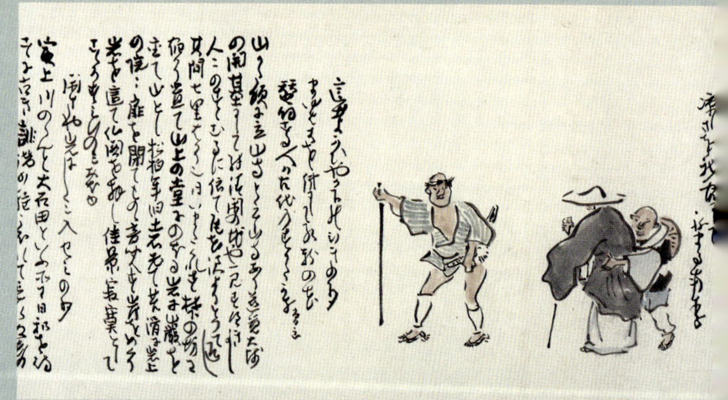

「奥之細道図」重文　与謝蕪村
京都国立博物館蔵
Oku no Hosomichi, Important
Cultural Property, Yosa Buson,
Kyoto National Museum / ColBase
(https://colbase.nich.go.jp)

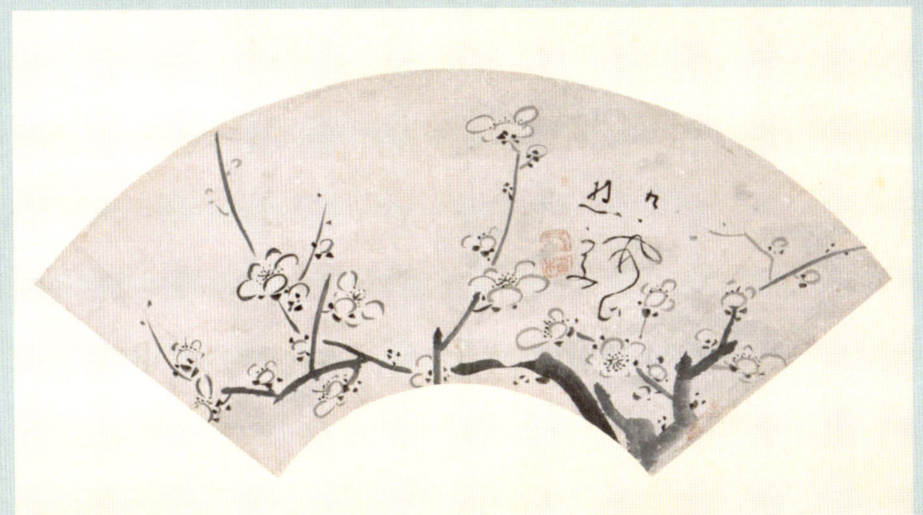

「扇面画類聚」池大雅・与謝蕪村等　江戸時代（18世紀）東京国立博物館蔵
Fan-shaped paintings Collaboration, Ike no Taiga, Yosa Buson, 18th century, Tōkyō
National Museum / ColBase (https://colbase.nich.go.jp)

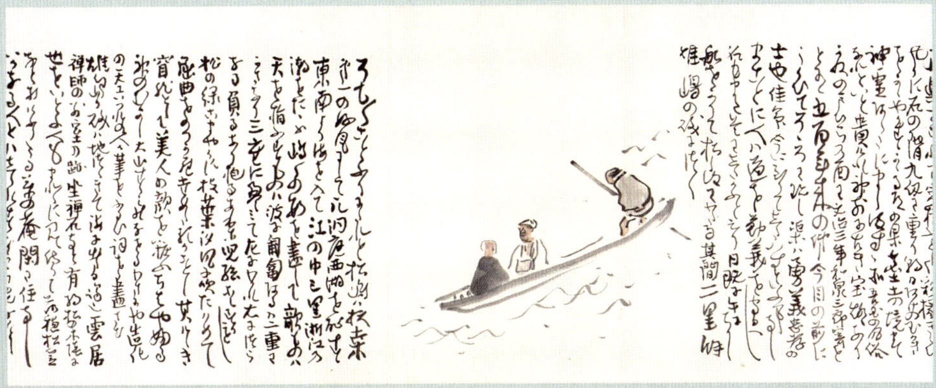

葛蛇玉

Katsu Jagyoku

鯉の絵を得意とし、
鯉翁とよばれた画家

かつ じゃぎょく
享保20〜安永9年（1735〜80）

　江戸時代中期の画家。玉泉寺
という浄土真宗の寺の次男とし
て生まれ、後に長嶋喜右衛門の
婿養子となった。絵ははじめ
橘 守国や鶴亭に学び、のちに
宋元の古画を研究して一家を成
した。好んで鯉の絵を得意とし
たため鯉翁とよばれ、上田秋成
著『雨月物語』にある「夢応の
鯉魚」のモデルといわれる。

"The Old Carp Man"

The mid Edo period painter Katsu
Jagyoku (1735-80) was born as the
second son of a priest at a Jodo Shin-
shu temple, the Gyokusenji. He later
became the adopted son-in-law of
Nagasaki Kiemon. He initially studied
painting with Tachibana Morikuni
and Kakutei, but later researched
Song and Yuan paintings and formed
his own school. His skill at painting
carp earned him the name "The Old
Carp Man." He was the model for the
"dream-come-true carp" in Ueda Aki-
nari's Tales of *Moonlight and Rain*.

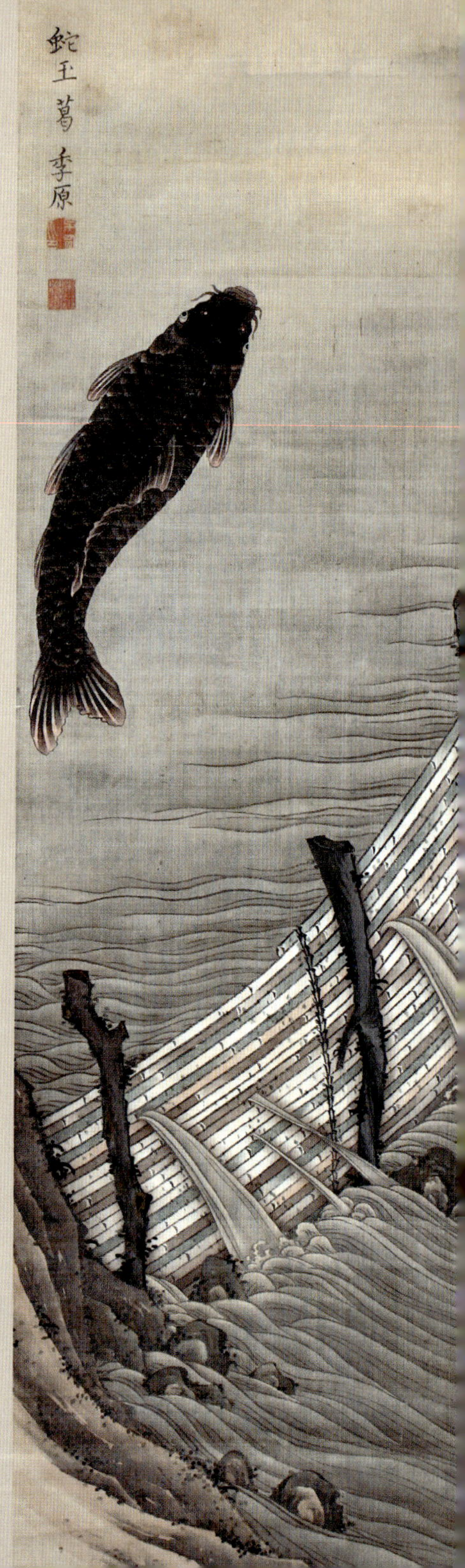

「鯉魚図」葛蛇玉
江戸時代（18 世紀）曹源寺蔵
Carps, Katsu Jyagyoku 18th century, Sogen-ji

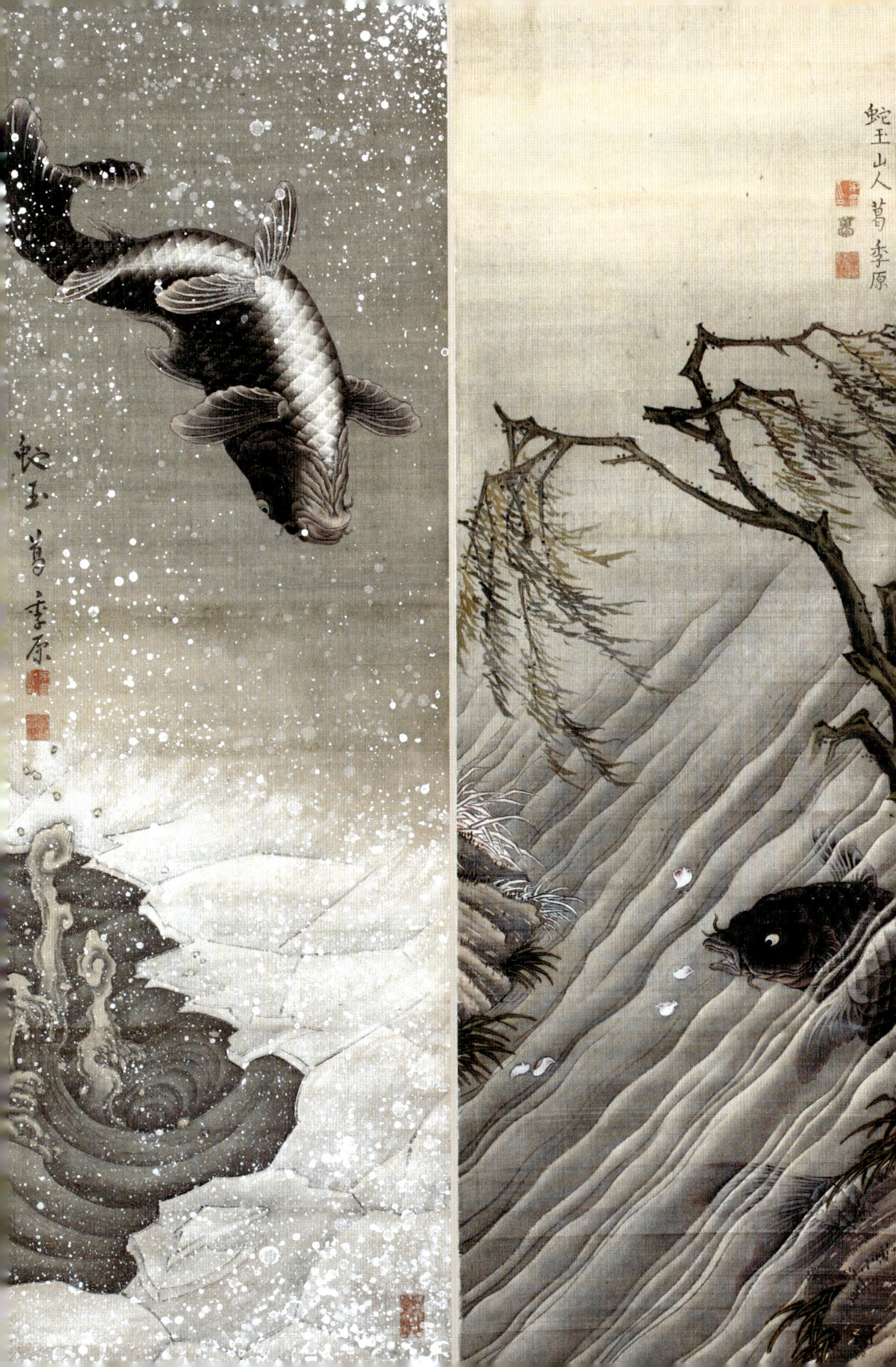

蛇王山人葛季原
蛇王葛季原

月僊
Gessen

応挙や蕪村の作風に影響を受けた画家

げっせん　寛保元年〜文化6年（1741〜1809）

　江戸時代中期の画僧。尾張名古屋に生まれる。浄土宗の僧となり、江戸へ出て増上寺に入り、桜井雪館のもとで絵を学び、大僧正妙誉より月僊の号を与えられた。上洛して円山応挙や与謝蕪村などの作風に影響を受け、さまざまな流派を取り入れた鋭い筆法の作風で一家をなした。安永3年（1774）伊勢（三重県）寂照寺の住職となり社会事業につくした。

A painter influenced by Ōkyo and Buson

A priest painter active in the mid Edo period, Gessen (1741-1809) was born in Nagoya, Owari province, and became a Pure Land priest. He came to Edo, entered Zōjōji Temple, and studied painting with Sakurai Sekkan. He received the art name Gessen from Daisōjōgyō Myōo. Moving to Kyoto, he was influenced by the styles of Maruyama Ōkyo and Yosa Buson, among others, and founded a school with his distinctive acute style of brushwork. In 1774 he became the chief priest at Jukushōji Temple in Ise (Mie prefecture) and dedicated himself to projects to benefit society.

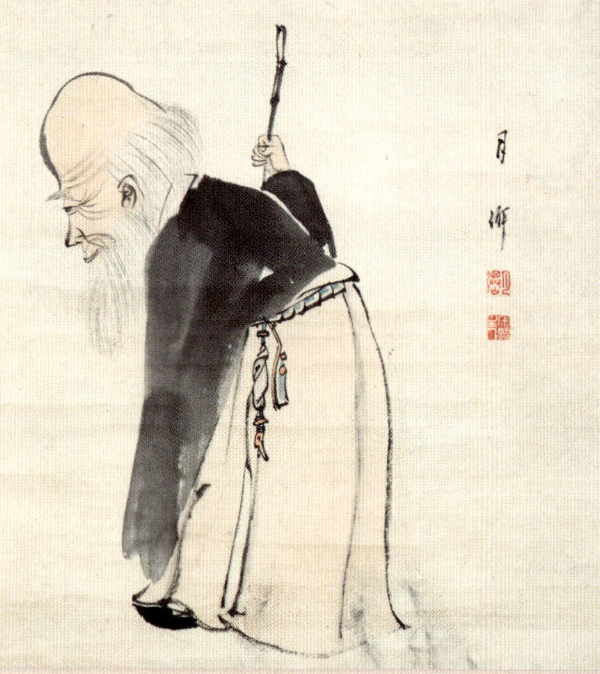

「寿老人図」月僊　制作年不詳　三重県立美術館蔵
Shou Laoren, Gessen, Mie Prefectural Art Museum

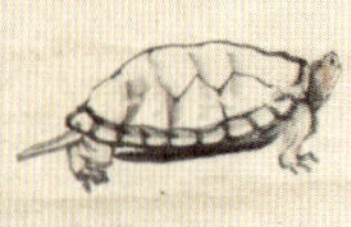

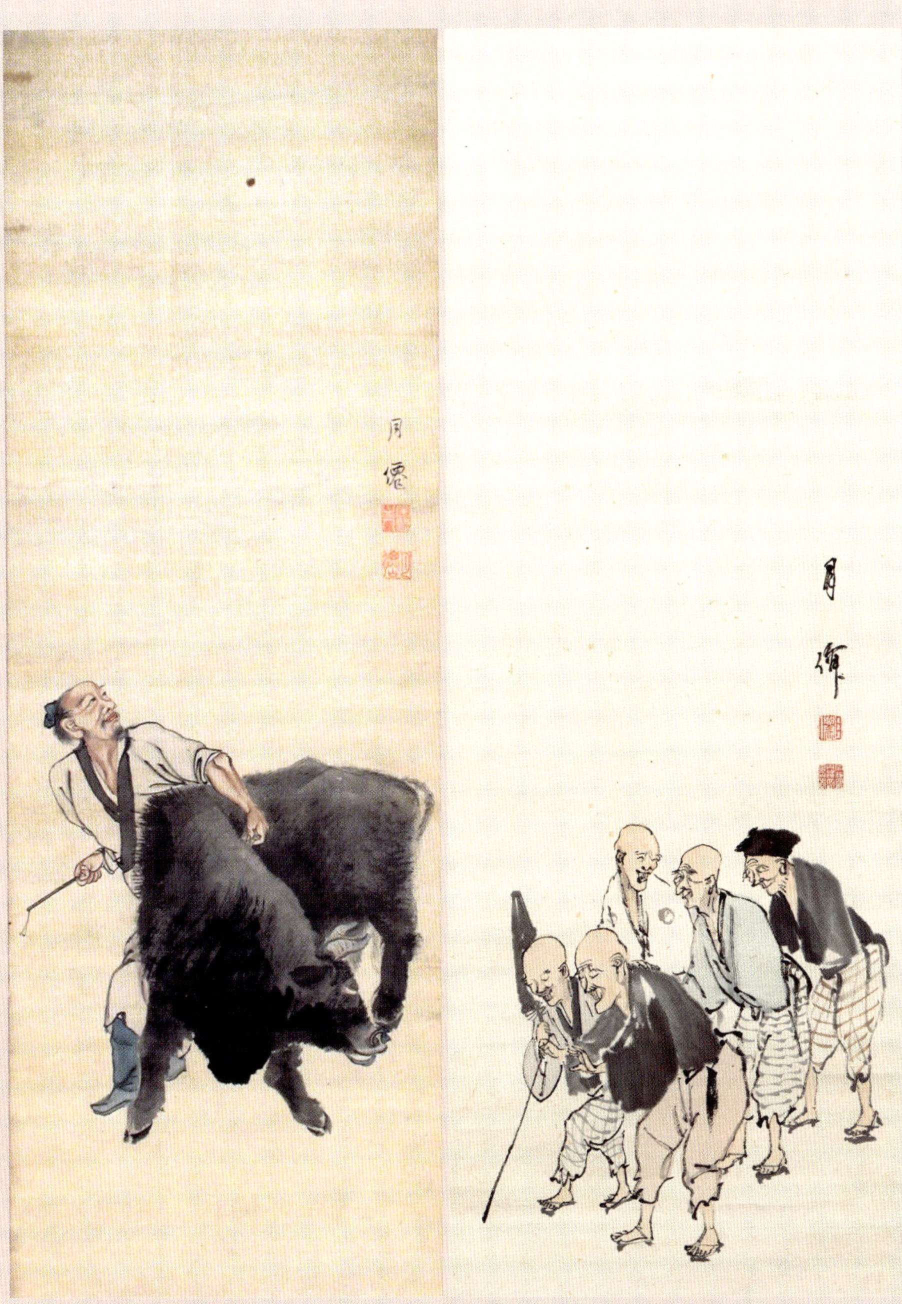

「人物と牛（曳牛人物図）」月僊
制作年不詳 三重県立美術館蔵
Men pulling a Calves, Gessen, Mie Prefectural
Art Museum

「盲人図」月僊　東京国立博物館蔵
Blind Peoples, Gessen, Tōkyō National Museum /
ColBase (https://colbase.nich.go.jp)

自らの心象を詩的な感性で描いた画家

うらがみ ぎょくどう
延享2～文政3年（1745～1820）

　江戸時代中期・後期の南画家。備前（岡山県）池田藩の支藩鴨方藩の武家に生まれる。7歳で家督を継ぎ、藩主池田政香の側近として重用された。50歳のとき、春琴と秋琴の二人の子どもをつれ脱藩。以後、京都に居を定めるまで琴をたずさえ各地を遍歴した。絵はほぼ独学で、音楽的ともいえる独特の作風は最晩年にようやく開花した。

A pinter who poetically depicted his own mindscape

A Nanga (southern Chinese style) painter active in the mid and late Edo period, Uragami Gyokudō (1745-1820) was born to a samurai family in the Kamogata domain, a branch of the Ikeda domain in Bizen (Okayama prefecture). He inherited the family headship at the age of seven and was valued as an aide to Ikeda Masaka, the lord of the domain. At the age of fifty, he left the domain, taking his two children with him. From then on, he made Kyoto his base while traveling all over the country, playing his *kin*, a seven-string lute. He was almost entirely self taught as a painter. His distinctive, musical style blossomed near the end of his life.

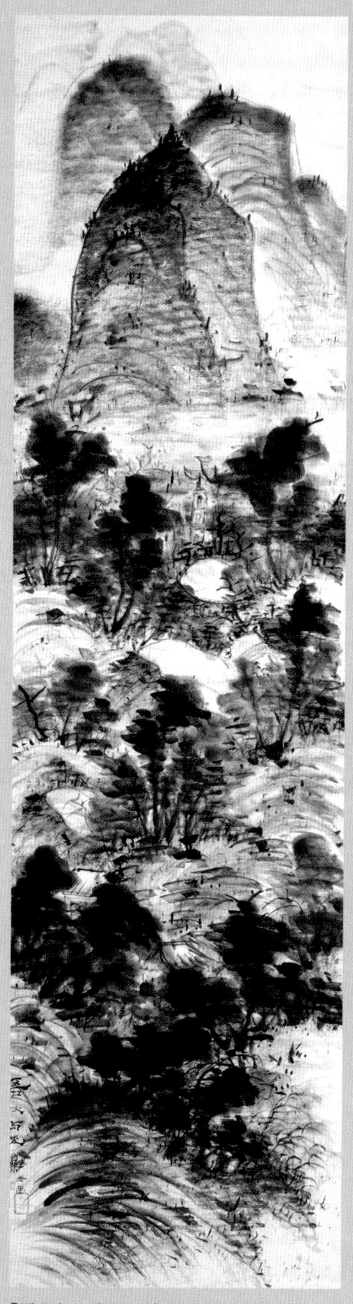

「吾心与山楽図」浦上玉堂
岡山県立博物館蔵
Goshin Yo Sanraku-Zu, Uragami Gyokudō,
Okayama Prefectural Museum

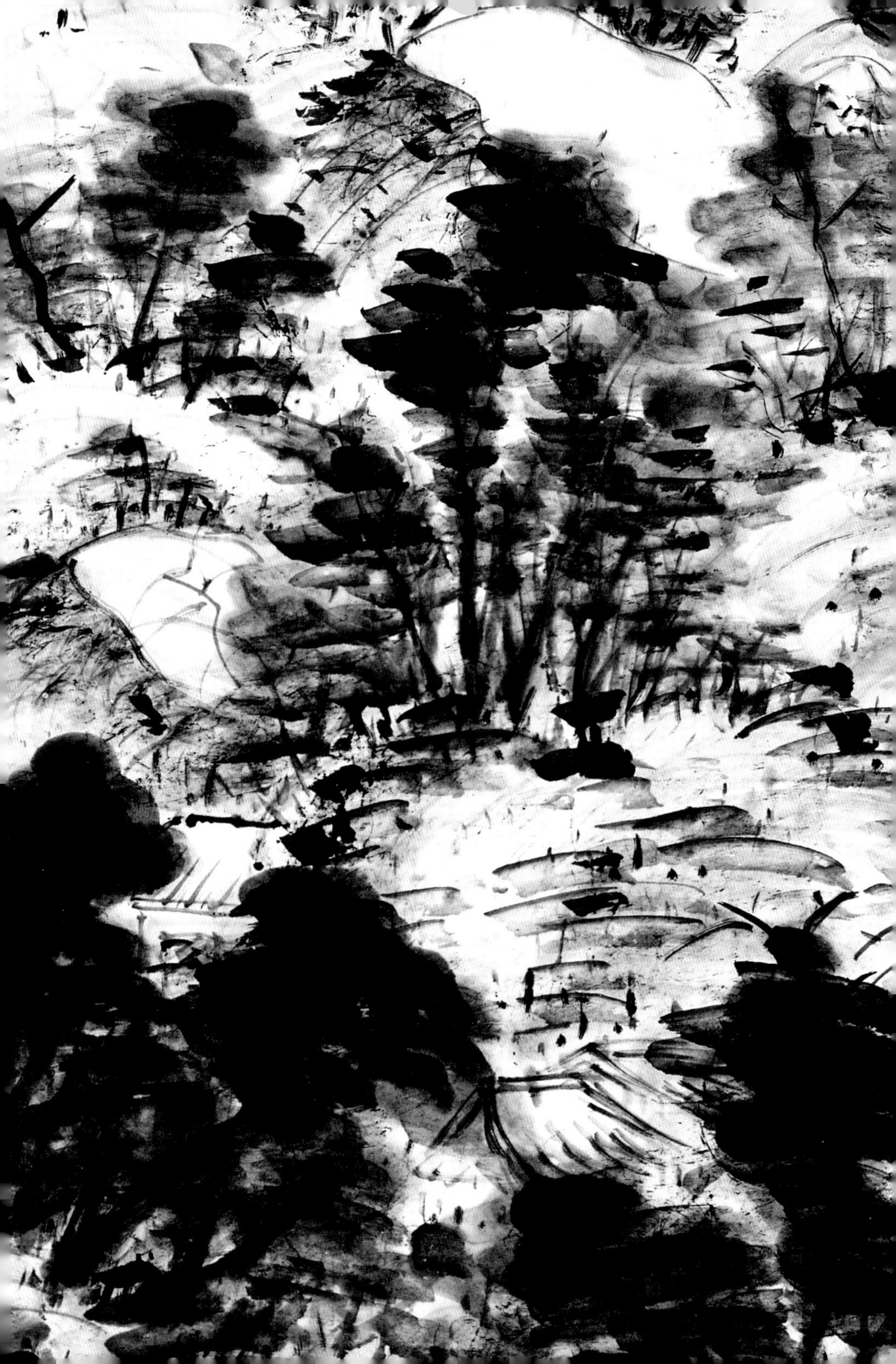

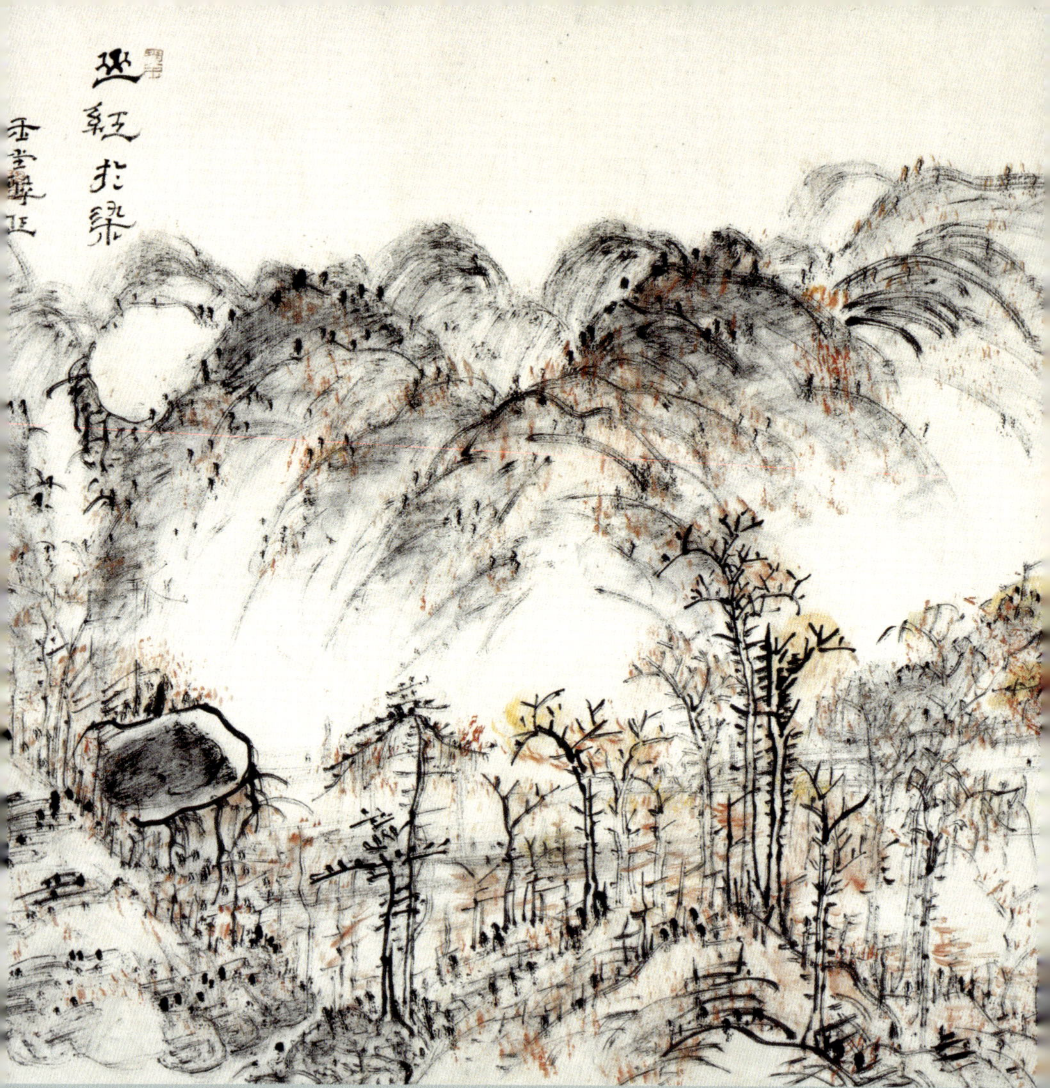

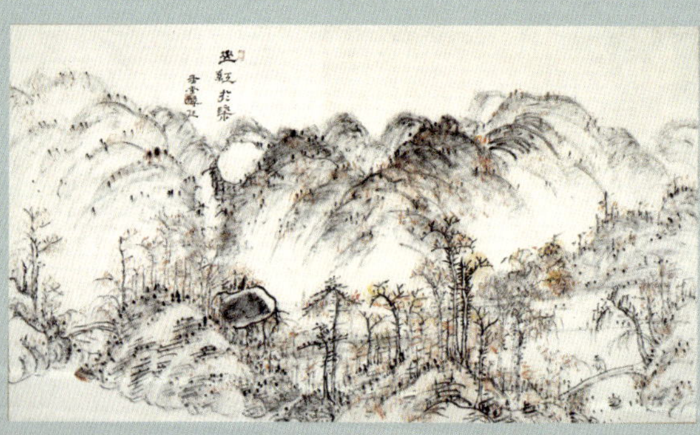

「山紅於染図」重文　浦上玉堂
19世紀初期　愛知県美術館蔵
（木村定三コレクション）
Mountains Dyed Red by Autumn
Foliage, Important Cultural Property,
Uragami Gyokudō, Early 19th century,
Aichi Prefectural Museum of Art/ Kimu-
ra Teizo Collection

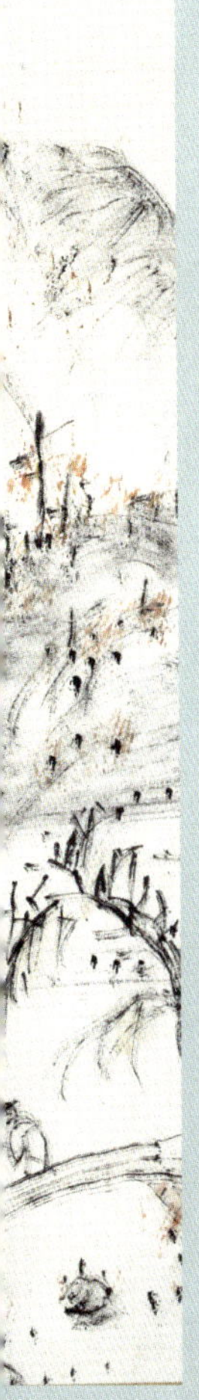

「高下数家図」浦上玉堂
19 世紀初期　愛知県美術館蔵
（木村定三コレクション）
Several Houses, Uragami Gyokudō, Early
19th century, Aichi Prefectural Museum
of Art/ Kimura Teizo Collection

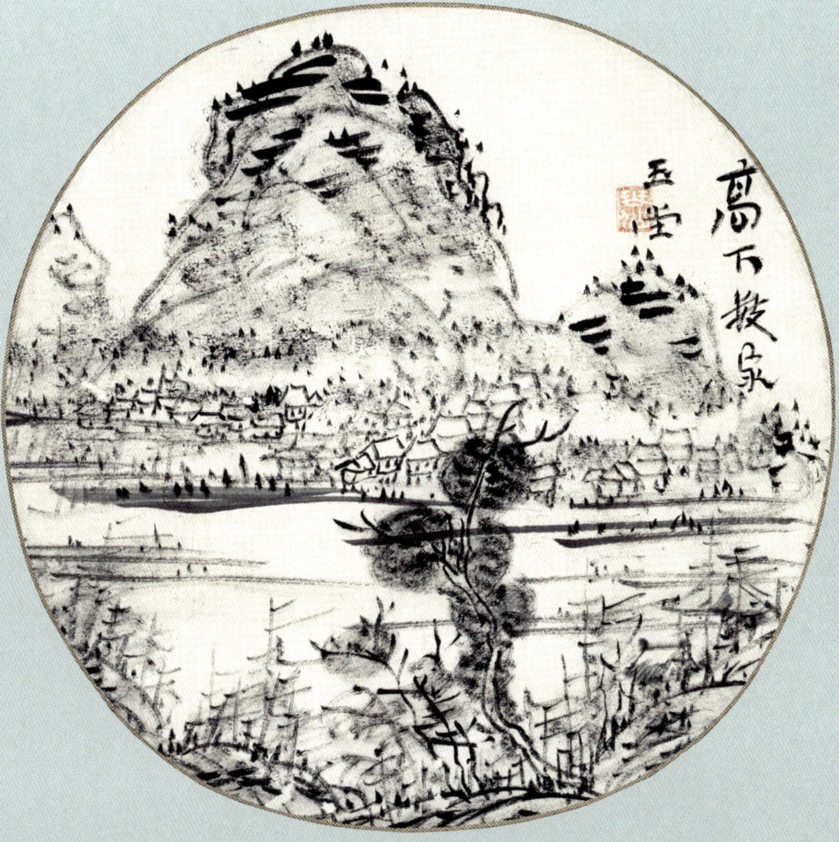

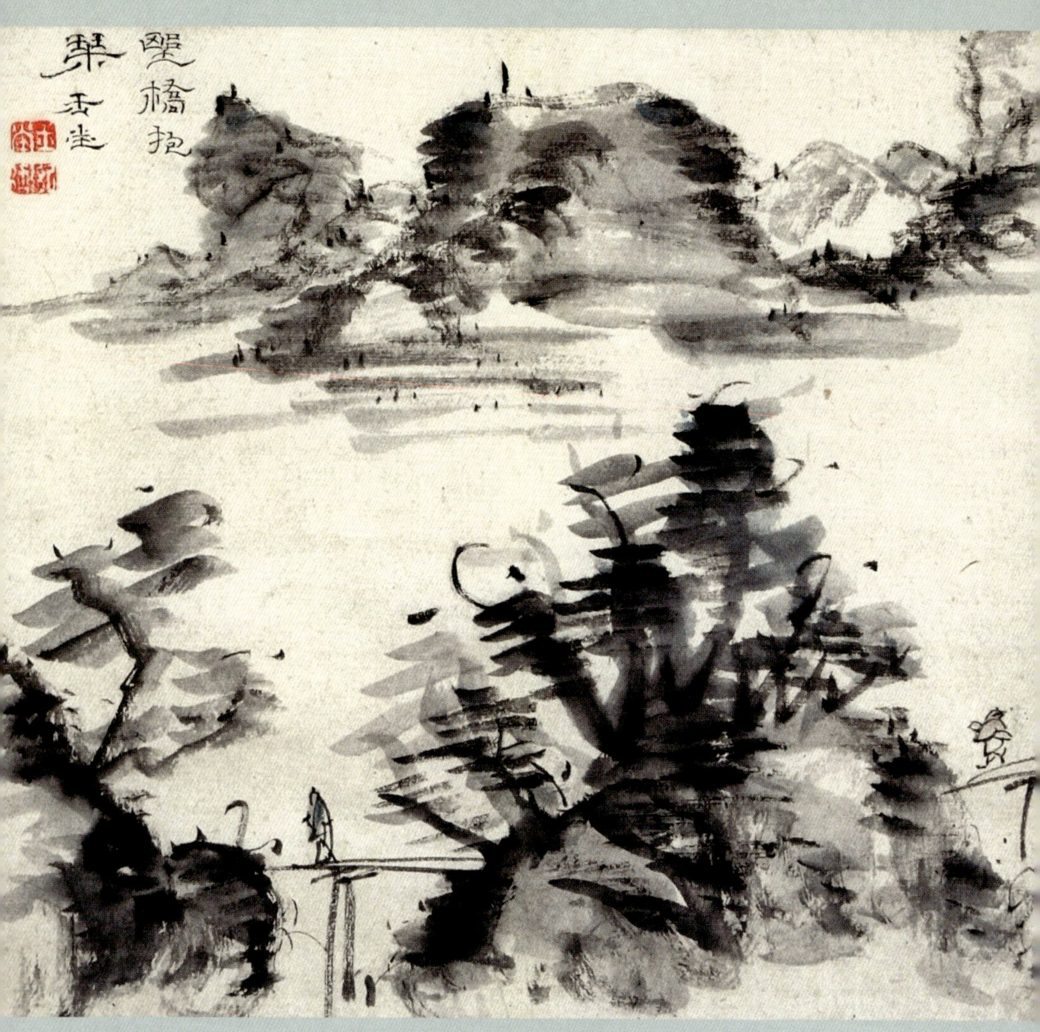

「野橋抱琴図」浦上玉堂　文化 11 年（1814）頃　岡山県立博物館蔵
Yakyo Houkin-Zu, Uragami Gyokudō, ca.1814, Okayama Prefectural Museum

「春山欲雨図」浦上玉堂　江戸時代（19 世紀）東京国立博物館蔵
Shunzan Yokuu-Zu, Uragami Gyokudō, 19th century, Tōkyō National Museum / ColBase (https://colbase.nich.go.jp)

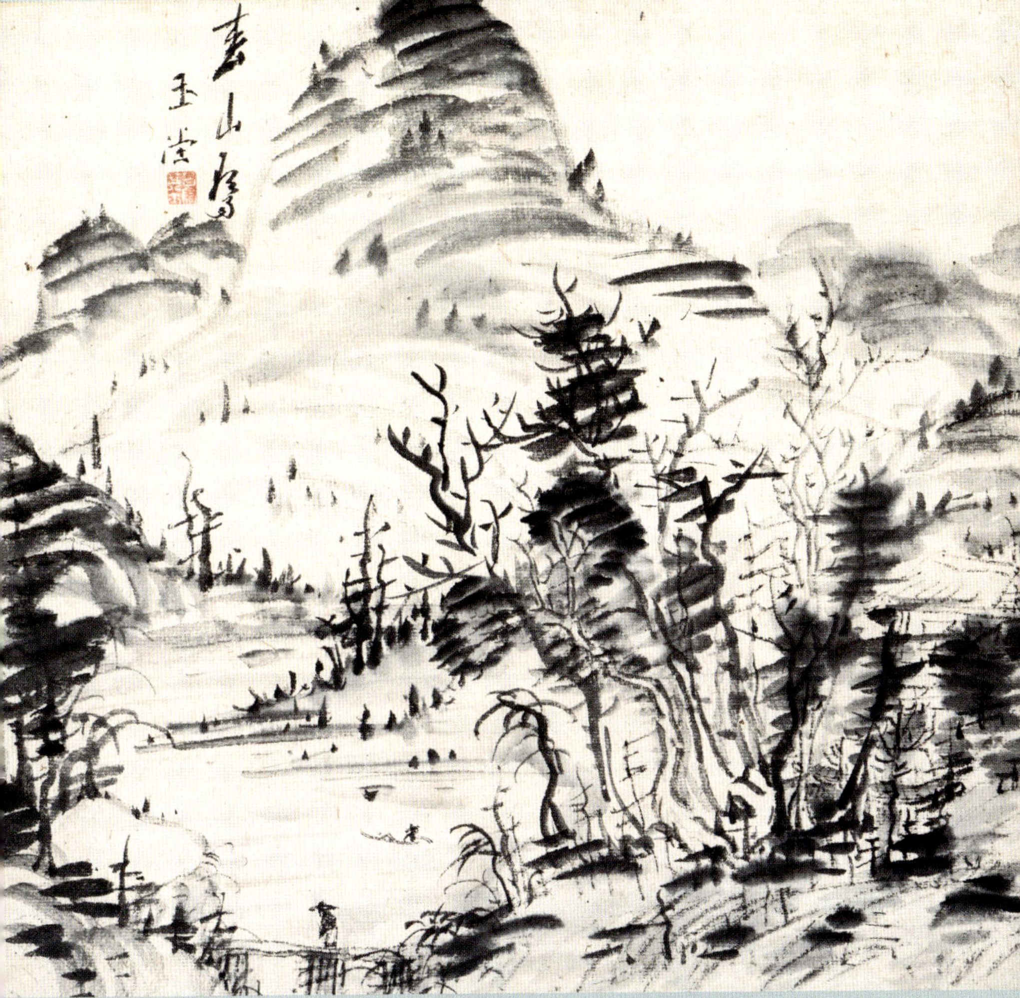

精細克明な毛描きにより、写実的な猿を得意とした

もり そせん　延享4~文政4年（1747~1821）

　江戸時代後期の画家。生地は長崎または摂津（兵庫県）西宮とされるが、大坂を中心に活躍した。はじめ長兄の陽信、次兄の周峰と狩野派の山本如春斎に学ぶが飽き足らず、写生に励み円山応挙の影響を受ける。動物画、とくに精細克明な毛描きにより、写実的に表現した猿の絵で名高い。

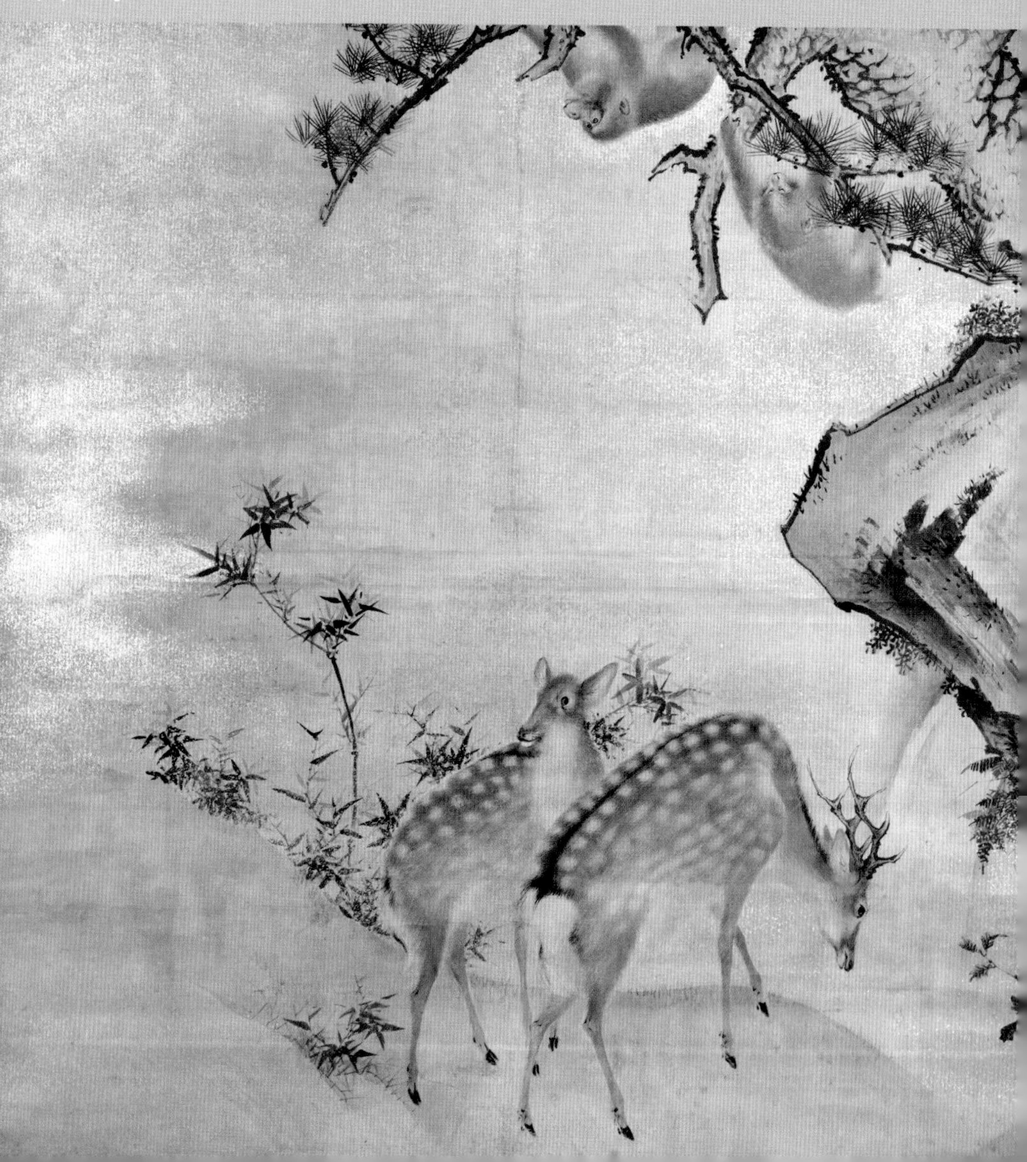

Depicting gibbons realistically with fine brushwork

Mori Sosen (1747-1821) a painter in the latter half of the Edo period, is said to have been born in Nagasaki or Nishimiya, Settsu (now Hyogo prefecture), but he made Osaka the center of his activities. His oldest brother was Takanobu, the next older brother Shūhō; they all studied with Yamamoto Joshunsai of the Kanō School, but Sosen was dissatisfied; stimulated by sketching, he was influenced by Maruyama Ōkyo. He was famous for his paintings of animals and particularly his realistic depictions of gibbons, their fur rendered with precisely detailed brushwork.

「秋山遊猿図」（部分）森狙仙　江戸時代（19 世紀）東京国立博物館蔵
Monkeys playing in the autumn mountains, Mori Sosen, 19th century, Tōkyō National Museum / ColBase (https://colbase.nich.go.jp)

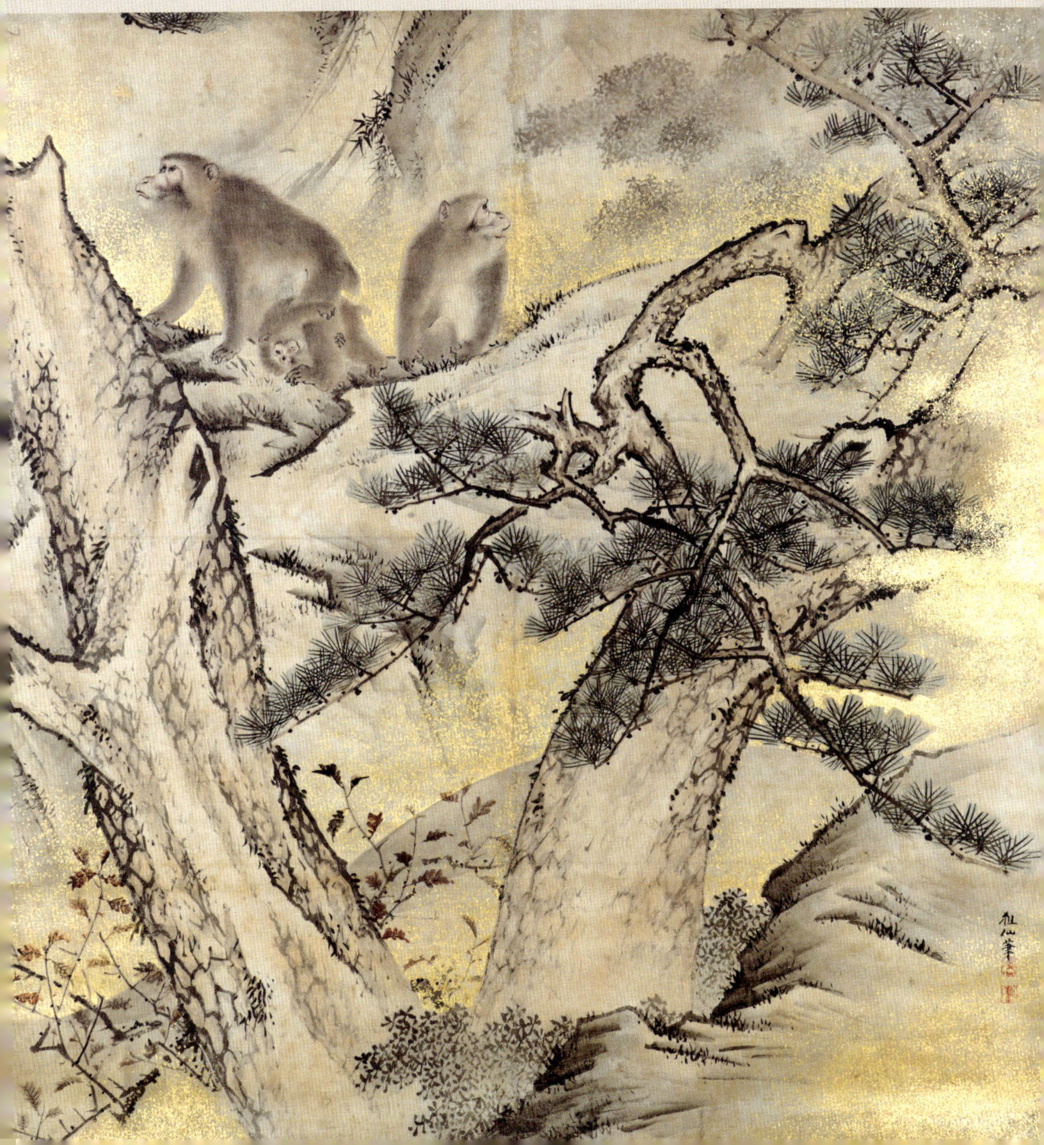

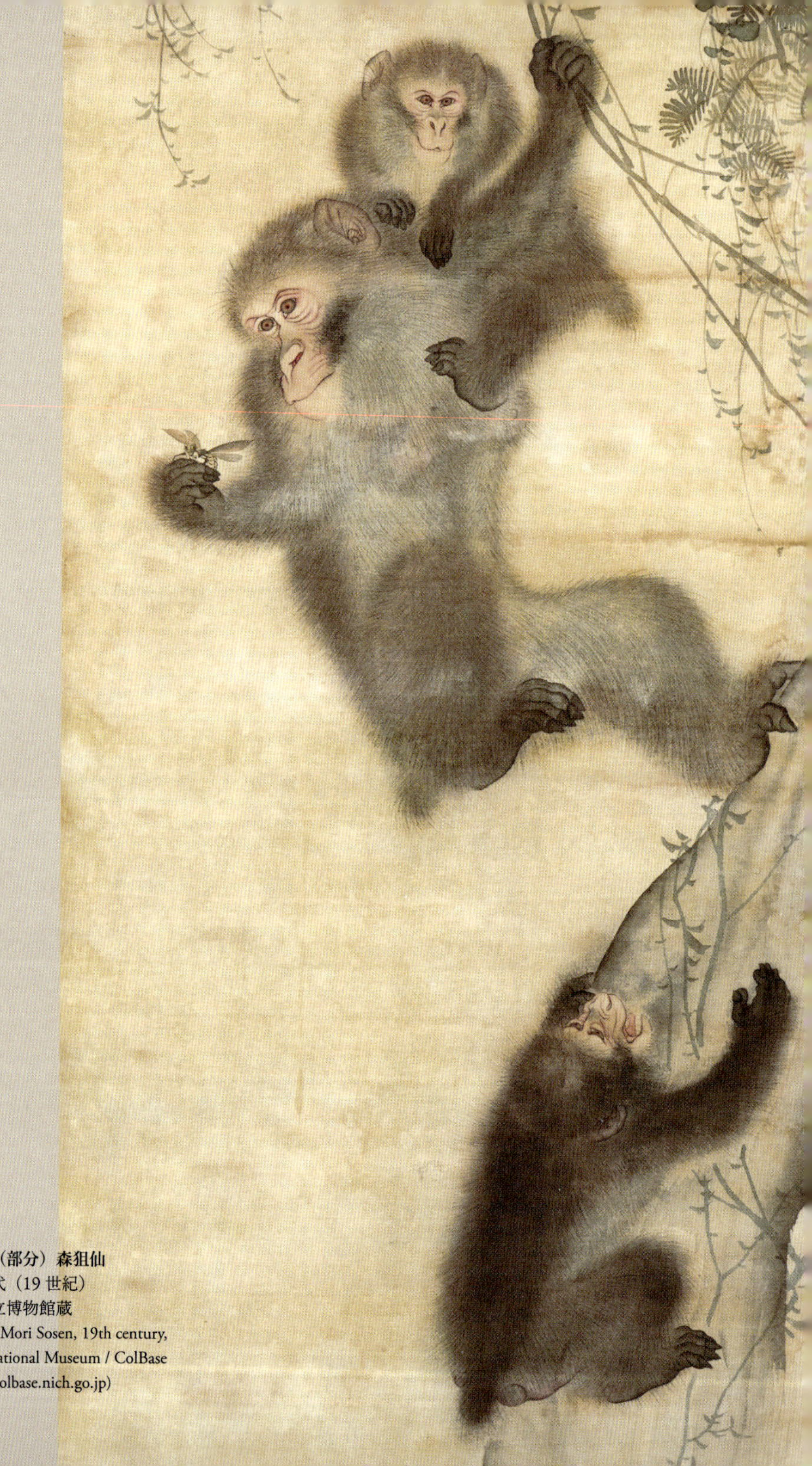

「猿図」（部分）森狙仙
江戸時代（19 世紀）
東京国立博物館蔵
Monkey, Mori Sosen, 19th century,
Tōkyō National Museum / ColBase
(https://colbase.nich.go.jp)

円山応挙に学び、応門十哲のひとり

もり てつざん　安永4～天保12年（1775～1841）

　江戸時代後期の画家。森周峯の長男として大坂に生まれ、森狙仙の養子となる。円山応挙の門に入り、応門十哲のひとり。狙仙の精緻な客観的描写に軽淡な情趣性のある作品を描く。晩年は宮廷の画用に従い、また熊本藩の庇護をうけた。動物画を得意とした。

One of Maruyama Ōkyo's top ten students

Mori Tetsuzan (1775-1841), a painter active in the latter half of the Edo period, was born in Osaka as the oldest son of Mori Shūhō and became the adopted son of Mori Sosen. Tetsuzan studied with Maruyama Ōkyo and was regarded as one of his top ten students. His work combined Sosen's detailed, objective style with a lighthearted sentimentality. In his later years, he served in the imperial court's painting bureau and also received the patronage of the Kumamoto domain. He too made paintings of animals his forte.

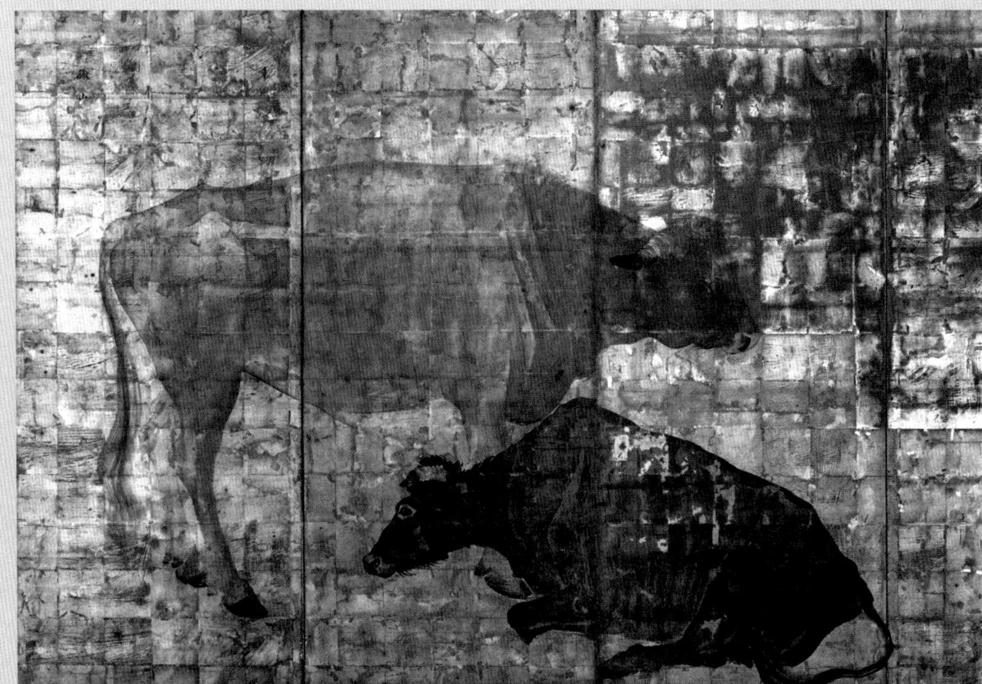

「牛図屏風」（部分）森徹山　江戸時代（19世紀）東京国立博物館蔵
Standing Screens of the Cows, Mori Tetsuzan, 19th century, Tōkyō National Museum / ColBase (https://colbase.nich.go.jp)

呉春

応挙と蕪村を融合した画風の画家

ごしゅん（松村月渓　まつむら げっけい）
宝暦2~文化8年（1752~1811）

　江戸時代中・後期の画家。京都金座の年寄役松村匡程の子。家業を継ぐが、そのかたわら大西酔月に絵を、与謝蕪村に俳諧と絵を学ぶ。36歳のときに父と妻を失い、摂津池田の呉服里に移る。その地で春を迎えたことにより呉春と改名した。その後、京都に戻り円山応挙と接し、その写生画風の影響を受けて独自の画風を確立した。

An Ōkyo-Buson fusion style

Goshun (1752-1811) was active in the mid to late Edo period. He was the son of an official at the Kyoto mint and carried on the family profession while also studying painting with Ōnishi Suigetsu and painting and *haikai* poetry with Yosa Buson. After losing his father and his wife when he was 36, he moved to Kureha no Sato in Ikeda, Settsu. Since he welcomed the spring there, he changed his name to Goshun ("honorable spring"). He later moved back to Kyoto, encountered Maruyama Ōkyo, was influenced by his realistic style, and established his own style of painting.

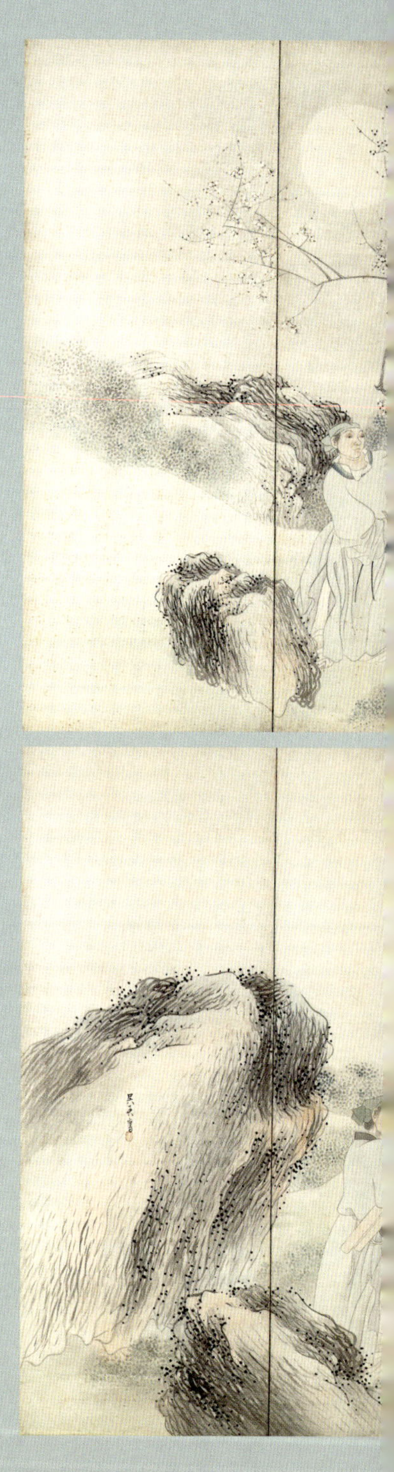

「桃李園夜宴・西園題石図屏風」呉春
江戸時代（18世紀）九州国立博物館蔵
Standing Screens of Tori-en Banquet, Sei-en Title Stone, Goshun, 18th century, Kyushu National Museum / Col-Base (https://colbase.nich.go.jp)

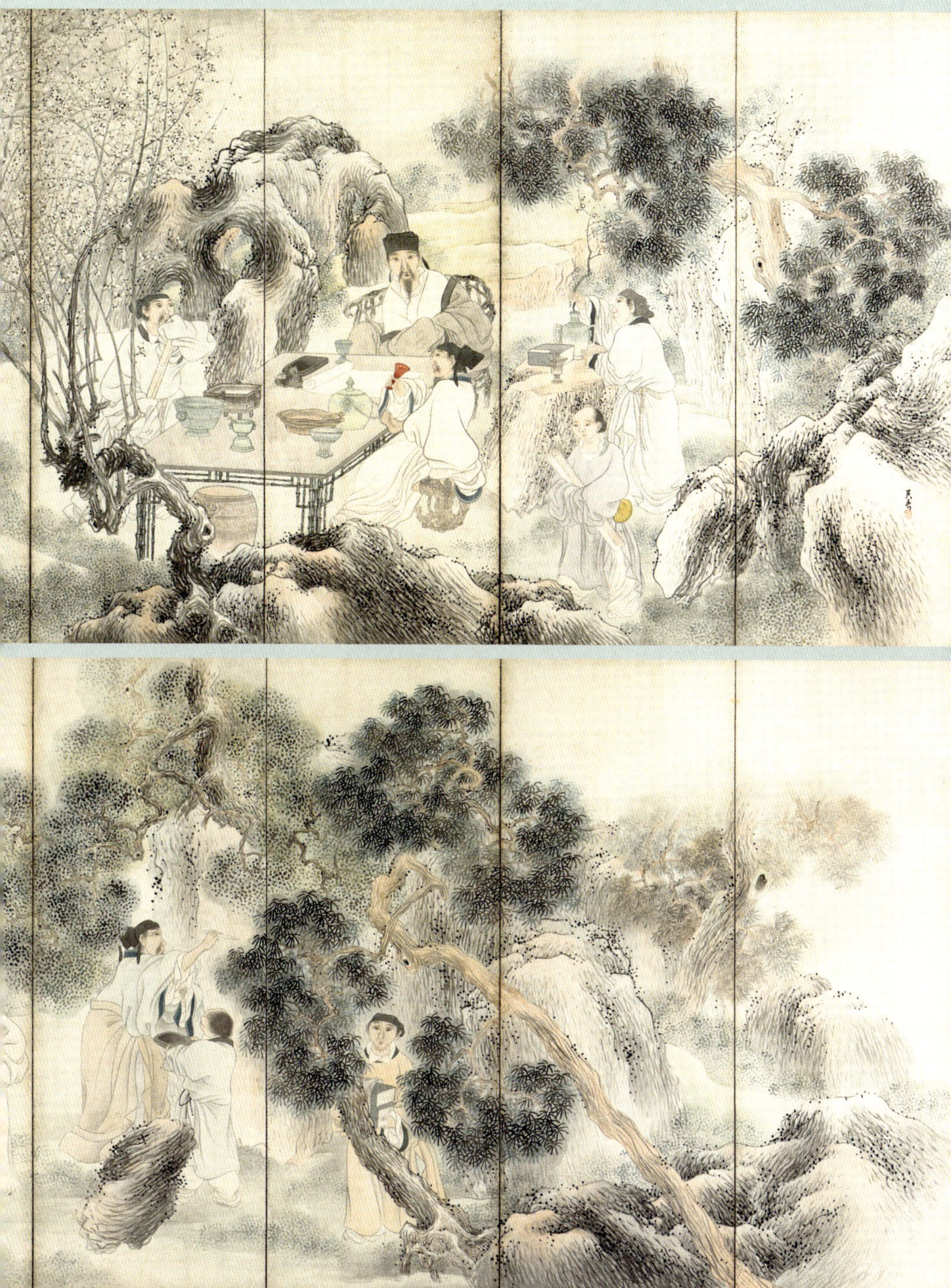

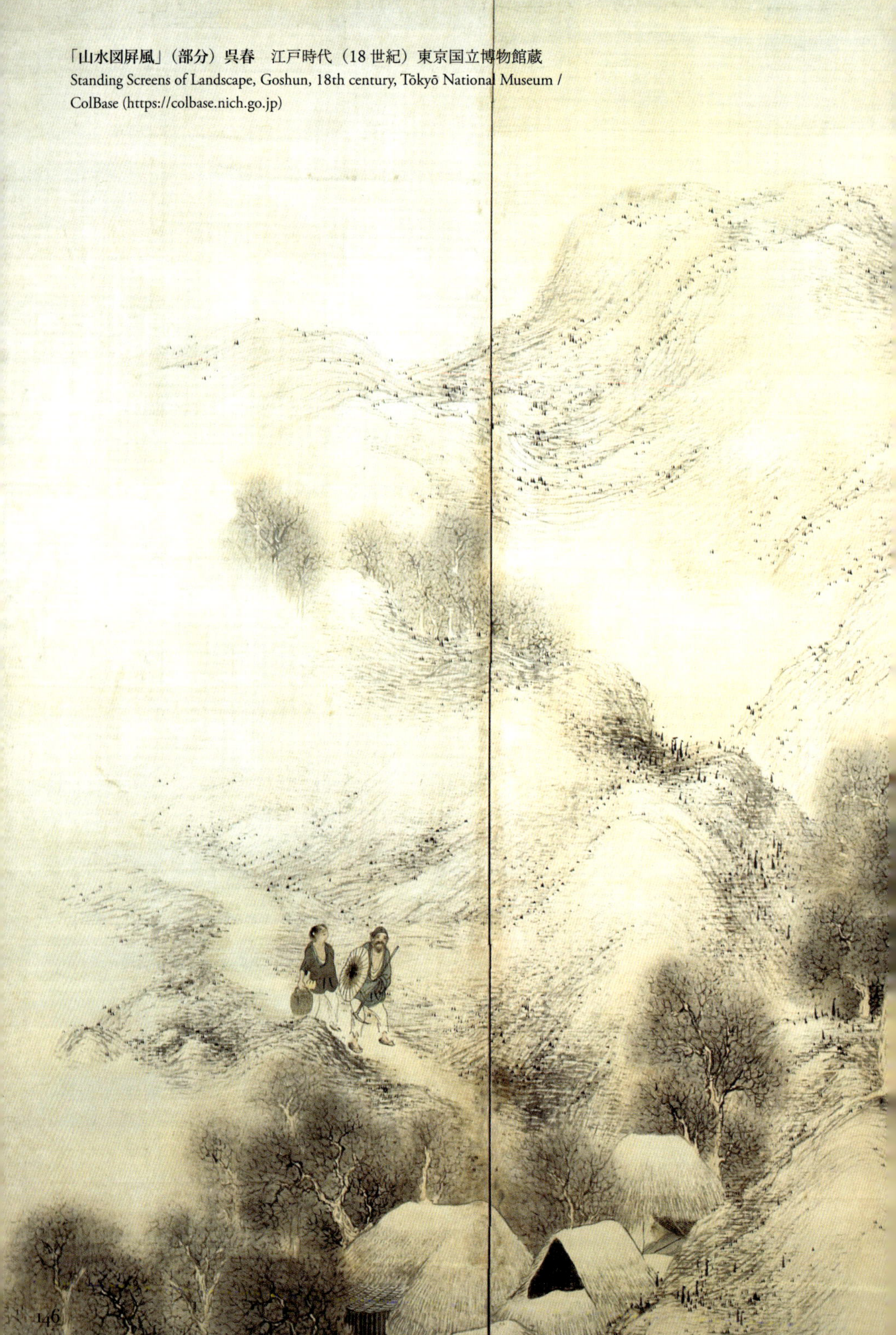

「山水図屏風」（部分）呉春　江戸時代（18世紀）東京国立博物館蔵
Standing Screens of Landscape, Goshun, 18th century, Tōkyō National Museum /
ColBase (https://colbase.nich.go.jp)

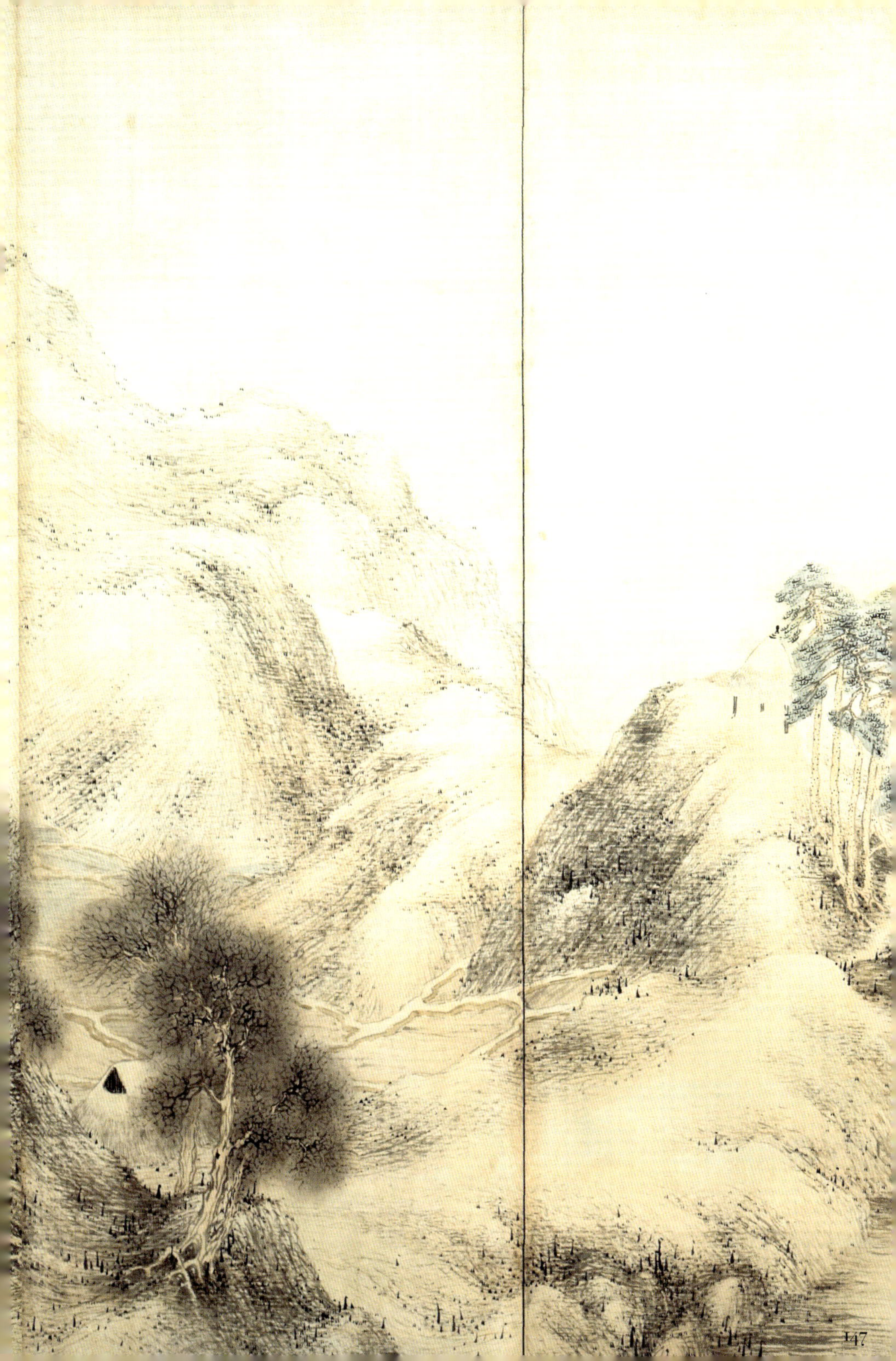

精緻で構成的な写生を原点に、奇想で諧謔的な世界を描く

ながさわ ろせつ　宝暦4~寛政11年（1754~99）

　江戸時代中期・後期の画家。山城国（京都府）淀藩に仕えた武士上杉和左衛門を父として生まれる。京都に出て円山応挙に学び、卓抜した筆致で応挙門下のなかで異彩を放つが、個性のつよい作風と奇行のため破門されたという。南紀の無量寺や草堂寺をはじめ、兵庫県大乗寺などに絵筆を振るい多くの襖絵を遺した。

Painting a humorous world eccentrically, with detailed, constructive realism

Nagasawa Rosetsu (1754-99) was active in the mid to late Edo period. His father was Uesugi Kazuemon, a samurai who served the Yodo domain in Yamashiro province (now Kyoto prefecture). Rosetsu moved to Kyoto and studied with Maruyama Ōkyo. He stood out among Ōkyo's students for his superb brushwork, but his highly individual style and eccentric behavior led to his being expelled from the Maruyama school. He produced many sliding door paintings, wielding his brush at, for example, Muryōji and Sōdōji temples in what is now southern Wakayama prefecture and Daijōji Temple in Hyogo prefecture.

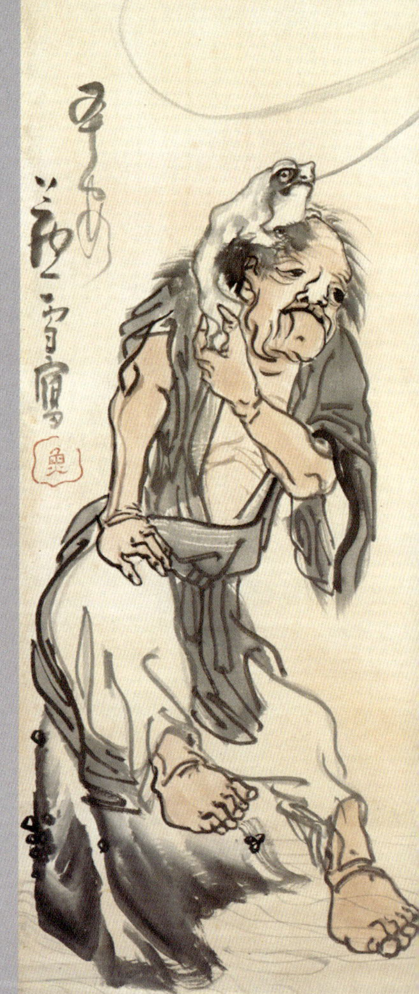

「双僊図」長澤蘆雪
江戸時代（18世紀）東京国立博物館蔵
Two-Hermit, Nagasawa Rosetsu, 18th century, Tōkyō National Museum / ColBase (https://colbase.nich.go.jp)

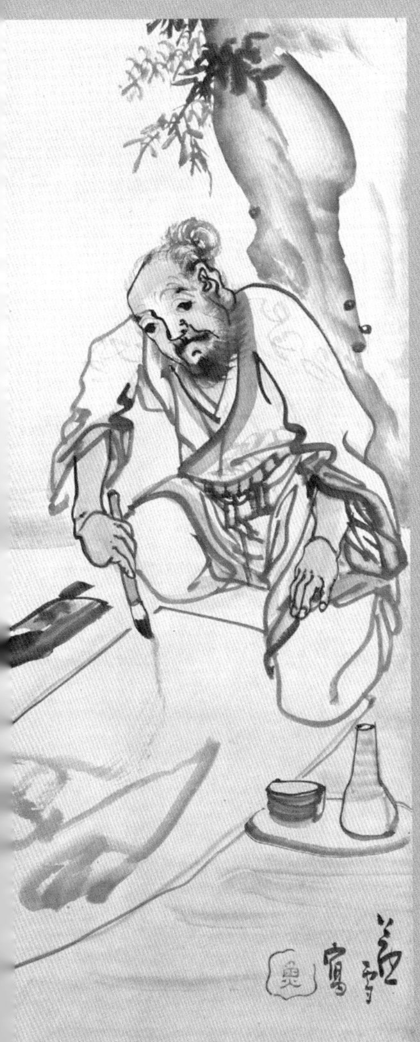

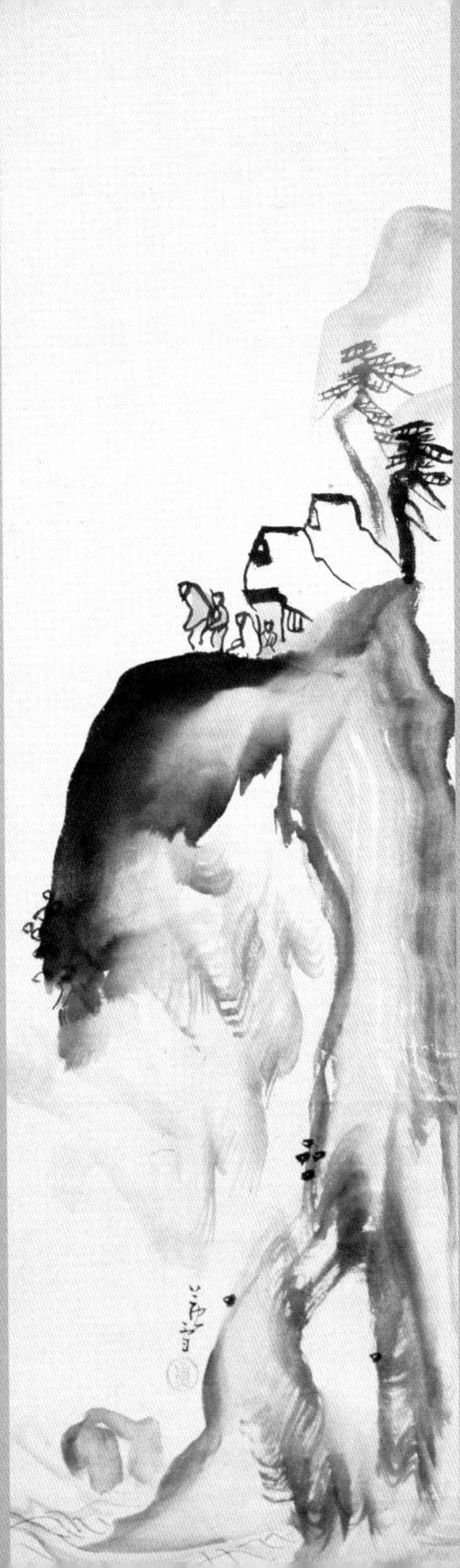

「眼下千丈図」長澤蘆雪
18世紀後半　愛知県美術館蔵
（木村定三コレクション）
Sheer Cliff, Nagasawa Rosetsu, Latter
half the 18th century, Aichi Prefectur-
al/ Kimura Teizo Collection

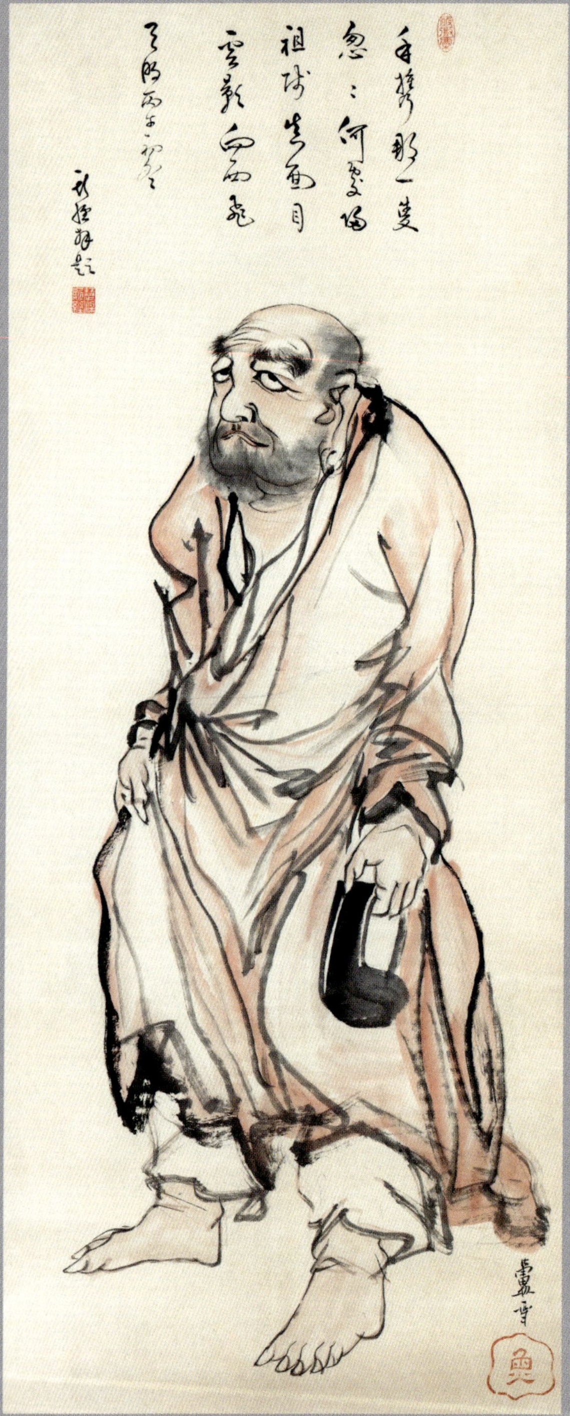

「隻履達磨図」長澤蘆雪
天明 6 年（1786）頃
豊橋市美術博物館蔵
Bodhidharma Holding a Shoe, Nagasawa Rosetsu, ca.1786, Toyohashi City Museum of Art & History

「呉美人図」長澤蘆雪
江戸時代（18 世紀）
東京国立博物館蔵
Tang Beauties, Nagasawa Rosetsu, 18th century, Tōkyō National Museum / ColBase (https://colbase.nich.go.jp)

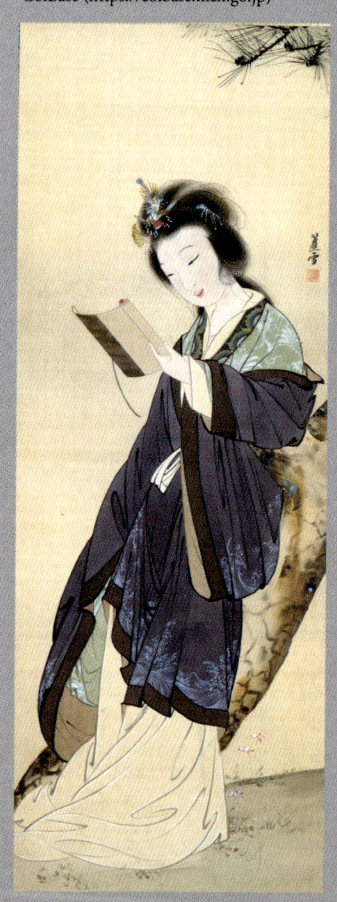

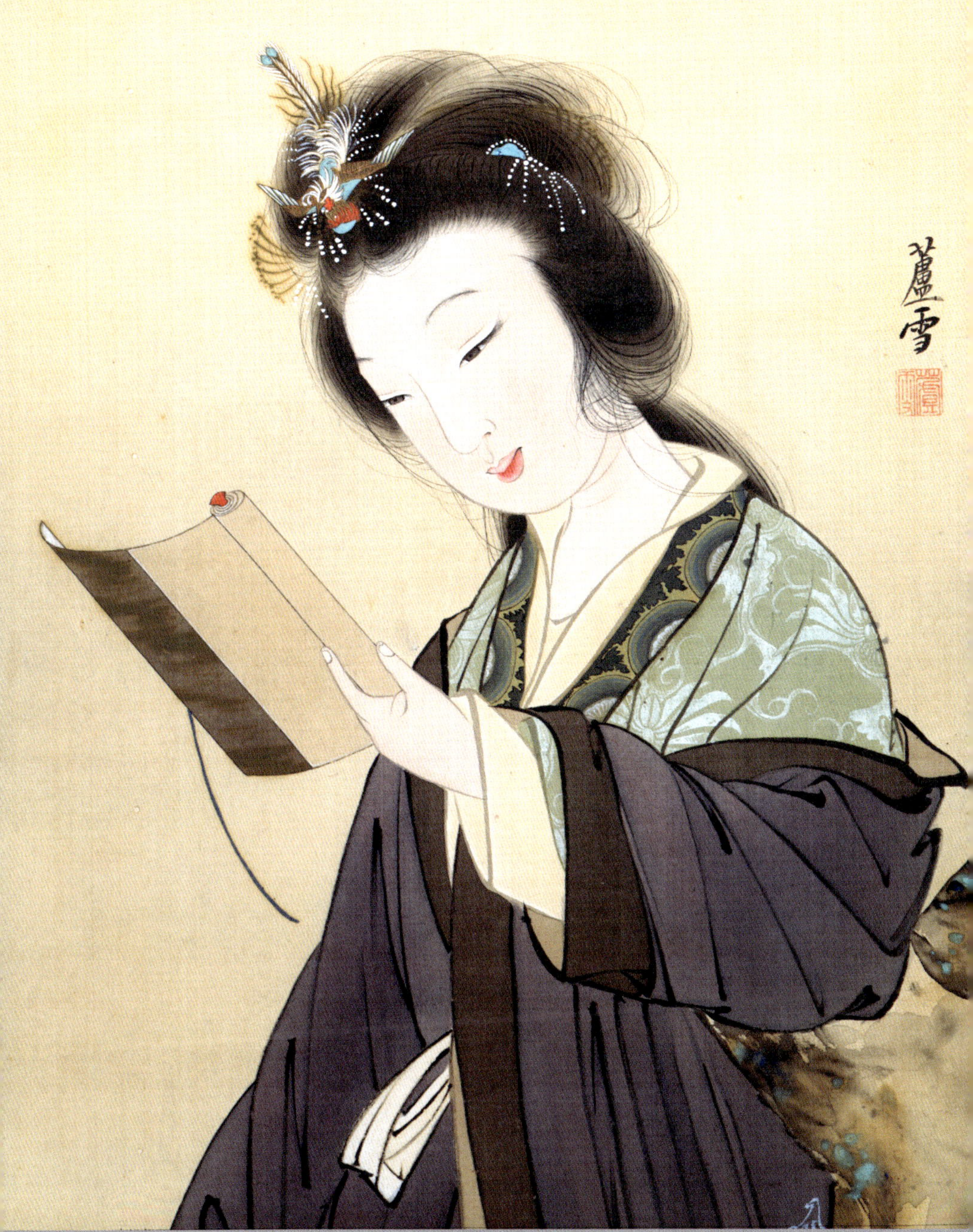

水墨画の技法
Ink Wash Painting Techniques

水墨は墨をおもな顔料にして、これの濃淡や潤渇（じゅんかつ）を利用して描くもので、人物や動物、山川草木など森羅万象を描きだすことができます。それには筆による技法や、墨と水のバランスなど、かなり高度なテクニックが要求されますが、ここではその一部を紹介します。

In ink wash painting, *sumi* ink is the principal pigment; its gradations and smoothness are used to depict human figures, animals, landscapes, plants, everything. These paintings require sophisticated techniques both for using the brush and for keeping the right balance between ink and water. Here we introduce some of those techniques.

「米点　べいてん」 *Beiten*

水墨山水画の筆法のひとつで点葉法ともいい、山や樹木、竹や水草などのかたちを、筆を横にして平たく墨点を打ってあらわす描法です。室町時代以降しばしば見られましたが、かなり高度な技術が必要なため、江戸時代の南画の池大雅や与謝蕪村たちからようやく駆使できるようになりました。

This technique is used in ink wash landscape paintings to depict the forms of mountains, trees, bamboo, and plants. The brush is held horizontally and simple dots of ink applied.

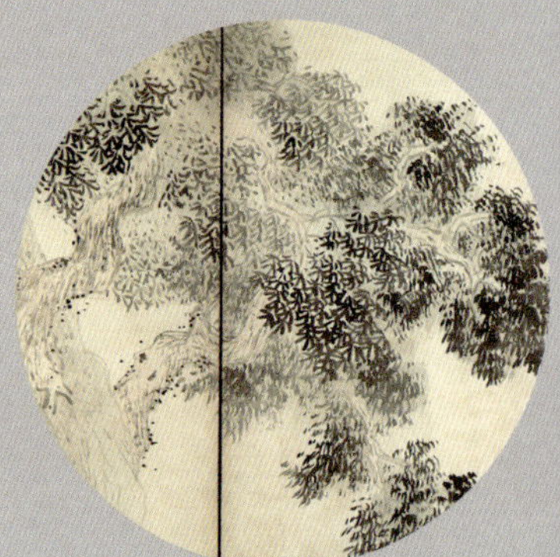

「山野行楽図屏風」（部分）重文
与謝蕪村　東京国立博物館蔵
ColBase (https://colbase.nich.go.jp)

「たらしこみ」 *Tarashikomi*

日本画の技法のひとつで、にじみの効果に着目した描法です。はじめに墨を塗って乾かないうちに、水やまたは水を多く含んだ墨をその上に重ねると、両者が自然に混ざり合ってにじみが生まれます。俵屋宗達の創案と考えられ、のちの琳派などでも多く用いられました。

This technique is also used in *Nihonga*, to produce pooled, blurred ink (or colors, in *Nihonga*). First ink is applied; before it dries, water or very diluted ink is dropped over it. The two components mingle, creating pooled gradations with softly blurred edges.

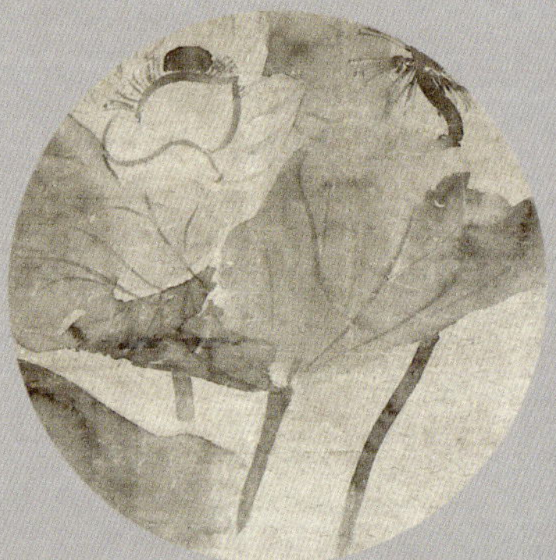

「蓮池水禽図」（部分）国宝
俵屋宗達　京都国立博物館蔵
ColBase (https://colbase.nich.go.jp)

「付立　つけたて」 *Tsuketate*

濃淡二種の墨を筆につけ、一気呵成に対象を描き、樹木の枝ぶりや竹などの陰影表現を立体感に表現します。円山応挙が意識的に用いたのにはじまり、呉春が洗練を加え、円山四条派が得意とするようになりました。

Two types of ink, darker and lighter, are applied to the brush, which is then used to depict the subject at a single stroke, creating a shaded or textured effect of tree bark or bamboo stalks.

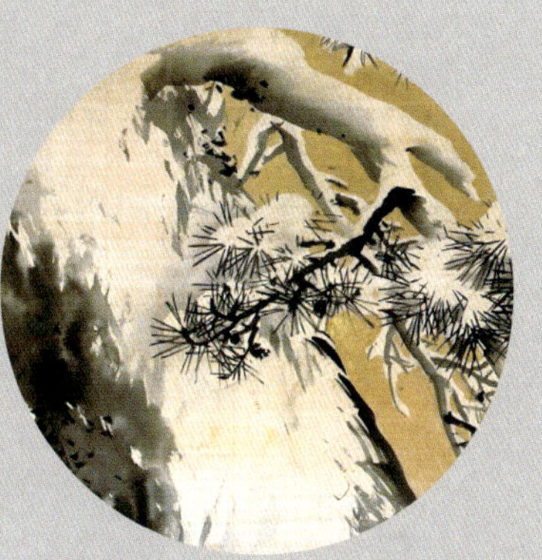

「雪中老松図」（部分）円山応挙
東京国立博物館蔵
ColBase (https://colbase.nich.go.jp)

「没骨　もっこつ」 *Mokkotsu*

対象の形態の輪郭線を用いないで、水墨や彩色の濃淡だけでかたちをあらわす描法で、室町時代初期の水墨画から用いられた技法です。

The the *mokkotsu* ("boneless") technique renders the shapes of the subjects without outlines. Only shades of ink (or colors) are used to depict the subjects. This technique has been used since early ink wash paintings in the Muromachi period.

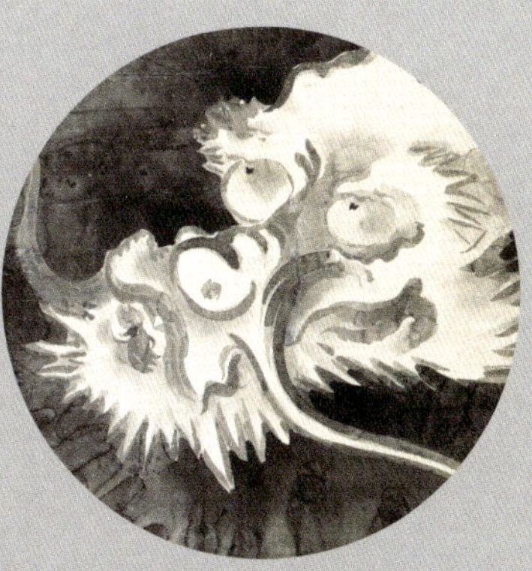

「雲龍図」（部分）尾形光琳
黎明教会資料研修館蔵

「潑墨　はつぼく」 *Hatsuboku*

潑墨とは墨を潑ぐことで、画面に墨をばらまき、一気に着衣の人物像や山や岩、樹木などのかたちを捉えると同時に、その濃淡で立体感をあらわす描法です。日本では南宋の玉澗を学んだ雪舟あたりから作例が見られますが、桃山時代以降はあまり用いられなくなりました。

The *hatsuboku* ("splashed ink") technique scatters ink over the picture plane, the splashes capturing the forms of humans in robes, mountains, rocks, and trees while producing, through the ink's gradations, a three-dimensional effect.

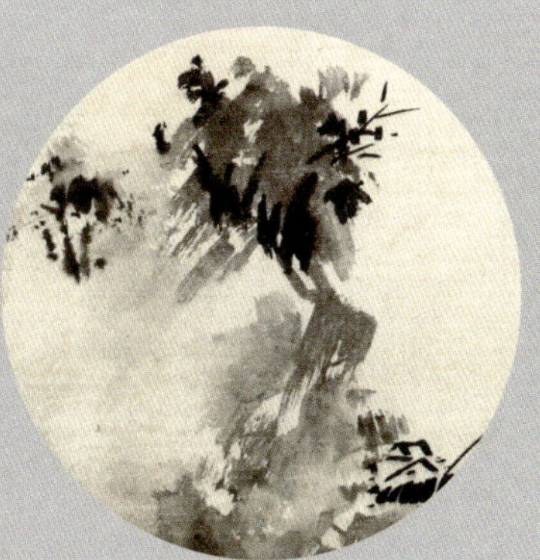

「破墨山水図」（部分）国宝
雪舟等楊　東京国立博物館蔵
ColBase (https://colbase.nich.go.jp)

酒井抱一

光琳の作品に接し、その芸術の再興を志した画家

さかい ほういつ　宝暦11〜文政11年（1761〜1828）

　江戸時代後期の画家。酒井忠仰の次男として江戸に生まれる。37歳で出家し、江戸根岸に雨華庵をいとなむ。絵は狩野高信から狩野風を学び、また南蘋派の花鳥画や浮世絵、円山派、土佐派などの画技も広く身につけた。のち尾形光琳の作品に接し深く傾倒し、その芸術の再興を志した。

The painter who aimed to revive Kōrin's art

Sakai Hōitsu (1761-1828) was an artist active in the latter half of the Edo period. He was born in Edo, the second son of Sakai Tadamochi. At 37, he entered the Buddhist priesthood and established the Ugean in Negishi, Edo. He studied the Kanō style with Kanō Takanobu, and a broad range of other painting styles, including the Nanpin School's bird-and-flower paintings, *ukiyo-e*, the Maruyama School, and the Tosa School. Later encountering the work of Ogata Kōrin, he was profoundly impressed and set his sights on reviving Kōrin's art.

右：「寒山図」酒井抱一
江戸時代（19 世紀）
東京国立博物館蔵
Hanshan, Sakai Hōitsu,19th century,
Tōkyō National Museum / ColBase
(https://colbase.nich.go.jp)

右頁左：「正月飾り物図」酒井抱一俳賛　鈴木其一・鈴木蠣潭・大西椿年・山崎鯉隠・長橋文桂
文化 13 年（1816）
東京国立博物館蔵
New Year's decorative map, Sakai Hōitsu, 1816, Tōkyō National Museum / ColBase (https://colbase.nich.go.jp)

右頁右：「白梅に雀図」酒井抱一
江戸時代　敦賀市博物館蔵
White Plum and Sparrow, Sakai Hōitsu, Edo period, Tsuruga Municipal Museum

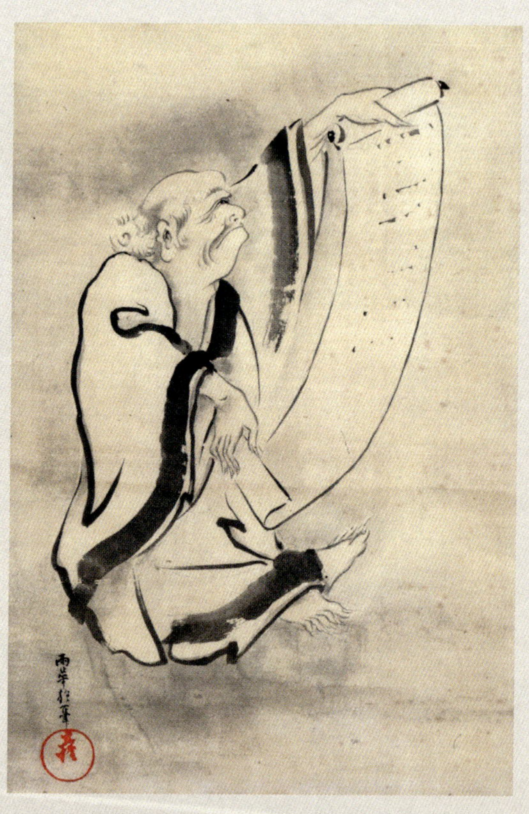

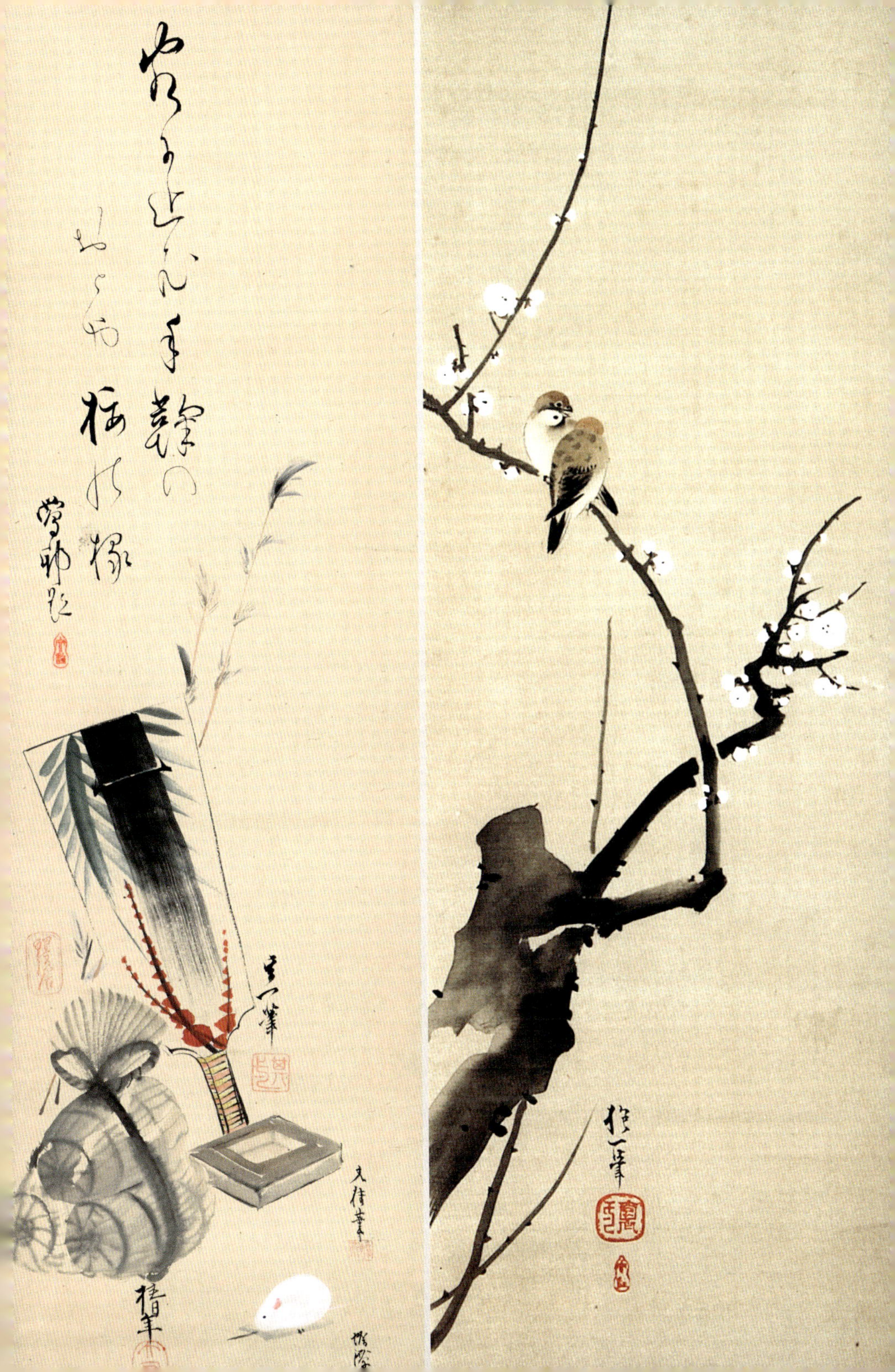

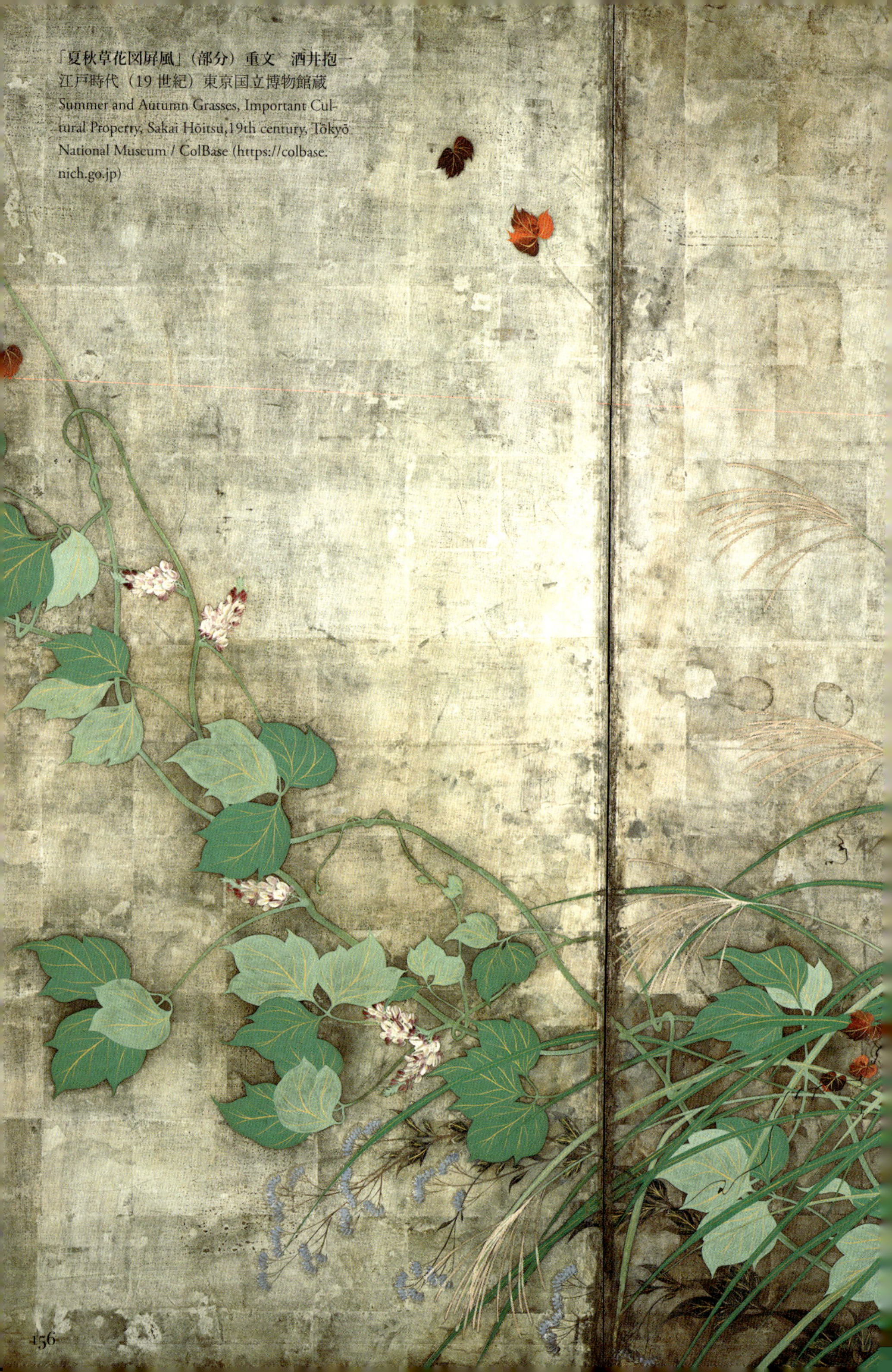

「夏秋草花図屏風」（部分）重文　酒井抱一
江戸時代（19世紀）東京国立博物館蔵
Summer and Autumn Grasses, Important Cultural Property, Sakai Hōitsu,19th century, Tōkyō National Museum / ColBase (https://colbase.nich.go.jp)

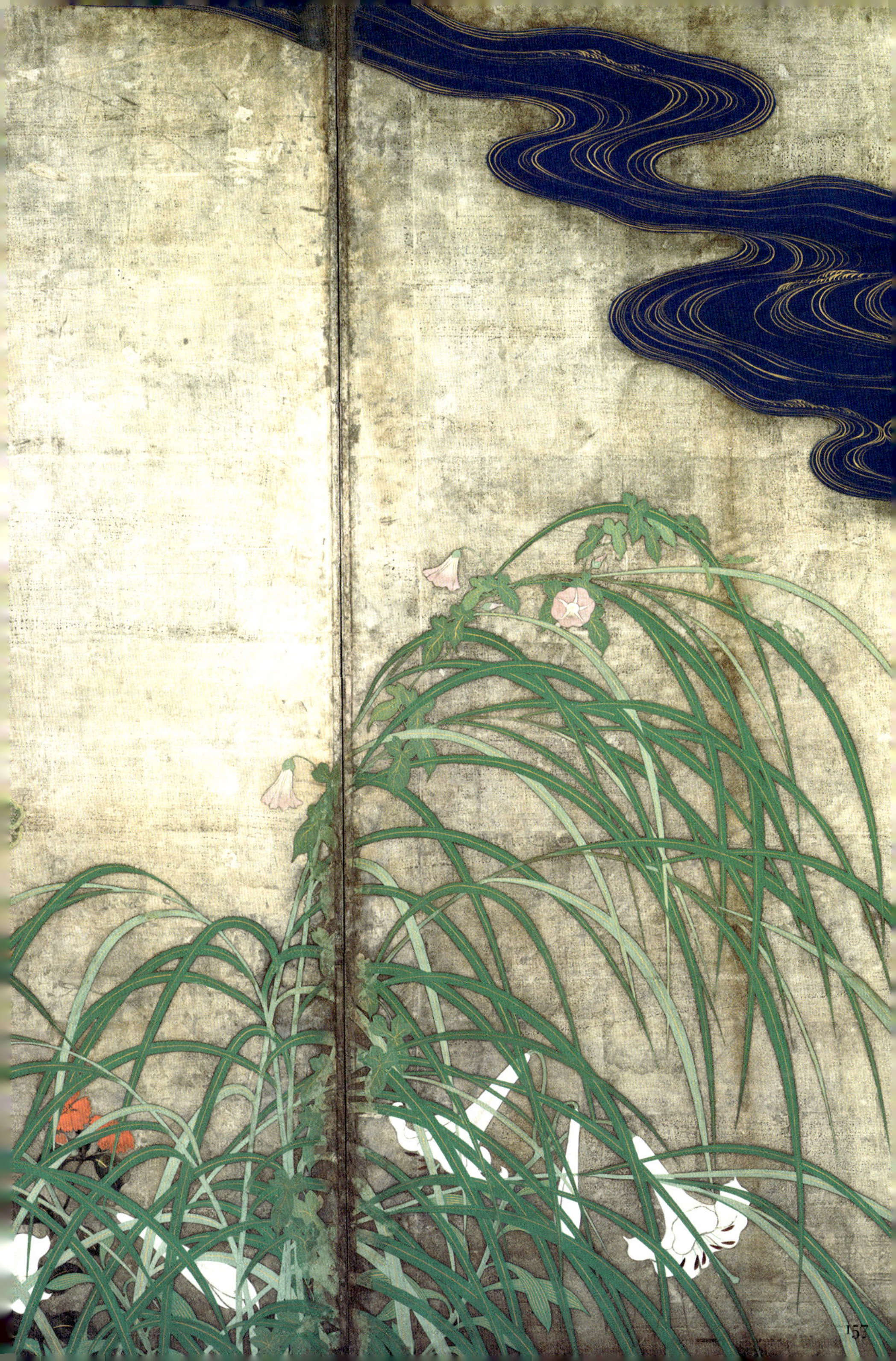

谷文晁

Tani Bunchō

雄渾な筆墨による覇気ある作風の画家

たに ぶんちょう

宝暦13～天保11年（1763～1840）

　江戸時代後期の文人画家。江戸下谷根岸に生まれる。漢詩人の谷麓谷の長男。はじめ狩野派の加藤文麗に学び、次いで長崎派の渡辺玄対らに師事した。以後、中国南宋や北宋画、西洋画などの諸画派を研究して独自の画風を創出し、江戸文人画壇の重鎮となる。弟子は非常に多く、渡辺崋山、立原杏所などがいる。

Forceful brushwork, vigorous style

A literati painter in the latter half of the Edo period, Tani Bunchō (1763-1840) was born in Shitaya Negishi, Edo. He was the eldest son of Tani Rokukoku, who was known for composing *kanshi* (Chinese poetry). Bunchō began studying with Katō Bunrei of the Kanō School, then shifted to Watanabe Gentai and other Nagasaki School painters. He also researched other types of painting, including Southern and Northern Song and Western influences in creating his distinctive style. He had a great many students, including Watanabe Kazan and Tachihara Kyōsho.

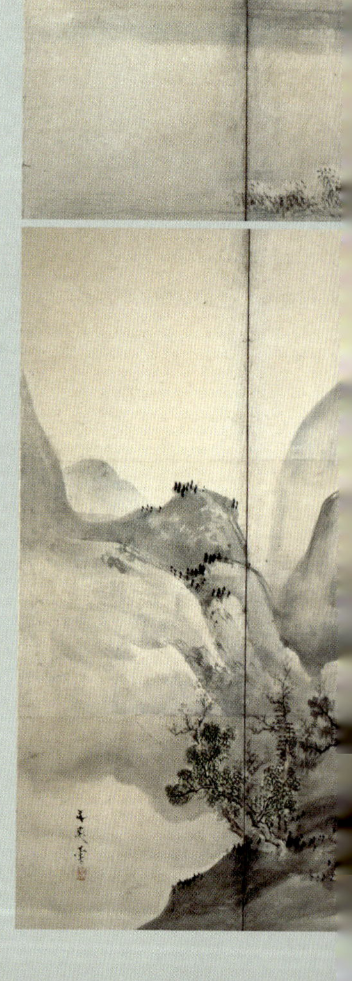

「山水図屛風」谷文晁
江戸時代（19世紀）栃木県立博物館蔵
Standing Screens of Landscape, Tani Bunchō,
19th century, Tochigi Prefectural Museum

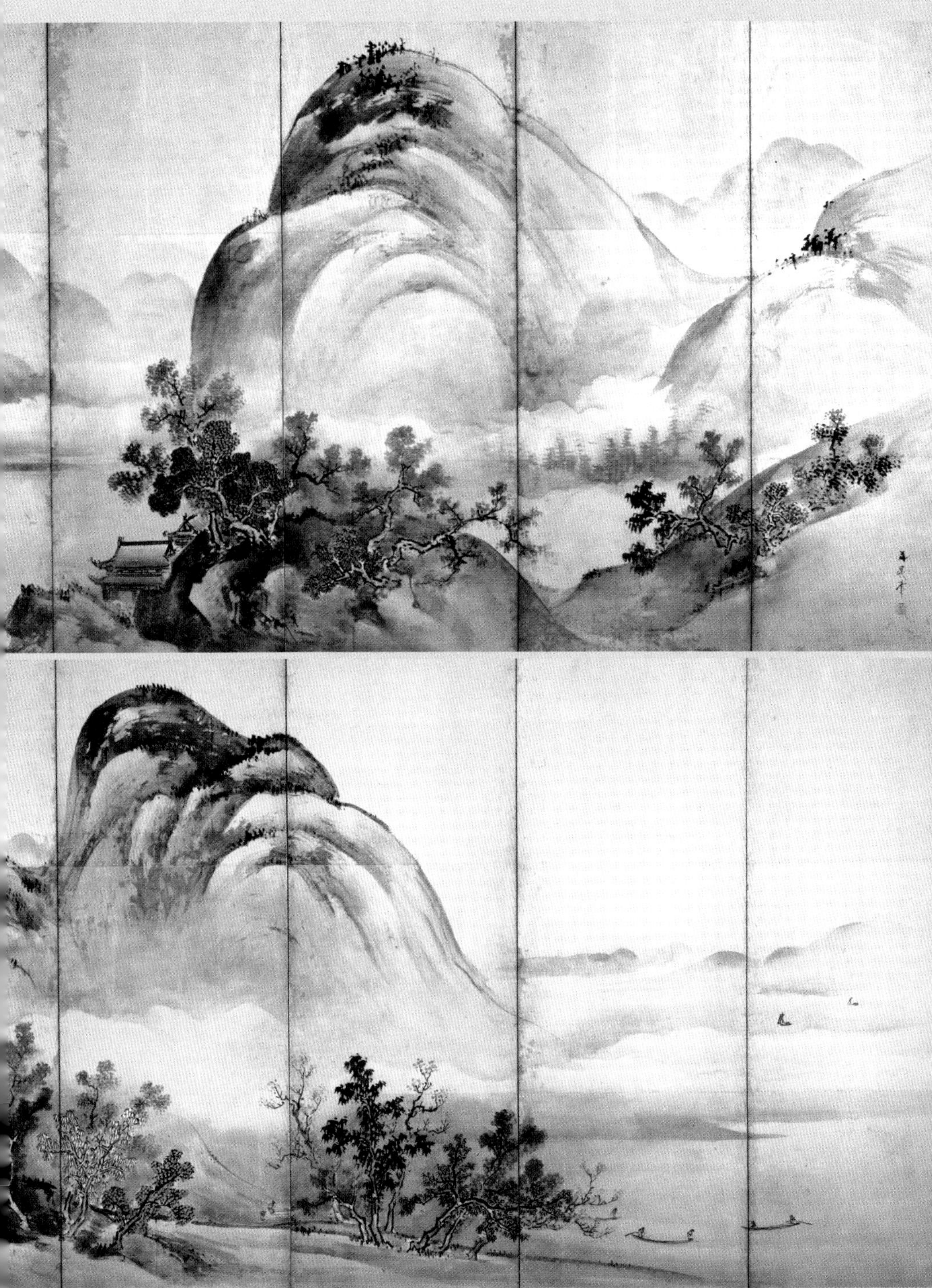

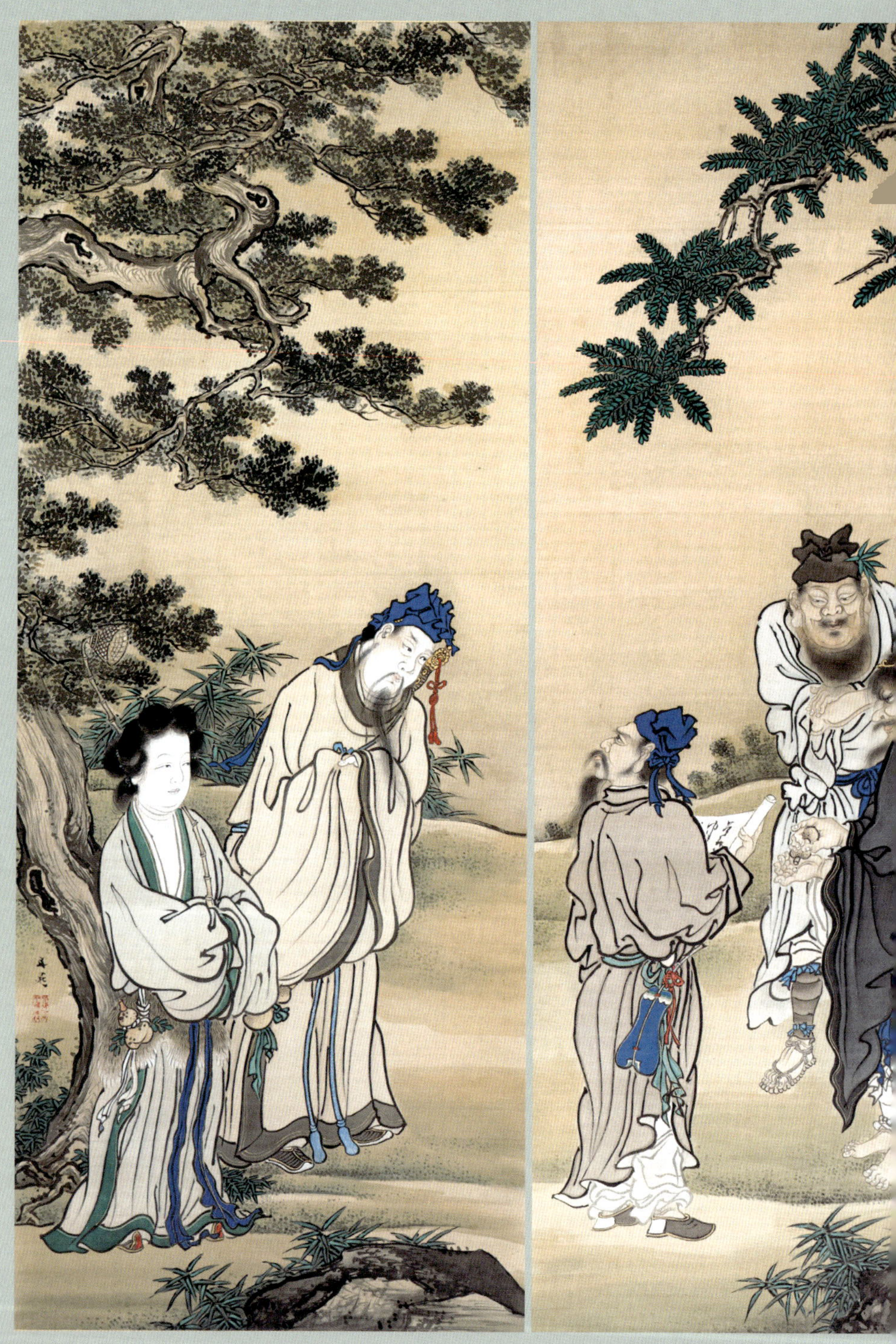

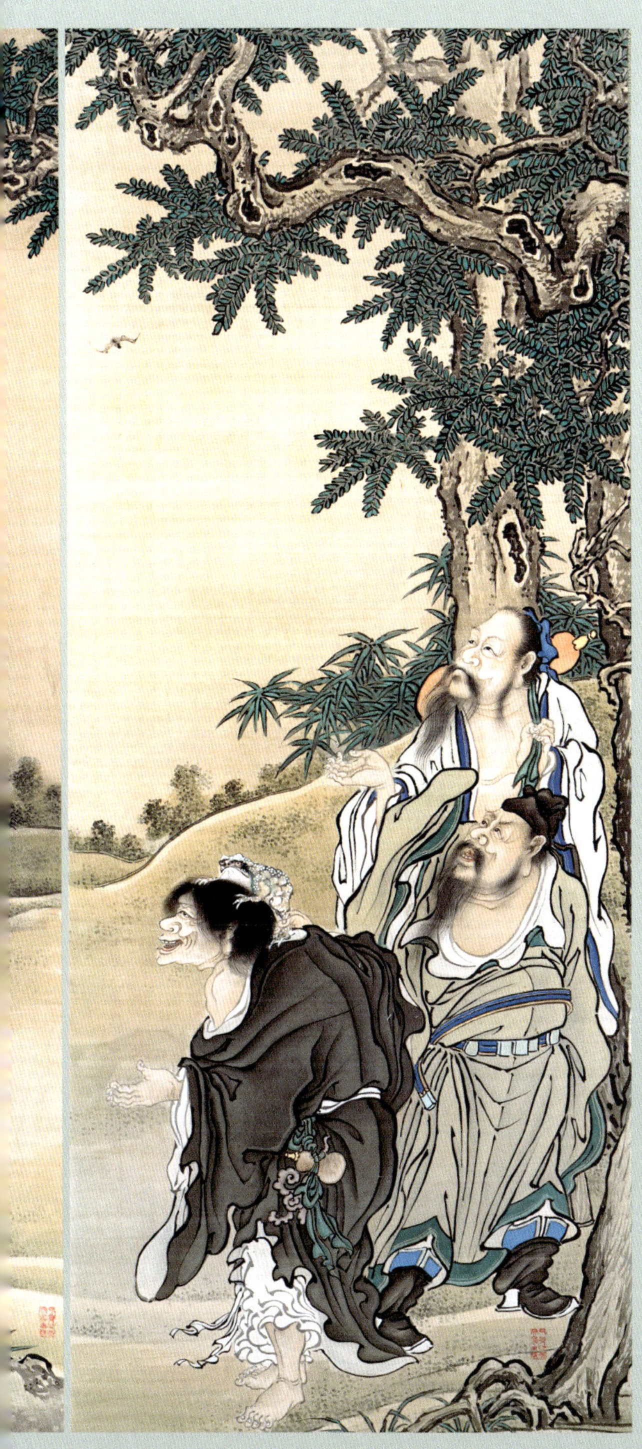

「八仙人図」谷文晁
文政 8 年（1825）
福島県立博物館蔵
Eight Hermit, Tani Bunchō, 1825,
Fukushima Museum

文人墨客との交遊から生まれた
繊細な水墨を描く

たのむら ちくでん
安永6~天保6年（1777~1835）

　江戸時代後期の南画家。豊後（大分県）竹田の岡藩の藩医の家に生まれる。儒者をこころざし藩校由学館に学び、のち同館の頭取となる。藩内の農民一揆の際、藩政改革の建言がいれられず隠退。絵は郷里の渡辺蓬島や淵野真斎に手ほどきを受け、谷文晁らに師事したが、多くは明清画に学び、中国南宗画に近い独自の画風を形成した。幕末文人画壇の代表的な作家である。

Creating detailed ink wash paintings, inspired by interactions with literati painters

Tanomura Chikuden (1777-1835), a Nanga (southern Chinese style) painter active in the latter half of the Edo period, was born in Taketa, Bungo province (Oita prefecture). His father was the Oka domain physician. Wanting to become a Confucian scholar, Chikuden studied at the Yugakkan, the domain academy, and later became its head. He retired when suggestions he made for reforming the domain's policies when a peasant uprising broke out were not accepted. He was taught painting in his home town by Watanabe Hōtō and Fuchino Shinsai, and also by Tani Bunchō and others, but he mainly studied Ming and Qing Chinese painting and achieved a style similar to Southern Song painting.

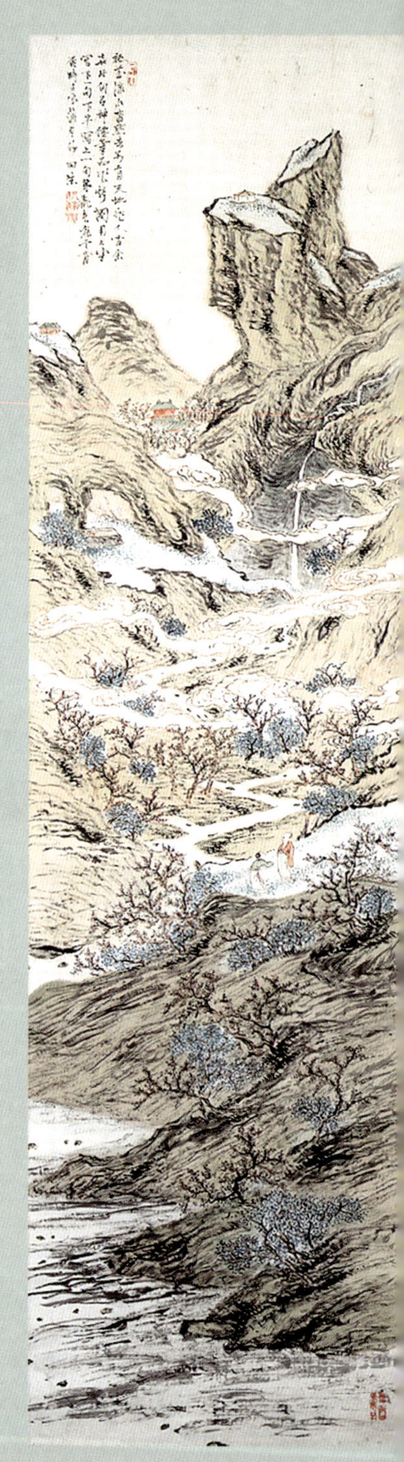

「桃花流水図」重文　田能村竹田
天保3年（1832）大分市美術館蔵
The Stream of Peach and Flower, Important Cultural Property, Tanomura Chikuden,1832, Oita Art Museum

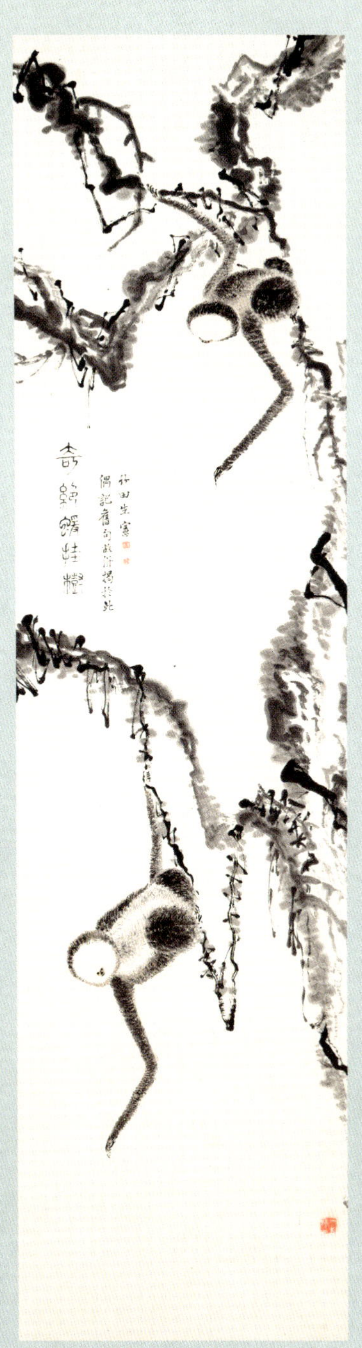

「猿猴挂樹図」田能村竹田
文政後期頃　大分県立美術館蔵
Monkeys, Hanging Down from Branchs, Tanomura Chikuden, Late Bunsei period, Oita Prefectural Art Museum

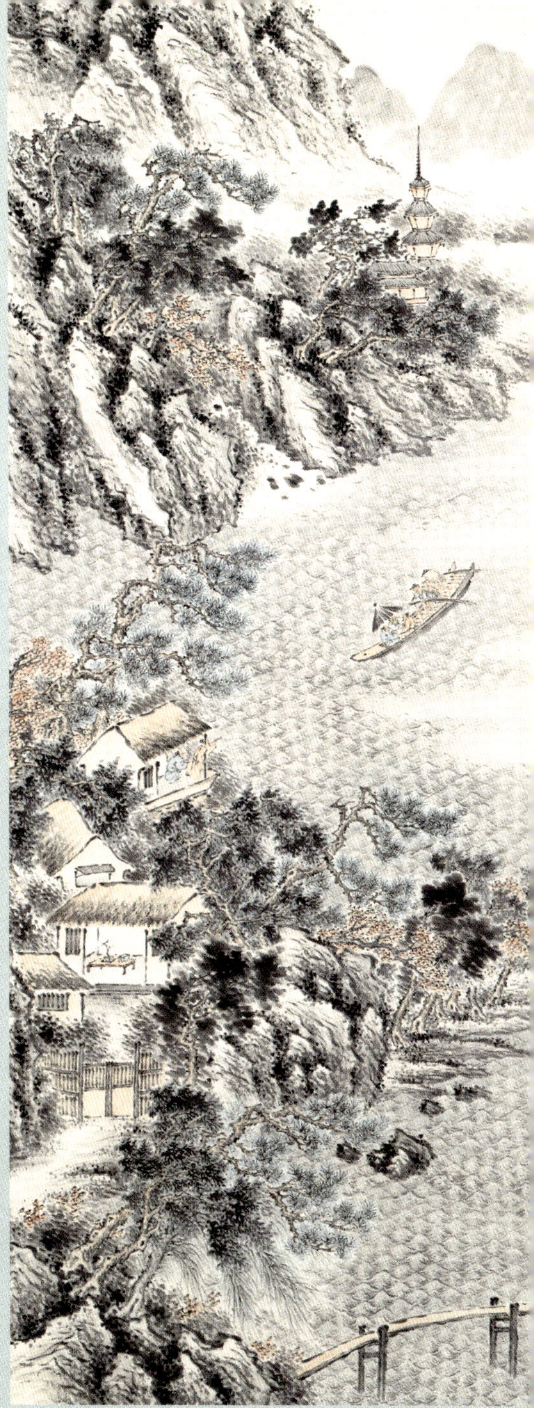

「風雨渡舟図」（部分）田能村竹田
文政 12 年（1829）東京国立博物館蔵
Windy Ferry, Tanomura Chikuden, 1829, Tōkyō National
Museum / ColBase (https://colbase.nich.go.jp)

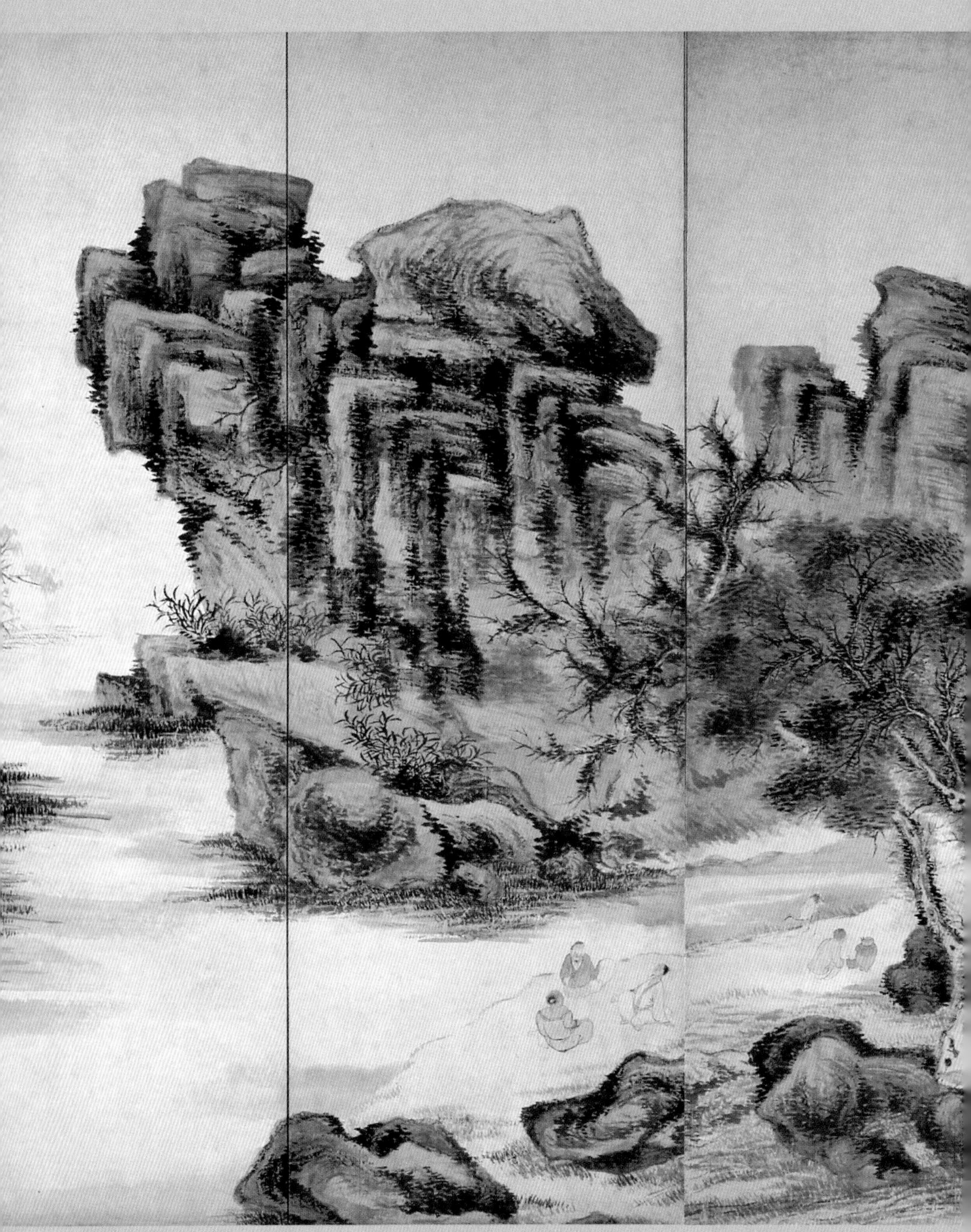

「高客聴琴図」田能村竹田　文政 5 年（1822）大分県立美術館蔵
Guests Listening to the Ch'in, Tanomura Chikuden, 1822, Oita Prefectural Art Museum

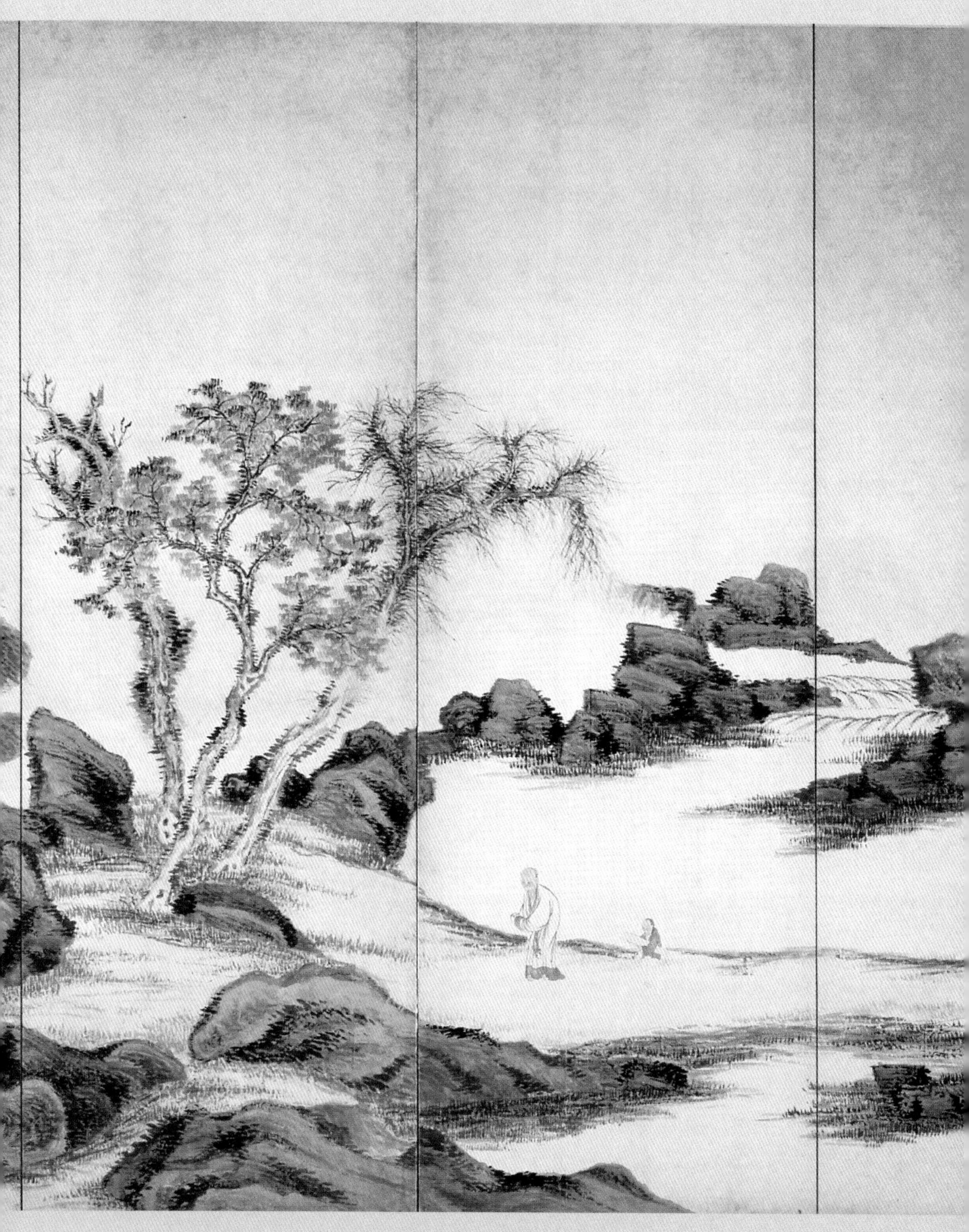

山本梅逸

巧みな描写と鮮麗な色彩で優品を残した画家

やまもと ばいいつ　天明3~安政3年（1783~1856）

　江戸時代後期の南画家。尾張名古屋に生まれる。はじめ山田宮常、山本蘭亭に学び、当地の豪商で古画収集家であった神谷天遊の元に出入りした。中林竹洞らと元明の古画を模写。その後、竹洞とともに京都にでて画業にはげむ。色彩豊かで技巧を駆使した花鳥画を得意とし、晩年は帰郷して名古屋藩絵師格となった。

Masterpieces with skillful depictions and vivid colors

Yamamoto Baiitsu (1783-1856), a Nanga artist active in the latter half of the Edo period, was born in Nagoya, Owari province. He studied first with Yamada Kyū-jō and Yamamoto Rantei; then, visiting Kamiya Ten'yū, a wealthy merchant and collector of antique paintings in Nagoya, he, Nakabayashi Chikutō, and other artists copied Chinese paintings from the Yuan and Ming periods. Later, he and Chikutō moved to Kyoto and concentrated on painting. Baiitsu's forte was bird-and-flower paintings using rich colors and his splendid skills. Late in life, he returned to Nagoya, where served as a painter by appointment to the Nagoya domain.

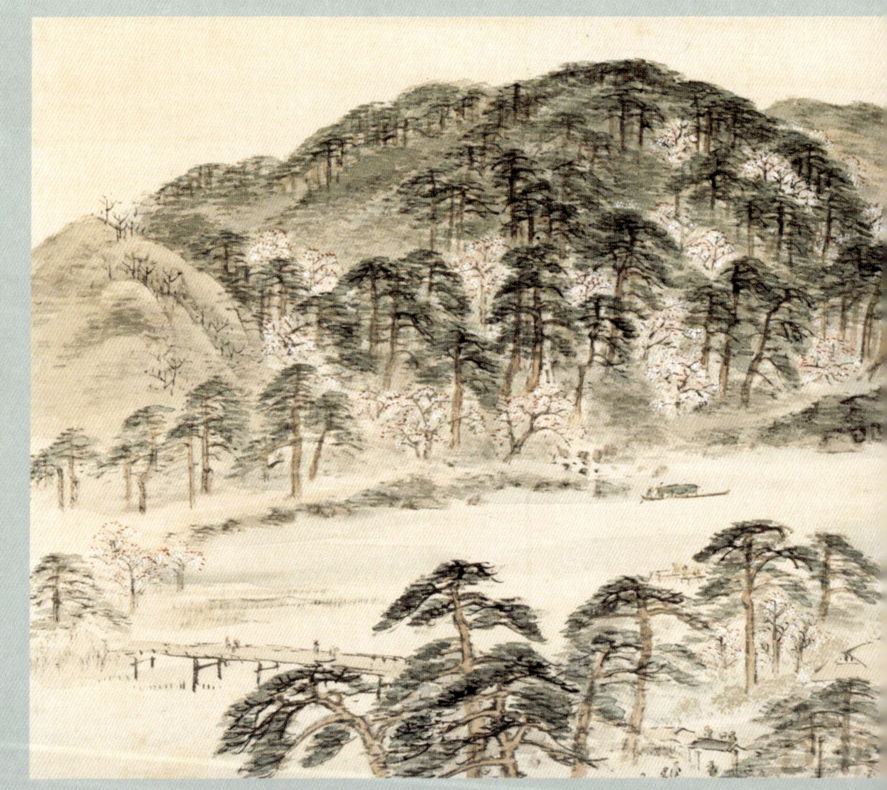

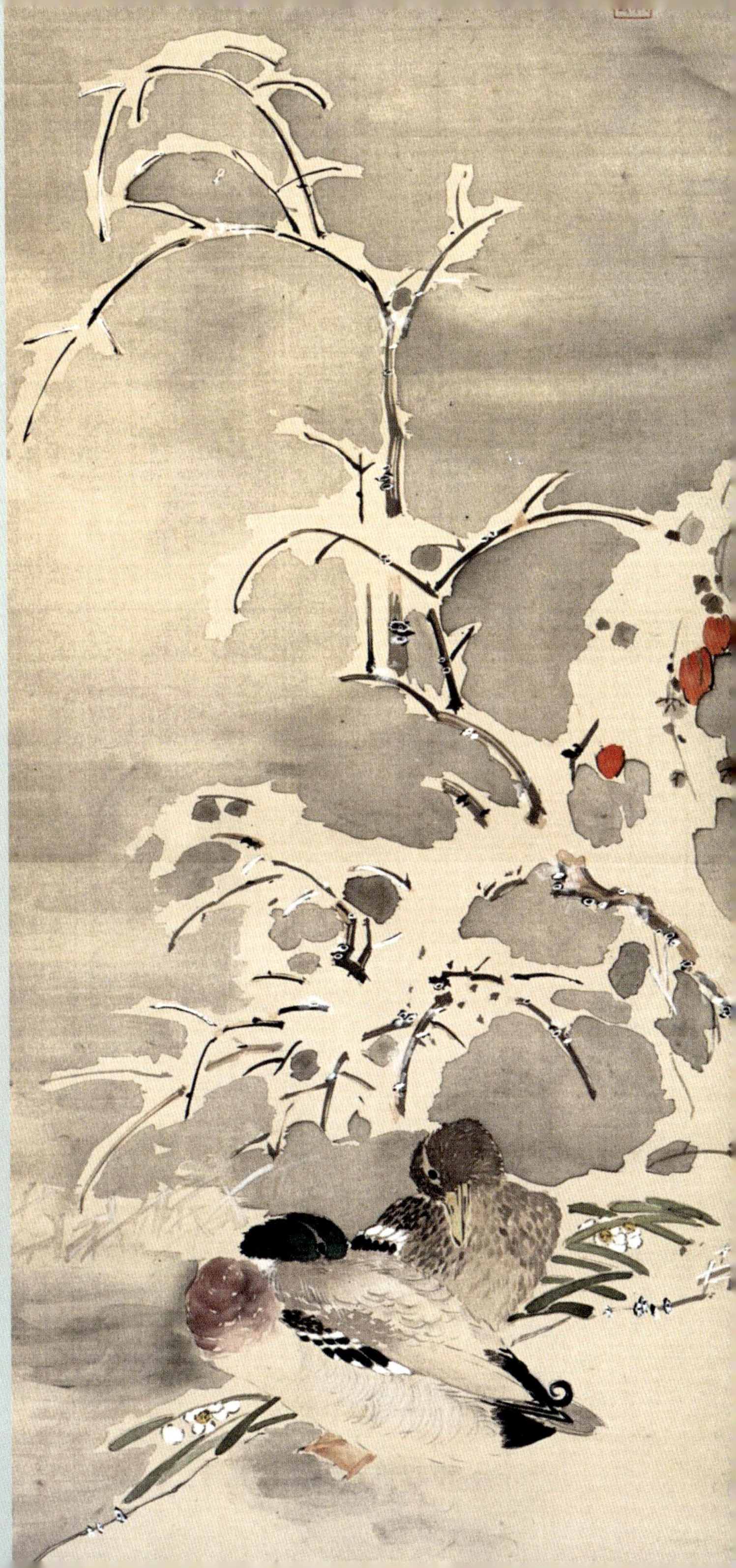

「雪中鴨図」（部分）
山本梅逸
江戸時代（19 世紀）
東京国立博物館蔵
The Ducks in the Snow, Yamamoto Baiitsu, 19th century,
Tōkyō National Museum /
ColBase (https://colbase.nich.
go.jp)

「嵐山春景図」山本梅逸
江戸時代（19 世紀）
愛知県美術館蔵（木村定三
コレクション）
Spring View of Arashiyama,
Yamamoto Baiitsu, 19th
century, Aichi Prefectural
Museum of Art/ Kimura Teizo
Collection

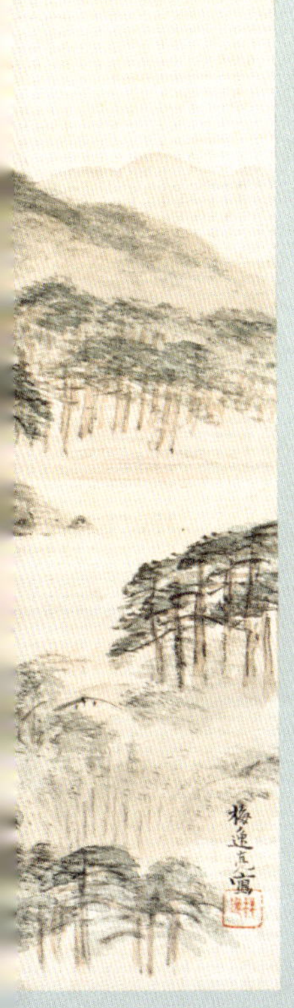

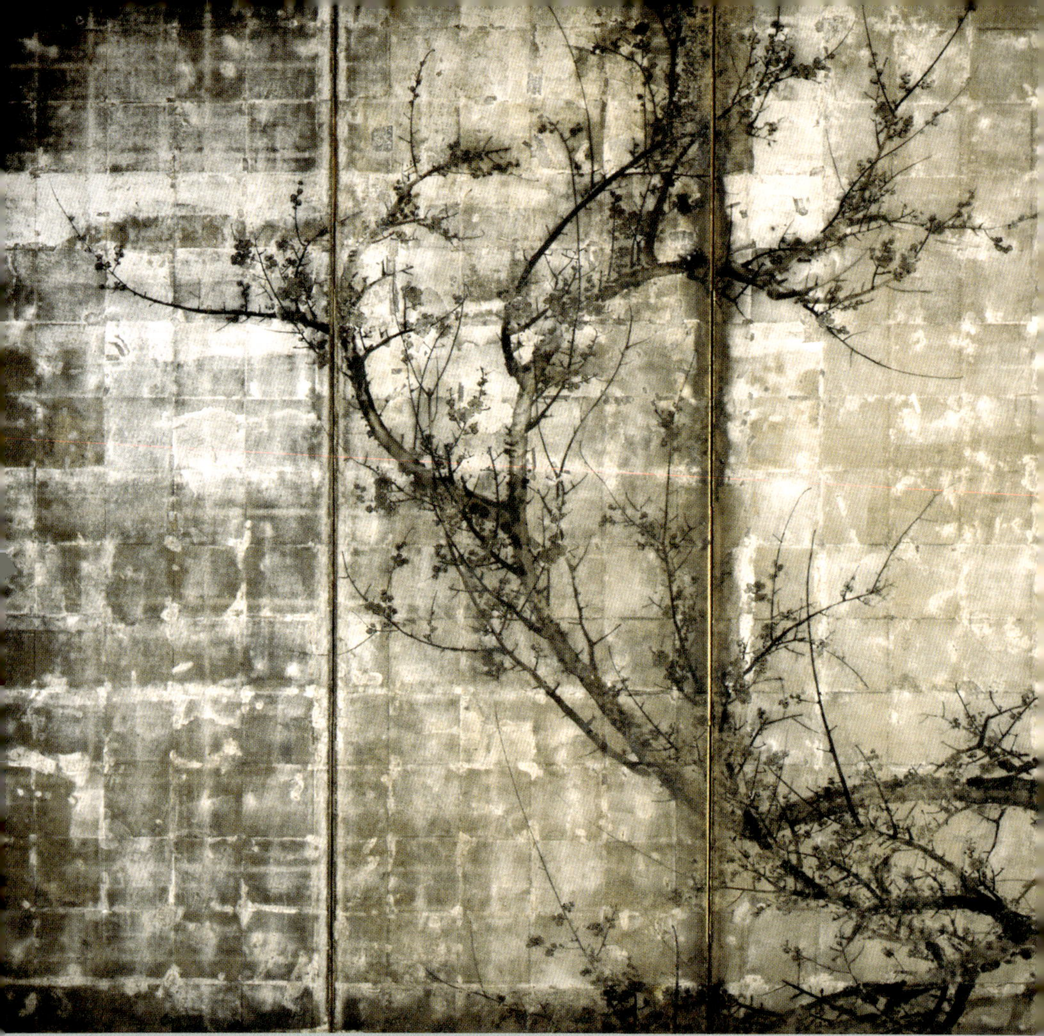

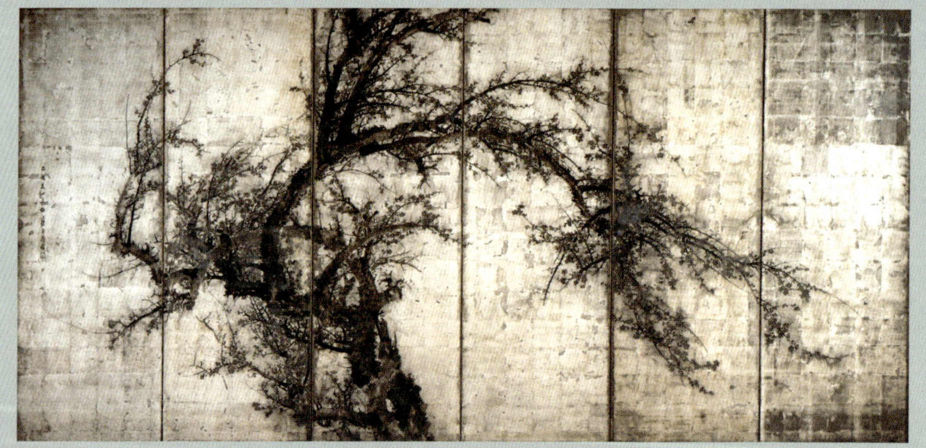

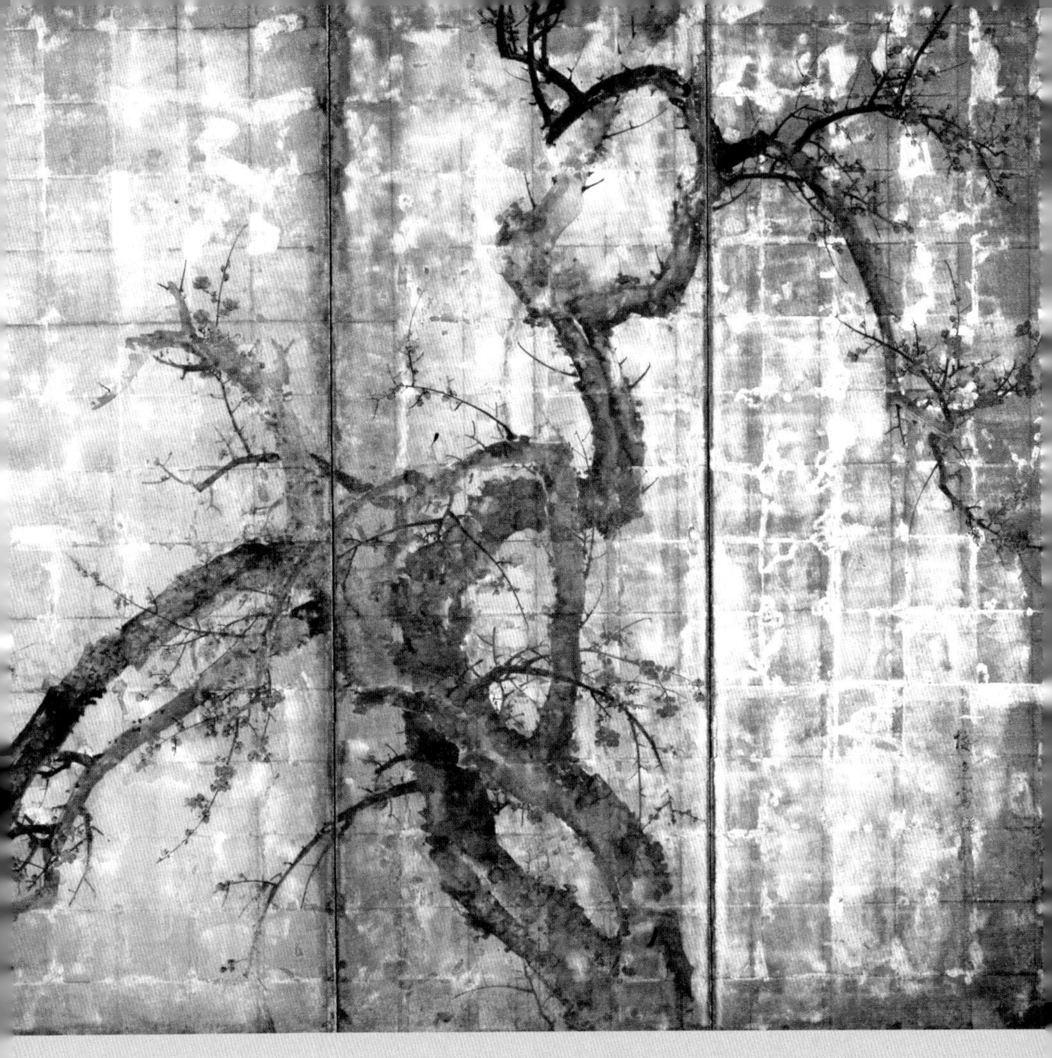

「紅白梅図」山本梅逸
文政 2 年（1819）島根県立美術館蔵
Red and White Plums, Yamamoto Baiitsu, 1819,
Shimane Art Museum

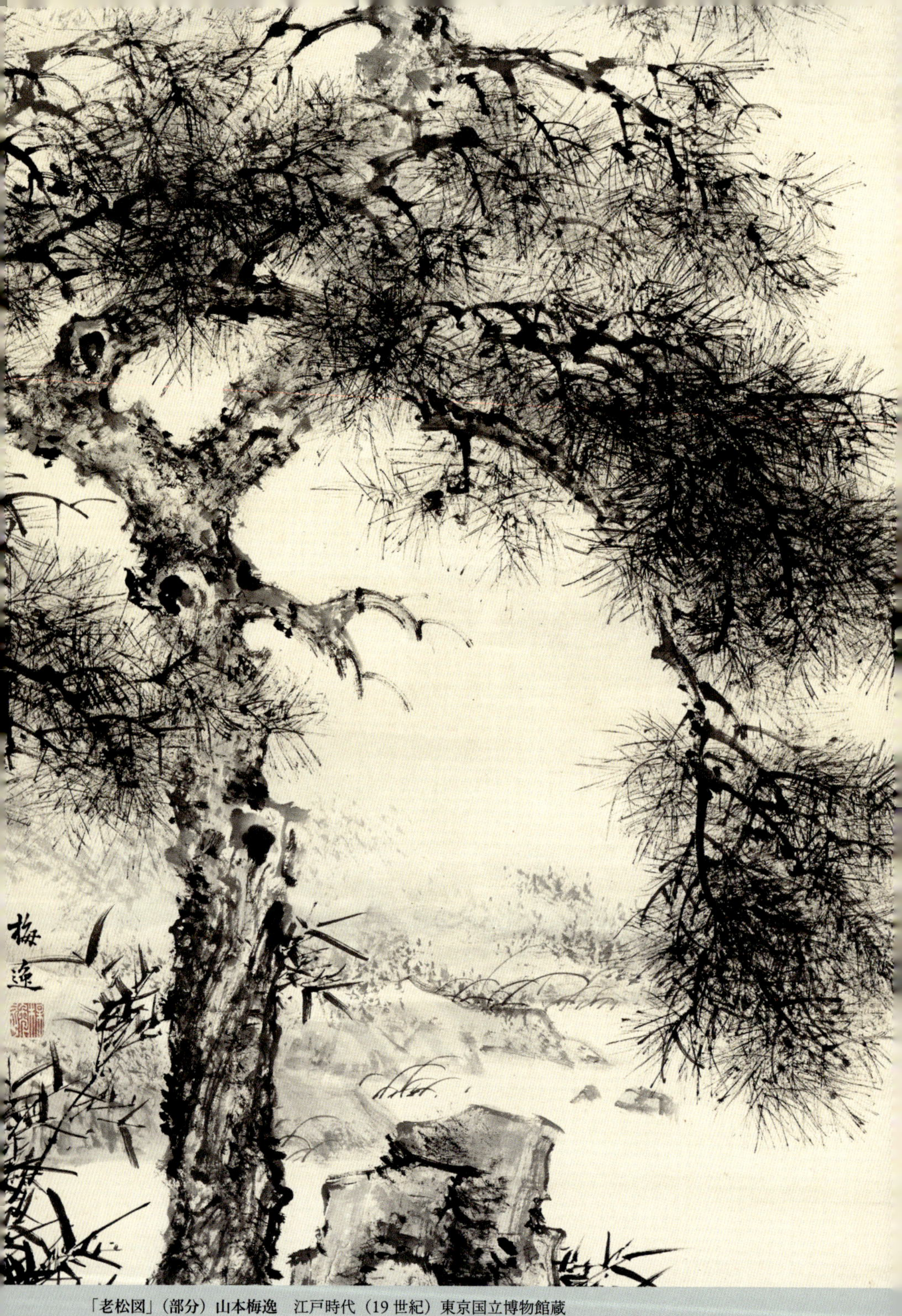

「老松図」（部分）山本梅逸　江戸時代（19世紀）東京国立博物館蔵
Old Pine Tree, Yamamoto Baiitsu, 19th century, Tōkyō National Museum/ ColBase (https://colbase.nich.go.jp)

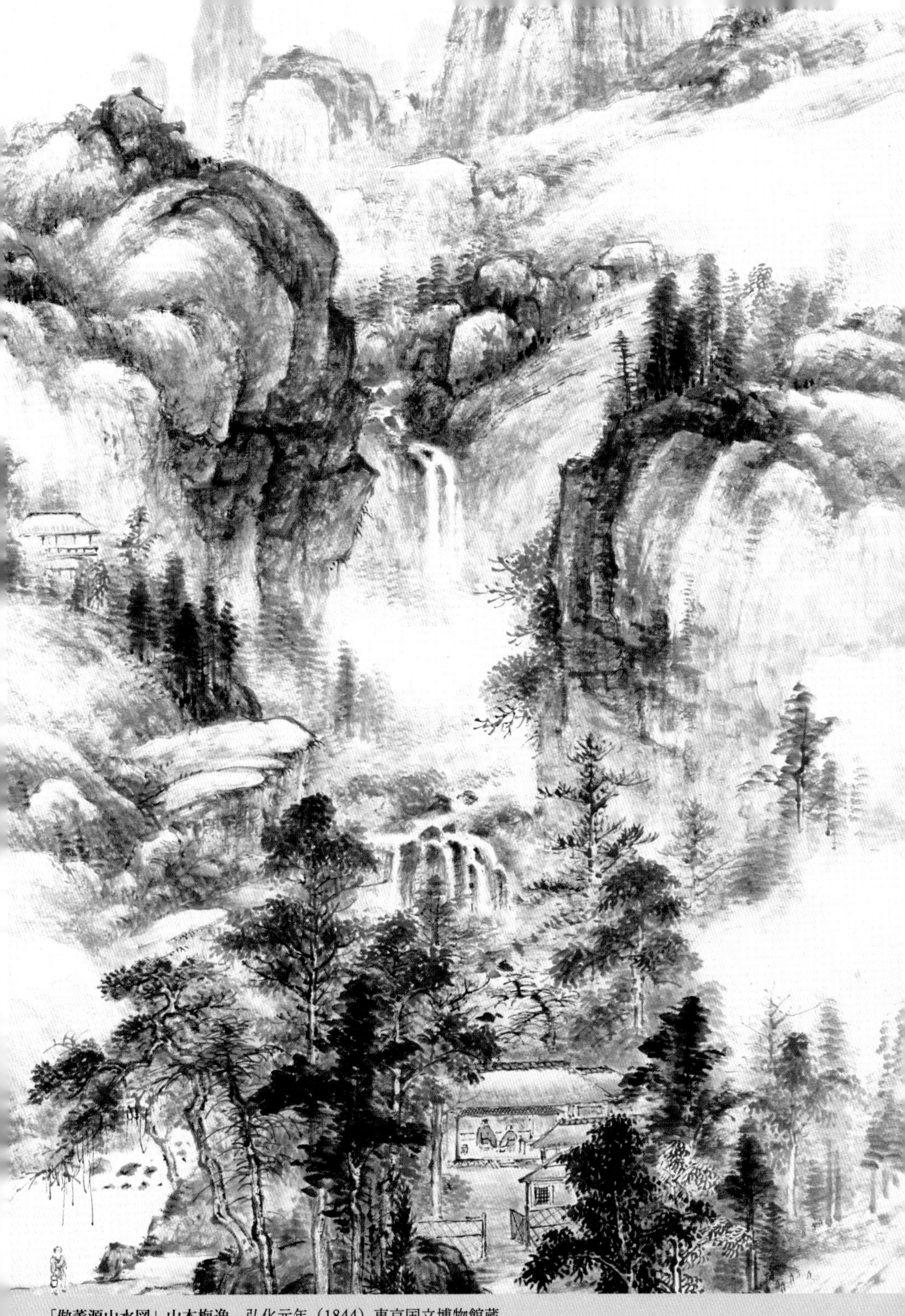

「倣董源山水図」山本梅逸　弘化元年（1844）東京国立博物館蔵
Landscape in the Manner of Dong Yuan, Yamamoto Baiitsu, 1844, Tōkyō National Museum/ ColBase (https://colbase.nich.go.jp)

菅井梅関

Sugai Baikan

豪快で荒々しい筆致に
特色のある画家

すがい ばいかん
天明4〜天保15年（1784〜1844）

　江戸時代後期の南画家。陸奥仙台に生まれる。絵ははじめ根元常南につき、のち江戸に出てからは谷文晁に学ぶ。その後長崎に赴き、清の江稼圃に師事する。大坂で画名をあげて40余歳で帰郷するが、晩年は不遇のうちに死去。剛健な筆触に特色があり、山水画や梅の絵をよくした。

A painter with hearty, rough brushwork

Sugai Baikan (1784-1844) was a Nanga painter active in the latter half of the Edo period. Born in Sendai, in Mutsu province, he first worked with Nemoto Jōnan, then moved to Edo and studied with Tani Bunchō. Later, he moved on to Nagasaki, where he took lessons from the Chinese painter Jiang Jiapu. He became well known as a painter in Osaka, returned to Sendai in his forties, and died in obscurity. He created many landscape and bird-and-flower paintings in his distinctively vigorous brushwork.

右：「牡丹猫図」菅井梅関
江戸時代　東北歴史博物館蔵
Cats and Buttons, Sugai Baikan, Edo period,
Tohoku History Museum

右頁左：「梅花小禽図」菅井梅関
江戸時代後期　東北歴史博物館蔵
Bird on a Plum Flower, Sugai Baikan, Late Edo
period, Tohoku History Museum

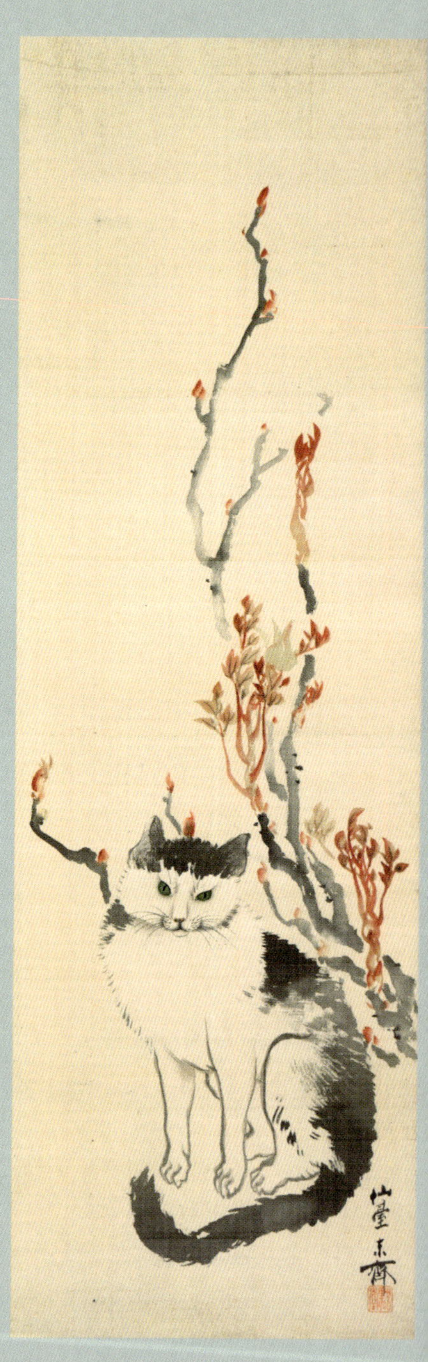

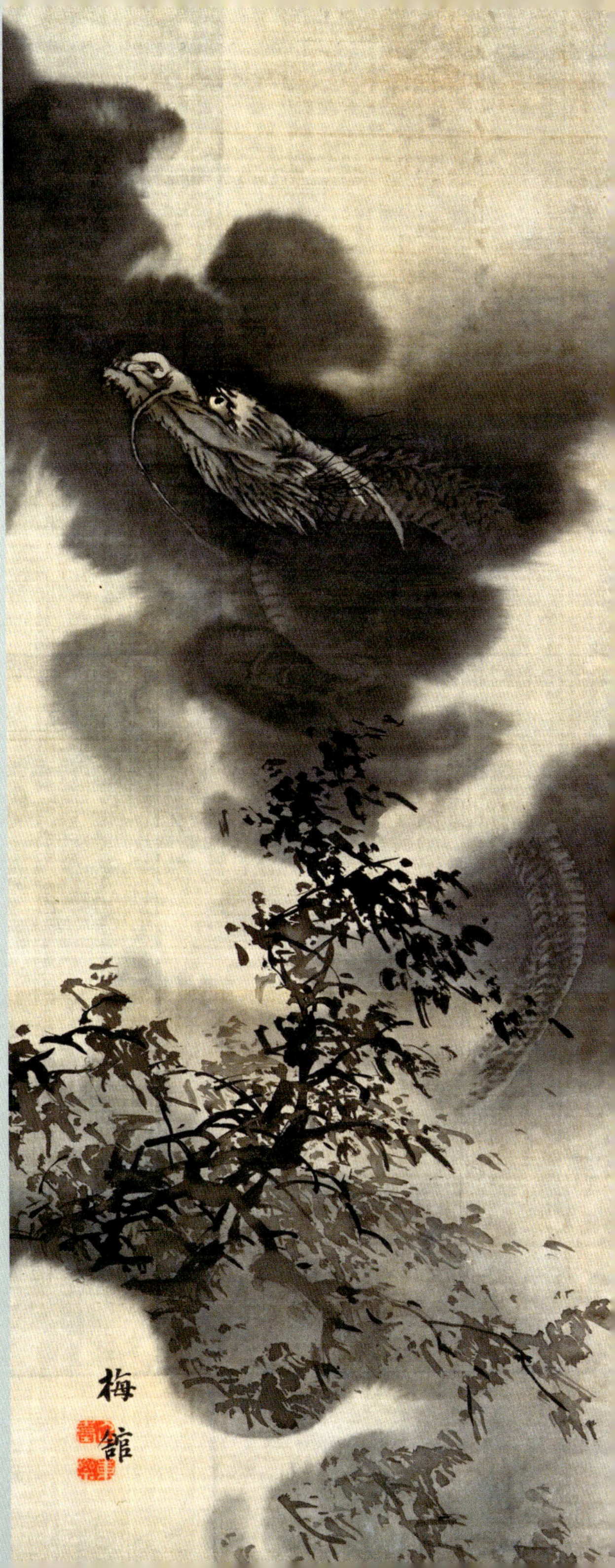

「龍図」菅井梅関
江戸時代後期　東北歴史博物館蔵
Dragon, Sugai Baikan, Late Edo period,
Tohoku History Museum

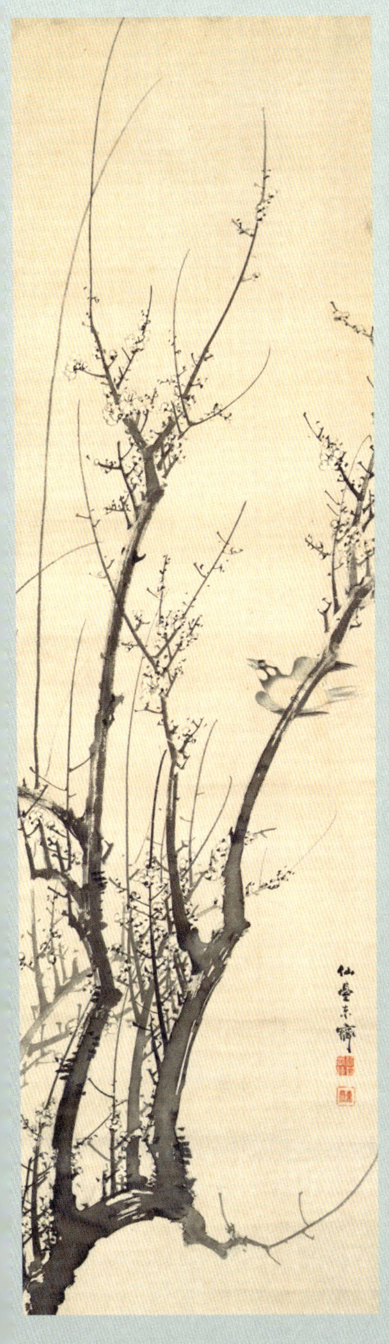

西洋画の描法を取り入れ、独自の肖像画を創造した画家

わたなべ かざん　寛政5〜天保12年（1793〜1841）

　江戸時代後期の画家、蘭学者。渡辺巴洲の長男。家が貧しく内職のため白川芝山、金子金陵らに絵を学び、谷文晁に入門する。初期には文晁や沈南蘋の影響を受けたが、西洋画法をとりいれた独自の様式を創造し、肖像画「鷹見泉石像」（国宝）などをのこす。『慎機論』を著して幕府の鎖国政策を批判し、蛮社の獄で捕らえられた。

A painter who incorporated Western techniques in creating unique portraits

Watanabe Kazan (1793-1841) was a painter and Dutch studies scholar active in the latter half of the Edo period. The eldest son of Watanabe Hashū, a poor samurai, he became a painter to help support his family. He studied painting with Shirakawa Shizan and Kaneko Kinryō before studying under Tani Bunchō. Initially influenced by Bunchō and Shen Nanpin, a Chinese artist in Nagasaki, he created his own style, incorporating Western techniques, and produced Portrait of *Takami Senseki* (National Treasure) and other works. He also wrote the *Shinkiron* (Arguments for Restraint in Critical. Times) criticizing the Tokugawa shogunate's closed-country policy, for which he was exiled to his home province.

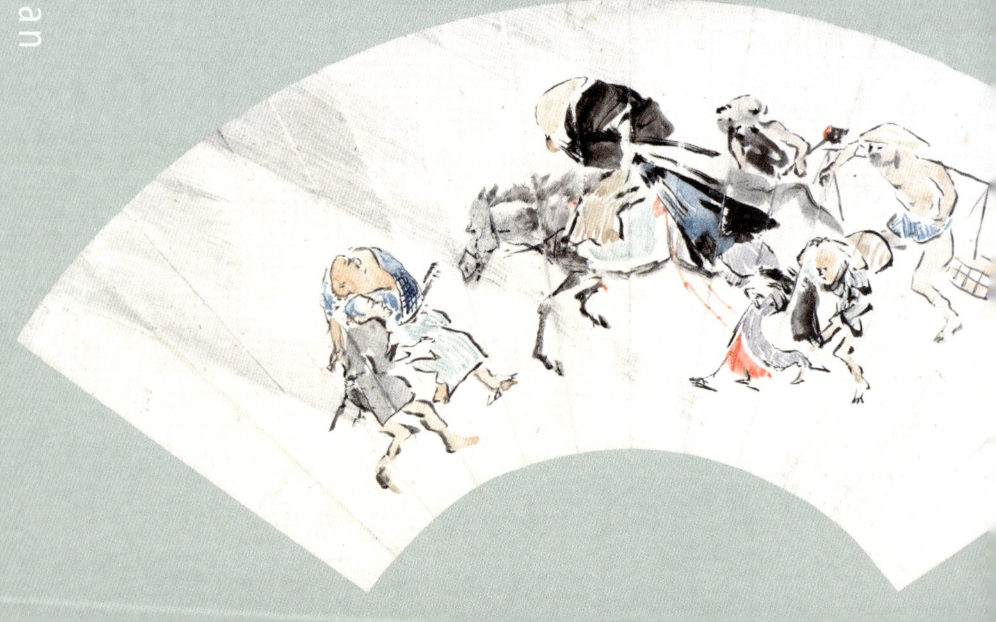

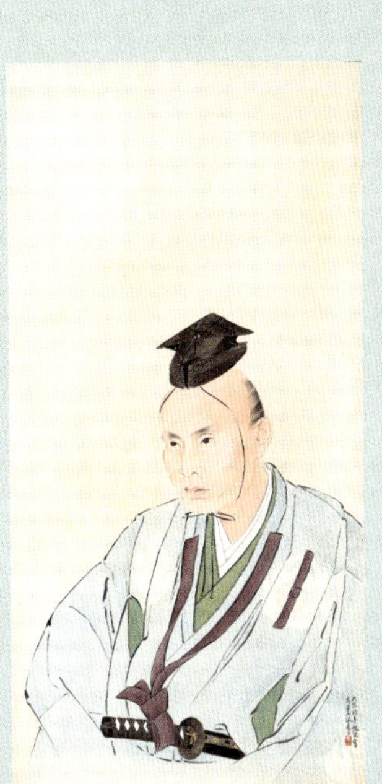

「鷹見泉石像」国宝　渡辺崋山
天保 8 年（1837）
東京国立博物館蔵
Statue of *Takami Senseki*, National
Treasure, Watanabe Kazan, 1837,
Tokyo National Museum / ColBase
(https://colbase.nich.go.jp)

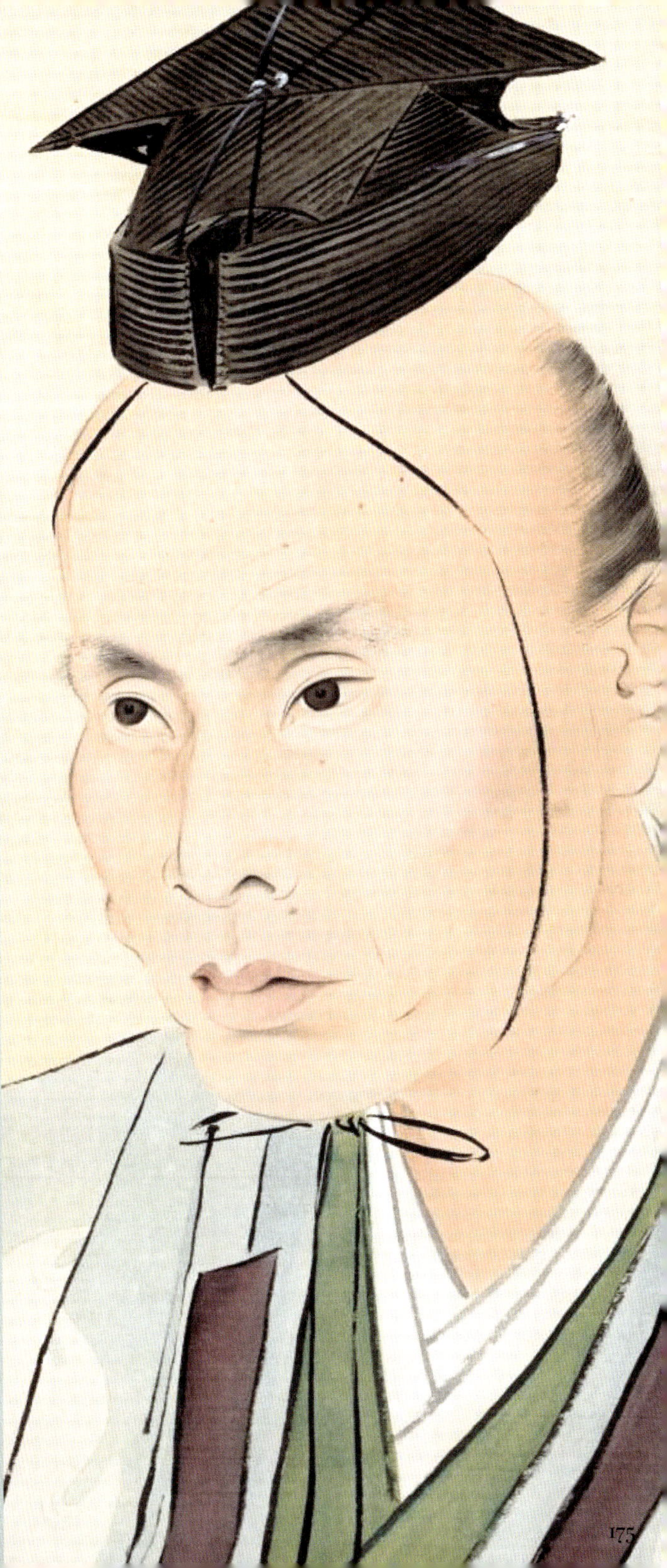

「驟雨図扇面」渡辺崋山
江戸時代（19 世紀）
東京藝術大学大学美術館蔵
画像提供：東京藝術大学 / DNPartcom
Fan with a Sudden Rain Shower,
Watanabe Kazan, 19th century, The
University Art Museum

河鍋暁斎
Kawanabe Kyōsai

縦横の奇才を達筆に表現し、反骨諷刺を描いた画家

かわなべ きょうさい　天保2～明治22年（1831～89）

　幕末・明治時代の日本画家。下総古河に生まれる。幼い頃から絵を好み、7歳で歌川国芳に入門、11歳で前村洞和門、のち狩野洞白に学ぶ。和漢古画や初期肉筆浮世絵などを研鑽して独自の画風を築く。狩野派と浮世絵を取り入れた鋭い写実と特異な画風で、縦横の奇才ぶりを達筆に発揮して反骨諷刺を描いた。

Brilliant, free brushwork by a rebellious, satyrical artist

A *nihonga* (modern Japanese-style painting) artist, Kawanabe Kyōsai (1831-1889) was active in the closing years of the Tokugawa shogunate and then the Meiji period. Born in Furukawa, Shimousa (now Ibaraki prefecture), he enjoyed painting from early childhood and, at the age of seven, began studying with Utagawa Kuniyoshi. At eleven, he studied with Maemura Tōwamon and later with Kanō Dōhaku. He diligently studied antique paintings from both Japan and China and early brush-drawn *ukiyo-e* as he developed his own style. His acute realism, incorporating elements from the Kanō School and *ukiyo-e*, displays his brilliant, free brushwork in rebellious and satyrical works.

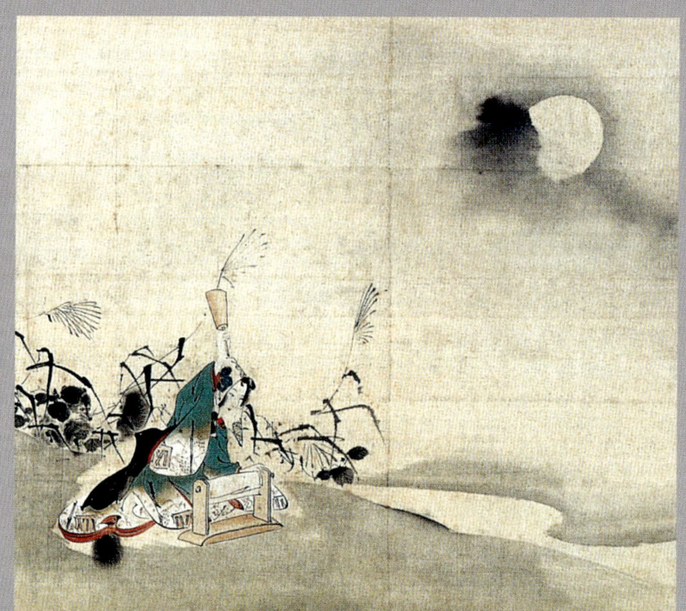

「狸砧図」 河鍋暁斎　江戸～明治時代　敦賀市博物館蔵
Raccoon *Kinuta-Zu*,　Kawanabe Kyōsai, Edo to Meiji period, Tsuruga City Museum

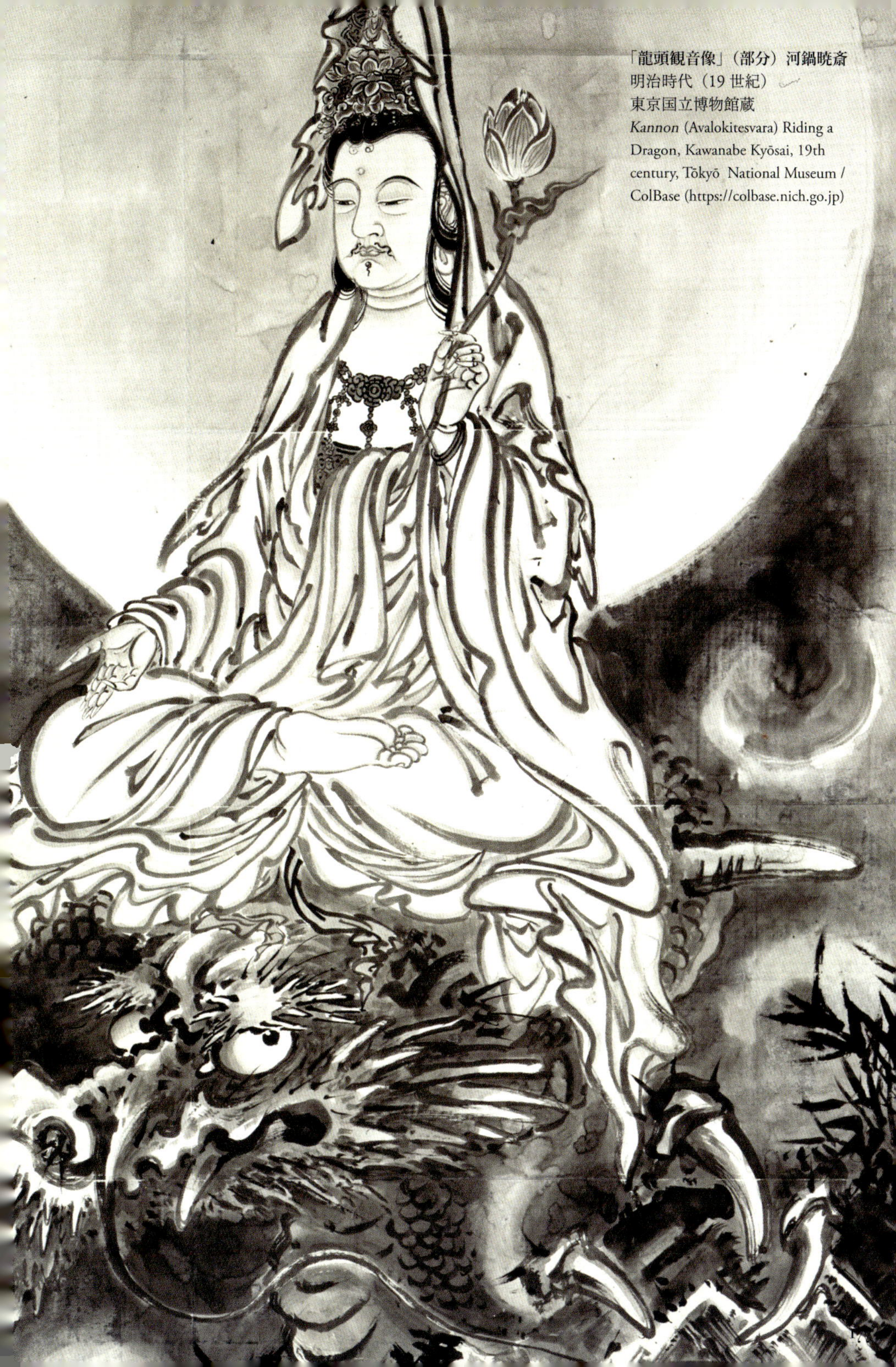

「龍頭観音像」（部分）河鍋暁斎
明治時代（19世紀）
東京国立博物館蔵
Kannon (Avalokitesvara) Riding a
Dragon, Kawanabe Kyōsai, 19th
century, Tōkyō National Museum /
ColBase (https://colbase.nich.go.jp)

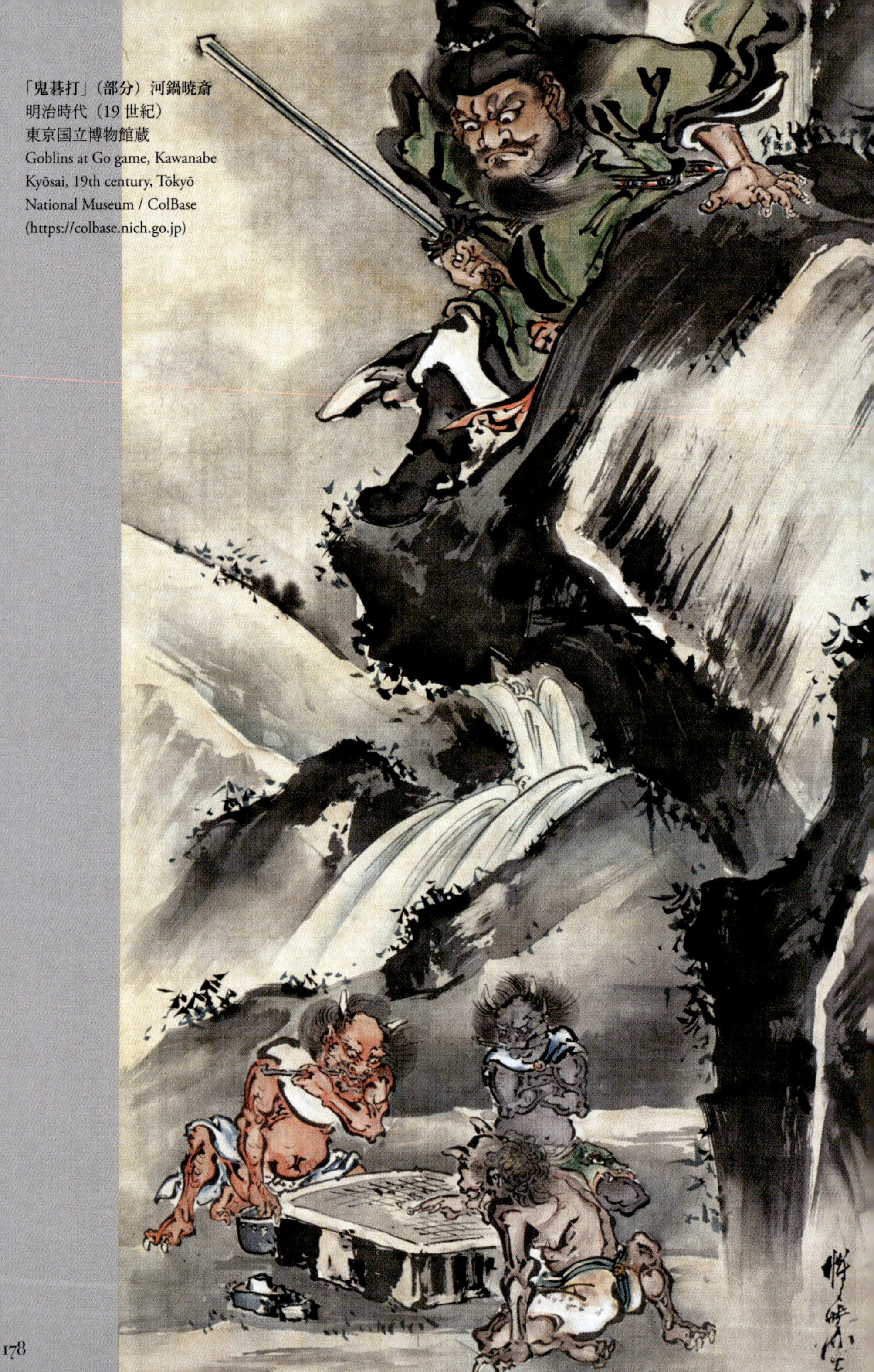

「鬼碁打」（部分）河鍋暁斎
明治時代（19 世紀）
東京国立博物館蔵
Goblins at Go game, Kawanabe
Kyōsai, 19th century, Tōkyō
National Museum / ColBase
(https://colbase.nich.go.jp)

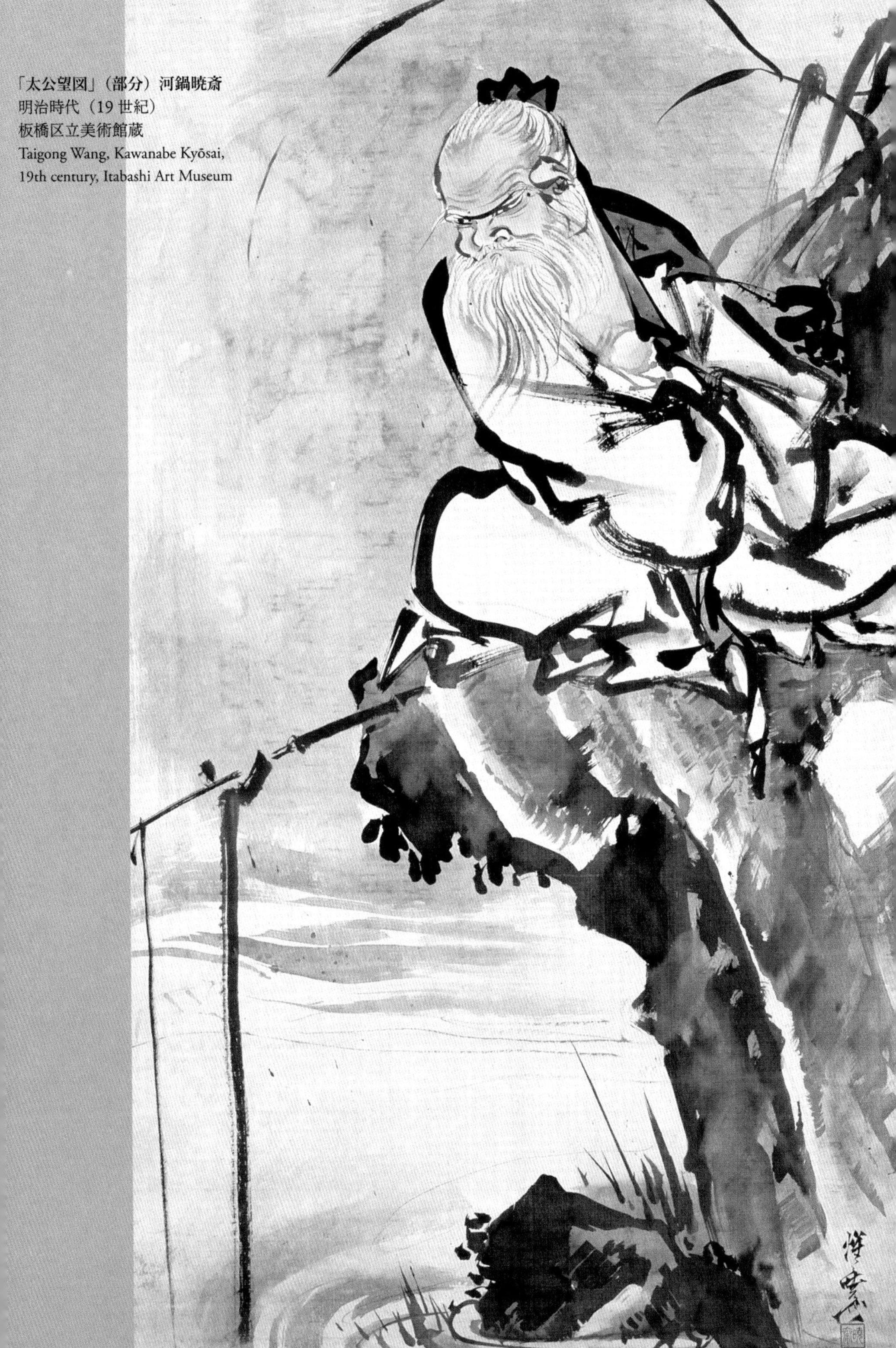

「太公望図」（部分）河鍋暁斎
明治時代（19 世紀）
板橋区立美術館蔵
Taigong Wang, Kawanabe Kyōsai,
19th century, Itabashi Art Museum

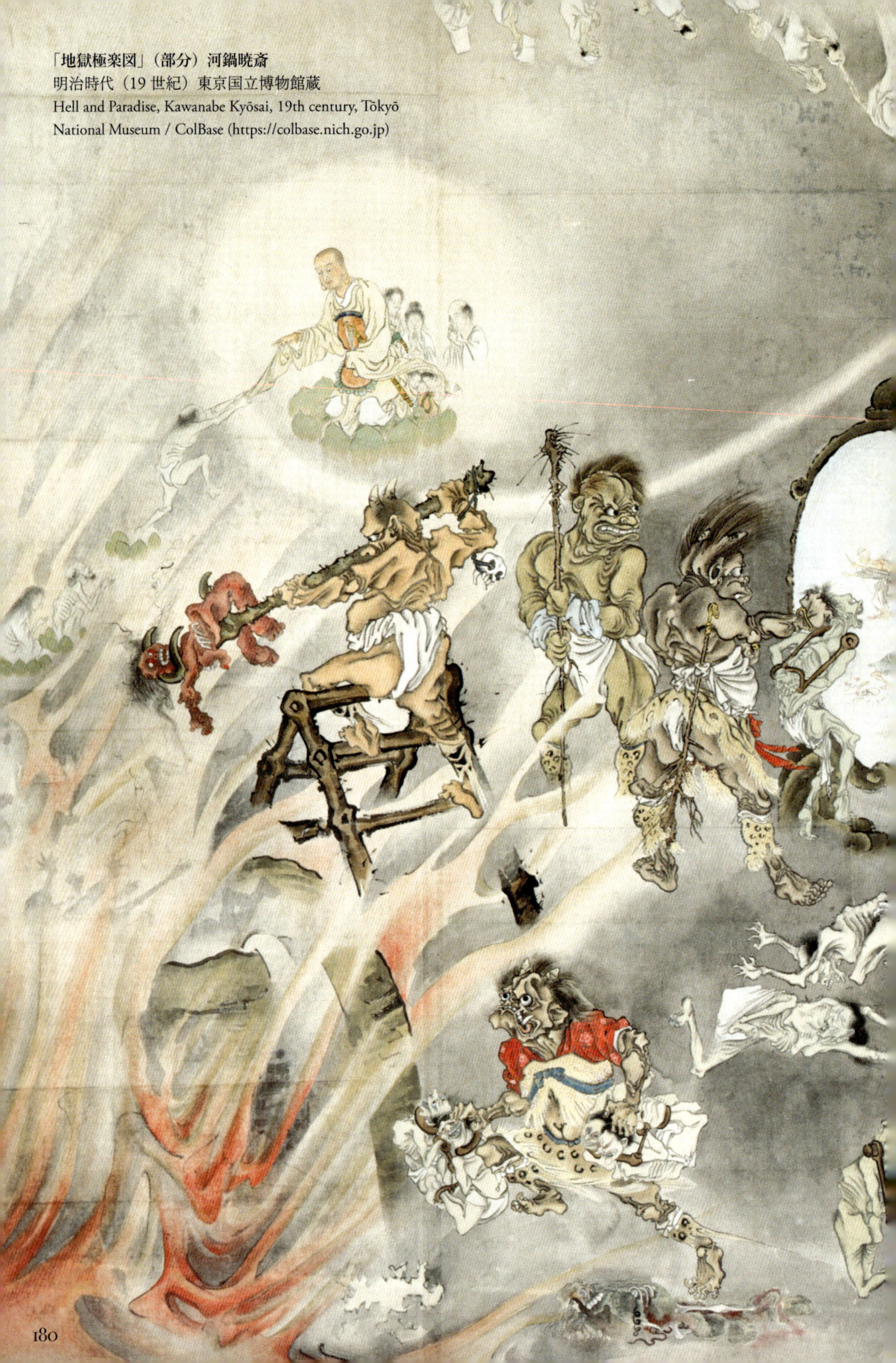

「地獄極楽図」（部分）河鍋暁斎
明治時代（19世紀）東京国立博物館蔵
Hell and Paradise, Kawanabe Kyōsai, 19th century, Tōkyō
National Museum / ColBase (https://colbase.nich.go.jp)

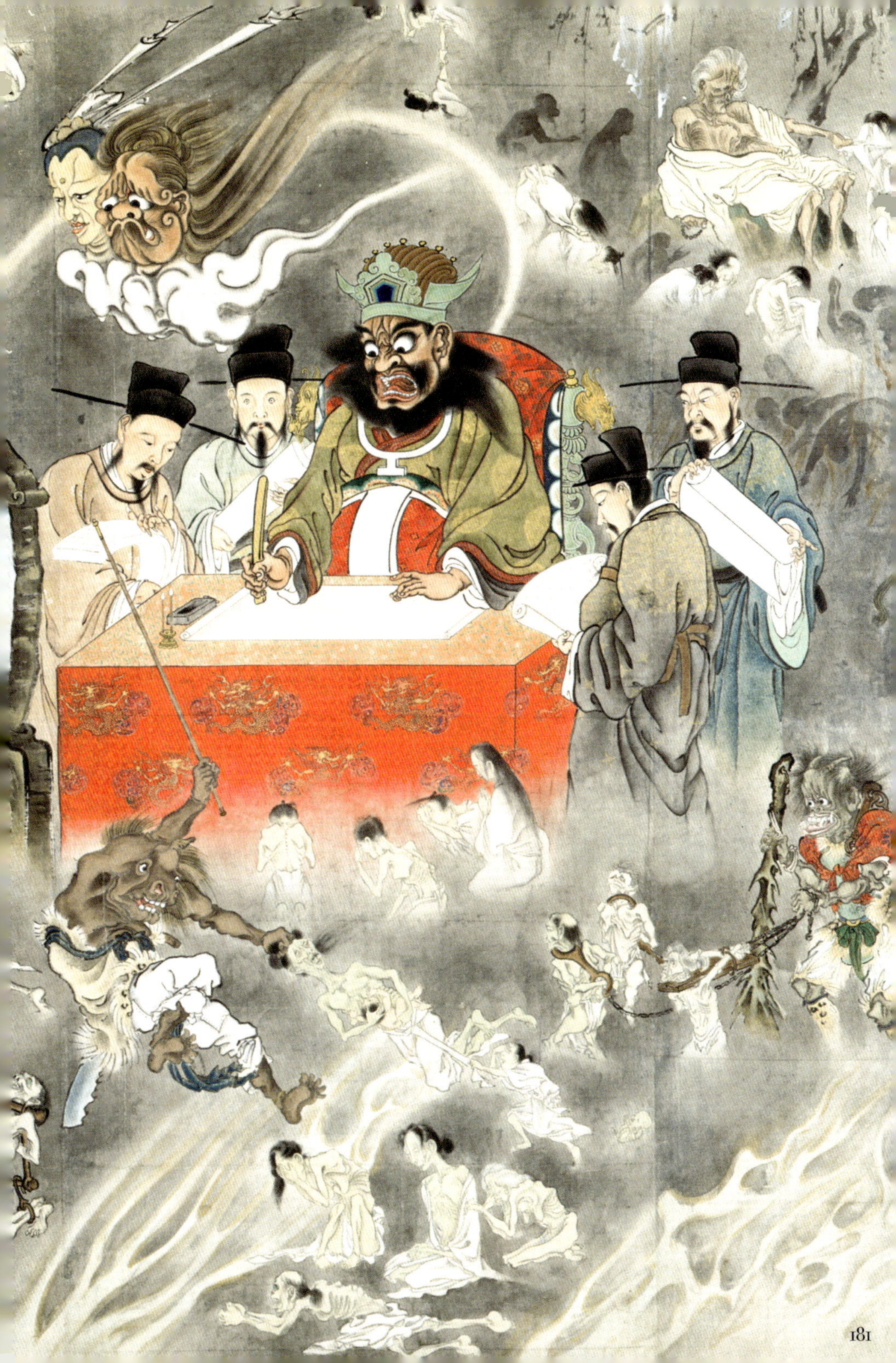

近代日本画に独自の地位を築いた文人画家

とみおか てっさい
天保7~大正13年（1836~1924）

　明治・大正期の日本画家。京都の法衣商十一屋伝兵衛の二男。20歳のころ太田垣蓮月の学僕となる。国学、漢学を修め、窪田雪鷹、小田海僊に南画、浮田一惠に大和絵を学ぶ。維新後、各地の神社の大宮司となって神道復興に尽くすが、兄の死にともない京都に帰り画業に専念し、近代日本画のなかで独自の地位を占めた。

The literati painter with a unique position in modern *Nihonga*

Tomioka Tessai (1837-1924) , a *Nihonga* artist active in the Meiji and Taisho periods, was the second son of Jūichiya Denbei, a Kyoto merchant dealing in sacerdotal robes. At around 20, he admitted as a working student by the Buddhist nun Ōtagaki Rengetsu. He mastered both Japanese and Chinese studies, then went on to study Nanga with Setsuyō and Oda Kaisen and Yamato-e with Ukita Ikkei. After the Meiji Restoration, he became a Shinto priest serving at various shrines, dedicating himself to a Shinto revival. At his elder brother's death, however, he returned to Kyoto, dedicated himself to painting, and established his unique position in modern *Nihonga*.

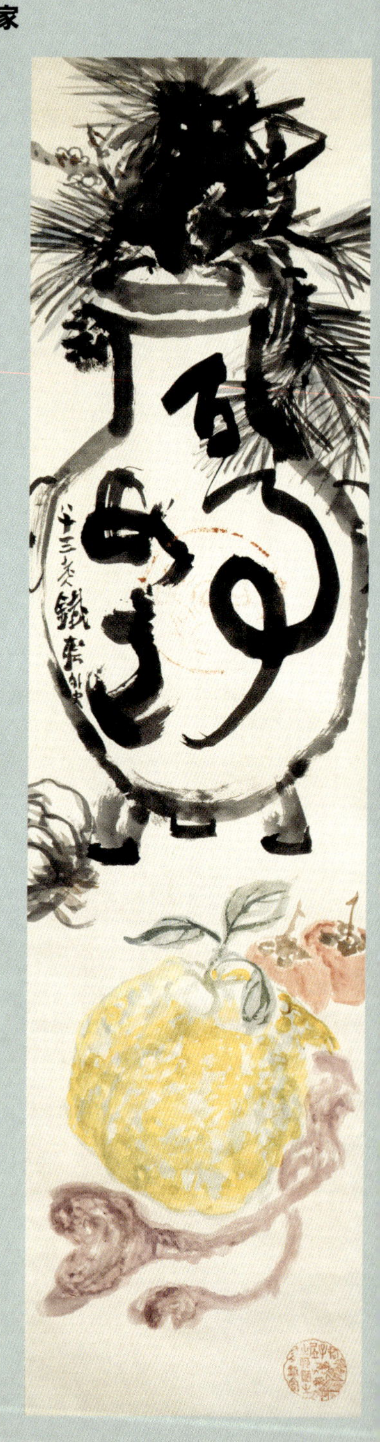

右：「百事如意図」富岡鉄斎
大正 7 年（1918）愛知県美術館蔵（木村定三コレクション）
Various Matters being one's Own Will, Tomioka Tessai, 1918,
Aichi Prefectural Museum of Art/ Kimura Teizo Collection

右頁：「二神会舞」（部分）富岡鉄斎
大正 12 年（1923）東京国立博物館蔵
Two Dancing Deities, Tomioka Tessai, 1923, Tōkyō National
Museum / ColBase (https://colbase.nich.go.jp)

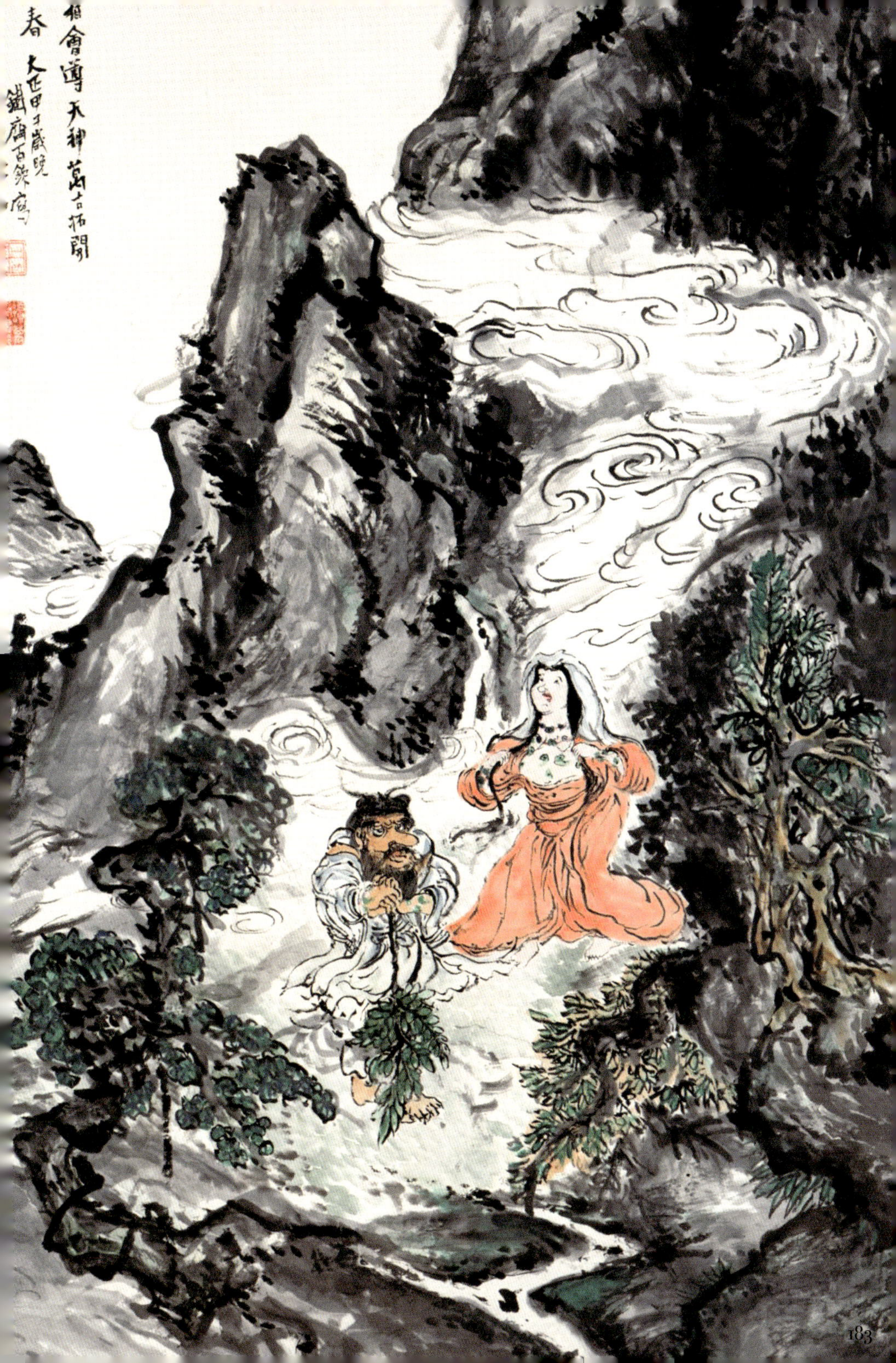
相會傳天神萬古拓開
春
大正甲子歲晚
鐵廟百鍊寫
183

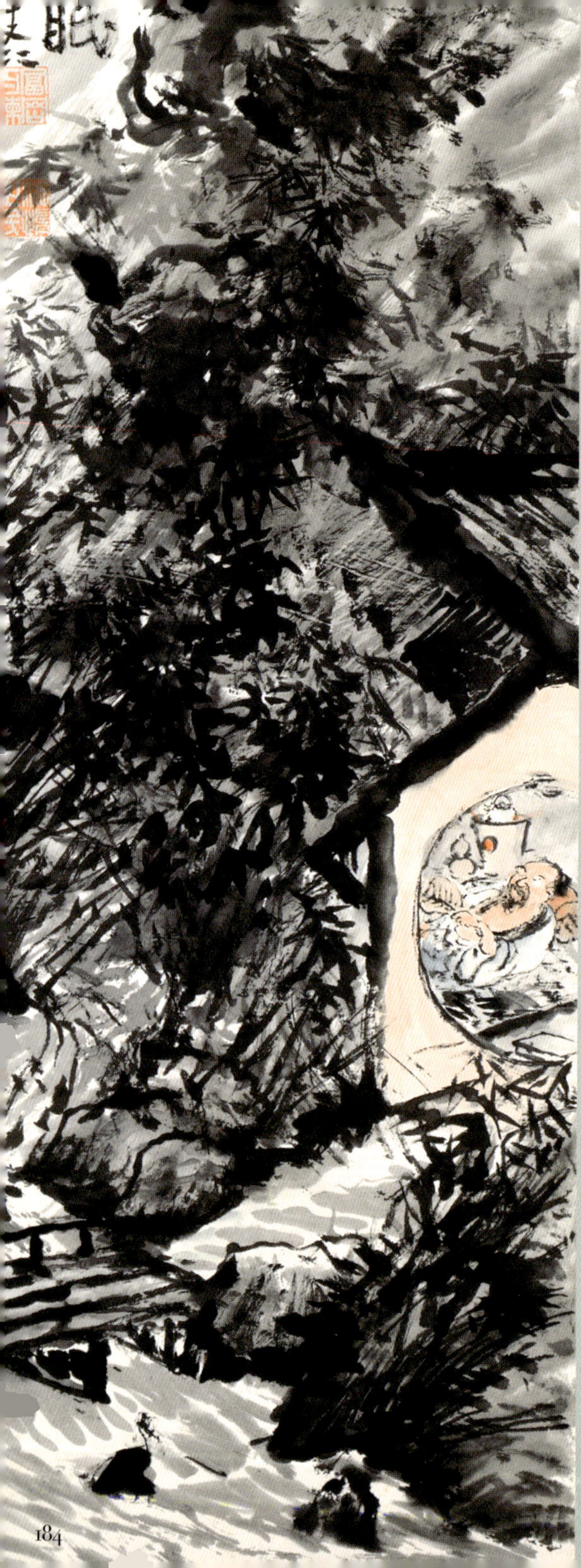

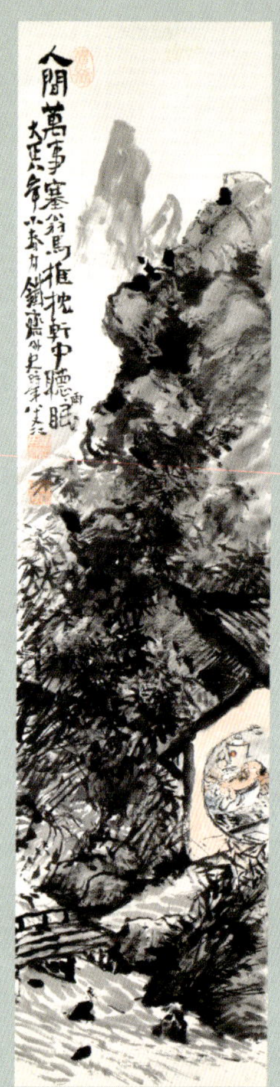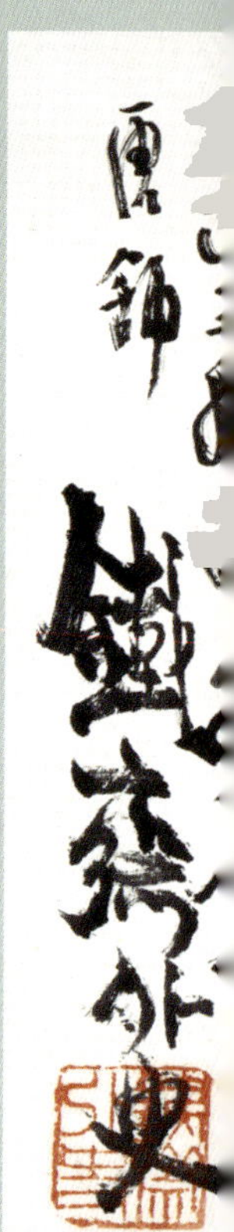

「竹窓高臥図」富岡鉄斎
大正 8 年（1919）
富山県水墨美術館蔵
Sleeping Hermit, Tomioka Tessai,
1919, The Suiboku Museum Toyama

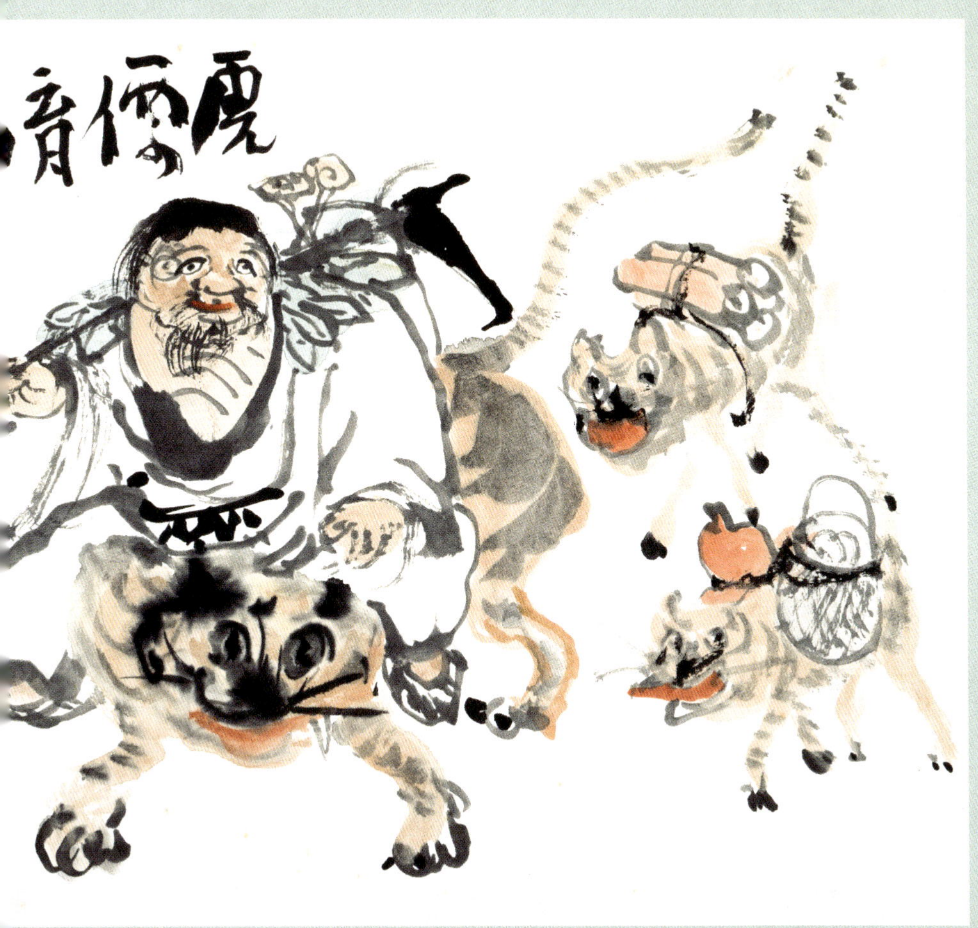

「虎僊育孺子図」富岡鉄斎
大正 3 年（1914）
愛知県美術館蔵（木村定三コレクション）
Legendary Wizards Nurturing Tiger Cubs,
Tomioka Tessai, 1914, Aichi Prefectural Museum
of Art/ Kimura Teizo Collection

横山大観 Yokoyama Taikan

近代日本画壇の中心的な存在の画家

よこやま たいかん　明治元~昭和33年（1868~1958）

　明治から昭和期の日本画家。水戸に生まれ、のち東京に移って母方の横山家を継いだ。東京美術学校に第 1 期生として入学、岡倉天心、橋本雅邦の指導を受けた。西洋画法を取り入れた「朦朧体（もうろうたい）」とよばれる没骨賦彩（もっこつふさい）の画法を開発し、大胆な没線描法を試みたが、朦朧派と悪評されて苦闘を強いられた。日本美術院を再興して中心作家として活躍。東洋の伝統に基づく近代日本画の創成を目ざして画壇に重きをなした。

「雨後之山」横山大観　昭和 16 年（1941）富山県水墨美術館蔵
Mountains After the Rain, Yokoyama Taikan, 1941, The Suiboku Museum Toyama

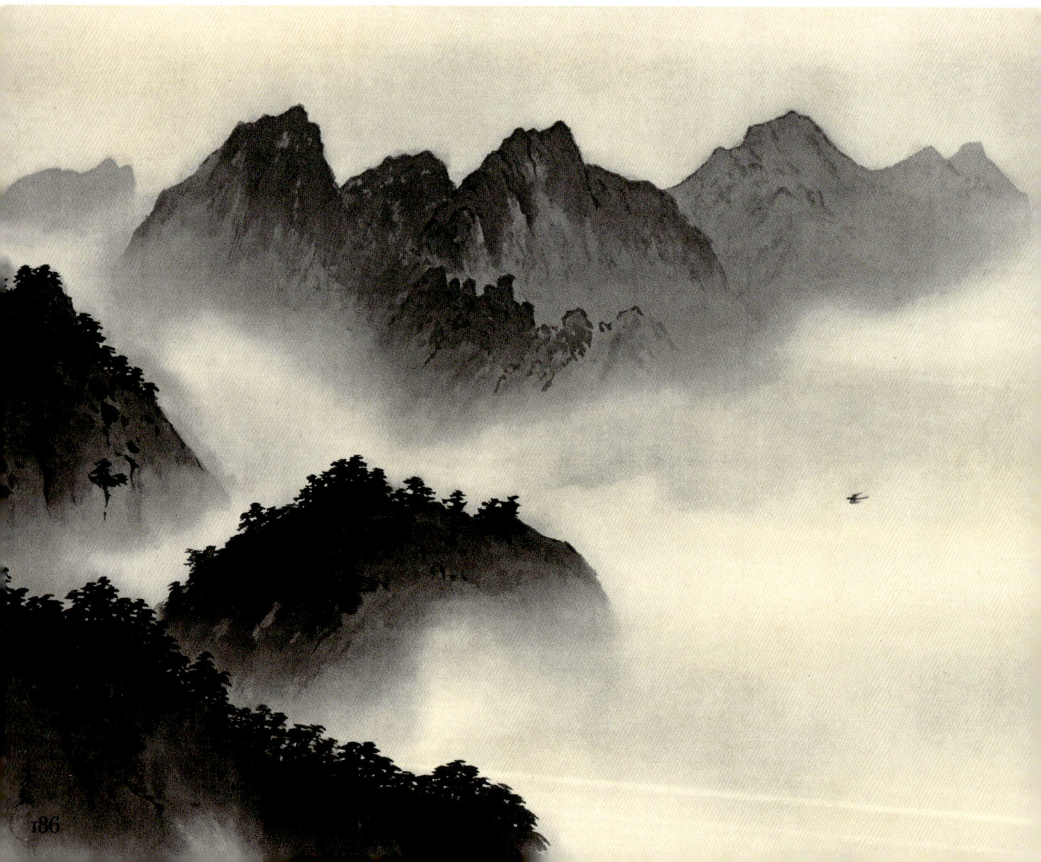

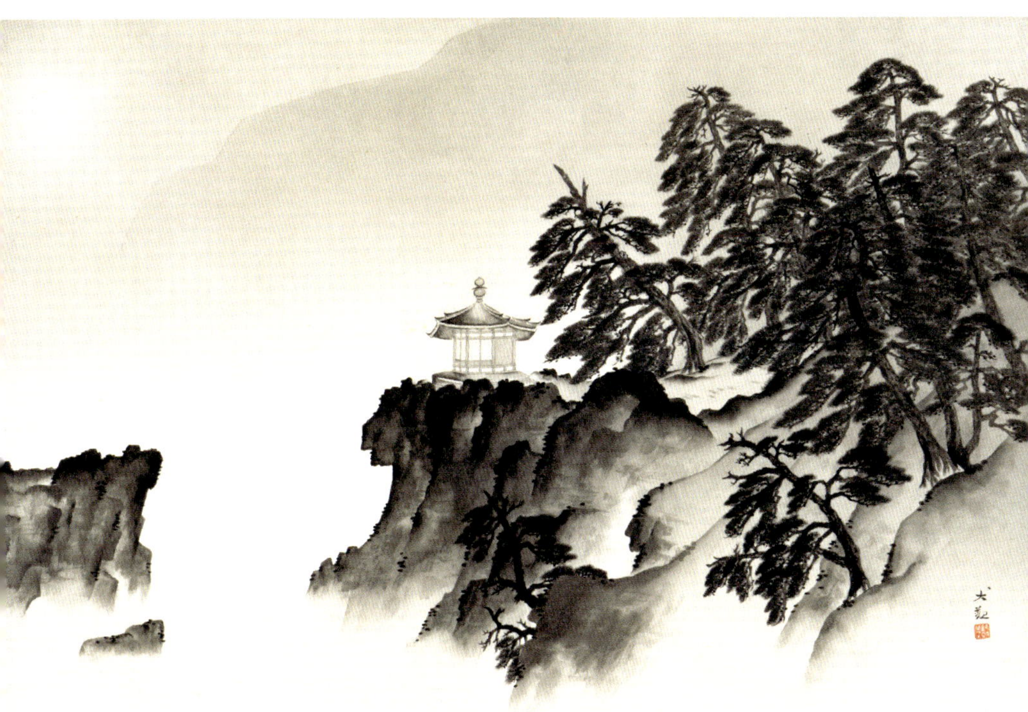

「五浦の月」横山大観　昭和 10 年（1935）東京国立博物館蔵
Izura no Tsuki, Yokoyama Taikan, 1935, Tōkyō National Museum / ColBase (https://colbase.nich.go.jp)

A central presence in the modern *Nihonga* world

A *Nihonga* artist active from the Meiji to the Showa periods, Yokoyama
Taikan (1868-1958) was born in Mito and later moved to Tokyo, where he
became the heir of his mother's family, the Yokoyama. He was in the first
class to enter the Tokyo Fine Arts School (now Tokyo University of the
Arts), where he received instruction from Okakura Tenshin and Hashimoto
Gahō. He developed the painting technique called *mokkotsu fusai* (outline-free polychromes), which was dubbed *mōrōtai* ("blurred style") and
experimented with a bold line-free style. Having revived the Japan Art Insti-
tute, he made it his main platform. Aiming to create modern *Nihonga* based
on Eastern traditions, he became a prominent figure in the art world,

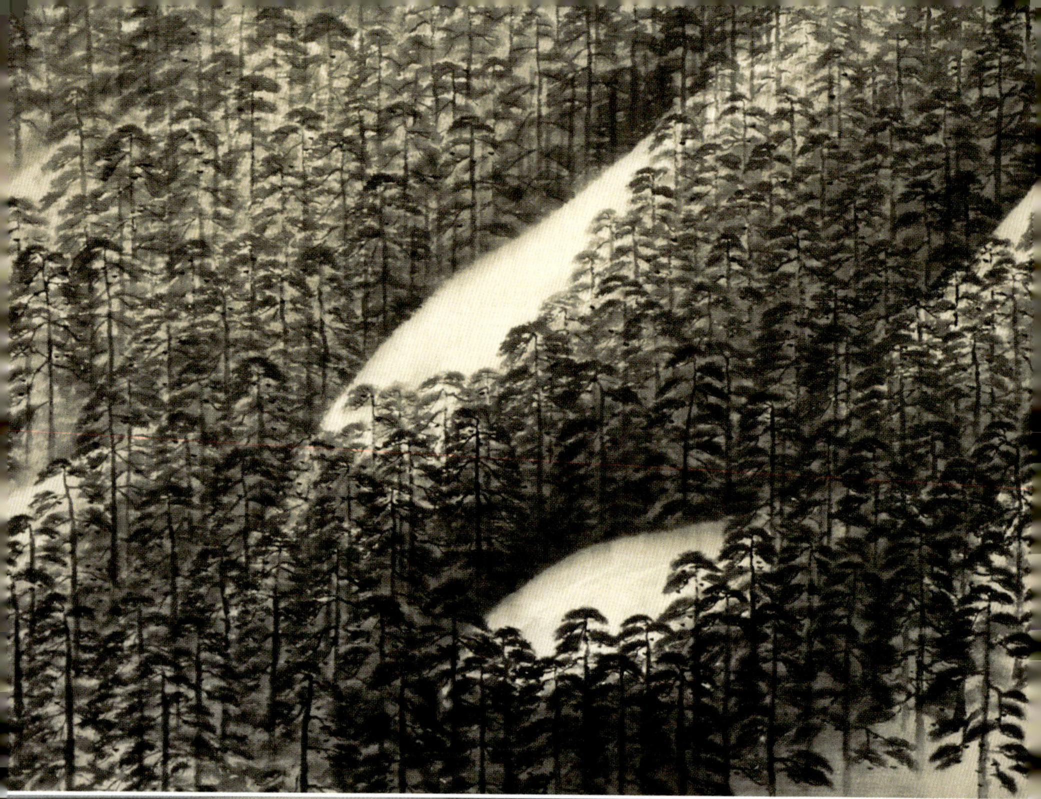

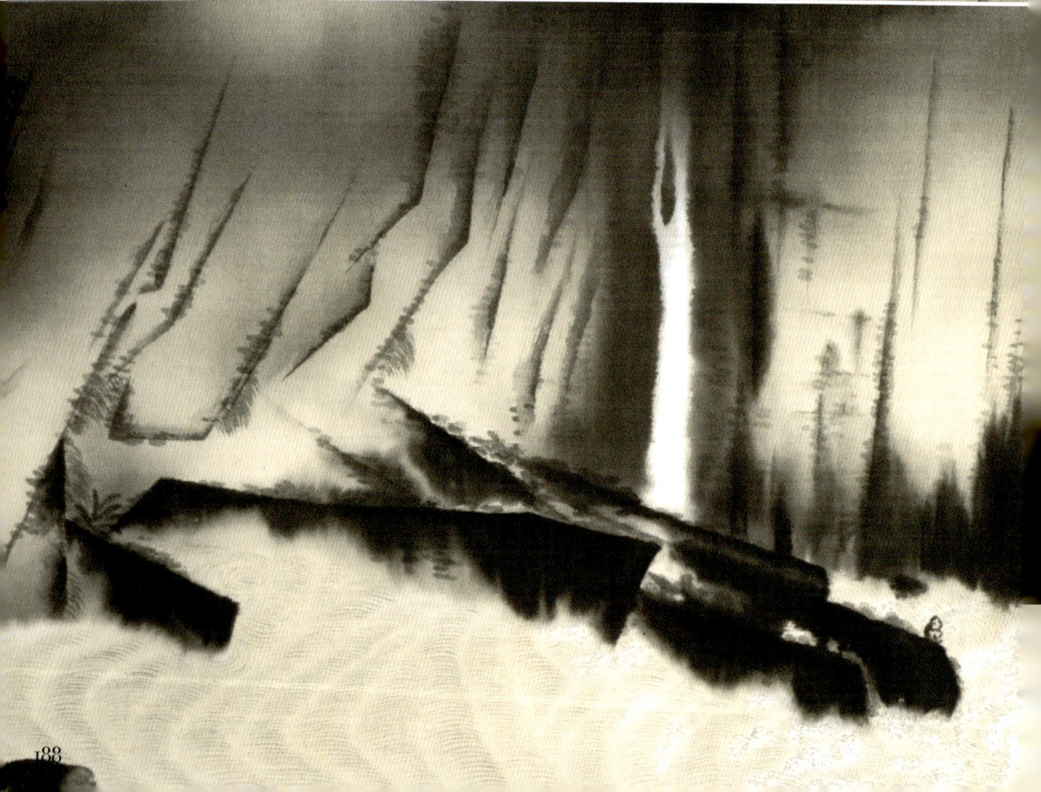

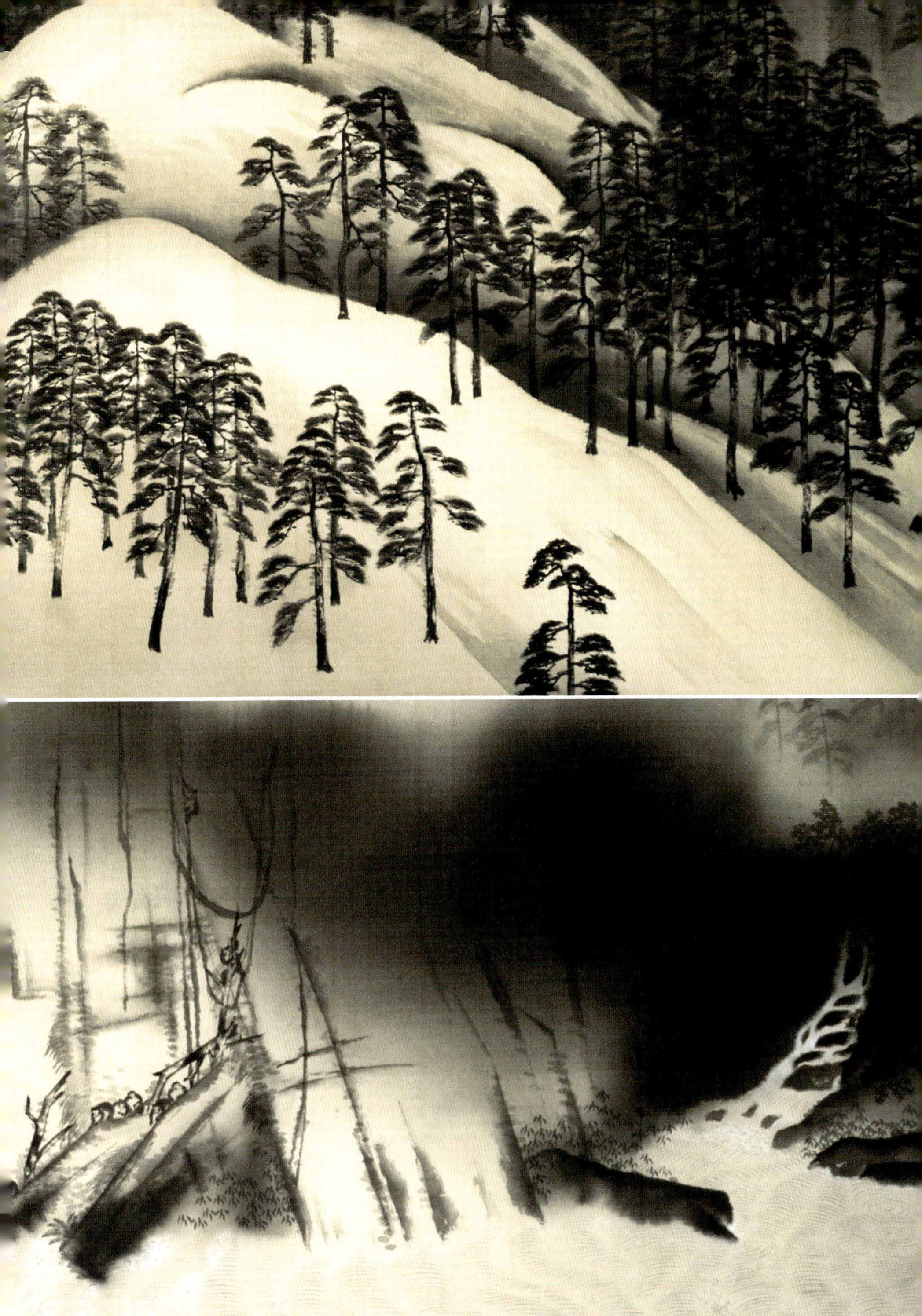

「生々流転」（部分）重文　横山大観　大正 12 年（1923）東京国立近代美術館蔵　Photo: MOMAT/DNPartcom
Metempsychosis, Important Cultural Property, Yokoyama Taikan, 1923, National Museum of Modern Art, Tokyo

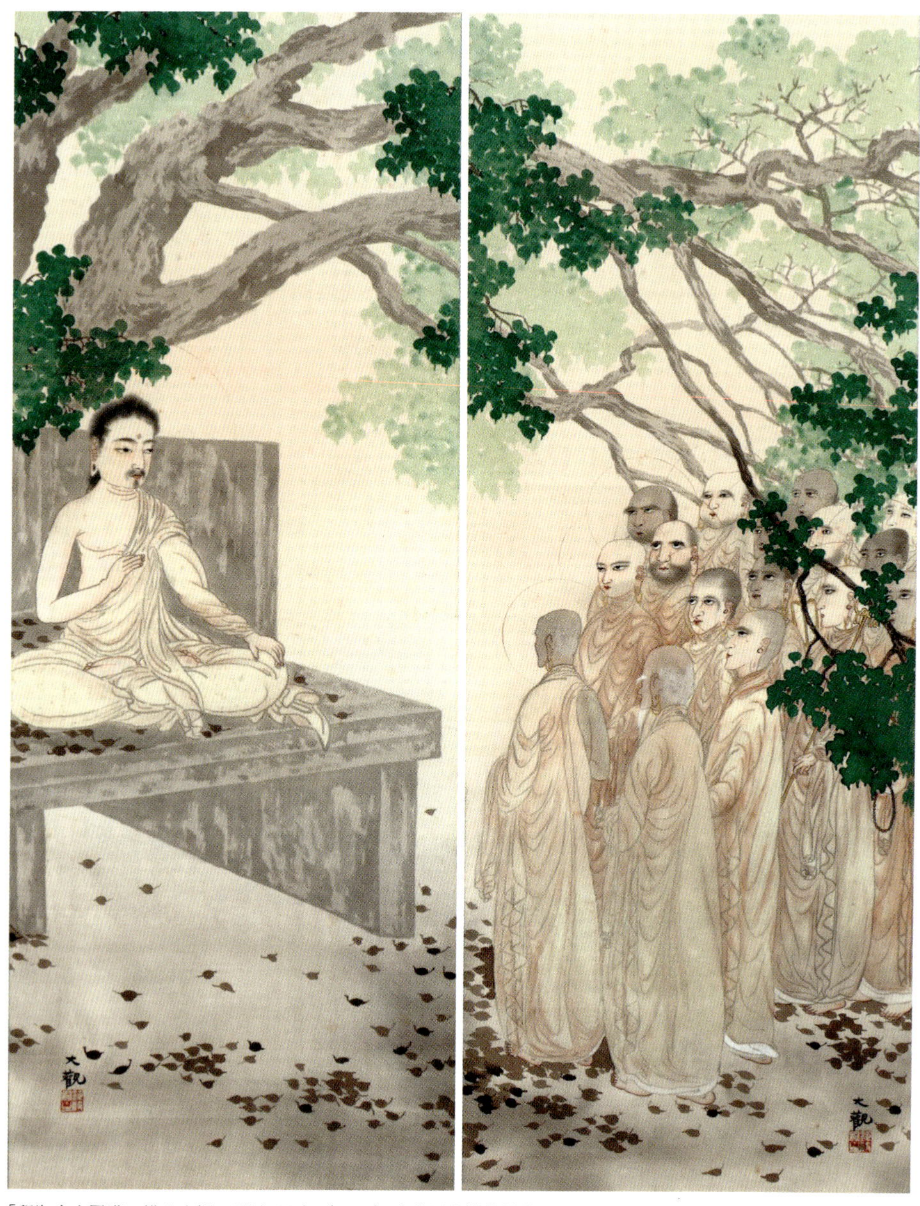

「釈迦十六羅漢」横山大観　明治 44 年（1911）東京国立博物館蔵
Sakyamuni and Sixteen Arhats, Yokoyama Taikan, 1911, Tōkyō National Museum / ColBase (https://colbase.nich.go.jp)

「松並木」（部分）横山大観　大正 2 年（1913）
東京国立博物館蔵
Rows of Pine Trees, Yokoyama Taikan, 1913, Tōkyō National Museum / ColBase (https://colbase.nich.go.jp)

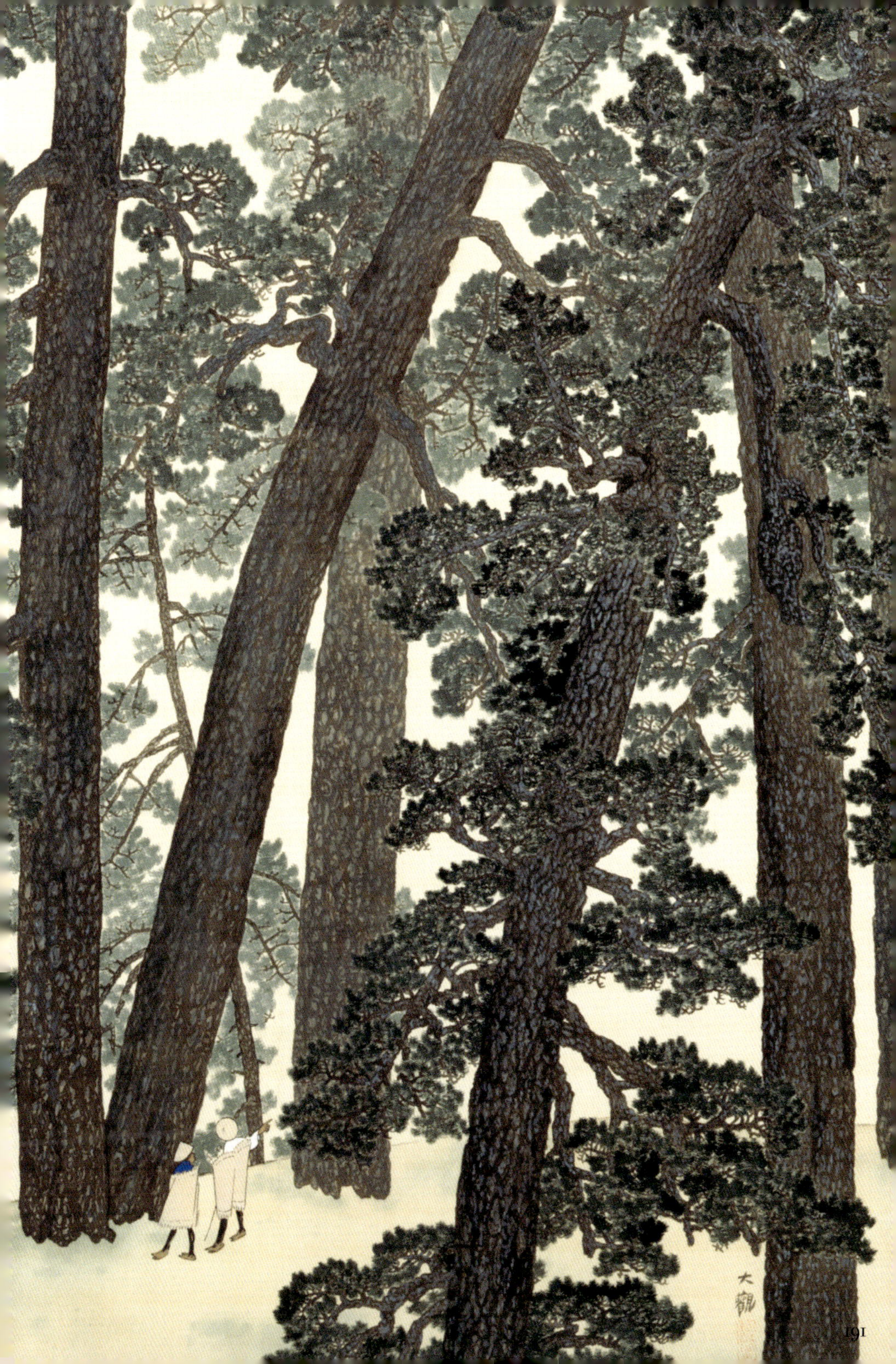

「木立に白鷺」横山大観　明治 37 年（1904）富山県水墨美術館蔵
Rows of Pine Trees, Yokoyama Taikan, 1904, The Suiboku Museum Toyama

［図版データ・作品解説］

図版データは、作品名、文化財指定、作者名、制作年、員数、種類、
材質、法量（縦・横、単位はセンチメートル）、所蔵家の順に掲載する。
制作年代は所蔵先の資料のため、不明なものは省略した。

雪舟等楊

14・15p「秋冬山水図」国宝　雪舟等楊　室町時代（15 世紀末
～16 世紀初期）軸双幅　紙本墨画　各 47.7 x 30.2cm　東京国立博物館
蔵　Landscape of Autumn and Winter, National treasure, Sesshū Tōyō, Late
15th century-early 16th century, Pair of hanging scrolls, Ink on paper, 47.7
x 30.2cm each, Tōkyō National Museum ●岩容の輪郭線が激しくぶつか
り合い、その相互がせり合うかたちで深奥の調和がみごとに保たれた構
図が魅力的な作品である。双幅の山水図のうち、「秋景」には川沿いに
道が奥へと伸び、遠くに楼閣が描かれる。モチーフは画面の下半分にま
とめられ、上部の空間には無限を感じさせる広大な秋空がある。一方の
「冬景」では、大胆に切り立った崖を中心に据え、対照的に建物を小さ
く見せることで、厳しい冬枯れの様子が描き出されている。雪舟の画風
の老成を知るに足る山水画で、67 歳で描いた「山水長巻」よりはあとの、
70 歳代の作品ではないかと思われる。

16・17p「天橋立図」国宝　雪舟等楊　室町時代（15～16 世紀）軸
1 幅　紙本墨画淡彩　89.5cm x 169.5cm　京都国立博物館蔵　Scene
at Ama no Hashidate, National treasure, Sesshū Tōyō, Late 15th century-
early 16th century, Hanging scroll, Ink and light colors on paper, 89.5cm x
169.5cm, Kyoto National Museum ●雪舟の傑作として名高い天橋立の景
観を鳥瞰（ちょうかん）的に描いた大作である。画面の中央には天橋
立の白砂青松の情景と智恩寺がとらえられ、その上方に阿蘇海をはさん
で寺社の林立する府中の町並み、さらにその背後には巨大な山塊と成相
寺の伽藍（がらん）が配されている。その重厚な筆致と卓越した画面
構成や緻密な描き込みが、異色ながら特別に力のこもった雪舟の自筆で
あることを強く示唆する。制作期については智恩寺に多宝塔が描かれて
いることから、現存する塔が再建された文亀元年（1501）以降を一つ
の目安とし、雪舟 80 歳代の最晩年期とする説がある。

18・19p「恵可断臂図」国宝　雪舟等楊　明応 5 年（1496）軸 1 幅
紙本墨画淡彩 199.9 x 113.6cm 齋年寺蔵　Hui-ke and Bodhidharma,
National treasure, Sesshū Tōyō, 1496, Hanging scroll, Ink and light colors
on paper, 199.9 x 113.6cm, Sainen-ji ●少林寺において、禅宗の初祖で
ある達磨が面壁座禅中に、慧可（えか）という僧が彼に参禅を請うた
が許されず、自ら左腕を切り落として決意のほどを示したところ、よう
やく入門を許されたという有名な禅機の場面を描いている。達磨のリア
ルな面貌と一点を凝視する鋭いまなざし、そして動きの少ない構図が画
面全体に息苦しいまでの緊張感を生み出している。77 歳の折に描いた
もので、老禅僧雪舟のたどりついた境地がここにあらわれている。本
図は幅裏の墨書から、雪舟没後まもない天文元年（1532）に尾張国知
多郡宮山城主である佐治為貞によって齋年寺に寄進されたことが知られ
る。

コラム［水と墨の無限の階調］

21p「破墨山水図」国宝　雪舟等楊　雪舟自序・月翁周鏡ら六僧
賛　明応 4 年 (1495)　軸 1 幅　紙本墨画　148.9 x 32.7cm 東京国立博
物館蔵　Haboku Landscape, National treasure, Sesshū Tōyō, Inscriptions
by Sesshū, Getto Shukyo, Ran'pa, Keishi, Ten'in Ryutaku, Ryoan Keigo, and
Keijo Shurin, 1495, Hanging scroll, Ink on paper, 148.9 x 32.7cm, Tōkyō
National Museum ●墨一色の濃淡で風景を描いた水墨画であるが、何が
描かれているかよくわからない。細部に目を凝らすと、いちばん上に薄
く描かれているのが遠くにそびえる岩山、真ん中の少し濃い墨がその手
前の小高い山で、いちばん下が近くの山と穏やかな水面である。このよ
うに画面の上にいくほど遠い景色というのが山水画とよばれる風景画の
基本である。よく見ると手前の山に一軒の家が建っており、軒先から右

に枝のようなものが張り出している。これは食事を出す店のしるしの旗
である。雪舟 76 歳のときの作品で、弟子の宗淵（そうえん）に求めら
れて本図を描いたこと、中国では李在（りざい）と長有声（ちょうゆう
せい）に画法を学んだことなどを自叙伝風に図上の賛に記している。

雪村周継

22・23p「蝦蟇鉄拐図」雪村周継　室町時代（16 世紀）軸 2 幅　紙
本墨画淡彩　各 151.5 x 205.9cm　東京国立博物館蔵　Immortais
Tieguai and Xiama, Sesson Shūkei, 16th century, Pair of hanging scrolls,
Ink and light colors on paper, 151.5 x 205.9 cm each, Tōkyō National
Museum ●蝦蟇鉄拐（がまてっかい）は蝦蟇仙人と鉄拐仙人の二人を
主題にした中国道釈（どうしゃく）人物画の画題である。蝦蟇仙人は
中国渤海（ぼっかい）の人で劉海蟾（りゅうかいせん）といい、金王
朝に仕えて大臣となったが、のちに終南山（しゅうなんざん）にこもっ
て道術を学び、三本足の蝦蟇を使う妖術を行なった。李鉄拐は八仙の一
人で、若いとき道術を得て自分の分身、つまり「魄（たましい）」を空
中に吐き出したという。この二人は道教特有の怪奇性の代表者で、一対
で描かれることが多い。本図はもと水戸徳川家の衝立の表裏に貼られて
あった。

24・25p「花鳥図屏風」雪村周継　室町時代（16 世紀）6 曲 1
隻　紙本着色　91.5 x 351.0cm 栃木県立博物館蔵　Standing Screen of
Flowers and Birds, Sesson Shūkei, 16th century, Single six-fold screen, Ink
and colors on paper, 91.5 x 351.0cm, Tochigi Prefectural Museum ●屏風の
右端からは太い幹の松樹が枝を広げ、その勢いに隠れるように牡丹の大
輪がおごそかに佇んでいる。第二扇から第三扇にかけて松の枝が直線的
に交差し、その樹枝の向こうの水辺には芦の生える土坡（どは）を描き、
つがいの鴛鴦（おしどり）を配している。左に目を移すと、二扇には
雪村独特の角のとがった岩を水中に立て、その上に黄蜀葵（とろろあお
い）の白い花を咲かせている。また紅の薔薇や三羽の白鷺を描くなど、
彩り豊かな画面に仕上げている。ただ第四扇は画面がつながらず、上下
の紙つぎも他とは異なっていることから、明らかに他の部分が挿入され
たものと思われる。

26p「布袋図」雪村周継　室町時代（16 世紀）軸 1 幅　紙本墨画
淡彩　25.5 x 34.5cm　板橋区立美術館蔵　Budai, Sesson Shūkei, 16th
century, Hanging scroll, Ink and light colors on paper, 25.5 x 34.5 cm,
Itabashi Art Museum ●七福神の一つである布袋は、中国の唐末五代の頃
の伝説的な禅僧で、名は契此（かいし）。腹が大きく膨れた肥大な体躯
であった。いつも大きな袋を持ち、杖をついて市中に喜捨を求め、食
物その他のもらい物を袋の中に入れ、あちらこちらを歩き回り吉凶や天
気を占ったという。日本には鎌倉時代にその図がもたらされ、禅の精神
を体現する仏尊として禅宗のなかで礼拝された。ここに描かれた布袋
さんは喜色満面の表情で、まるで雲に乗って飛んでいるかのように大きな
袋に杖を立てている。晴れやかなその姿がとても滑稽である。

27p「松鷹図」重文　雪村周継　室町時代（16 世紀）軸 2 幅　紙
本墨画　125.9 x 53.6cm/126.5 x 53.6cm　東京国立博物館蔵　Hawks
and Pines, Important cultural property, Sesson Shūkei, 16th century,Tow
hanging scrolls, Ink on paper, 125.9 x 53.6 cm / 126.5 x 53.6 cm, Tōkyō
National Museum ●松樹の太い枝に止まった二羽の鷹の精悍な勇姿が描
かれる。鷹の姿態や顔の向きなどにも動きがあり、構図の安定したバラ
ンスのよさが感じられる。勇猛な鷹の姿は雪村の気性があらわされてお
り、戦国武将の好尚と時代性がよく反映されている。鷹狩りに用いる鷹
は、猟犬と同様に武士にとって重要な存在であった。上下に描かれた松

葉は、藁筆（わらふで）を用いた粗豪な筆致がほどこされてこの猛禽の雄姿をいっそう助長している。一方の鷹の羽毛は柔らかい毛筆を使って描かれ、対照的な筆技の面白さを演じている。雪村の楷体による花鳥画の傑作である壮年期の制作と考えられる。

長谷川等伯

28・29p「**松林図屏風**」**国宝　長谷川等伯**　安土桃山時代（16世紀）6曲1双　紙本墨画　各156.8 x 356.0cm　東京国立博物館蔵 Standing Screens of Pine Grove, National treasure, Hasegawa Tōhaku, 16th century, Pair of six- fold screens, Ink on paper, 156.8 x 356.0 cm each, Tōkyō National Museum ●霧に包まれた松林の情景を詩情豊かに描いた水墨画の傑作である。松を横長の画面に配した並列的な構成ではあるが、手前に厳然と姿を見せる松と、後方に影のように描かれた松とを墨の濃淡で見事に描き分けている。右隻左隻の中央上方にうっすらとあらわした雪山が限りなく深奥な空間を演出している。禅林の観念的な水墨画法から脱し、漢画の決め事にもとらわれず、身近な題材を新鮮な感覚で描き出しているところに素朴な共感を覚える。松の葉叢は藁筆の粗い筆致で描き、手前の松を濃墨で力強くはね上げているところは、全体の静閑なイメージに比べて躍動感が伝わってくる。

30・31p「**瀟湘八景図屏風**」**長谷川等伯**　安土桃山時代（16世紀）6曲1双　紙本墨画淡彩　各159.0 x 354.8cm　東京国立博物館蔵 Standing Screens of Eight Sceneries of Xiao and Xiang, Hasegawa Tōhaku, 16th century, Pair of six-fold screens, Ink and light colors on paper, 159.0 x 354.8 cm each, Tōkyō National Museum ●雲霞にかすんだ山水の広大な風景のなかに瀟湘（しょうしょう）八景などの諸景物がちりばめられた、真体手法の山水図屏風である。中国湖南省の瀟水と湘水の合流点付近にある八つの佳景は、古来より画題として好まれた。北宋時代の文人画家宋迪（そうてき）が創始したものとされ、王洪、牧渓（もっけい）らの作品が知られる。広大な景観のなかに、平沙落雁・遠浦帰帆・山市晴嵐・江天暮雪・洞庭秋月・瀟湘夜雨・煙寺晩鐘・漁村夕照などのモチーフを散りばめた本図は、等伯の50歳代半ばごろの力作である。

32・33p「**枯木猿猴図**」**重文　長谷川等伯**　安土桃山時代（16世紀）軸双幅　紙本墨画　各157.0 x 104.0cm　龍泉庵蔵 Monkeys in Withered Tree, Important cultural property, Hasegawa Tōhaku,16th century, Pair of hanging scrolls, Ink painting on paper, 157.0 x 104.0 cm each, Ryūsen-an ●本図は、もと前田利長所持の六曲一双屏風であったが、世にいわれる「腕切りの猿」の一隻が焼失してしまい、残りの一隻から双幅に仕立てられたという。画面を対角線上に横切る老木、そして斜め左に伸びる藁筆様の枝は荒々しく力強い描線で描かれている。墨をはね散らし、その濃淡で立体感をあらわす溌墨（はつぼく）の技法をも併用し、画面にリズミカルな調和を感じさせている。掛幅にしては描かれた対象が大きいが、等伯の筆力と構成力が絶頂期の作品といえよう。

海北友松

34・35p「**雲龍図屏風**」**重文　海北友松**　桃山時代（17世紀）6曲1双　紙本墨画　各149.4 x 337.5cm　北野天満宮蔵 Standing Screens of a Dragon and Tigers, Important cultural property, Kaihō Yūshō, 17th century, Pair of six-fold screens, Ink painting on paper, 149.4 x 337.5cm each, Kitano Tenmangu Shrine ●六曲一双の大画面には全体に濃厚な墨色がほどこされ、墨の広がりや滲み、流れる効果などを巧みに活かしながら、空間の深い奥行きを暗示する墨雲のなかから二頭の龍の姿を現出させている。龍は雲を起こし、雨を降らせる神性の象徴とされ、友松はその霊獣を好んだようで、雲龍図は琴棋書画図とともに多く描かれた。ほかに建仁寺本坊方丈の襖八面に描かれたものや勧修寺の作品が知られる。本図では雲中に顕現する龍におどろおどろしさではなく、ある種の凄みやユーモラスな感じをあらわすなど、友松晩年の境地をうかがわせ

る。

36・37p「**宮女琴棋書画図屏風**」**重文　海北友松**　安土桃山～江戸時代（16~17世紀）6曲1双　紙本墨画着色　各154.0 x 358.6cm　東京国立博物館蔵　Kyujyo Standing Screens of Four Elegant Pastimes, Important cultural property, Kaihō Yūshō, 16th to 17th century, Pair of six-fold screens, Ink painting and colors on paper, 154.0 x 358.6cm each, Tōkyō National Museum ●琴棋（囲碁）書画は、中国で士大夫の身につけるべきものとされた琴と碁、書と画の四芸のことで、日本でも室町時代以後、掛け物や襖絵、屏風絵などの題材として盛んに描かれた。普通は男性が描かれるが、ここでは中国の官女の姿に換え色鮮やかな衣を着たたくさんの女性が描かれているところがこの作品のユニークさである。着色と水墨の並置も独特で、桃山絵画を代表する友松の魅力あふれる傑作である。友松は同時代に活躍した狩野永徳や山楽とは違い、武家の出身で本格的に絵画の制作を始めたのは60歳代と遅咲きであった。武士らしい勢いのある力強い線と丸みを帯びた岩や幹のかたちが特徴的に描かれている。

コラム［禅問答と禅画の世界］

39p「**南泉斬猫**」（「**禅宗祖師図**」襖十六面の内　部分）重文　伝長谷川等伯　慶長7年（1602）襖1面　紙本墨画　天授庵蔵 Nansen Cuts the Cat in Two, Important cultural property, Attributed to Hasegawa Tōhaku, 1602, One sliding door, Ink painting on paper, Tenju-an ●「南泉斬猫（なんせんざんみょう）」は禅宗の公案の一つで、中国の唐時代の禅僧南泉普願に関する話。ある時、東堂西堂の両堂で猫の仏性の有無を争ったところ、南泉はその猫の首をぶら下げて、剣を片手に、「皆の者、何とでも言ってみろ、言えればよし、言えなければこの首をぶった切るぞ」と問答した。しかし返答がなかったのでその猫を斬ったという故事である。

狩野元信

40・41p「**楼閣山水図屏風**」**伝狩野元信**　室町時代（16世紀）6曲1隻　紙本墨画淡彩　東京国立博物館蔵 Landscape with Pavilion, Attributed to Kanō Motonobu, 16th century, Single six-fold screen, Ink and light colors on paper, Tōkyō National Museum ●宝形造の屋根を持つ楼閣を画面の右に片寄せ、左方を広大な水景となしている。背景にはわずかに樹林と山並みが添えられているにすぎない。すっきりとまとめられた作品である。美しい水辺に臨む楼閣のなかには、山水画を描く主人たちの姿がある。人里離れた環境で文雅な生活を送るという、中国的な隠逸（いんいつ）への憧れをあらわしている。南宋の宮廷絵画様式に基づき、狩野派の二代目である元信の周辺で制作された。

42・43p「**囲碁観瀑図屏風**」**伝狩野元信**　室町時代（16世紀）6曲1双　紙本墨画淡彩　各162.0 x 347.5cm　東京国立博物館蔵 Standing Screens of Igo and Kanbaku, Attributed to Kanō Motonobu, 16th century, Pair of six-fold screens, Ink and light colors on paper, 162.0 x 347.5cm each, Tōkyō National Museum ●右側に碁（ご）を打つ人を、左側に滝とそれを眺める人を描く。いずれも中国知識人の文雅の集いを、南宋の宮廷絵画様式に倣っている。右側の屏風では、水辺の伸びやかな風景のなかで碁盤をはさんで向き合う人物、山仕事の帰りなのか大きな柴の束をかたわらに置き観戦している。左側の屏風は、雪が降り積もる山中の景色で、高い崖から流れ落ちる滝と、家の中からそれを眺める人物が描かれている。滝つぼのあたりは水煙けがぶっていて、ごうごうという音まで聞こえてきそうだ。画面左端の下には大きな笠をかぶり、雪仕度をした人物がお供をつれて歩いてくる様子が伺える。

44・45p「**禅宗祖師図**」**重文　伝狩野元信**　室町時代（16世紀）軸2幅　紙本墨画淡彩　各175.2 x 137.4cm　東京国立博物館蔵

Patriarchs of Zen Buddhism, Important cultural property, Attributed to Kanō Motonobu, 16th century, Pair of hanging scrolls, Ink and light colors on paper, 175.2 x 137.4 cm each, Tōkyō National Museum ●祖師図とは仏教の修行上の教師であり、模範とすべき先輩の姿を描いたもので、中国の唐時代に活躍した禅僧のエピソードが基になっている。画面右に描かれているのが「香厳撃竹（きょうげんげきちく）」というエピソードの祖師図。このエピソードは、禅僧である香厳智閑（ちかん）がなかなか悟りきれず、墓守として生活をしていた時、箒（ほうき）で掃いた小石が竹に当った音を聞き悟りを得たというもの。この場面は、香厳がその音を聞いた瞬間を捉えたものであろう。ひっそりとした山間に佇む香厳とその奥に広がる山々は空間の奥行きを感じさせる。本図はもと大仙院の衣鉢の間の障壁画で、禅宗祖師図 (現在は全六幅) の一部である。

狩野永徳

46・47p「許由巣父図」重文　狩野永徳　安土桃山時代（16 世紀）軸 2 幅　紙本墨画　各 124.2 x 25.4cm 東京国立博物館蔵　Xuyou Washing His Ears and Chaofa with His Ox, Important cultural property, Kanō Eitoku, 16th century, Pair of hanging scrolls, Ink painting on paper, 124.2 x 25.4 cm each, Tōkyō National Museum ●右が許由（きょゆう）で、左が巣父（そうほ）の図。「許由巣父」の故事は、聖天子と仰がれた堯（ぎょう）帝が、許由の高士であることを聞いて天下を譲ろうと言うと、許由は、汚れたことを聞いたとして、潁水（えいすい）で耳を洗い、箕山（きざん）に隠れた。また巣父も、堯から天下を譲られようとして拒絶した高士であったが、耳を洗っている許由を見て、そのような汚れた水は牛にも飲ませることができないと言って、引いていた牛を連れて帰ったという。栄貴を忌み嫌うことのたとえである。

48・49p「松に叭叭鳥・柳に白鷺図屏風」狩野永徳　室町 ～ 安土桃山時代（16 世紀）6 曲 1 双　紙本墨画　各 160.5 x 351.0cm　九州国立博物館蔵　Standing Screens of Crested Myna on a Pine Tree and White Egret on a Willow Tree, Kanō Eitoku, 16th century, Pair of six-fold screens, Ink painting on paper, 160.5 x 351.0 cm each, Kyushu National Museum ●右隻には流れ落ちる渓流に松の巨木がしっかりと根を張り、その根元の土坡（どは）や岩上に叭叭鳥（ははちょう）たちが羽を休めている。池面に流れ落ちる水量から激しい水音が聞こえてくるようだ。左隻に目を移せばそこは静寂の世界である。柳の古木が枝を広げ、その幹と岸辺には白鷺たちが集まり鳴きあっている。空中には三羽の白鷺が岸辺を目指して舞い降りてきた。叭叭鳥の羽の黒と白鷺の羽の白、そして水流の動と静などの対比が画面構成にリズムを生み出し、装飾効果を高めている。永徳は作画活動の大半を金碧障壁画の制作に費やしたと思われるが、水墨による襖絵や大作の屏風絵も遺している。

雲谷等顔

50・51p「山水図屏風」重文　雲谷等顔　安土桃山 ～ 江戸時代（16~17 世紀）6 曲 1 双　紙本墨画淡彩　各 151.1 x 359.0cm　東京国立博物館蔵　Standing Screens of Landscape, Important cultural property, Unkoku Tōgan, 16th to 17th century, Pair of six-fold screens, Ink and light colors on paper, 151.1 x 359.0 cm each, Tōkyō National Museum ●右隻に冬、左隻に夏の景色を描いた山水図屏風である。こうした山水画では近景にある大きなモチーフを左右の端に寄せて描き、真ん中の空間をあけて遠近を強調するものが多いが、ここでは切り立った山を屏風の端に寄せず中央寄りに描くという大胆な構図がとられている。山や岩にみられる強い筆のタッチや、岩山や人家、舟などのモチーフの選び方にも雪舟の影響が見られるが、整然とした画面構成や温和で静謐な情景は等顔の特色がよくあらわれている。等顔は安芸広島城主毛利輝元に召し抱えられ御用絵師となり、輝元の命で雪舟筆「山水長巻」を模写、雪舟ゆかりの雲谷庵とこの山水長巻とが彼にゆだねられた。

52・53p「山水図屏風」雲谷等顔　安土桃山 ～ 江戸時代（16~17 世紀）6 曲 1 双　紙本墨画　各 153.5 x 342.8cm 東京国立博物館蔵 Standing Screens of Landscape, Unkoku Tōgan, 16th to 17th century, Pair of six-fold screens, Ink painting on paper, 153.5 x 342.8 cm each, Tōkyō National Museum ●本図も琴棋書画図のような世俗をはなれた清閑なところで、琴や棋を楽しむ文人の理想郷的な生活を彷彿とさせる情景を描いている。山や岩の直角三角形のかたちが反復して歯切れよいリズムを刻み、端正な画面をつくっている。生い茂る松樹のもとに舟をつけ、舟遊びや探梅を楽しむ人々の豊かな感性も描き出している。等顔は狩野永徳や山楽、長谷川等伯、海北友松とならぶ桃山画壇の巨匠で、毛利輝元に仕えて雪舟流を標榜した。江戸時代を通じて、その画系は中国地方から北九州の画壇に大きな影響力をもった。

本阿弥光悦

54・55p「蓮下絵和歌巻断簡」本阿弥光悦　江戸時代（17 世紀）1 巻　紙本墨書　東京国立博物館蔵　Fragment of a Lotus-illustrated *Waka* Scroll, Hon'ami Kōetsu, 17th century, 1 volume, Ink painting on paper, Tōkyō National Museum ●たっぷりとした筆使いで豊麗な白蓮の姿を描き、銀泥の濃淡によって花弁の厚みから鋭い先端の質感までを巧みに捉えている。もとは、色替わり料紙に百人一首の和歌を散らした巻子本で、蓮葉だけの描写からはじまり、蕾から満開に至り、やがて散っていく蓮の短い一生が写されていた。金銀泥を用いて大胆に描かれた蓮の下絵は、古くから俵屋宗達の筆といわれており、独特のたらし込みの手法が見られる。その上に光悦が『百人一首』の和歌を散らし、「前大僧正　慈円　おほけなく　浮世の民に　おほふかな　我立袖に黒染の袖」と書き記してある。その書は下絵と見事な調和を醸し出している。

56・57p「摺下絵和歌巻」本阿弥光悦　江戸時代（17 世紀）1 巻　彩箋墨書　34.1 x 1405.6cm 東京国立博物館蔵　Poem Anthology *Waka* Scroll Over Printed Design, Hon'ami Kōetsu, 17th century, 1 volume, Ink painting on colors on paper, 34.1 x 1405.6cm, Tōkyō National Museum ●光悦和歌巻の料紙には、肉筆の金銀泥下絵のほかに、木版による金銀泥摺絵を用いた作品も見られる。種々の花鳥の図様を長い巻物の画面に展開させ、光悦流の和歌を書き連ねたもので、大胆な画面構成や複雑な版木の使用法、図様の絵画表現などの特徴から、これらの版画制作にも宗達が関与したと考えられている。

57p「歌仙　凡河内躬恒」本阿弥光悦　江戸時代（17 世紀）軸 1 幅　紙本着色　27.1 x 20.5cm 黎明教会資料研修館蔵　*Kasen: Ōshikōchi no Mitsune*, Hon'ami Kōetsu. 17th century, Hanging screen, Colors on paper, 27.1 x 20.5cm, Reimei Art Gallery ●凡河内躬恒（おおしこうちのみつね）は平安時代の歌人。延喜 5 年（905）には、紀貫之や紀友則、壬生忠岑（みぶのただみね）と共に『古今和歌集』の撰者となり、同集には紀貫之につぐ六十首の歌がはいっている。三十六歌仙のひとりに数えられ、宮廷歌人としての名声は高い。

宮本武蔵

58p「周茂叔図」宮本武蔵　江戸時代（17 世紀前期）軸 1 幅　紙本墨画　94.5 x 42.0cm 岡山県立美術館蔵　Zhou Maoshu, Miyamoto Musashi, Early 17th century, Hanging scroll, Ink on paper, 94.5 x 42.0cm, Okayama Prefectural Museum of Art ●周茂叔（しゅうもしゅく）は蓮を愛した中国北宋の儒学者。周敦頤（あざなは茂叔）の故事を描いたもの。東洋画の画題である「四愛図」として知られていて、東晋（とうしん）の陶淵明（とうえんめい）の愛菊、北宋の周敦頤の愛蓮、林逋（りんぽ）の愛梅、黄庭堅（こうていけん）の愛蘭をいう。わが国では室町時代になってから障壁画に描かれるようになった。林羅山の賛が記されており、武蔵と当時の文化人との交際の一端が知られることは興味深い。

58p「**茄子図**」宮本武蔵　江戸時代（17世紀）軸 1 幅　紙本墨画 20.8 x 33.7cm　岡山県立美術館蔵　Eggplant, Miyamoto Musashi, 17th century, Hanging scroll, Ink on paper, 20.8 x 33.7cm, Okayama Prefectural Museum of Art ◉何気なく描かれたような一枝の茄子であるが、そのひしゃげた茄子のユーモラスな存在のなかに、一種の気迫と禅味がただよう作品である。武蔵の直接の画業の師は明らかではないが、南宋の梁楷や桃山時代の海北友松らの影響がうかがわれる。作品は減筆体の鋭い筆致で描いた人物や禽鳥の水墨画が多く、本図のような蔬菜（そさい）図は珍しい。

59p「**布袋観闘鶏図**」宮本武蔵　江戸時代（17世紀前期）軸 1 幅 紙本墨画　71.3 x 32.2cm　福岡市美術館蔵（松永コレクション）画像提供：福岡市美術館 / DNPartcom/ 撮影：山﨑信一　Priest Budai watching Cockfight, Miyamoto Musashi, Early 17th century, Hanging scroll, Ink on paper, 71.3 x 32.2cm, Fukuoka Art Museum/Matsunaga Collection ◉大きな袋を肩にかけ、杖に体を預けながら闘鶏に見入っている。いままさに飛びかかろうと睨み合っている二羽の鶏をただ悠然と見下ろしている。厳しい現実を見据えながら、布袋の表情から優しい笑いが洩れている。この作品の旧蔵者であった茶人の松永耳庵（じあん）は「布袋という絶対者が、争いの絶えない世間を見つめている」と喝破（かっぱ）した。

コラム［武士が描いた水墨画］

61p「**布袋竹雀枯木翡翠図**」宮本武蔵　江戸時代（17世紀）軸 3 幅　紙本墨画　各 111.1 x 37.9cm　岡山県立美術館蔵　Hotei, Sparrow on Bamboo and Kingfisher on Withered Branch, Miyamoto Musashi, 17th century, Three hanging scrolls, Ink on paper, 111.1 x 37.9cm each, Okayama Prefectural Museum ◉三幅対の軸もので、布袋図を中央に、左に翡翠（かわせみ）、右に竹雀が描かれている。岸辺の枯木に止まり、じっと水面を凝視する翡翠の姿。風に揺れる細竹に身をあずけながら岸辺の虫に狙いを定める雀が一羽。余白を充分に生かした空間に描かれた小禽たちの精神性までもが読み取れる作品である。武蔵の描く鳥禽には、小禽の一瞬の動態がみごとに捉えられ、親しみ深い雀や鳩などが多く、いずれも実に生き生きと描かれている。瞬時における的確な対象把握と、迅速な行動が要求される剣の道を極めた武蔵の眼力をもってして、はじめて描き出される世界がここにある。

狩野山雪

62・63p「**双龍図**」狩野山雪　江戸時代（17世紀）軸 2 幅　紙本墨画　各 115.1 x 51.2cm　東京国立博物館蔵　Twin Dragons, Kanō Sansetsu, 17th century,Pair of hanging scrolls, Ink on paper, 115.1 x 51.2 cm each, Tōkyō National Museum ◉昇龍（しょうりゅう）と降龍（こうりゅう）が渦巻く雲中で対峙（たいじ）する姿をとらえている。渦巻状に旋回する風、滞留する雲など大気の変化が絶妙な墨の濃淡によってあらわされ、動と静の対比が劇的な効果をあげている。山雪は狩野山楽を継ぐ京狩野第二代目で、山楽の装飾的画風を受け継ぎつつも、同時代の狩野探幽の優美さとは対照的に、理知的で明快な画面構成に独自の造形性を示した。

64p「**雪中騎驢図**」狩野山雪　寛永（1624～43）後期～正保期（1644～47）頃　軸 1 幅　紙本墨画　155.6 x 47.1cm　千葉市美術館蔵　Riding on Donkey's Back in Snow, Kanō Sansetsu, ca.1624-47, Hanging scroll, Ink on paper, 155.6 x 47.1cm, Chiba City Museum of Art ◉大きな笠をかぶり大きなマントを着て、驢馬（ろば）に跨ったうしろ姿の人物は、山雪の画にしばしば登場する、山雪の好む造形の登場人物のひとつになっていたようである。手慣れた筆により、数筆で、笠、マント、驢馬のかたちを見事にとらえて描き出している。雪山とそれを眺める人物のみで構成された画面には、驢馬の足が雪に埋もれたさまを描き、その周囲にわずかに淡墨と点描をほどこすことで積雪の厚みをあらわし得ている

のには驚く。また左上に中墨と濃墨で山の地肌をあらわすことにより山の実在を示しながら、その黒との対比によって雪を輝かせ、重なる雪山とそれを包み込む大気までも描きこんでいる。

64・65p「**猿猴図**」狩野山雪　江戸時代（17世紀）軸 1 幅　紙本墨画　107.1 x 42.7cm　東京国立博物館蔵　Monkey, Kanō Sansetsu, 17th century, Hanging scroll, Ink on paper, 107.1 x 42.7 cm, Tōkyō National Museum ◉柏の樹の枝に腰掛け、水に映る月をとろうとする手長猿。牧渓（もっけい）画をもとに多くの画家が手長猿を描いたが、この猿の微笑に向き合えば、思わず「かわいい」と叫びそうになる。これは「猿猴捉月（えんこうそくげつ）」すなわち、猿が水中に映った月を取ろうとして瀕死したという、仏教の摩訶僧祇律（まかそうぎりつ）の故事から描かれたもので、身のほどをわきまえず、能力以上の事を試みて失敗することのたとえであるが、そのような教訓はどうでもよいくらい猿の表情はとても愛くるしい。山雪は墨の和紙への浸透をコントロールし、滲みによって毛のふくらみを見事にあらわしている。

狩野探幽

66・67p「**波濤図**」狩野探幽　寛永末期（1642～44）6 曲 1 双　紙本墨画淡彩　各 151.0 x 339.6cm　島根県立美術館蔵　Waves, Kanō Tan'yū, ca.1642-44,Pair of six-fold screens, Ink and light colors on paper, 151.0 x 339.6 cm each, Shimane Art Museum ◉大画面に大きく余白とって波濤が渦巻く大海原を描き、左右に奇岩を配している。狩野派の筆法による岩や波の描写や簡潔な構図表現は、探幽画の特徴がよくあらわれている。後年の作品にはこの構図をもとに、いささか混みあった波濤を描き、鵜、鷗、鴨、鴛鴦を配した「波濤水禽図」（静嘉堂文庫美術館蔵）があり、画様の変容が窺える作品である。探幽の作品は、作風と落款の変遷から三期に分けられるが、この作品は 34 歳から 59 歳頃にかけて探幽斎と称した「斎書き時代」中頃の作と考えられる。

68・69p「**四季耕作図屏風**」狩野探幽　江戸時代（17世紀）6 曲 1 双　紙本墨画淡彩　各 159.8 x 352.8cm　東京国立博物館蔵　Agriculture in the Four Seasons, Kanō Tan'yū, 17th century, Pair of six-fold screens, Ink and light colors on paper, 159.8 x 352.8cm each, Tōkyō National Museum ◉稲の種まきから収穫までの農作業の様子が、季節の景観のなかに描かれている。こうしたモチーフはわが国に請来された伝梁楷（りょうかい）筆「耕織図巻」を参考にされたもので、そっくりそのまま、ないしは季節を反転させるかたちで引用されている。元信時代の狩野派はこの四季折々の農作業の情景を屏風にまとめた四季耕作図を頻繁に手懸けたことが知られている。徳川将軍家の御用絵師である探幽は、農業を立国の基本とする幕府の政策を絵画で体現しているのである。

70p「**鯉図**」狩野探幽　江戸時代（17世紀）軸 3 幅対　絹本淡彩　各 125.5 x 54.7cm　敦賀市博物館蔵　Carp, Kanō Tan'yū, 17th century,Three hanging scrolls, Light colors on silk, 125.5 x 54.7cm each, Tsuruga City Museum ◉三幅対の軸もので、掲載されていないが中軸は白衣の観音が岩座に坐す姿を描いたもの。左右幅には、瀧を登る鯉と落下する鯉がそれぞれに描かれている。これは中国の龍門という急流を鯉が登りきることができると龍に変化するという登龍門の故事に由来する。

71p「**鸕鷀草葺不合尊降誕図**」狩野探幽　江戸時代（17世紀）軸 1 幅　紙本淡彩　101.2 x 31.8cm　東京国立博物館蔵　The Birth of *Ugayafukiaezu no Mikoto* , Kanō Tan'yū, 17th century, Hanging scroll, Ink and light colors on paper, 101.2 x 31.8cm, Tōkyō National Museum ◉画面の大きく広がって描かれた波打ち際に、赤ん坊が横たわっている。そして粗末な小屋の前には男が立っている。この場面は、海の神の娘である豊玉姫（とよたまびめ）が、産屋に鵜の羽を葺（ふ）き終らないうちに産気づき出産。その時、夫である彦火火出見尊（ひこほほでみのみこと）に、本来の姿である八尋和邇（やひろわに）の姿をみられた姫は、赤

子を残して海に帰ってしまった。八尋和邇は巨大な鰐とも鮫ともいわれている。神話の時空を、長い波打ち際に示すその劇的な手法は見事である。

久隅守景

72・73p「納涼図屏風」国宝　久隅守景　江戸時代(17世紀) 2曲1隻　紙本墨画淡彩　149.1 x 165.0cm　東京国立博物館蔵　*Nōryōzu (A Peasant Family Beneath a Hanging Gourd Trellis)*, National treasure, Kusumi Morikage, 17th century, Single two-fold screen, Ink and light colors on paper, 149.1 x 165.0cm, Tōkyō National Museum ●大きな白い満月が朧（おぼろ）げにあたりの闇をも引き込んだ夏の夕暮れ時、地べたに筵（むしろ）を敷いて寝ころべばひんやりと居心地がよく、知らぬ間に一日の疲れも癒される。夕顔棚の風景と柔らかい白黒の対比が醸し出す情景がいかにも清新な趣である。月、夕顔、男、女、子ども、屋根、壁と、どれも異なる筆使いでありながら一つに溶けあうように優しく響きあうのは、夕闇を意識して描かれた淡墨が基調となっているからなのだろう。この絵ほど夏の夕暮れの一刻を情趣豊かに謳いあげた絵はほかにない。

74・75p「許由巣父図屏風」久隅守景　江戸時代（17世紀）2曲1隻　紙本墨画淡彩　153.3 x 168.8cm　東京国立博物館蔵　*Xuyou Washing His Ears and Chaofa with His Ox*, Kusumi Morikage, 17th century, Single two-fold screen, Ink and light colors on paper, 153.3 x 168.8cm, Tōkyō National Museum ●「許由巣父」は、許由が潁水（えいすい）で耳のけがれを洗い落としているのを見た巣父が、そのような汚れた水は牛にも飲ませられないとして牛を連れて帰ったという、中国古代の故事を描いている。屏風の中央には大きな瀧が滔々と流れ落ち、二人の人物と牛が右側に、左側には余白が取られている。手前の岩の朴訥（ぼくとつ）とした筆遣いは守景の特徴である。守景は狩野派の探幽の弟子で、探幽の姪の国（くに）と結婚をするなど期待された。しかし、子どもたちの起こした不祥事から探幽の元を去ったと考えられている。安定した地位や家族を失った後も多くの作品を描き、晩年は金沢に滞在していたことが知られている。

俵屋宗達

76・77p「関屋図屏風」重文　俵屋宗達・烏丸光弘　江戸時代（17世紀）6曲1隻　紙本金地着色　95.5 x 273.0cm　東京国立博物館蔵　*Standing Screens of the Tale of Genji: Sekiya*, Important cultural property, Tawaraya Sōtatsu, praised by Karasuma Mitsuhiro, 17th century, Single six-fold screen, Ink and gold foil on paper, 95.5 x 273.0 cm, Tōkyō National Museum ●光源氏が石山寺詣の途中、逢坂（おうさか）の関でかつての愛人空蝉（うつせみ）の一行と出会う場面で、往時をしのぶ「関屋」帖とわかる。絵は背景を一切省いた金地に、源氏らに道を譲るために牛車を止めて待つ空蝉の一行のみを描く。さまざまな姿態に描かれる従者たちは、先行するやまと絵作品から図様を転用していることが指摘されている。図上に烏丸光広が「関屋」の一節と自詠の和歌を書きつけている。

78・79p「蓮池水禽図」国宝　俵屋宗達　江戸時代（17世紀）軸1幅　紙本墨画　119.0 x 48.3cm　京都国立博物館蔵　*Water Birds in Lotus Pond*, National treasure, Tawaraya Sōtatsu, 17th century, Hanging scroll, Ink on paper, 119.0 x 48.3cm, Kyoto National Museum ●静かな水面には二羽の鳰（かいつぶり）が泳ぎ、しっとりと湿気を含んだ白い蓮の花が匂うように咲き誇る。花弁を縁取る描線はふっくらとして柔らかい。葉の表と裏を描き分ける墨面の処理、水中から出てきた水禽の濡れた頭の毛の表現は絶妙である。次なる餌を求めて小波をたてる一羽と、静かに足を休める一羽という対照の妙を、柔らかい筆づかいときらめくような墨色をもって描き得ている。南宋時代の頃から愛好された伝統画題を宗達独特の穏やかで潤いのある筆で描き、日本的な水墨画を完成させている。宗達の水墨技法の極を示す作品といえよう。

79p「駒引図扇面」俵屋宗達　江戸時代（17世紀）軸1幅　紙本着色　19.5 x 53.0cm　黎明教会資料研修館蔵　*Fan painting of a Horse pulling*, Tawaraya Sōtatsu, 17th century, Hanging scroll, Ink and colors on paper, 19.5 x 53.0cm, Reimei Art Gallery ●「駒引」は平安時代、毎年4月に武徳殿で天皇が馬寮（めりょう）の馬を御覧になり、5月の騎射に備えた儀式のこと。前庭を通る馬を御覧になり、その後で楽舞の演奏、饗宴などが行なわれた。馬を曳く馬方やその様子を見る男たちの朗らかさから、その場の和やいだ様子が伝わってくる。馬の動きも細やかに捉えられ、それぞれの質感を見事に表現している。

尾形光琳

80・81p「竹梅図屏風」重文　尾形光琳　江戸時代（18世紀）2曲1隻　紙本金地墨画　65.2 x 181.0cm　東京国立博物館蔵　*Standing Screens of Bamboo plums*, Important cultural property, Ogata Kōrin, 18th century, Single two-fold screen, Ink and colors on gold ground on paper, 65.2 x 181.0cm, Tōkyō National Museum ●吉祥のモチーフである「松竹梅」のうち、金地画面の上に墨で竹と梅を描いている。竹は幅広の筆致でゆっくりと描き下し、節のところで筆を止め、濃墨で節部分の線を引いて質感を高めている。竹の幹は種々の太さで、かつ微妙に濃淡を変えて描かれている。余白のバランスも絶妙に配置されている。梅は速筆を走らせて簡略に描かれており、稲妻のように枝を鋭く屈曲させている。梅樹は竹林の後方にあるのがわかるが、竹の上下を絶妙に調節し、対照的な墨の表情を同一画面のなかで統合させているのである。光琳独自の視覚効果が発揮された水墨画の代表作といえよう。

82・83p「風神雷神図」重文　尾形光琳　江戸時代（18世紀）2曲1双　紙本金地着色　各164.5 x 182.4cm　東京国立博物館蔵　*Standing Screens of Wind and Thunder Gods*, Important cultural property, Ogata Kōrin, 18th century, Pair of two-fold screens, Colors on gold decorated paper, 164.5 x 182.4cm each, Tōkyō National Museum ●宗達が描いた「風神雷神図屏風」（京都・建仁寺蔵）を、尾形光琳が忠実にトレースした作である。右に風神、左に雷神が描かれた屏風が二枚組になっている。自然現象から起こる風や雷といった人間には抗えない大きな力を、神の姿を借りてユーモラスに描いている。宗達の風神雷神図との違いはいくつかある。二神はほぼ同じ大きさであるが、光琳版では画面は一回り大きく広げられ、宗達版で下界を見下ろしていた雷神の視線の向きが、光琳版では風神をまっすぐ見るように描かれている。風神と雷神は視線を交錯させ、まるで息を合わせて踊っているかのようである。光琳の特徴は、風神と雷神を一体として捉え、調和性を重視して描いている。この屏風の裏には酒井抱一の「夏秋草図屏風」が描かれている。

84p「布袋図」尾形光琳　江戸時代（18世紀）軸1幅　紙本墨画　31.8 x 58.6cm　黎明教会資料研修館蔵　*Budai*, Ogata Kōrin, 18th century, Hanging scroll, Ink on paper, 31.8 x 58.6 cm, Reimei Art Gallery ●江戸時代の画家は布袋を好んで描いたが、なかでも光琳は素敵な布袋図を数多く残している。布袋は中国の唐時代末の禅僧で、いつも半裸で太鼓腹を出して大きな袋を背負い、市中を歩いて喜捨（きしゃ）を求め、弥勒の化身ともいわれた。日本には室町時代からこの奇僧のことが知られるようになり、絵画や詩文に描かれるようになった。満面溢れるような笑みを浮かべる布袋さんの表情と、こちらに歩む姿をすばやい描線で軽やかに捉えている。

84p「寿老人図扇面」尾形光琳　江戸時代（18世紀）軸1幅　紙本墨画　19.0 x 43.3cm　黎明教会資料研修館蔵　*Fan-shaped paintings of Shou Laoren*, Ogata Kōrin, 18th century, Hanging scroll, Ink on paper, 19.0 x 43.3 cm, Reimei Art Gallery ●寿老人は長頭の老人で、鹿を伴い巻物をつけた杖（つえ）を携えるというのが定型の姿であるが、ここでは老樹の下に寿老人だけが簡略な筆致で描かれている。中国の道教に由来して福禄寿とともに南極星の化身とされる。日本には禅宗伝来後における水墨画の画題の一つとして移入された。

85p「雲龍図」尾形光琳　江戸時代（18 世紀）軸 1 幅　紙本墨画　112.5 x 47.0cm　黎明教会資料研修館蔵　Dragon and Clouds, Ogata Kōrin, 18th century, Hanging scroll, Ink on paper, 112.5 x 47.0 cm, Reimei Art Gallery ◉黒雲から龍が姿を現わす。墨は素地の白と溶け合って微妙な階調を作り、さらにたらし込みを加えることによって画面に厚みと生動感を与えている。「たらし込み」は墨の乾かぬうちに濃度の異なる墨を注してにじみやむらを意図的に作り出す技法で、宗達などが得意とした技法である。本図はこの技法を駆使し、黒々とした暗雲を外隈（そとぐま）風に用い、白い龍の巨体を浮き上がらせている。

白隠慧鶴

86・87p「大応・大燈・関山像」白隠慧鶴　江戸時代（18 世紀）軸 3 幅　紙本着色　大応国師像 123.3 x 53.5cm　大燈国師像 122.8 x 53.5cm　関山像 121.2 x 53.5cm　九州国立博物館蔵　Statue of Daio, Daito, Sekizan, Hakuin Ekaku, 18th century, Three hanging scrolls, Colors on paper, Statue of Daio Kokushi, 123.3 x 53.5cm, Statue of Daito Kokushi, 122.8 x 53.5cm, Statue of Sekizan, 121.2 x 53.5cm, Kyushu National Museum ◉大宰府の崇福寺の住持を長く務めた大応国師、その法を継いだ大燈国師、さらにその法を継いだ関山慧玄は、日本臨済宗草創期における鎌倉時代の重要な三禅僧である。白隠は臨済宗中興の祖に位置づけられる名禅僧で、江戸時代中期に活躍した。禅の教えを民衆に広めるべく、生命感あふれるユニークな禅画や書を数多く描き、国内はもとより海外からも注目されている。本図は、その白隠が自らにつながる臨済宗の法系の最も尊重すべき高僧を描いたもので、数少ない貴重な着色画である。柔らかな筆致や下書き線を隠さない大らかさが、独特の魅力を生んでいる。

88p「寿老人図」自賛　白隠慧鶴　江戸時代（18 世紀）軸 1 幅　紙本墨画　83.0 x 28.9cm　愛知県美術館蔵（木村定三コレクション）Shou Laoren, Hakuin Ekaku, 18th century, Hanging scroll, Ink on paper, 83.0 x 28.9cm, Aichi Prefectural Museum of Art/ Kimura Teizo Collection ◉笑みを浮かべた頭の長い寿老人が、頭の上に「壽」の大きな文字をのせている。また衣の袖の部分も、「老」の字をアレンジした隠し文字を描いているようである。なかなか乙な発想がユニークである。

88p「渡唐天神図」自賛　白隠慧鶴　江戸時代（18 世紀）軸 1 幅　紙本墨画　92.0 x 25.8cm　愛知県美術館蔵（木村定三コレクション）Tenjin Visiting China, Hakuin Ekaku, 18th century, Hanging scroll, Ink on paper, 92.0 x 25.8cm, Aichi Prefectural Museum of Art/ Kimura Teizo Collection ◉渡唐天神は、天神にまつられた菅原道真が渡唐し、室町時代に流行した中国の径山の無準師範（ぶしゅんしばん）に参禅したという説話によるもの。一般的には正面立像の頭部に幅巾を戴き、両手を拱手して道服を着て、一囊を腰に付けて一朵の梅花を袖間に持つ姿で描かれる。衣の文様など、細かく描き込む描写は白隠の絵のなかでは異色である。

仙厓義梵

89p「富嶽図」仙厓義梵　文政 7 年（1824）軸 1 幅　紙本墨画　37.5 x 56.1cm　東京国立博物館蔵　Mt. Fuji, Sengai Gibon, 1824, Hanging scroll, Ink on paper, 37.5 x 56.1 cm, Tōkyō National Museum ◉富嶽図とは、富士山を描いた絵のことで、画面の上には富士と城のような城郭が描かれ、江戸市中は簡略化されて屋根の姿が点在している。甲申（きのえさる）の元旦に日本橋から富嶽を描いたとあるから、文政 7 年（1824）の作とわかる。本図を描いた仙厓は、軽妙洒脱な水墨画をよくした。特有のユーモアに富んだ画風を確立し、世事を気にせず親しみやすく味わいがある禅画を描いた。晩年は博多の聖福寺の住職となり、幅広い学識で

弟子を育成し、博多の町人とも親しく交わった。布教活動の一環として人々の求めに応じて軽妙な禅画を数多く描いている。

90p「寒山拾得図」自賛　仙厓義梵　江戸時代（18 世紀後半 ~19 世紀前半）軸 1 幅　絹本墨画　107.9 x 33.9cm　愛知県美術館蔵（木村定三コレクション）Hanshan and Shide, Sengai Gibon, Latter half of the 18th century-first half of the 19th century, Hanging scroll, Ink and colors on silk, 107.9 x 33.9cm, Aichi Prefectural Museum of Art/ Kimura Teizo Collection ◉仙厓の絵はほとんどが紙に描かれるが、「寒山拾得図」は珍しく絹本に描かれている。拾得が墨を磨り、寒山が崖に詩を書き付ける伝統的な図柄によるが、本図では、寒山が拾得の上につま先立ちしてしまっている。

90p「姫御前図」仙厓義梵　江戸時代（18 世紀後半 ~19 世紀前半）軸 1 幅　紙本墨画　32.5 x 22.5cm　愛知県美術館蔵（木村定三コレクション）Princess, Sengai Gibon, Latter half of the 18th century-first half of the 19th century, Hanging scroll, Ink on paper, 32.5 x 22.5cm, Aichi Prefectural Museum of Art/ Kimura Teizo Collection ◉「姫御前図」は、熱心に寺に参詣する姫君を描いたもので、賛には「姫御前のねがいのほどをききわけて 南無妙法の蓮華開かむ」と墨書されている。

91p「滝図自画賛」仙厓義梵　文政 10 年（1827）軸 1 幅　紙本墨画　136.2 x 30.2cm　東京国立博物館蔵　Waterfall, Sengai Gibon, 1827, Hanging scroll, Ink on paper, 136.2 x 30.2cm, Tōkyō National Museum ◉この作品は晩年に故郷である美濃（みの）国の水で墨を磨り、胸中に浮かんだ滝を描き、自詠の和歌を書き添えたものである。書かれている賛は「散る玉を星とおもひぬ　白雲の中より瀧のながれ出れば　養老水を以て画出（かきいだ）す」。白い雲のような水煙をあげ、星のようにきらめく水しぶきをあげて滝が流れ出していると、養老の水をつかって描いたことが書き添えられ、描かれているのが養老の滝であることが暗示されている。岐阜県にある養老の滝は、その水が長生きをもたらす酒になったという伝説のある滝である。

91p「趙州狗子図」自賛　仙厓義梵　江戸時代（18 世紀後半 ~19 世紀前半）軸 1 幅　紙本墨画　94.3 x 30.8cm　愛知県美術館蔵（木村定三コレクション）Catechetical Question about Puppies, Sengai Gibon, Latter half of the 18th century-first half of the 19th century, Hanging scroll, Ink on paper, 94.3 x 30.8cm, Aichi Prefectural Museum of Art/ Kimura Teizo Collection ◉「趙州狗子（ちょうしゅうくし）」は禅の公案で、犬の仔に仏性があるかどうかと問われた中国唐時代の趙州和尚が、ないと答えたという故事による。犬に仏性があるかないかという質問を出し、有無にとらわれる心を破するのが目的の有名な公案の一つである。人物は丸みを帯びて描かれ、中央の趙州はまだ重々しいが、周りの僧は完全に戯画である。もちろん仔犬は、自分達をテーマに難しい禅問答が行われているとは露知らず、楽しげな様子である。

風外慧薫

92p「半身達磨図」自賛　風外慧薫　江戸時代（16 世紀後期 ~17 世紀）軸 1 幅　紙本墨画　68.0 x 28.8cm　愛知県美術館蔵（木村定三コレクション）Bodhidharma, Fūgai Ekun, Latter half of the 16th century-17th century, Hanging scroll, Ink on paper, 68.0 x 28.8cm, Aichi Prefectural Museum of Art/ Kimura Teizo Collection ◉首から肩にかけてたっぷりの墨を含んだ簡潔な筆さばきで、一気呵成に線を走らせている。おおらかな墨の線とその上に浮かぶ達磨の細やかな表情。緩急の筆の技がみごとに交わっている。

93p「芦葉達磨図」自賛　風外慧薫　江戸時代（16 世紀後期 ~17 世紀）軸 1 幅　紙本墨画　85.3 x 44.6cm　愛知県美術館蔵（木村定三コレクション）Bodhidharma on a Reed, Fūgai Ekun, Latter half of the 16thcentury-

17th century, Hanging scroll, Ink on paper, 85.3 x 44.6cm, Aichi Prefectural Museum of Art/ Kimura Teizo Collection ◉芦葉達磨は東洋画の画題のひとつで、禅宗の初祖である達磨が梁の武帝との問答の後、一枚の芦の葉に乗って揚子江を渡り魏に入ったという説話をもとにして描かれたものである。顔や足の部分は細かく描写する一方、衣は太く濃い墨線で粗く描いている。また達磨の衣を太い線で囲まれた白い面のようにあらわす表現は、雪舟の「慧可断臂図」に先例が見られる。禅宗絵画の伝統をよく踏まえた上で、衣の抽象的なかたちの面白さと癖のある賛の書体を呼応させ、風外の禅画の世界を作り上げている。

93p「指月布袋図」自賛　風外慧薫　江戸時代（16 世紀後期 ~17 世紀）軸 1 幅　紙本墨画　63.2 x 26.7cm　愛知県美術館蔵（木村定三コレクション）Bodai Pointing at the Moon, Fūgai Ekun, Latter half of the 16th century-17thcentury, Hanging scroll, Ink on paper, 63.2 x 26.7cm, Aichi Prefectural Museum of Art/ Kimura Teizo Collection ◉「指月布袋」は月を指さす布袋を画題とする禅画の総称で、禅の根本を説いた教訓の図である。月は円満な悟りの境地を指し示し、指は経典を象徴している。月が指の遥か彼方の天空にあるように、「不立文字」を説く禅の悟りは経典学習などでは容易に到達できず、厳しい修行を通して獲得するものであることを説いている。布袋が持つ大きな袋の抽象的なかたちが、画面全体に安らぎをあたえている。

コラム［禅僧が描いた水墨画］

95p「布袋図」白隠慧鶴　江戸時代（18 世紀）軸 1 幅　紙本墨画　42.3 x 57.7cm　愛知県美術館蔵（木村定三コレクション）Budai, Hakuin Ekaku, 18th century, Hanging scroll, Ink on paper, 42.3 x 57.7cm, Aichi Prefectural Museum of Art/ Kimura Teizo Collection ◉布袋の袋のなかに「壽」の字が入り、それに合わせて印も寝かせて捺しているのが面白い。「壽」の入った袋の口を持ち、力一杯吹き込んで袋を膨らませようとする、布袋のうれしそうな姿がユニークである。

大津絵

96p「大津絵 猫とねずみ図」江戸時代　軸 1 幅　紙本墨画淡彩　33.7 x 23.3cm　大津市歴史博物館蔵　Ōtsu-e: Cat Drinking with Mouse, Edo period, Hanging scroll, Ink and colors on paper, 33.7 x 23.3cm, Otsu City Museum of History ◉自分の体ほどもある大きな盃で酒を飲むねずみに、猫が唐辛子をつまんで、さらに酒をすすめている。猫はねずみが酒に酔ったところを食べようと目論んでいる。これは酒を飲んでも酒に飲まれるなという教訓である。

97p「大津絵・為朝」江戸時代　軸 1 幅　紙本墨画淡彩　61.1 x 24.4cm　大津市歴史博物館蔵　Ōtsu-e: Tametomo, Edo period, Hanging scroll, Ink and colors on paper, 61.1 x 24.4cm, Otsu City Museum of History ◉源為朝（みなもとのためとも）は平安時代後期の武将で、為義の子。あまりの荒武者であったため父に九州へ追放され、ここで勢力をはり鎮西八郎と称した。勇猛さの象徴として、あるいは病魔退治の人物として描かれた。大津絵としては、疱瘡（ほうそう）（天然痘）除けとして人気があった。

97p「大津絵 鬼の念仏」江戸時代　軸 1 幅　紙本墨画淡彩　大津市歴史博物館蔵　Ōtsu-e: Goblin praying to Buddha, Edo period, Hanging scroll, Ink and colors on paper, Otsu City Museum of History ◉大津絵のシンボルともいえる画題で、恐ろしい形相の鬼が念仏を唱えながら布施を乞う姿が描かれる。その善と悪の相違の面白さが好評を博して人気画題となった。通常は胸に鉦（かね）を掛け、左手には奉加帳（ほうがちょう）、右手に撞木（しゅもく）を持ち、片方の角が折れている姿で描かれる。江戸時代の旅行ガイドブックであった「東海道名所図会」に描かれた大津絵の店では、この鬼の念仏を看板として掲げている。幕末の大津絵で

は、慈悲のない心にもかかわらず、形だけの善行を積む偽善の諷刺として扱われている。子供の夜泣き止めの護符ともされた。

曾我蕭白

98・99p「虎渓三笑図」曾我蕭白　安永期（1772~81）頃　軸 1 幅　紙本墨画　132.5 x 56.3cm　千葉市美術館蔵　The Three Laughters of Tiger Ravine, Soga Shōhaku, ca.1772-81, Hanging scroll, Ink on paper, 132.5 x 56.3cm, Chiba City Museum of Art ◉「虎渓三笑（こけいさんしょう）」は、中国画と室町時代後期以後の日本画との人物図の画題の一つで、中国、東晋の慧遠（えおん）は廬山に白蓮社の東林寺を開いて 30 余年も近くの虎渓橋から外に出なかった。ある時、訪ねてきた詩人の陶淵明、道士の陸修静を送りながら話に夢中になり、日頃渡るのを避けていた虎渓を過ぎてしまい、虎の声に初めて気がつき、三人で大笑いしたという伝説的逸話がある。儒仏道の三教一体をあらわす故事で、陶淵明は儒教、慧遠法師が仏教、陸修静が道教をあらわす。太筆で描いたような山容水態、塗り残しの白さを生かした岩肌や雲の描き方もみどころである。画風、印章から蕭白晩年の安永期の作品とみられる。

100・101p「群童遊戯図屏風」曾我蕭白　江戸時代（18 世紀）6 曲 1 双　紙本銀地着色　各 166.8 x 369.0cm　九州国立博物館蔵　Standing Screens of the Children at Playing, Soga Shōhaku, 18th century, Pair of six-fold screens, Colors on silver decorated paper, 166.8 x 369.0 cm each, Kyushu National Museum ◉珍しく銀地を背景にした六曲一双の大画面に、右隻では半裸の子どもたちが相撲に熱中し、柳の根本では牛が不安げな目つきでそれを眺めている。左隻では魚獲りに興じる子どもたちの自由奔放な姿が捉えられている。そのなかには亀を捉えた子から奪い取った者、その側では鰻を捉えた子がぬるぬるした獲物を逃すまいと必死の程である。そんな子どもたちに呆れ顔の女性二人が涼しげに様子を眺めている。本図は、近年まで秘蔵されていた幻の屏風絵である。

102・103p「林和靖図屏風」右隻　曾我蕭白　宝暦 10 年（1760）6 曲 1 双　紙本墨画淡彩　各 172.0 x 364.0cm　三重県立美術館蔵　The Recluse Lin Hejing with Cranes, Right, Soga Shōhaku, 1760, Pair of six-fold screens, Ink and color on paper, 172.0 x 364.0cm each, Mie Prefectural Art Museum ◉本図は、鶴と梅を愛し、西湖のほとり孤山に庵を結び隠遁（いんとん）した北宋の詩人林逋（りんぽ）（967~1028）を描いた屏風。名利を好まず、若いときから学問に励み、郷里杭州の西湖の孤山に廬を立てて住み、詩作を事とし、20 年間町に出ず、生涯独身で、梅を植え、鶴を飼って「梅妻鶴子」といわれる。理想の高士としてしばしば絵画化されたが、蕭白が描く林和靖（りんなせい）は、隠棲に嫌気がさしたのか、うつろな表情をかくそうともしない。梅の巨木は画面を突き抜け左隻に枝を伸ばし、その下で二羽の鶴が遊ぶ。大樹の表現は狩野永徳の「四季花鳥図襖」や彭城百川の「旧慈門院障壁画」に影響を受けたと指摘されている。

コラム［曾我蕭白の水墨画］

104・105p「群仙図屏風」重文　曾我蕭白　明和元年（1764）6 曲 1 双　紙本着色　各 172.0 x 378.0cm　文化庁蔵　Standing Screens of the Immortals, Important cultural property, Soga Shōhaku,1764, Pair of six-fold screens, Colors on paper, 172.0 x 378.0cm, each, Agency for Cultural Affairs ◉この屏風は京都の大名である京極家に伝わったといわれており、長寿や富貴のモティーフである、仙人、唐子、鶴や鯉などが描かれていることから、若君の誕生を祝った絵ではないかと推定されている。純度の高い高級な岩絵具をふんだんに使い、中国の道教にまつわる説話集『列仙伝』に出てくる仙人が描かれている。右隻には笙（しょう）を吹いている蕭史（しょうし）と龍に乗る青い衣の呂洞賓（りょどうひん）はわかるが、あとは何だかよくわからない混沌の世界である。左隻に描かれているのは子どもたちに囲まれ、そのうちの一人を抱きかかえて鶴

の前に立っているのが林和靖、水をはった大鉢に跳ねる鯉を手にする左
茲（さじ）、大きな白蝦蟇（がま）を背負い耳掃除をしてもらっている
のが劉海蟾（りゅうかいせん）、桃を眺めながら休んでいるのが西王母（せ
いおうぼ）である。モティーフとなっている鶴や亀、西王母は長寿を、
鯉は龍になるということから出世を象徴するなど縁起物として描かれた
ものと思われる。款記から蕭白 35 歳の作とわかる。

106・107p「**松梅孤鶴図**」**伊藤若冲**　江戸時代（18 世紀）軸 1 幅
紙本着色　136.5 x 60.9cm　東京国立博物館蔵　Pine, Plum and Solitary
Crane, Itō Jakuchū, 18th century, Hanging scroll, Colors on paper, 136.5 x
60.9 cm, Tōkyō National Museum ◉直立不動の鶴の姿は、逆さの卵から
まっすぐ足が生えているようなかたちの、不思議な見返り鶴である。鶴
の足元には毛の割れた筆先で勢いよくはらったように描いた特徴のある
松葉が描かれている。また樹皮は連なった蛸の吸盤のように描かれ、墨
に濃淡があり、淡い墨の上に濃い墨が重ねられている。鶴の足元からは、
ほっそりとした白梅が枝を伸ばし、黄色い蕊（しべ）の連なりがリズ
ミカルである。水墨を基調としているが、鶴の頭部に色彩が使われるな
どいいアクセントになっている。本図は、京都、大雲院に伝わる明時
代の「松上双鶴図　陳伯冲（じんはくちゅう）筆」を原図に用いるが、
極端なデフォルメを加えて斬新な作品に仕上げている。

108・109p「**松梅群鶏図屏風**」**伊藤若冲**　江戸時代（18 世紀）6 曲
1 双　紙本墨画淡彩　各 154.0 x 354.0cm　東京国立博物館蔵　Standing
Screens of the Pine, Plum Blossoms and Fowls, Itō Jakuchū, 18th century,
Pair of six-fold screens, Ink and colors on paper, 154.0 x 354.0 cm each,
Tōkyō National Museum ◉若冲は鶏の絵を得意とした画家で「動植綵絵
（どうしょくさいえ）」の群鶏図をはじめ多くの鶏図を描いている。本
図には、正面や後ろを向いたもの、雄々しく立つ姿や座る姿など、雌
雄の鶏と雛のさまざまな姿態が克明にとらえられている。特に雄鶏が尾
羽を振り上げた姿はユニークで愛らしさを感じさせる。また石燈籠は、
大小の無数の点描がほどこされ、御影石の表面が真に迫ってくるようで
ある。若冲の水墨画には軽妙でユーモラスな作品が多く、画箋紙に墨が
にじむ性質などを巧みに利用しており、こうした技法が生む表現効果に
は濃彩の作品に通じるマチエールの画家としての側面がうかがえる。

110p「**付喪神図**」**伊藤若冲**　江戸時代（18 世紀）軸 1 幅　紙本
墨画 129.2 x 27.9cm　福岡市博物館蔵　画像提供：福岡市博物館 /
DNPartcom *Tsukumo-gami*（Spirits of Used Items）, Itō Jakuchū, 18th
century, Hanging scroll, Ink on paper, 129.2 x 27.9cm, Fukuoka Municipal
Museum ◉薄暗い闇の空間にぼんやりと光があたった付喪神（つくもが
み）たち。前の方には茶釜や水指、茶碗など茶道具の妖怪がいならび
これから茶会でもやろうというのか。その後ろには燭台や鳥兜（とりか
ぶと）、鼓や琴、琵琶などの妖怪が続く。どの面々も恐ろしいというよ
りは愛らしく、ユーモラスである。「付喪神」は、器物が作られてから
百年を経過すると精霊が宿り、人に害を加えるという俗信からその精霊
のことをいう。毎年新年になると、古い道具類を路地に捨てる煤払いと
いう行事があるが、これは付喪神の災難に遭わないようにと行われるも
のである。

110p「**伏見人形図**」**伊藤若冲**　江戸時代（18 世紀後半）軸 1 幅
紙本着色　95.0 x 26.7cm　愛知県美術館蔵（木村定三コレクション）
Fushimi Dolls, Itō Jakuchū, Latter half of the 18th century, Hanging scroll,
Ink and colors on paper, 95.0 x 26.7cm, Aichi Prefectural Museum of Art/
Kimura Teizo Collection ◉縦長の画面に布袋が連なって行進しているよう
だ。ぽっちゃりとした表情のなんとも大らかな伏見人形の布袋さんであ
る。団子状態で描かれているが、前後の重なり具合を綿密に考え、リ
ズミカルに配置されている。若冲の描く伏見人形図には七体の布袋さん
が描かれることが多い。これは、初午（はつうま）の日に買い求めた

伏見人形は、その年に不幸にあえば河原で割り砕き、なければ毎年買い
足して、七体揃ったら無事を感謝して稲荷社に納めたことからきている。

110p「**雷神図**」**伊藤若冲**　宝暦 ～ 明和期（1751~72）頃　軸 1
幅　紙本墨画　110.0 x 30.0cm　千葉市美術館蔵　God of Thunder, Itō
Jakuchū, ca.1751-72, Hanging scroll, Ink on paper.110.0 x 30.0cm, Chiba
City Museum of Art ◉太鼓をしっかり掴んだ雷神が真っ逆さまに落ちて
行く。右手に太鼓、左手にバチを持ち、腕と足には輪をつけて、虎の
皮の褌をなびかせて筋骨隆々の脚が見えている。太鼓には雷をあらわす
三つ巴の模様が描かれる。この作品は大津絵の画題である「雷と太鼓」
で、空から落ちて波に浮かぶ太鼓を雷神が錨で釣り上げようとする図か
ら取ったのであろう。賛には「雲くらき　そらにふきくる風みえて　神
なりさはく　をともすさまし」とある。

111p「**六歌仙図**」**伊藤若冲**　寛政 3 年（1791）軸 1 幅　紙本墨
画 137.2 x 64.8cm　愛知県美術館蔵（木村定三コレクション）Six
Poetic Immortals, Itō Jakuchū, 1791, Hanging scroll, Ink on paper, 137.2
x 64.8cm, Aichi Prefectural Museum of Art/ Kimura Teizo Collection ◉『古
今和歌集』の序に論評された六人の歌人、つまり在原業平、僧正遍昭、
喜撰法師・大友黒主、文屋康秀、小野小町が、田楽を焼き、酒の肴に
している様子をユーモラスに描いた戯画である。78 歳の時に描いたと
記されるが、還暦後の若冲は改元のたびに一歳加算したとする説 (狩野
博幸『若冲』、紫紅社、1993 年) により、寛政 3 年（1791）の制作と
知られる。

111p「**雨龍図**」**伊藤若冲**　1760 年代前半　軸 1 幅　紙本墨画
130.5 x 53.0cm　秋田市立千秋美術館蔵　Rain Dragon, Itō Jakuchū,
Early 1760s, Hanging scroll, Ink on paper, 130.5 x 53.0 cm, Akita Senshu
Museum of Art ◉見たこともない龍の姿を墨一色でユーモアたっぷりと、
躍動感あふれる姿でとらえている。幅の狭い画面を巧みに利用し、画面
からはみ出た部分はどうなのかと、見るものの想像力を駆り立てる作品
である。龍は思いっきり口を開けて叫んでいるようで、下顎がはずれそ
うなほど力んでいる。そして黒眼は下を向いて開きすぎた口を見ている
ようだ。胴体の鱗は若冲の筋目描（すじめがき）の技術を駆使し、一
気に描き切っている。若冲得意の濃密な色彩の絵画とは異なる、より自
由な造形を見ることができる。

112・113p「**仙山観花図**」**円山応挙・高芙蓉賛**　安永 7 年（1778）
軸 1 幅　絹本着色　55.6 x 114.3cm　九州国立博物館蔵　Seeing the
Flowers in Hermit Mountains, Maruyama Ōkyo,Praised by Kofuyou, 1778,
Hanging scroll, Colors on silk, 55.6 x 114.3 cm, Kyushu National Museum
◉画面には滝や渓流、蛇行して流れ来る川、また近景を横断する幅広の
川といった具合に、様々な水の流れが描かれ、藍で彩られた水面には淡
墨で細やかに波を描き、浅深や緩急など水の変化がとらえられている。
写生を重視する応挙らしい表現である。この作品は、応挙 46 歳時の大
作で、賛には、池大雅の親友である高芙蓉（こうふよう）が、応挙の
亡くなる前月に書している。応挙の水の表現がいかに素晴らしいかが
切々と賛美されている。

114p「**雪中老松図**」**円山応挙**　明和 2 年（1765）軸 1 幅　紙本墨画
123.0 x 71.6cm　東京国立博物館蔵　Ancient Pine in the Snow, Maruyama
Ōkyo, 1765, Hanging scroll, Ink on paper, 123.0 x 71.6 cm, Tōkyō National
Museum ◉墨の濃淡によって松の幹と枝の立体感をみごとにとらえ、背
景に薄く金泥を刷（は）いて絹地の白さを生かし、枝上の雪を美しく
浮かび上がらせている。応挙の特質である平易な画風がよくあらわれた
作品である。当時の京都において、この画風で応挙は一世を風靡した。

115p「**双鶴図**」**円山応挙**　天明 6 年 (1786) 軸 1 幅　紙本淡彩　東京

国立博物館蔵　Cranes, Maruyama Ōkyo,1786, Hanging scroll, Light colors on paper, Tōkyō National Museum ●丹頂鶴と真鶴という二羽の組み合わせだけで、他のモチーフは一切描いていない。頭頂が赤く尾羽が白い丹頂鶴は、胸を膨らませて天に向かって鳴き声をあげ、羽が暗灰色の真鶴は頭をひねって正面を向く。この正面を向く真鶴は応挙の得意としたものでしばしば見受けるが、立体感を出す描写への応挙の自信が窺えるだろう。二羽の鶴を重ねるという難しい構図だが、破綻無くまとめているところに応挙の技巧の的確さを認めることができる。

116・117p「遊虎図」重文　円山応挙　天明 7 年（1787）襖 4 面　紙本墨画淡彩金砂子撒　各 182.5 x 139.0cm　金刀比羅宮蔵　Leisurely Tiger, Important cultural property, Maruyama Ōkyo, 1787, Four sliding doors, Ink,light colors and gold sand on decorated paper, 182.5 x 139.0 cm each, Kotohira-Gu ●金刀比羅宮表書院の「鶴の間」に続く「虎の間」は、三十畳の大広間に、東、北、西の方向に向かって絵画空間が作り出されている。実物大に近い虎が、眠ったり横たわったりと様々な肢体を見せてくれる。なかでもとくに「水飲みの虎」の描写は素晴らしく名高い作品である。広い座敷を虎たちがゆったりとたたずむ姿を見ていると、獰猛であるはずの虎に取り囲まれているのに、なぜか落ち着いた雰囲気が感じられる。

池大雅

118p「西湖図」池大雅　江戸時代 (18 世紀) 軸 1 幅　紙本墨画淡彩　94.3 x 19.5cm　東京国立博物館蔵　Landscape in the Xī hú, Ike no Taiga, 18th century, Ink and light color on paper, Hanging scroll, 94.3 x 19.5 cm, Tōkyō National Museum ●西湖は中国浙江省の杭州西部にある湖で、林和靖（りんなせい）ら文人ゆかりの湖である。日本においても漢画系の画家によってしばしば描かれている。縦長の画面には、本来は円環状に描かれる岩山や樹木が縦に点在している。大雅の造形力が描き出した情景のハーモニイが美しい作品である。

119p「春景山水図」池大雅　江戸時代 (18 世紀) 軸 1 幅　紙本墨画淡彩　130.6 x 33.0cm　東京国立博物館蔵　Spring Landscape, Ike no Taiga, 18th century, Hanging scroll, Ink and light colors on paper, 130.6 x 33.0 cm, Tōkyō National Museum ●穏やかな春の景色を描いた作品で、芽吹いたばかりの柳には彩色され、風に揺らいでいる。本図は、当時の画家たちが手本として活用していた中国明時代後期に出版された版本『八種画譜』を参考にして描かれたようである。実業家であり美術コレクターでもあった原富太郎（三溪）の旧蔵品である。

119p「酔李白図」池大雅　江戸時代 (18 世紀)　軸 1 幅　紙本墨画　118.8 x 40.3cm　東京国立博物館蔵　Drunken Li Bai, Ike no Taiga, 18th century, Hanging scroll, Ink on paper, 118.8 x 40.3 cm, Tōkyō National Museum ●酒好きの詩人として知られる李白を背後から支える童子たち。その姿を行列のように重ね描いている。款記によれば、冬の日にたまたま描き、大雅みずから杜甫の五言律詩「冬日有懐李白（とうじつにりはくをおもうあり）」を書き添えたという。李白は、中国、盛唐期の詩人で放浪の一生を送った。好んで酒や月、山を詠み、道教的幻想に富む作品を残している。玄宗と楊貴妃の牡丹の宴で、酔中に「清平調詞」三首を作った話は有名である。

120・121p「楼閣山水図屏風」国宝　池大雅　江戸時代 (18 世紀)　6 曲 1 双　紙本金地墨画着色　各 168.7 x 745.2cm　東京国立博物館蔵　Landscape with Pavilion, National treasure, Ike no Taiga, 18th century, Pair of six-fold screens, Ink and colors on gold paper, 168.7 x 745.2 cm each, Tōkyō National Museum ●中国の景勝地で景色のよいことで知られる場所を屏風の左右に描いている。右隻には、孟浩然（もうこうねん）、李白ゆかりの洞庭湖を眺望する岳陽楼、左隻には、欧陽修（おうようしゅう）が安徽省琅琊山（あんきしょうろうやさん）に建てた酔翁亭であ

る。大雅は清時代の中国で描かれた画帖のなかの二図を参考に描いているが、原図より建物や人物を大写しにして、群青や朱などの鮮やかな色で服を彩り、金地に輝く文人生活を映し出している。中国には行ったことのない大雅だが、憧れの世界を想像力で描ききっている。

122・123p「唐子遊図扇面・蘭図扇面」池大雅・池玉瀾　江戸時代 (18 世紀) 扇面 2 面　紙本墨画淡彩　紙本墨画　44.7 x 17.5cm/16.8 x 29.6cm 44.2 x 17.3cm,16.8 x 29.6cm　東京国立博物館蔵　Fan with Chinese Children Playing and Orchids, Ike no Taiga and Ike no Gyokuran, 18th century, Two fan panels, Ink and light colors on paper, Ink on paper, 44.7 x 17.5cm, 16.8 x 29.6cm, 44.2 x 17.3cm,16.8 x 29.6cm, Tōkyō National Museum ●簡略な筆墨による、山中で唐子が遊ぶ様子を淡彩で描いた池大雅の「唐子遊図」と池玉瀾の「蘭図」の扇面である。大雅堂五世定亮の長文の記された箱に一対で納められている。

123p「茄子糸瓜図賛」池大雅　江戸時代 (18 世紀)　軸 1 幅　絹本墨画　29.2 x 55.2cm　東京国立博物館蔵　Eggplant and Melon, Ike no Taiga, 18th century, Hanging scroll, Ink on silk, 29.2 x 55.2 cm, Tōkyō National Museum ●即席で筆を取って描かれたような茄子と糸瓜を墨でとらえ、端歌を添えている。賛には、「闇に窓うつ時雨も　よいわいな　独寝さめ　のさしきにゆかり　思へは茄子もよいわいな　色も一しほ小紫　霞樵墨戯」とある。

与謝蕪村

124p「富嶽列松図」重文　与謝蕪村　江戸時代（18 世紀後半）軸 1 幅　紙本墨画淡彩　29.6 x 138.0cm　愛知県美術館蔵（木村定三コレクション）Mt.Fuji Seen beyond Pine Trees, Yosa Buson, Important cultural property, Latter half of the 18th century, Hanging scroll, Ink and light on paper, 29.6 x 138.0cm, Aichi Prefectural Museum of Art/ Kimura Teizo Collection ●暗い背景に松林から真っ白な姿を覗かせる富士を描いている。墨の微妙な階調は、空間に満ちた湿潤な大気までも感じさせている。前景の松林は左右に広く横に伸び、左奥の淡く描かれた松林へと続いている。松の幹は力強い墨線で描かれ、整えられた構図と墨色を生かした描写には、文人画家としての蕪村独特の味わいがある。横長の本図は、「夜色楼台図」（国宝）、「峨眉露頂図巻」（重文）と合わせ、「三大横物」とよばれる蕪村晩年の代表作の一点である。

125p「薄に鹿図」与謝蕪村　江戸時代（18 世紀後半）軸 1 幅　絹本着色　129.0 x 60.0cm　愛知県美術館蔵（木村定三コレクション）Eulalias and Deer, Yosa Buson, Latter half of the 18th century, Hanging scroll, Ink and colors on silk, 129.0 x 60.0cm, Aichi Prefectural Museum of Art/ Kimura Teizo Collection ●生い茂る薄（すすき）のなかを歩む鹿を描く。少し不安げでお茶目な表情は、人の表情を思い出させる。蕪村は宝暦初年に京に上り、画業に専念して国内のさまざまな流派はもとより、中国諸家の作品や版本類を研究して自己の画風を形成していった。池大雅とならぶ文人画の大成者といわれた。

126・17p「山野行楽図屏風」重文　与謝蕪村　江戸時代（18 世紀）6 曲 1 双　紙本淡彩　各 155.1 x 388.0cm　東京国立博物館蔵　Standing Screens of the Old Scholar's Travels, Important cultural property, Yosa Buson, 18th century, century, Pair of six-fold screens, Light color on paper, 155.1 x 388.0 cm each, Tōkyō National Museum ●右隻に、まだ月の浮かぶ夜明け前の山野を馬に任せながら進む三人の旅人を描き、左隻には子どもの手を借りながら、清流を越え、急な山道を登り、遅々として進まぬ四人の老いた高士を描いている。風景や人物には墨に加えて透明感のある淡彩がほどこされ、風そよぐ清々しい空気が画面いっぱいに流れているようだ。中国風の主題を俳趣あふれる描写に置き換えた蕪村の代表作である。

128p「紫陽花にほととぎす図」与謝蕪村　江戸時代（18 世紀後半）軸 1 幅　紙本墨画淡彩　38.7 x 64.3cm　愛知県美術館蔵（木村定三コレクション）Eulalias and Deer, Yosa Buson, Latter half of the 18th century, Hanging scroll, Ink and light colors on paper, 38.7 x 64.3cm Aichi Prefectural Museum of Art/ Kimura Teizo Collection ◉鋭く啼き渡る杜鵑（ほととぎす）と、それを見上げるように紫陽花が大きく描かれる。たっぷりと墨をふくんだ筆で一気に描いた紫陽花の葉には、爽やかな藍色がほどこされている。飛びゆく杜鵑に、自画賛の「岩くらの　狂女戀せよ　ほととぎす」の句がそえられる。移り気な紫陽花の花が、描かれていない恋の情景を感じさせる。みずみずしい俳画の世界である。

128・129p「奥之細道図」重文　与謝蕪村　2 巻　各 29.2 x 31.0cm 京都国立博物館蔵　Oku no Hosomichi, Important cultural property, Yosa Buson, Two volumes, 29.2 x 31.0cm each, Kyoto National Museum ◉元禄 2 年 3 月、門人の曽良とともに江戸深川を出発。奥州、北陸の名所や旧跡を巡り、9 月に大垣に至るまでの俳諧紀行文である芭蕉の『奥の細道』の全文を与謝蕪村が書写し、これに合わせた絵を描いたもの。二人が行く先々で出会った人々の姿が、簡潔ながら実に生き生きと描かれている。蕪村独特のスタイルによる書と、軽妙な挿図の調和がこのうえなく魅力的な作品である。

129p「扇面画類聚」池大雅・与謝蕪村等　江戸時代（18 世紀）東京国立博物館蔵　Fan-shaped paintings Collaboration, Ike no Taiga, Yosa Buson, 18th century, Tōkyō National Museum ◉軽やかな筆さばきで梅の古木をみごとに描き出している。淡い薄墨のタッチが咲き始めた梅の花弁をリズミカルのとらえ、爽やかな気分にさせてくれる扇面である。

葛蛇玉

130・131p「鯉魚図」葛蛇玉　江戸時代（18 世紀）軸 3 幅　絹本着色　各 33.2 x 99.6cm　曹源寺蔵　Carps, Katsu Jyagyoku 18th century, Three hanging scrolls, Colors on paper, 33.2 x 99.6cm each, Sōgen-ji ◉三幅の軸には、風になびく柳の下を流れる早瀬に、頭をもたげた一尾の鯉が顔を見せ、瞬く間に竹の堰を飛び越えて空に舞う。そして最後は川面に張り詰めた氷を砕き宙に身体を翻すという物語のある構図である。鯉の躍動感がまるで映像のストップモーションを見るよう、生きるものの命を謳歌している。上田秋成の『雨月物語』の中にもその存在が伝説的に反映された葛蛇玉は、当時大坂の地では「鯉翁（りおう）」とよばれたほどの「鯉描きの名手」であった。

月僊

132p「寿老人図」月僊　制作年不詳　紙本淡彩　軸 1 幅　57.0 x 83.6cm　三重県立美術館蔵　Shou Laoren, Gessen, Hanging scroll, Light colors on silk, 57.0 x 83.6cm, Mie Prefectural Art Museum ◉動きの遅い亀の姿に何かを感じ取ったのであろうか、寿老人がじっと亀を見つめる。寿老人は中国の伝説中の人物で、宋代、元祐年間の人である。頭が長く白髪で、団扇と巻物をつけた杖を持ち、鹿や鶴を連れていたといわれる。長寿を授ける神様だから長寿の亀を登場させたようだ。

133p「人物と牛（曳牛人物図）」月僊　制作年不詳　軸 1 幅　絹本淡彩　105.0 x 32.8cm　三重県立美術館蔵　Men pulling a Calves, Gessen, Hanging scroll, Light colors on silk, 105.0 x 32.8cm, Mie Prefectural Art Museum ◉まだ成牛にならない子牛だろうか、なかなか動こうともしないので牛使いも慌てている様子だ。人物の描写も的確で、牛との動きのバランスが絶妙にとらえられている。上洛して知恩院門主の知遇を受け、円山応挙の影響を受けたせいか観察眼はすばらしい。月僊はさまざまな流派を取り込んだ鋭い筆法の作風で一家をなした。

133p「盲人図」月僊　軸 2 幅　東京国立博物館蔵　Blind Peoples,

Gessen, Two hanging scrolls, Tōkyō National Museum ◉余白を十分に取った軸に六人の盲人たちの歩く姿を描く。顔の表情は齢を重ねた老人の容姿で、穏やかな話し声が聞こえるようだ。月僊の作品は、擦筆によるゴツゴツした描線を多用しているため、人物画ではその卑俗な顔貌も相まってむしろ情趣に乏しい画面に陥りやすいようである。7 歳で仏門に入り、浄土宗の僧となる。のちに京都に上り、知恩院に住するようになった。知恩院には現在でも「百盲図巻」をはじめとする月僊画が数点遺存している。

浦上玉堂

134・135p「吾心与山楽図」浦上玉堂　軸 1 幅　紙本墨画淡彩　167.0 x 46.2cm　岡山県立博物館蔵　Goshin Yo Sanraku-Zu, Uragami Gyokudō, Hanging scroll, Ink and light colors on paper, 167.0 x 46.2cm, Okayama Prefectural Museum ◉黒々とした濃墨で描かれた樹々が左右に配され、画面を上に向かって駆け登るリズミカルな筆致がこの作品を特色づけている。中心をなす山頂の山が三つにも見え、二つの山が重なり透けているようでもある。山間の寺院のところどころの屋根に彩色された代赭と墨の強い対比が絶妙なバランスをとっている。筆の勢いがとまらないような玉堂の昂揚感が伝わる作品である。

136p「山紅於染図」重文　浦上玉堂　19 世紀初期　軸 1 幅　紙本着色　36.5 x 65.5cm　愛知県美術館蔵（木村定三コレクション）Mountains Dyed Red by Autumn Foliage, Important cultural property, Urakami Gyokudō, Early 19th century, Hanging scroll, Ink and colors on paper, 36.5 x 65.5 cm, Aichi Prefectural Museum of Art/ Kimura Teizo Collection ◉紅葉真っ盛りの風景を代赭や黄色の雌黄を加えて描いている。また墨線は渇筆と擦筆（さっぴつ）を用いており、濃墨との調和が絶妙で、白い紙の質感が生かされている。画面右下に描かれた高士の視点で、この秋の山を歩みたくなるような作品である。題名は「山は紅で染めたよりも紅い」という意味で、玉堂作品のなかでも、もっとも色彩あふれる一点ある。

137p「高下数家図」浦上玉堂　19 世紀初　軸 1 幅　紙本墨画　27.7 x 28.4cm　愛知県美術館蔵（木村定三コレクション）Several Houses, Urakami Gyokudō, Early 19th century, Hanging scroll, Ink on paper, 27.7 x 28.4 cm, Aichi Prefectural Museum of Art/ Kimura Teizo Collection ◉「高下数家図」の題名は、中国北宋時代の文人、王安石の桃源郷のような風景を詠った詩に由来している。本図にもまた理想郷のイメージが映し出されているといえよう。一幅の画面のなかに円形や矩形の界線を引き、複数の小さな独立した山水画を描くことは、晩年の玉堂がしばしば試みていたことである。

138p「野橋抱琴図」浦上玉堂　文化 11 年（1814）頃　軸 1 幅　28.8 x 30.5cm　岡山県立博物館蔵　Yakyo Houkin-Zu, Uragami Gyokudō, ca.1814, Hanging scroll, 28.8 x 30.5cm, Okayama Prefectural Museum ◉野にかけられた橋を、琴をたずさえた玉堂が行く。近景の濃墨の筆致と、遠景の薄く粗に描かれた山並みとの遠近感がみごとな風景である。玉堂の号は、35 歳の時に得た明の明人顧元昭の作になる「玉堂清韻」と銘をもつ七弦琴を入手したことによる。寛政 6 年（1794）50 歳の時、春琴と秋琴の二人の子どもをつれて脱藩。以後文化 8 年（1811）京都に居を定めるまで、琴をたずさえ東北から九州まで各地を遍歴した。

139p「春山欲雨図」浦上玉堂　江戸時代（19 世紀）軸 1 幅　紙本墨画　29.0 x 33.4cm　東京国立博物館蔵　Shunzan Yokuu-Zu, Uragami Gyokudō, 19th century, Hanging scroll, Ink on paper, 29.0 x 33.4cm, Tōkyō National Museum ◉「春山欲雨 玉堂」と画題を記し、これから降りはじめるであろう、春雨の潤いを待つ春山の情景を描く。60 歳代前半頃の作品と考えられ、息子である春琴による識語（しきご）が付属している。玉堂の特徴である横に長い米点（べいてん）を用い、リズミカルに山と樹葉を描いた独創的な作品である。

森狙仙

140・141p「秋山遊猿図」森狙仙　江戸時代（19 世紀）軸 2 幅　紙本着色　各 164.0 x 135.8cm　東京国立博物館蔵　Monkeys playing in the autumn mountains, Mori Sosen, 19th century, Two hanging scrolls, Colors on paper, 164.0 x 135.8cm each, Tōkyō National Museum ◉松の老樹が画面中央から左右にのび、背景の岩には猿たちが休んでいる。また岩陰には鹿たちが描かれ、秋を感じさせるモチーフである。岩を描くごつごつとした輪郭線のタッチは荒々しく、それとは対照的に、「狙仙の猿」といわれる通り猿や鹿たちの毛並みは細い描線で一本一本丁寧に描かれ、その柔らかさを十分にあらわしている。

142p「猿図」森狙仙　江戸時代（19 世紀）軸 1 幅　絹本着色　92.0 x 36.2cm　東京国立博物館蔵　Monkey, Mori Sosen, 19th century, Hanging scroll, Colors on silk, 92.0 x 36.2cm, Tōkyō National Museum ◉猿の親子が檜に登り、戯れる姿を描いている。小猿は親の肩にしがみつき、親猿は藤の蔓にぶら下りながら捕まえた虫を繁々と見つめている。もう一匹の子猿は遅れまいと、必死の形相で幹を駆け登る。狙仙が描いた猿の絵は大変人気があったので、今日でもたいへん多く残っている。毛並みを細かく描きかさねてふわりとした感触をあらわし、体躯や動きを巧みに捉え、立体感や臨場感を見事にあらわした作品が多い。

森徹山

143p「牛図屏風」森徹山　江戸時代（19 世紀）4 曲 1 隻　紙本銀地着色　164.8 x 70.3cm　東京国立博物館蔵　Standing Screens of the Cows, Mori Tetsuzan, 19th century, Pair of four-fold screens, Colors on silver decorated paper, 164.8 x 70.3cm, Tōkyō National Museum ◉銀地の屏風に、立ち姿の茶の牛と首をのばし寝そべる黒牛を描いている。画面いっぱいに描かれた牛はほぼ実物大のサイズであり、まるでそこにいるかのような不思議な感覚にとらわれる。顔のまわりの毛やしっぽ、脚など、よく見ると勢いを感じさせるかすれた筆づかいである。徹山は義理の父の森狙仙とともに円山応挙に学び、猿を得意とした狙仙の写生のたくみさと、円山派の写実的な描写の技術を身につけて対象をとらえている。

呉春（松村月渓）

144・145p「桃李園夜宴・西園題石図屏風」呉春　江戸時代 (18 世紀) 6 曲 1 双　紙本墨画淡彩　各 166.2 x 372.0cm　九州国立博物館蔵　Standing Screens of Tori-en Banquet, Sei-en Title Stone, Goshun, 18th century, Pair of six-fold screens, Ink and light colors on paper, 166.2 x 372.0 cm each, Kyushu National Museum ◉六曲の屏風には、右に唐の李白が催した花見の宴、左に宋の文人らが王詵（おうせん）の西園に会した「西園雅集」中、米芾（べいふつ）が岩壁に書を認める場面が描かれる。西園雅集は、友人を招いて開く宴会をいい、宋代に、蘇軾、黄庭堅、秦観、晁无咎（ちょうむきゅう）らの風流人が、しばしば西園に集まったという故事からきている。岩の配置や樹木の彩色のバランスが小気味よく、清々しい淡い藍や緑、代赭による彩色が華やかな雰囲気を醸し出す。人物や卓上の器物の細墨線による描写は実に丁寧に描かれる。

146・147p「山水図屏風」呉春　江戸時代 (18 世紀) 6 曲 1 双　絹本墨画淡彩　各 163.7 x 364.2cm　東京国立博物館蔵　Standing Screens of Landscape, Goshun, 18th century, Pair of six-fold screens, Ink and light colors on silk, 163.7 x 364.2cm each, Tōkyō National Museum ◉右隻に野良仕事を終えて家路につく親子らしき二人の農夫、左隻には、少し寒そうな景色のなかに滝が落ち、驢馬（ろば）に跨り旅する文人がいる。光沢のある滑らかな絹本（こうほん）というサテン地に描かれ、歯切れよい墨と透明感のある淡彩で彩色される。柔らかく澄んだ秋の爽やか

な空気と光をとらえている。蕪村に学んだ呉春の池田時代の傑作である。

長澤蘆雪

148p「双僊図」長澤蘆雪　江戸時代（18 世紀）軸 2 幅　紙本墨画淡彩　各 131.9 x 56.0cm　東京国立博物館蔵　Two-Hermit, Nagasawa Rosetsu, 18th century, Two hanging scrolls, Ink and light colors on paper, 131.9 x 56.0cm each, Tōkyō National Museum ◉僊は山中で修行をして不老不死の術を修めた仙人のこと。左には蝦蟇鉄拐図に鉄拐仙人とともに描かれる蝦蟇仙人、右には寒山拾得図でお馴染みの寒山である。蝦蟇仙人は肩の蝦蟇で妖術を使い、寒山はひたすら筆をとって書を認めている。これは中国の道釈人物画の画題としてよく知られる。やわらかい筆運びと水墨の美しい諧調は芦雪独自の作品に仕上がっている。

149p「眼下千丈図」長澤蘆雪　18 世紀後半　軸 1 幅　紙本墨画淡彩　99.7 x 28.6cm　愛知県美術館蔵（木村定三コレクション）Sheer Cliff, Nagasawa Rosetsu, Latter half the 18th century, Hanging scroll, Ink and light colors on paper, 99.7 x 28.6cm, Aichi Prefectural/ Kimura Teizo Collection ◉懸崖に佇む家屋から出て崖下を望む人物が認められる。なんとも殺風景な様子である。即興的な筆運びで崖を描き、濃墨で崖の先端の厚みをあらわし、あとは薄墨で山容をとらえている。座興として描いたものと想像される。崖下の隠れるような落款もユニークである。

150p「隻履達磨図」長沢蘆雪　天明 6 年（1786）頃　軸 1 幅　紙本墨画淡彩　134.8 x 56.0cm　豊橋市美術館蔵　Bodhidharma Holding a Shoe, Nagasawa Rosetsu, ca.1786, Hanging scroll, Ink and light colors on paper, 134.8 x 56.0 cm, Toyohashi City Museum of Art & History ◉隻履達磨（せきりだるま）は片方の履物をもった達磨のことで、禅宗祖師の達磨伝説のひとつである。衣に朱をさして達磨の朱衣とし、肉身にも朱をさしている。即興的に描かれたものと思われるが、しっかりとした墨線でとらえられている。画面上には「手携履一隻　怱々何處帰　祖師真面目　雲影向西飛　天明丙午初冬　斯経拝題印」と妙心寺直指庵住職であった斯経（しきょう）の題がある。

150・151p「呉美人図」長澤蘆雪　江戸時代（18 世紀）軸 1 幅　絹本着色　170.4 x 46.0cm　東京国立博物館蔵　Tang Beauties, Nagasawa Rosetsu, 18th century, Hanging scroll, Colors on silk, 170.4 x 46.0cm, Tōkyō National Museum ◉美人は松の幹に寄りかかり、巻子の文字に集中する。女性の口元は少しほころんでいる。顔にほのかに差された朱色、長いまつ毛やほつれ髪の描写は繊細で色香を放っている。華やかさはないが、切れ長の目は非常に可憐で奥ゆかしさが感じられる。目を凝らすと足元には蓮華草が咲き、春を感じさせている。芦雪の比較的早い時期の優品である。

酒井抱一

154p「寒山図」酒井抱一　江戸時代（19 世紀）軸 1 幅　紙本墨画　113.5 x 50.1cm　東京国立博物館蔵　Hanshan, Sakai Hōitsu, 19th century, Hanging scroll, Ink on paper, 113.5 x 50.1 cm, Tōkyō National Museum ◉思案気の表情で寒山が経典を広げて見入っている。着衣した袈裟は、袖口は太筆でゴツゴツと、衣の輪郭は細筆で素早く描きとめられている。簡略化された描写であるが、顔の表情は綿密に仕上げられている。寒山は中国の禅僧で、奇行で知られる。拾得とともに「寒山拾得図」として中国や日本では古くから描かれている画題である。

155p「正月飾り物図」酒井抱一俳賛　鈴木其一・鈴木蠣潭・大西椿年・山崎鯉隠・長橋文桂　文化 13 年（1816）軸 1 幅　紙本墨画　95.9 x 27.7cm　東京国立博物館蔵　New Year's decorative map, Sakai Hōitsu, 1816, Hanging scroll, Ink on paper, 95.9 x 27.7cm, Tōkyō National Museum ◉羽子板に供物を守る器、米俵に白鼠の玩具など、正月の飾

り物が描かれる。羽子板には竹と紅梅が描かれ、竹の枝は羽子板からはみ出している。賛は酒井抱一によるもので、子年の正月にあわせ、抱一とその仲間たちが集まり一緒に制作したことが想像される。

155p 「白梅に雀図」酒井抱一　江戸時代　軸1幅　絹本着色　97.5 x 32.6cm　敦賀市博物館蔵　White Plum and Sparrow, Sakai Hōitsu, Edo period, Hanging scroll, Colors on Silk, 97.5 x 32.6cm, Tsuruga Municipal Museum ●抱一は十二図を一組とした十二ヶ月花鳥図をいくつか描いているが、この白梅に雀図もその流れのものであろう。老木がのばした枝に清楚な花をつけた白梅、その枝の花に魅せられたつがいの雀が憩う姿が描かれる。余白を十分にとった本図は、瀟洒な趣と梅の馥郁とした香りを感じさせる作品である。

156・157p 「夏秋草花図屏風」重文　酒井抱一　江戸時代（19世紀）2曲1双　紙本銀地着色　各167.0 x 184.0cm　東京国立博物館蔵　Summer and Autumn Grasses, Important cultural property, Sakai Hōitsu,19th century, Pair of two-fold screens, Colors on silver decorated paper, 167.0 x 184.0 cm each, Tōkyō National Museum ●この屏風は、尾形光琳の「風神雷神図屏風」の裏にあとから描き加えたもので、抱一の光琳への敬慕が込められた作品である。月の光を思わせる銀地を背景にして、「雷神図」の裏には突然の驟雨に打たれた百合や昼顔などの夏草を描き、「風神図」の裏には葛や藤袴、薄や野葡萄といった秋草の姿が野分にふかれ靡いている。このように季節の草花を描くだけではなく、風立つ一瞬の情景を切り取る表現で、夏秋の季節感の対比をより際立たせている。

谷文晁

158・159p 「山水図屏風」谷文晁　江戸時代（19世紀）6曲1双　紙本着色　各159.4 x 338.5cm　栃木県立博物館蔵　Standing Screens of Landscape, Tani Bunchō, 19th century, Pair of six-fold screens, Colors on paper, 159.4 x 338.5 cm each, Tochigi Prefectural Museum ● 6曲1双の大画面には、中央に水をたたえた湖に舟を浮かべ、奥深い水辺の空間には霞がたなびき、背後には深い谷をいだいた高山がそびえている。きめのこまかい筆致と微妙に潤った墨、澄んで明るい淡彩が加えられ、静かな叙情が感じられる清爽な作品になっている。

160・161p 「八仙人図」谷文晁　文政8年（1825）軸3幅対　絹本着色　各124.2 x 49.6cm　福島県立博物館蔵　Eight Hermit, Tani Bunchō, 1825, Three hanging scrolls, Colors on silk, 124.2 x 49.6cm each, Fukushima Museum ●本図は漢の八仙人である、鍾離・張果老・韓湘子・李鐵拐・曹國舅・呂洞賓・藍采和・何仙姑の八人を描いたものであろう。右幅には、瓢をかつぐのは張果老、将軍姿の鍾離、ひきがえるを頭に載せるのが李鐵拐。中幅には呂洞賓・藍采和・韓湘子、左幅の貴人の姿は曹國舅、女性は何仙姑と想定されるが、いずれの仙人たちも特に奇矯な姿には描かれていない。細緻な描写と安定した構図、練達した筆法は仙人に人間らしさと品格を与えている。

田能村竹田

162p 「桃花流水図」重文　田能村竹田　天保3年（1832）軸1幅　紙本淡彩　114.0 x 31.0cm　大分市美術館蔵　The Stream of Peach and Flower, Important cultural property, Tanomura Chikuden,1832, Hanging scroll, Light colors on paper, 114.0 x 31.0 cm, Oita Art Museum ●画中の識語によると、中国の詩人李白から引用した二句「桃花流水沓然去　別有天地非人間」からイメージを受けて制作されたことが知られる。「桃花流水沓然去」は画面の下半分を、「別有天地非人間」によって上半分を描いたということである。竹田は李白の詩が気に入っており、世俗を離れた理想郷である桃源郷を描くことにより、その忘我の心境を本作品に表現したものである。

163p 「猿猴挂樹図」田能村竹田　文政後期頃　軸1幅　紙本墨画淡彩　143.0 x 38.9cm　大分県立美術館蔵　Monkeys, Hanging Down from Branchs, Tanomura Chikuden, Later Bunsei period, Hanging scroll, Ink and light colors on paper, 143.0 x 38.9cm, Oita Prefectural Art Museum ●縦長の画面に淡い墨でブラシのように描かれた樹木に、二頭の手長猿が楽しそうにぶら下がっている。手長猿の身体も簡略化されスポンジのような丸いかたちで描かれる。猿の顔は鼻口目が点のように小さく、近寄りよく見ないと判別できない。挂樹は楷樹といい、別称「ナンバンハゼ」ともよばれる。

163p 「風雨渡舟図」田能村竹田　文政12年（1829）軸1幅　紙本墨画淡彩　178.8 x 51.9cm　東京国立博物館蔵　Windy Ferry, Tanomura Chikuden, 1829, Hanging scroll, Ink and light color on paper, 178.8 x 51.9 cm, Tōkyō National Museum ●精緻な描写で山肌や樹木を描き、流れる川面には細やかな波頭が立つ。突然の風雨の激しさをあらわしている。竹田は同じようなテーマの作品を何点か描いているが、そのなかでも本図は大作で質が高い。画中の賛によると、文政12年(1829)2月、長崎において描いたことがわかり、竹田の動向を知るうえでも貴重な作品である。

164・165p 「高客聴琴図」田能村竹田　文政5年（1822）10曲1隻　紙本墨画淡彩　167.0 x 438.2cm　大分県立美術館蔵　Guests Listening to the Ch'in, Tanomura Chikuden, 1822, Single ten-fold screen, Ink and light colors on paper, 167.0 x 438.2cm,　Oita Prefectural Art Museum ●竹田の作品のなかでは珍しい屏風に描かれる。大画面をもてあますことなく構築的に描く。画面右には供を従えた男が向かう先で、三人の高士たちが語り合っている。背景に描かれた奇怪な岩の表現は、皴法（しゅんぽう）を使い分けるように描かれ、竹田の若々しい意欲が感じられる作品である。文政5年（1822）の杵築旅行の折に同地の森本甚右衛門のために描かれ、もとは四面の襖仕立てであった。

山本梅逸

166p 「嵐山春景図」山本梅逸　江戸時代（19世紀）軸1幅　絹本着色　32.7 x 50.7cm　愛知県美術館蔵（木村定三コレクション）Spring View of *Arashiyama*, Yamamoto Baiitsu, 19th century, Hanging scroll, Ink and colors on silk, 32.7 x 50.7cm,Aichi Prefectural Museum of Art/ Kimura Teizo Collection ●嵐山を流れる大堰川の両岸の山々には青々とした松が美しく点在し、渡月橋からの眺めも素晴らしいことであろう。実際にはこの真景図のような高い場所から嵐山を眺めるところがなく鳥瞰図として描かれている。梅逸はこの構図の作品を何点も描いており、人気の高い画題であったことがうかがわれる。

167p 「雪中鴨図」山本梅逸　江戸時代（19世紀）軸1幅　絹本着色　軸1幅　125.7 x 41.2cm　東京国立博物館蔵　The Ducks in the Snow, Yamamoto Baiitsu, 19th century, Hanging scroll, Colors on silk, 125.7 x 41.2cm, Tōkyō National Museum ●重い雪が降り積もった岸辺につがいの鴨が羽を休めている。すべてが雪の覆われているため水面の様子も定かではない。ただ木の枝に残った朱色の木の実が寒中のなかで暖かさを感じさせてくれている。

168・169p 「紅白梅図」山本梅逸　文政2年（1819）6曲1双　紙本銀地墨画　各163.3 x 344.0cm　島根県立美術館蔵　Red and White Plums, Yamamoto Baiitsu, 1819, Pair of six-fold screens, Colors on silver decorated paper, 163.3 x 344.0cm each, Shimane Art Museum ●銀箔地の大画面に、清香漂う紅白梅の妖艶な姿を浮かび上がらせている。銀箔の冴えた輝きが月光に照らされたようで、幻想的な夜を想い出させる。梅逸は若いころ、名古屋の富商である神谷天遊に連れられ、近隣の寺で王冕（おうべん）の「墨梅図」に接して感銘を受け、天遊より「梅逸」の号を与えられたと伝えられる。

170p「老松図」山本梅逸　江戸時代（19 世紀）軸 1 幅　絹本墨画 132.1 x 60.1cm　東京国立博物館蔵　Old Pine Tree, Yamamoto Baiitsu, 19th century, Hanging scroll, Ink on silk, 132.1 x 60.1cm, Tōkyō National Museum ●岸辺に立つ老松の樹形を、幹の荒々しい樹皮から先端の細やかな葉先まで、詳細に描き上げてみごとである。葉先は淡い墨をほどこして立体的にボリュームを出し、木の生命力を出している。

171p「倣董源山水図」山本梅逸　弘化元年（1844）軸 1 幅　紙本墨画 179.0 x 95.5cm　東京国立博物館蔵　Landscape in the Manner of Dong Yuan, Yamamoto Baiitsu, 1844, Hanging scroll, Ink on paper, 179.0 x 95.5cm, Tōkyō National Museum ●まことにどっしりとした山容はみごとで、前後に重なって描く山々の存在感は迫力満点である。渇筆（かっぴつ）と潤筆（じゅんぴつ）で描かれた山の量感表現など、充実の筆技をみせている。梅逸は尾張の文人画家で、京に上って名をなした。本図はその京都時代の作品で、得意の花鳥画にとどまらない優れた実力をみせている。

菅井梅関

172p「牡丹猫図」菅井梅関　江戸時代　軸 1 幅　絹本淡彩　101.1 x 32.9cm　東北歴史博物館蔵　Cats and Buttons, Sugai Baikan, Edo period, Hanging scroll, Light colors on silk, 101.1 x 32.9cm, Tohoku History Museum ●牡丹の新芽がまっすぐに伸び、その前に愛らしい猫がじっと座る。牡丹に猫は中国起源の画題であり、多くの場合、このモチーフは眠り猫で描かれる。梅関は 20 歳代以降、仙台から江戸、関西、長崎など巡って様々な流派の絵画を学んだ。そして長崎に来日中の清の画家、江稼圃（こうかほ）から本格的な文人画の指導を受けている。

173p「梅花小禽図」菅井梅関　江戸時代後期　軸 1 幅　絹本墨画 123.2 x 35.7cm　東北歴史博物館蔵　Bird on a Plum Flower, Sugai Baikan, Late Edo period, Hanging scroll, Ink on silk, 123.2 x 35.7cm, Tohoku History Museum ●画面いっぱいに枝をのばす梅樹の花がほころびはじめたようで、一羽の小禽が羽を休ませている。枝を描いた筆の運びと剛健な筆触はみごとなもので、生き生きとした生命感をとらえている。何気ない画題であるが、味わい深い作品である。

173p「龍図」菅井梅関　江戸時代後期　軸 1 幅　絹本墨画 89.2 x 36.2cm　東北歴史博物館蔵　Dragon, Sugai Baikan, Late Edo period, Hanging scroll, Ink on silk, 89.2 x 36.2cm, Tohoku History Museum ●龍は想像上の動物であるが、水に潜み、空を飛んで雲を起こし、雨をよぶ霊力があるとされる。五本の指のついた四本足の大蛇で、頭には二本の角があり、顔が長く耳を持ち、口のあたりに長いひげがある。本図の龍も雨をよぶため水中から空を目指して駆け登っている。暗雲からのぞく神々しい姿をとらえている。

渡辺崋山

174p「驟雨図扇面」渡辺崋山　江戸時代（19 世紀）額 1 面　紙本着色 16.3 x 46.5cm　東京藝術大学大学美術館蔵　画像提供：東京藝術大学／ DNPartcom　Fan with a Sudden Rain Shower, Watanabe Kazan, 19th century, One frame, Colors on paper, 16.3 x 46.5cm, The University Art Museum ●崋山ははじめ沈南蘋風の花鳥画を描いたが、のちに西洋画の技法を学び遠近法や陰影法をとり入れた作品を描き、従来の文人画から脱皮した独自の画風を確立した。扇面に描かれたこの作品には、幼少より培われた絵を速く描く技術と、写実性へのこだわりがあらわれている。

175p「鷹見泉石像」国宝　渡辺崋山　天保 8 年（1837）軸 1 幅　絹本着色 114.2 x 56.9cm　東京国立博物館蔵　Statue of *Takami Senseki*, National treasure, Watanabe Kazan, 1837, Hanging scroll, Colors on silk, 114.2 x 56.9 cm, Tōkyō National Museum ●眼光鋭く正面を見据えているのが、江戸時代後期の武士で洋学者の鷹見泉石（たかみせんせき）。崋山にとって蘭学の先輩というべき下総（しもうさ）古河藩家老である。本図は、藩主の使いとして寺院に参拝した折、泉石の正装した姿を崋山が描いた。あっさりとした線描と色彩のなかにも細やかな技術が駆使されており、人物の高い教養と強い意思が伝わってくる。

河鍋暁斎

176p「狸砧図」河鍋暁斎　江戸～明治時代　軸 1 幅　絹本着色 41.0 x 46.5cm　敦賀市博物館蔵　Raccoon *Kinuta-Zu*, Kawanabe Kyōsai, Edo to Meiji period, Hanging scroll, Colors on silk, 41.0 x 46.5 cm, Tsuruga City Museum ●満月が顔を出した野辺で、砧（きぬた）を打つ女性の姿が描かれる。常は農婦が作業をするが、本図は小袖を着た狸が美女に化けた姿で描かれた戯画である。砧を逆さに読むと狸（たぬき）であり、また小袖の文様に鳥獣を追い払う鳴子が描かれているのも暁斎ならではの趣向である。

177p「龍頭観音像」河鍋暁斎　明治時代（19 世紀）軸 1 幅　紙本墨画 354.0 x 199.9cm　東京国立博物館蔵　*Kannon (Avalokitesvara) Riding a Dragon*, Kawanabe Kyōsai, 19th century, Hanging scroll, Ink on paper, 354.0 x 199.9cm, Tōkyō National Museum ●観世音菩薩は人々の訴えを観じ、ただちにすくうという菩薩。三十三応化身（おうげしん）する観世音菩薩のうちの、龍に乗る龍頭観音を暁斎はしばしば描いている。とくに本図は、狩野派の画風が生かされた力強い筆線で描かれる。

178p「鬼碁打」河鍋暁斎　明治時代（19 世紀）軸 1 幅　絹本淡彩 128.7 x 55.1cm　東京国立博物館蔵　Goblins at Go game, Kawanabe Kyōsai, 19th century, Hanging scroll, Light colors on silk, 128.7 x 55.1cm, Tōkyō National Museum ●崖下で碁を楽しむ鬼たちを、剣片手に鍾馗が睨む。鍾馗は、疫鬼を退治する一種の神として中国でもわが国でも信仰された。ここでは碁を愉しんでいる鬼たちを邪魔する無学な奴として描かれる。碁は知識人の遊びであるから鍾馗もそうなるのである。

179p「太公望図」河鍋暁斎　明治時代（19 世紀）軸 1 幅　絹本墨画淡彩 191.0 x 83.5cm　板橋区立美術館蔵　Taigong Wang, Kawanabe Kyōsai, 19th century, Hanging scroll, Ink and light colors on silk, 191.0 x 83.5 cm, Itabashi Art Museum ●太公望（たいこうぼう）は釣り好きの人を指していう俗称であるが、本来は周の文王の師、呂尚（りょしょう）の称。周の文王が狩りに出て、釣りをしている呂尚にあい、これこそ太公（文王の父）が待ち望んでいた賢人であるとして太公望と称した。この作品では、気迫のこもった老人像に仕立て、のんびりと釣り糸を垂れるのではなく、水面下の世界を見つめる哲人として描かれる。太公望の姿をとらえた暁斎の筆さばきはみごとである。

180・181p「地獄極楽図」河鍋暁斎　明治時代（19 世紀）軸 1 幅　麻布着色 199.6 x 342.4cm　東京国立博物館蔵　Hell and Paradise, Kawanabe Kyōsai, 19th century, Hanging scroll, Ink and color on hemp, 199.6 x 342.4 cm, Tōkyō National Museum ●混沌とした地獄での閻魔大王の審判が描かれる。閻魔は死者を裁く裁判官十王のうちの一人で、使者たちは死後 35 日目に閻魔庁で犯した罪を裁かれた。画面右上には奪衣婆（だつえば）に衣服を剥がされた亡者。左上ではさまざまな責め苦を受けながら地蔵に救われる光景が描かれる。怖く暗い地獄世界であるが、諷刺と笑いでコミカルに描き上げたところは、さすが暁斎は天才絵師である。

富岡鉄斎

182p「百事如意図」富岡鉄斎　大正 7 年（1918）軸 1 幅　紙本墨画 130.0 x 33.3cm　愛知県美術館蔵（木村定三コレクション）Various

Matters being one's Own Will, Tomioka Tessai, 1918, Hanging scroll, Ink on paper,130.0 x 33.3cm, Aichi Prefectural Museum of Art/ Kimura Teizo Collection ◉鉄斎の描く吉祥図である。鼎（かなえ）に松と梅をたて、その前に百合根、柿、橙、霊芝が置かれている。それぞれには意味があり、松は不老長寿、梅は安産と子孫繁栄、橙は代々繁栄を象徴する。また百合根の「百」は多くをあらわし、柿は「事」の通音、霊芝はそのかたちから「如意」をあらわし、以て「百事如意」の語呂合わせとなる謎語画題である。そして大字で書かれた「百事如意（百事、意の如し）」はすべて願いどおりになるという意味である。

183p **「二神会舞」富岡鉄斎**　大正 12 年（1923）軸 1 幅　絹本着色 168.8 x 85.5cm　東京国立博物館蔵　Two Dancing Deities, Tomioka Tessai, 1923, Hanging scroll, Colors on silk, 168.8 x 85.5 cm, Tōkyō National Museum ◉『古事記』の神話に拠る作品で、邇邇芸命 (ににぎのみこと) が高天原から降るとき、高天原と葦原の中つ国との間にあった天の八衢 (やちまた) で、猿田彦神 (さるたひこのみこと) が先頭に立って道案内した。黒々とした渓谷を雲が流れるなか、猿田彦神が先導し横には彼の名を明かした天宇受賣命（アメノウズメ）が描かれる。

184p **「竹窓高臥図」富岡鉄斎**　大正 8 年（1919）軸 1 幅　紙本墨画淡彩　131.5 x 32.0cm 富山県水墨美術館蔵　Sleeping Hermit, Tomioka Tessai, 1919, Hanging scroll, Ink and light colors on paper,131.5 x 32.0cm, The Suiboku Museum Toyama ◉人里離れた山里の竹林に囲まれた庵では、枕を高くして眠る文人が丸窓から望める。画中の賛には、「人間萬事塞翁馬」などと書かれていることから、人生の幸不幸は前もって分からないものだから、くよくよせず家の中で雨音を聴きながら眠る、といった意味が読みとれる。中国の古典からとった教訓的な題材を、画と賛で描いている。

185p **「虎僊育馬子図」富岡鉄斎**　大正 3 年（1914）軸 1 幅　紙本墨画淡彩　31.8 x 42.6cm　愛知県美術館蔵（木村定三コレクション）Legendary Wizards Nurturing Tiger Cubs, Tomioka Tessai, 1914, Hanging scroll, Ink and light colors on paper, 31.8 x 42.6 cm, Aichi Prefectural Museum of Art/ Kimura Teizo Collection ◉本作品は、京都の老舗菓子屋である虎屋から木村氏が直接に譲り受けたもので、虎屋京都店の主人であった黒川正弘と、その近所に居を構えていた鉄斎との深い交流はよく知られている。鉄斎は奔放な筆使いと、自由な発想による独自の作品を数多く手掛けた。仔を連れた虎にまたがるおおらかな人物は鉄斎自身であるのだろう。

横山大観

186p **「雨後之山」横山大観**　昭和 16 年（1941）軸 1 幅　紙本墨画　54.0 x 71.0cm　富山県水墨美術館蔵　Mountains After the Rain, Yokoyama Taikan, 1941, Hanging scroll, Ink on paper, 54.0 x 71.0cm, The Suiboku Museum Toyama ◉晴れゆく空と山容の雲の動き、また光と空気の変化を墨の濃淡だけで描写し、柔らかい墨の味わいで大気の雰囲気をみごとに描く。大観は墨絵について「墨には五彩ありと申しますが、墨はただ一色でありながら其中には濃淡渇潤の千変万化があり、これが色彩以上の複雑さをあらわして、色彩を超絶したる実在感を端的に微妙に表現するのであります」と語っている。

187p **「五浦の月」横山大観**　昭和 10 年 (1935)　軸 1 幅　紙本墨画 76.9 x 124.0cm　東京国立博物館蔵　*Izura no Tsuki*, Yokoyama Taikan, 1935, 76.9 x 124.0cm, Tōkyō National Museum ◉五浦は茨城県北東部にある海岸で、太平洋を臨む美しい入江がある。明治 39 年（1906）、岡倉天心は大観らとともに五浦で日本美術院の活動を繰り広げた。描かれているこの六角堂で天心はしばしば瞑想に耽った。本図からは、恩師を追慕する大観の強い想いが感じとれる。

188・189p **「生々流転」重文　横山大観**　大正 12 年（1923）画巻　絹本墨画　55.3 x 4070.0cm　東京国立近代美術館蔵　Photo: MOMAT/ DNPartcom Metempsychosis, Important cultural property, Yokoyama Taikan, 1923, Scroll, Ink on silk, 55.3 x 4070.0 cm, National Museum of Modern Art, Tokyo ◉生々流転とは、万物がたえず生まれ変わり死に変わっていつまでも変化しつづけることで、大観は水の一生をテーマとして描いた。霧から生まれた水滴があつまり渓流となり川となる。さらに大河になって大海に注ぎ、龍となって天に昇るまでを描く。水の流れに万物の移り変わりを見る壮大な自然観、人生観が語られている。全長 40 メートルにもおよぶ日本最大、最長の絵巻物として知られる。

190p **「釈迦十六羅漢」横山大観**　明治 44 年 (1911) 軸 2 幅　絹本着色　各 130.9 x 70.5cm　東京国立博物館蔵　Sakyamuni and Sixteen Arhats, Yokoyama Taikan, 1911, Two hanging scrolls, Colors on silk, 130.9 x 70.5 cm each, Tōkyō National Museum ◉釈迦と弟子たちの羅漢を軸二幅に描き分けて対置させる。十六羅漢は、釈迦の命によりこの世に長くいて正法を守り、衆生（しゅじょう）を導く十六人の大阿羅漢のこと。十六羅漢図は、古来、仏画の伝統的な画題であるが、大観は独特な構成を試みている。色鮮やかに描かれた画面には、大正期にあらわれる新たな日本画の思潮をみてとることができる。

191p **「松並木」横山大観**　大正 2 年 (1913) 軸 1 幅　絹本着色 194.8 x 85.7cm　東京国立博物館蔵　Rows of Pine Trees, Yokoyama Taikan, 1913, Hanging scroll, Colors on silk, 194.8 x 85.7cm, Tōkyō National Museum ◉黒々とした松の巨木が街道に立ちはだかる。その大きさを強調するように画面には旅人の姿が描き添えられている。大観は明治期には朦朧体 (もうろうたい) を提唱し、大正期には琳派を探求、昭和にはいると水墨画を数多く描くなど、常に日本画の新しい表現を追求した。

192p **「木立に白鷺」横山大観**　明治 37 年（1904）軸 1 幅　紙本墨画淡彩　71.0 x 49.0cm　富山県水墨美術館蔵　Rows of Pine Trees, Yokoyama Taikan, 1904, Hanging scroll, Ink and light color on paper, 71.0 x 49.0cm, The Suiboku Museum Toyama ◉霧が立ち込める森に、もくもくと雲のように木立が伸び、月が顔を出しはじめた。地上に目を移せば白い描線で水の流れが描かれたその場所に、数羽の白鷺が佇む。本図は明治 37 年（1904）、岡倉天心に従い渡米し、大観が滞米中に描いたとされ、ボストンから日本に里帰りした貴重な作品である。

［画家略歴］

池大雅　いけのたいが　享保8～安永5年（1723～76）

　江戸時代中期の南画家、書家。京都西陣菱屋町に銀座役人の手代池野嘉左衛門の子として生まれる。姓は池野、名は勤、無名、字は公敏、貸成、通称は秋平。号は大雅堂、九霞山樵、三岳道者など。7歳の頃、黄檗山萬福寺で書を披露、中国人の住職に才能を認められ、15歳の頃には画扇屋、篆刻を業とし、中国南宗画を独学した。柳沢淇園や祇園南海の影響を受ける一方で日本各地を旅し、明るく新鮮な色彩で独自性と風格に富んだ詩情豊かな作品を生み出した。木村蒹葭堂や桑山玉洲、野呂介石など門人も多く、また妻の玉瀾に教えて女流の文人画家に育て、おしどり夫婦として聞こえた。

伊藤 若冲　いとうじゃくちゅう　享保元～寛政12年（1716～1800）

　江戸時代中期の画家。京都高倉錦小路の青物問屋「枡源」の長男として生まれる。本名源左衛門、名は汝鈞、字は景和。また絵を依頼する人は必ず米一斗をもって謝礼としたことから斗米庵、そして心遠館と号した。初め狩野派を学び写生の重要性を認識、さらにその後、中国の宋、元、明の花鳥画を模写した。また尾形光琳の画風を研究し独自の画風を開いた。とくに鶏の絵を得意とし、写生を基礎にした装飾性のある作品を描いた。生涯独身で、晩年は京都深草の石峯寺の近くに隠棲し、五百羅漢を制作した。代表作に「動植綵絵」30幅（皇居三の丸尚蔵館）、「仙人掌群鶏図襖絵」（西福寺）などがある。

浦上 玉堂　うらかみぎょくどう　延享2～文政3年（1745～1820）

　江戸時代中期、後期の南画家。備中鴨方藩の武家に生まれる。名は孝弼、字は君輔、通称は兵右衛門。別号は穆斎。玉堂の号は、35歳の時に得た明の顧元昭の作になる「玉堂清韻」と銘をもつ七弦琴を入手したことによる。7歳で家督を継ぎ、藩主池田政香の側近として重用され、江戸にもしばしば出府する機会を得て、谷文晁らと往来、文人画に関心をもつ。寛政6年（1794）、50歳の時、春琴、秋琴の二人の子どもをつれて脱藩。以後文化8年（1811）京都に居を定めるまで琴をたずさえ東北から九州まで各地を遍歴した。絵はほぼ独学で、音楽的ともいえる韻律的な筆致を微妙にたたみ込む独特の作風は、最晩年にようやく開花したものである。

雲谷等顔　うんこくとうがん　天文16～元和4年（1547～1618）

　織豊、江戸時代前期の画家。肥前能古見の城主原直家の次男と伝えられる。名を直治、通称を治兵衛。天正年間（1573～92）父直家は肥前国有馬で戦死。一族の滅亡後、またはその少し前に画家へ転向し、京都ではじめ狩野永徳あるいは松栄について絵を学んだと伝える。その後再び西国に戻り、天正元年（1573）、安芸広島城主毛利輝元に召し抱えられ御用絵師となる。この頃から雪舟に私淑、輝元の命で雪舟筆「山水長巻」を模写し、その恩賞によって、文禄2年（1593）、雪舟ゆかりの雲谷庵とこの山水長巻とが彼にゆだねられ、既に途絶えていた雪舟画の再興を命じられた。雲谷の姓を名のり雪舟の正当な継承者として雲谷派を立ち上げる。雲谷派は中国地方から北九州にかけての画壇に影響力を保持し、幕末まで続く。

尾形光琳　おがたこうりん　万治元～享保元年（1658～1716）

　江戸時代前期の画家。京都有数の呉服商雁金屋に生まれ、幼少より能や絵に造詣の深かった父宗謙の影響を受けた。名は惟富、方祝、号は澗声、道崇、青々、寂明など。初め山本素軒に狩野派を、のち生家に伝わる俵屋宗達画の美に出合いその画風を学んだ。元禄14年（1701）法橋となり、「燕子花図屏風」（根津美術館）を描いて独自の世界を確立した。俵屋宗達の「風神雷神図」の模写を経て、「紅白梅図屏風」（MOA美術館）の代表作を完成させた。晩年は弟尾形乾山の陶器の絵付、蒔絵、小袖の下絵など、工芸意匠にも優れた作品を残した。

海北友松　かいほうゆうしょう　天文2～元和元年（1533～1615）

　織豊時代の画家。近江国坂田郡に生まれる。浅井長政の重臣善右衛門尉網親の三男。名は紹益。天正元年（1573）、一族は織田信長により浅井家が滅ぼされた際に主家と運命をともにしたが、幼い友松は京都東福寺に修行中のため難を逃れた。画の師は狩野元信、あるいは永徳と伝えられるが、中国南宋の梁楷の画法などを学び、独自の画風を形成した。和歌や連歌、茶の湯にも通じ、当代一流の文化人としての高い教養を備え、大徳寺の春屋宗園、東福寺の集雲守藤、連歌師里村紹巴と親交を結んだ。慶長4年（1599）再建の建仁寺方丈に描いた水墨障壁画が代表作として知られる。武家の精神を失わない気迫のこもった鋭い表現をみせ、余白の中に豊かな情感を漂わせる作風の水墨画を得意とした。

葛蛇玉　かつじゃぎょく　享保20～安永9年（1735～80）

　江戸時代中期の画家。大坂生まれ。名は季原、字は子明、蛇玉、鯉翁と号した。玉泉寺という浄土真宗の寺の次男として生まれ、後に長嶋喜右衛門の婿養子となった。幼い頃から絵に親しみ橘守国に手解きを受け、僧鶴亭から南蘋画風を授けられる。後に宋元の古画を研究して一家を成した。明和3年（1766）2月22日の晩、蛇が玉を含んでくる夢を見て、目覚めてみればそこに玉があった。どのような吉祥であるのかわからなかったが、これにより蛇玉と称するようになった。好んで鯉を得意としたため「鯉翁」とよばれ、上田秋成著『雨月物語』にある「夢応の鯉魚」のモデルといわれる。

狩野永徳　かのうえいとく　天文12～天正18年（1543～90）

　織豊時代の画家。山城に生まれる。狩野松栄の長男。名は州信、通称は源四郎。狩野派宗家五代。天文21年（1552）祖父狩野元信と共に将軍足利義輝に伺候。永禄9年（1566）大徳寺聚光院方丈の装飾に従事し、水墨襖絵「琴棋書画図」、「花鳥図」を描く。永徳の大画面様式は、織田信長、豊臣秀吉の注目するところとなり、安土城、桃山城、聚楽第など、当代を代表する建造物の障壁画はすべて永徳の指導下に制作された。代表作に、信長が上杉謙信に贈った「洛中洛外図屏風」（上杉家）、「唐獅子図屏風」（皇居三の丸尚蔵館）などがある。

狩野山雪　かのうさんせつ　天正17/18～慶安4年（1589/90～1651）

　江戸時代前期の画家。和歌山藩執政千賀道元の子として九州肥前に生まれ、父とともに大坂へ移住。名は光家、通称は縫殿助、号は蛇足軒、桃源子。慶長10年（1605）、狩野山楽の門人となり、のち婿養子になり京狩野家を継ぐ。山楽の装飾的画風を受け継ぎつつも、理知的で明快な画面構成に独自の造形性を示した。寛永6年（1629）頃「当麻寺縁起」を、同8年頃、山楽の指導を受けながら制作した天球院方丈画では、主力となって活躍。同12年、山楽没によって後を継ぎ、いわゆる京狩野の第二代となった。正保4年（1647）東福寺の「三十三観音図」を補作し、同年法橋となる。代表作に装飾的で造形性に富んだ「雪汀水禽図屏風」、「蘭亭曲水図屏風」などがある。

狩野探幽　慶長 7 ～延宝 2 年（1602 ～ 74）

　江戸時代前期の画家。鍛冶橋狩野家の祖。孝信の長男として京都に生まれる。名は四郎次郎、采女、守信、別号は生明、白蓮子。早熟の画家であり、11 歳の時に駿府で徳川家康に謁見、江戸移住後、数え年 16 歳の元和 3 年（1617）徳川幕府の御用絵師となり、同 7 年江戸城鍛冶橋門外に屋敷をもらい鍛冶橋狩野家を開いた。寛永 3 年（1626）二条城行幸殿の障壁画制作では一門を率いて活躍した。その後、名古屋城、江戸城、京都御所、日光東照宮などの障壁画を制作、指導的な役割を果たした。寛永 12 年（1635）、紅月宗玩と図って探幽斎を名のり、山水、人物、花鳥と画域広く描いた。同 15 年法眼、寛文 2 年（1662）には宮内卿法印となる。広い余白を設けた理知的な画面構成、簡潔で柔軟な筆墨は狩野派様式を一新し、その軽淡瀟洒な画風は豪壮華麗な桃山画風に代わり支持された。

狩野元信　文明 8 ～永禄 2 年（1476 ～ 1559）

　戦国時代の画家。山城出身。狩野正信の長男。幼名は四郎二郎。のち大炊助と称す。永正 10 年（1513）『鞍馬寺縁起』を制作。天文 10 年（1541）頃、越前守に任ぜられ、さらに法眼に叙せられ、永仙と号す。天文 8 年～ 22 年には弟子とともに石山本願寺の障壁画制作に活躍。中国画の諸様式に大和絵の色彩性、装飾性を合わせた、平明で装飾的な障壁画様式を打ち出した。障壁画のほか、扇面画なども手がけ、その作品は宮廷や公家、武家、町衆など幅ひろい層に支持された。代表作に、大仙院客殿襖絵「四季花鳥図」、「清凉寺縁起絵巻」（清凉寺）などがある。

河鍋 暁斎　天保 2 ～明治 22 年（1831 ～ 89）

　幕末、明治期の浮世絵師。下総古河藩士河鍋喜右衛門の次男として生まれる。幼名周三郎、俗称洞郁。江戸の火消同心屋敷で育つ。歌川国芳に入門、のち狩野派の前村洞和、狩野洞白陳信の門に入る。安政 5 年（1858）独立し本郷で開業。狩野派を基礎とした浮世絵風の狂画、諷刺画などを描く。明治 14 年（1881）内国勧業博覧会で「枯木寒鴉」が受賞。幕末から明治前期にかけての動乱した社会に対する厳しい観察を通して、その特異な時代感覚を表現した作品が多い。著書に『暁斎画談』がある。

久隅守景　生没年不詳

　江戸時代前期の画家。清原雪信の父。通称は半兵衛。号は無下斎、一陳翁、棒印など。狩野探幽門下の四天王の一人と称され、師からその才能を期待されたが、後には狩野一門を離脱。一説には破門されたとも伝えられる。寛永 19 年（1642）、近江（滋賀県）大津の聖衆来迎寺の障壁画の制作に参加する。明暦年間（1655 ～ 58）頃、加賀金沢藩主前田家に仕え、菩提所瑞龍寺の襖絵を描く。当時しだいに安易な粉本主義から創造性がなくなりつつあった江戸狩野派を離れ、農民の生活に取材した田園風俗の作品に本領を発揮した。代表作に「納涼図屏風」（東京国立博物館）、「四季耕作図屏風」（石川県立美術館）などがある。

月僊　寛保元～文化 6 年（1741 ～ 1809）

　江戸時代中期の画僧。尾張名古屋の味噌商の家に生まれ、7 歳で仏門に入り、浄土宗の僧となる。俗姓は丹家氏。名は玄瑞、字は玉成、号は月僊。別号に寂照主人、本祥寿がある。江戸へ出て増上寺に入り、桜井雪館について絵を学び、大僧正妙誉より月僊の号を与えられた。明和年間（1764 ～ 72）の初めに京都に移り円山応挙、与謝蕪村などの作風に影響を受け、さまざまな流派を取り込んだ鋭い筆法の作風で一家をなした。安永 3 年（1774）伊勢山田の寂照寺の住職となった後は、寺の再興に努め貧民救済にも尽力した。枯痩な渇筆に淡墨を加えた独特の作風で多くの作品を残している。

呉春　（松村月渓・まつむらげっけい）宝暦 2 ～文化 8 年（1752 ～ 1811）

　江戸時代中、後期の画家。四条派の祖。京都金座の年寄役松村匡程の子。名は豊昌、字は伯望、通称は文蔵、月渓と号す。家業を継いだが、そのかたわら大西酔月に絵を、また与謝蕪村に俳諧と絵を学んだ。後に職業画家となり、天明元年（1781）、36 歳のときに父と妻を失った彼は、摂津池田の呉服里に移り、その地で春を迎えたことにより呉春と改名した。この頃は蕪村から学んだ技法に平明な自然観察を加味して新しい画風を確立した。寛政元年（1789）5 月、京都に戻り、円山応挙らと交流を深め、その写生画風の影響を受けて独自の画風を確立した。

酒井抱一　宝暦 11 ～文政 11 年（1761 ～ 1828）

　江戸時代後期の画家。忠仰の次男として江戸に生まれる。播磨（兵庫県）姫路藩主酒井忠以の弟。名は忠因、字は暉真。号は鶯村、軽挙道人、通称は栄八など。37 歳のとき、西本願寺の文如の弟子となり、権大僧都に任ぜられた。絵は狩野高信から狩野風を学び、また南蘋派の花鳥画、浮世絵、円山派、土佐派なども広く学んだ。のち尾形光琳の作品に接し深く傾倒、その芸術の再興を志した。文化 12 年（1815）には光琳百年忌を催し、『光琳百図』、『尾形流略印譜』を刊行。代表作には尾形光琳「風神・雷神図屏風」の裏面に描いた「夏秋草図屏風」（東京国立博物館）がある。

菅井梅関　天明 4 ～天保 15 年（1784 ～ 1844）

　江戸時代後期の南画家。陸奥仙台の人。名は岳輔、字は正卿、通称は岳輔。別号は東斎。絵は初め根元常南につき、のち江戸に出てからは谷文晁に学び、その後長崎に赴き清の江稼圃に師事する。晩年は帰郷するが不遇のうちに死去。剛健な筆触に特色があり、山水画や梅の絵を得意とした。主な作品に「墨梅図」（東京国立博物館）、「高士観瀑図」（仙台市博物館）、「雪梅図」（仙台市博物館）、「夏冬山水図屏風」などがある。

雪舟 等楊　応永 27 ～永正 3 年（1420 ～ 1506）

　室町、戦国時代の画家。備中赤浜生まれ。禅僧としての諱は等楊、雪舟は中国元代の名僧楚石梵琦の二大字墨跡を入手してつけた雅号。永享年間はじめ頃（1429 ～）上洛、相国寺に入り春林周藤に禅の教えを受けるが、禅僧としては終生知客の位にとどまり、もっぱら画をもって名をなした。画技は周文に学んだとされる。40 歳前に相国寺を出て、大内氏の庇護を受けて山口に雲谷庵を開く。応仁元年（1467）48 歳の春、大内氏の貿易船に乗って明代の中国を旅する。帰国後は大分に天開図画楼という画房を開き、作画に専念するとともに諸国を遍歴して、日本の自然を対象とする真景図も描いた。後世の漢画系の画家たちに大きな影響を及ぼした。

雪村 周継　生没年不詳

　戦国、織豊時代の画僧。常陸辺垂郡田村生まれ。諱は周継。舟居斎、鶴船と号す。戦国武将佐竹氏の一族の長男として生まれたが、家督争いのわずらわしさを避けて禅僧となる。会津、小田原、鎌倉など東国を転々とし遊歴して、晩年 70 歳の頃から会津の芦名盛氏の知遇を得て、会津に近い三春に雪村庵を結び隠棲した。広く宋元画、ことに牧谿や玉潤などを学び、独自の様式を創

造したと推定される。雪舟に私淑したことは、天文 11 年（1542）
雪村自らがその画論を披瀝した『説門弟資』に述べられている。

せんがいぎぼん
仙厓義梵　寛延 3 ～天保 8 年（1750 ～ 1837）

　江戸時代後期の臨済宗の禅僧。美濃（岐阜県）谷口に生まれる。
法名は義梵。別号は円通、天民、百堂、虚白など。宝暦 10 年
（1760）、美濃清泰寺の空印円虚について得度。明和 5 年（1768）、
武蔵東輝庵の月船禅慧の法を継ぐ。その後、39 歳で博多に赴き、
栄西が開いた聖福寺住持となり、同寺の復興に努力した。禅僧と
して簡素な生活を送る一方、50 歳頃から書画の才をあらわした。
「厓画無法」といわれるように飄逸な画風が多く、禅の悟りの境
地を機知に富んだ筆墨であらわした。階層を問わず人々から親し
まれ、多くの揮毫した作品が遺る。

そがしょうはく
曾我 蕭 白　享保 15 ～天明元年（1730 ～ 81）

　江戸時代中期の画家。京都の商家に生まれ、本姓は三浦、名は
暉雄。蕭白のほか、蛇足軒、鬼神斎などと号す。初め京狩野派の
高田敬甫に師事し絵を学んだ。また室町時代の漢画系画派である
曾我派に私淑して、独自に曾我蛇足や曾我直庵の画風を学び、自
ら十世蛇足軒と号した。類い稀な想像力と力強い筆致、鮮烈な彩
色があふれる画風により、型破りな独自の世界を確立した。また
文人的な気質も兼ね備えており、詩趣を盛った山水画に沈潜する
こともあった。松阪を中心として伊勢地方を遊歴し、その奇行ぶ
りが今もその地に伝えられている。

たにぶんちょう
谷文晁　宝暦 13 ～天保 11 年（1763 ～ 1840）

　江戸時代後期の文人画家。江戸下谷根岸に生まれる。漢詩人の
谷麓谷の長男。通称は文五郎、別号は写山楼、画学斎など。初め
狩野派の加藤文麗に学び、長崎派の渡辺玄対に師事した。以後、
中国南宋、北宋画、西洋画などの諸画派を研究し、独自の画法を
生み出した。天明 8 年（1788）、田安徳川家に出仕し、田安家
から養子に入って白河藩主となった松平定信の近習として、その
絵画御用にたずさわる。寛政 4 年（1792）、松平定信に認められ、
定信編『集古十種』の挿絵も描く。洋風の手法をとりいれて独自
の画風を創出し、江戸文人画壇の重鎮となる。弟子は非常に多く、
渡辺崋山、立原杏所などがいる。

たのむらちくでん
田能村竹田　安永 6 ～天保 6 年（1777 ～ 1835）

　江戸時代後期の南画家。豊後（大分県）竹田の岡藩の藩医の家
に生まれる。名は孝憲、字は君彝、通称は行蔵。別号は田舎児、
老圃師。儒者をこころざし藩校由学館に学び、のち同館の頭取と
なる。文化 8 年（1811）、同 9 年に起こった藩内の農民一揆の際、
藩政改革の建言がいれられず致仕。絵は初め郷里の渡辺蓬島、淵
野真斎に手ほどきを受け、また谷文晁らに師事したが多くは明清
画に学び、中国南宗画に近い独自の画風を形成した。辞職後はし
ばしば京坂地方遊び、頼山陽、浦上春琴、岡田半江ら文人墨客ら
と親交をもった。画風は柔らかな描線を神経細かく行き届かせた
清雅なもので、江戸時代の南画家のなかではもっとも本格的な南
宗様式に近い。

たわらやそうたつ
俵屋宗達　生没年不詳

　桃山から江戸時代初期の画家。「伊年」印をもちい、号は対青軒。
京都で活躍した町絵師で「俵屋」はその屋号である。宗達の伝記
の詳細は不明であるが、絵師として活躍する一方、烏丸光広、千
少庵ら当時の公卿や文化人との広い交際があった。扇面や色紙、
短冊、巻子など、様々な形式の料紙装飾を手掛ける工房を主宰し、

金銀泥を用いた雅で大胆な構図の金地屏風や華麗な料紙装飾に新
しい画境を獲得した。また柔らかい筆致とたらし込みの技法で水
墨画にも比類ない傑作を残した。代表作に「蓮池水禽図」（京都
国立博物館）、「関屋・澪標屏風」（静嘉堂文庫美術館）、「風神雷
神図屏風」（建仁寺）などがある。

とみおかてっさい
富岡鉄斎　天保 7 ～大正 13 年（1836 ～ 1924）

　明治、大正期の日本画家。京都の法衣商十一屋の二男。本名は
猷輔のち百錬。字は無倦。別号は裕軒のちに鉄斎、ほかに鉄崖、
鉄道人がある。幼少の頃の病がもとで耳が遠くなり、書画を深く
嗜むようになる。20 歳のころ心性寺の太田垣蓮月尼と同居、そ
の清廉な人格と文雅の風韻に親炙、多くの影響を受ける。国学、
漢学を修め、窪田雪鷹、小田海僊に南画の手ほどきを受け、浮田
一蕙に大和絵を学ぶ。維新後は、大和石上神宮小宮司、和泉大鳥
神社の大宮司となって神道復興に尽くすが、明治 14 年（1881）、
兄の死にともない京都に帰り画業に専念、在野の文人画家として
後半生を送った。

ながさわろせつ
長澤蘆雪　宝暦 4 ～寛政 11 年（1754 ～ 99）

　江戸時代中期、後期の画家。山城国（京都府）淀藩に仕えた下
級武士の家に生まれる。名は政勝また魚、字は氷計、引裾、号は
于緝、蘆雪など。京都に出て円山応挙に絵を学び、個性的な表現
で応挙門下の中で異彩を放った。天明 6 年（1786）、暮から翌
春にかけて旅行した南紀の無量寺や草堂寺などに絵筆を振るい多
くの襖絵を遺した。代表作に正宗寺（豊橋市）旧丈障壁画、兵庫
県香住の大乗寺の障壁画、厳島神社（広島県）の「山姥図」、「花
鳥游魚図巻」、「海兵奇勝図」（メトロポリタン美術館）などがある。

はくいんえかく
白隠慧鶴　貞享 2 ～明和 5 年（1685 ～ 1768）

　江戸時代中期の臨済宗の禅僧。駿河浮島原（静岡県沼津市）に
生まれる。俗姓は杉山。禅僧としての諱は慧鶴。別号は鵠林、鵠
提窟。15 歳で同地松蔭寺の単嶺祖伝について得度。さらに美濃
瑞雲寺、越後、英巌寺など諸国を行脚して参禅し、松蔭寺へ戻る。
宝永 5 年（1708）、信濃飯山の正受老人こと道鏡慧端の法をつぐ。
以後、松蔭寺を中心に広く活動し、臨済宗中興の祖と称せられた。
還暦を過ぎた頃から禅画墨蹟を描くようになり、達磨、観音、布
袋などの祖師や、神仏や寓意画などを個性的な筆致で描いた。

はせがわとうはく
長谷川等伯　天文 8 ～慶長 15 年（1539 ～ 1610）

　織豊時代の画家。能登七尾の城主畠山氏の家臣奥村文之丞宗道
の子、染色家長谷川宗清の養子。名は久六、又四郎。能登で初め
雪舟門下の等春に学ぶ。元亀 2 年（1571）ごろ上京し、本法寺
の日通上人、茶人千利休と親交を結び、さらに武将たちから支持
されて頭角をあらわしていく。天正 17 年（1589）大徳寺塔頭
に多くの水墨画を描く。同 18 年内裏対屋の障壁画制作に関し、
狩野永徳と対立し排斥された。その後狩野派に強い対抗意識を燃
やし、その気性の激しさが気魄のこもった筆技を生んだともいえ
る。文禄 2 年（1593）、秀吉の長男鶴松の菩提寺である祥雲寺
の金碧障壁画を、一門を率いて制作した。金地に濃彩を用いた絢
爛豪華なその作品は、桃山盛期を代表する傑作の一つに数えられ
る。

ふうがいえくん
風外慧薫　永禄 11 ～没年不詳（1586 ～ 1654?）

　江戸時代前期の禅僧画家。上野国（群馬県）碓氷郡土塩村の人。
同国の乾窓寺、長源寺、双林寺などで修行の後、相模国小田原（神
奈川県）の成願寺住職。のち曾我山中の巌窟にすみ、遠江石岡に

移る。承応 3 年（1654）ごろ墓穴をほらせ、自らそこに投じて入寂したという。この間、墨戯を能くし、達磨や布袋、自画像など多くの禅画を描いた。

ほんあみこうえつ 本阿弥光悦 永禄元～寛永 14 年（1558 ～ 1637）

　織豊、江戸時代前期の芸術家。本阿弥家の分家として京都に生まれる。号は自得斎、徳友斎、太虚庵など。家職である刀剣の鑑定、浄拭を得意とした。書画、蒔絵、陶芸などにすぐれ、また古典、茶道に通じた幅広い教養と才能を持って新しい芸術の指導者となった。元和元年（1615）、徳川家康から洛北鷹峯を賜り、「光悦村」を開いた。書は尊朝法親王に青蓮院風を学んだが、古典を研究して独自の書風を開き、近衛信尹、松花堂昭乗とともに寛永の三筆にかぞえられた。陶芸は鷹峯隠棲の頃より楽焼の茶碗や香合などを作るようになったと見られる。蒔絵には斬新なデザインの「舟橋蒔絵硯箱」、墨跡に「立正安国論」などがある。

まるやまおうきょ 円山応挙 享保 18 ～寛政 7 年（1733 ～ 95）

　江戸時代中期の画家。丹波国桑田郡穴太村（京都府亀岡市）に円山藤左衛門の次男として生まれる。幼名は岩次郎、通称は主水、字は仲選。明和 3 年（1766）、応挙と改名する。幼い頃より絵を好み、早くから上洛して玩具商に奉公。絵は狩野探幽の流れをくむ鶴沢派の石田幽汀に入門したが、狩野派の形式化した画風に飽き足らず、眼鏡絵の制作を通じて西洋画法に親しみ、また中国画の沈南蘋にも影響されて写生の重要性に開眼する。本草学に関心深い近江円満院の門主祐常に見出され、写生を基本とした写実的作風に独自の画風をひらいた。以後京都画壇の中心的存在として旺盛な制作活動を展開させた。

みやもとむさし 宮本武蔵 天正 12 ～正保 2 年（1584 ～ 1645）

　江戸時代前期の剣術家。二刀流剣法（円明流・二刀一流・二天一流・武蔵流）の祖。美作（岡山県）宮本村に生まれる。名は玄信、号は二天。実歴は不明な部分が多く、生涯 60 余度の試合に不敗をほこり、豊前船島における佐々木小次郎との決闘は、伝説化されて武芸談になっている。晩年は熊本藩主細川忠利の客分に迎えられ、この地で没した。書画にもすぐれ、中でも水墨画は名手であった。南宋の梁楷や桃山時代の海北友松の影響をうかがわせる減筆体で、武人らしい簡潔でしかも気魄を感じさせる作品が多い。代表作に「鵜図」、「蘆雁図屏風」（永青文庫）、また武道の奥義を説く兵法書『五輪書』を著わした。

もりそせん 森狙仙 延享 4 ～文政 4 年（1747 ～ 1821）

　江戸時代後期の画家。生地は長崎または摂津（兵庫県）西宮とされるが、大坂を中心に活躍した。名は守象、字は叔牙。祖仙、如寒斎、霊明庵とも号した。父は橘如閑斎と名のる画家。はじめ長兄の陽信、次兄の周峰と狩野派の山本如春斎に学ぶが飽き足らず、写生に励み円山応挙の影響を受ける。動物画、とくに精細克明な毛描きにより写実的に表現した猿を得意とし、「狙仙の猿」として名高い。主な作品に「雪中獣禽図襖」（広誠院）、「猿鹿図」・「秋山遊鹿図」（東京国立博物館）、「藤に三匹猿之図」（一宮市博物館）などがある。

もりてつざん 森徹山 安永 4 ～天保 12 年（1775 ～ 1841）

　江戸時代後期の画家。名は守真、字は子玄、通称は文蔵、徹山は号。森狙仙の次兄で狩野派の森周峯の子として大坂に生まれ、森狙仙の養子となる。円山応挙に学び、門下十哲のひとり。狙仙の精緻な客観的描写に軽淡な情趣性を加えている。晩年は宮廷の

画用に従い、また熊本藩の庇護をうける。婿養子が一鳳、義子が寛斎で、それぞれ画系を継ぐ。主な作品に「牛図屏風」（東京国立博物館）がある。

やまもとばいいつ 山本梅逸 天明 3 ～安政 3 年（1783 ～ 1856）

　江戸時代後期の南画家。尾張名古屋に生まれる。彫刻師の子。名は亮、字は明卿。梅逸、玉禅と号する。22 歳の頃、当地の豪商で古画収集家であった神谷天遊の庇護を受け、中林竹洞と共に京都へ上がって長崎派や四条派の画風を取り入れ画技を磨いた。安政元年（1854）、名古屋に戻り藩の御用絵師格に任ぜられて士分に取り立てられた。明の周之冕に私淑し、色彩豊かで技巧を駆使した花鳥画を得意とした。竹洞とともに名古屋を中心とする尾張南画の代表的存在で弟子の育成にもつとめた。

よこやまたいかん 横山大観 明治元～昭和 33 年（1868 ～ 1958）

　明治、昭和期の日本画家。水戸藩士酒井捨彦の長男として水戸に生まれ、のち東京に移って母方の横山家を継いだ。明治 22 年（1889）、開校の東京美術学校に入学、岡倉天心、橋本雅邦の指導を受けた。卒業後、京都美術工藝学校で教鞭をとったのち、同 29 年、母校東京美術学校の助教授になった。同 31 年、美術学校に校長天心を排斥する騒動が起こると、天心、雅邦らと辞職。日本美術院創立に参加し、第一回展に出品の「屈原」が銀牌を受賞。同 33 年頃から西洋画法を取り入れた「朦朧体」とよばれる没骨賦彩の画法を開発、大胆な没線描法を試みたが、朦朧派と悪評されて苦闘を強いられた。天心没後の大正 3 年（1914）、下村観山らと日本美術院を再興、東洋の伝統に基づく近代日本画の創成を目ざして画壇に重きをなした。

よさぶそん 与謝蕪村 享保元～天明 3 年（1716 ～ 83）

　江戸時代中期の俳人、画家。摂津（大坂市）に生まれる。本姓は谷口、のち与謝。別号は宰鳥、落日庵、夜半亭二世。画号は四明、春星、謝寅など。20 歳の頃、江戸に出て夜半亭巴人の門に入って俳諧を学ぶ。巴人没後、関東、奥州を遊歴し、宝暦元年（1751）36 歳の時、京都に移る。明和 3 年（1766）、炭太祇らと三菓社を結び、同 7 年、夜半亭二世を襲名して宗匠の列につらなった。安永 2 年（1773）には『あけ烏』を刊行、俳諧新風を大いに鼓吹し、暁台、二柳ほか諸家と親交を結ぶ。純粋な南宋画ばかりでなく、文人画としては南蘋派など北宗画系の作風も取り入れ、変化に富んだ独自の画風を確立、また俳画にも新境地を開いた。

わたなべかざん 渡辺崋山 寛政 5 ～天保 12 年（1793 ～ 1841）

　江戸時代後期の三河田原藩士、画家、蘭学者。江戸生まれ。渡辺巴洲の長男。名は定静、字は伯登、子安、通称は登。別号は寓絵堂、全楽堂など。家が貧しく内職のため白川芝山、金子金陵らに絵を学び、文化 6 年（1809）、谷文晁に入門。絵の傍ら、佐藤一斎、松崎慊堂らに儒学を学ぶ。蘭学をおさめて高野長英、小関三英らと尚歯会に加わり西洋文物の研究を行う。『慎機論』を著して幕府の鎖国政策を批判し、天保 10 年（1839）、蛮社の獄で捕らえられる。田原に蟄居中の同 12 年に自刃した。西洋画法をとりいれた独自の画風を完成し、作品に「四洲真景」、「鷹見泉石像」（東京国立博物館）などを残す。弟子に椿椿山、岡本秋暉がいる。

［墨のいろ 年譜］ ＊太字は本文掲載作品を示す。

応永 27 年 （1420）	【雪舟】	・備中（岡山県）に生まれる。一説に生地は赤浜と伝える。
永享 2 年 （1430）	【雪舟】	・この頃、京都の相国寺に入って僧となり、春林周藤に師事したと思われる。
		・諱「等楊」を授かる。これ以降、画を相国寺の周文に学ぶ。
寛正 5 年 （1464）	【雪舟】	・この年より、周防雲谷庵にあり。
応仁 2 年 （1468）	【雪舟】	・「四季山水図」（東京国立博物館蔵）を描く。
文明 6 年 （1474）	【雪舟】	・「山水図巻（倣高彦敬）」（山口県立美術館蔵）を描く。
文明 8 年 （1476）	【元信】	・山城に生まれる。
	【雪舟】	・豊後の天開図画楼にあり。
文明 18 年 （1486）	【雪舟】	・周防にあり、天開図画楼を本拠に画作する。了庵桂悟、山口に到着し雪舟のために「天開図画楼記」を書く。「山水図巻（山水長巻）」（毛利博物館蔵）を描く。
明応 2 年 （1493）	【雪舟】	・「束帯天神図」（山口県立美術館蔵）を描く。
明応 4 年 （1495）	【雪舟】	・**「破墨山水図」**（東京国立博物館蔵）を描き、宗淵に与える。
明応 5 年 （1496）	【雪舟】	・**「慧可断臂図」**（齋年寺蔵）を描く。
文亀元年 （1501）	【雪舟】	・「渡唐天神図」（岡山県立美術館蔵）、「四季山水図屏風」（東京国立博物館蔵）を描く。
		・**「天橋立図」**（京都国立博物館蔵）この年以降に画かれる。
永正元年 （1504）	【雪村】	・この年を雪村の出生年とする説あり。常陸佐竹氏の一族という（『本朝画史』）。
永正 3 年 （1506）	【雪舟】	・この頃没（87 歳）。
天文 2 年 （1533）	【友松】	・近江国（滋賀県）坂田郡浅井家の武将、海北善右衛門綱親の子として生まれる。
天文 8 年 （1539）	【等伯】	・能登国七尾に生まれる。実父は奥村文之丞宗道、のちに長谷川宗清（法名道浄）の養子となる。
天文 11 年 （1542）	【雪舟】	・『設門弟資』を著す。
天文 12 年 （1543）	【永徳】	・山城に生まれる。
天文 16 年 （1547）	【等顔】	・肥前能古見（佐賀県）の城主原直家の次男として生まれる。
永禄元年 （1558）	【友松】	・東福寺において安国寺恵瓊との出会いこの頃か。
	【光悦】	・京都に生まれる。
永禄 2 年 （1559）	【元信】	・10 月 6 日死去（84 歳）。
永禄 3 年 （1560）	【雪村】	・この年以前、「山水図」（早雲寺第二世大室宗碩賛）を描く。
永禄 11 年 （1568）	【等伯】	・長男、久蔵生まれる。「涅槃図」（羽咋市、妙成寺）を描く（30 歳）。【風外】・上野国（群馬県）に生まれる。
元亀 3 年 （1572）	【等伯】	・「日堯上人像」（本法寺）を描く（34 歳）。
天正元年 （1573）	【雪村】	・70 歳のとき、すでに奥州田村（三春）に隠棲。
天正 2 年 （1574）	【雪村】	・この頃、「竹林七賢図屏風」（畠山記念館蔵）を描く。（款記に 71 歳とあり）。
天正 12 年 （1584）	【武蔵】	・播磨または美作に生まれる。
天正 13 年 （1585）	【雪村】	・この頃、「瀟湘八景図屏風」（六曲一隻）を描く（款記に 82 歳とあり）。この後、三春で没したか。
天正 17 年 （1589）	【友松】	・11 月、桂宮御別生業御造営。一説に友松、永徳とともに襖絵を描く。
	【山雪】	・肥前国に生まれる。
天正 18 年 （1590）	【永徳】	・9 月 14 日死去（48 歳）。
文禄 2 年 （1593）	【等伯】	・祥雲禅寺障壁画（現智積院蔵）を完成か（54 歳）。息子久蔵、26 歳で没す。
文禄 3 年 （1598）	【友松】	・5 月、石田三成に伴われ、筑紫へ旅する。
慶長 7 年 （1602）	【等伯】	・天授庵に「商山四皓図」**「禅宗祖師図」**「松鶴図」の襖絵を描く（64 歳）。
	【友松】	・この頃、しばしば八条宮智仁親王邸に出入りし、押絵の注文などを受ける。この頃「山水図屏風」（京都国立博物館蔵）「飲中八仙図屏風」（京都国立博物館蔵）「瀟湘八景図」を描く。
	【探幽】	・山城国に生まれる。
慶長 10 年 （1605）	【友松】	・この頃、妙心寺大通院客殿に襖絵を描く（焼失）。妙心寺との関係この頃盛んか。
		・「琴棋書画図屏風」（妙心寺蔵）、「三酸・寒山拾得図屏風」（妙心寺蔵）この頃か。
慶長 13 年 （1608）	【等伯】	・「日通上人像」（本法寺）を描く（70 歳）。
慶長 15 年 （1610）	【等伯】	・江戸下向到着後、没す（72 歳）。
慶長 17 年 （1612）	【探幽】	・父孝信にともなわれ、駿府で徳川家康に拝謁する（11 歳）。
慶長 18 年 （1613）	【友松】	・「禅宗祖師図屏風」（静岡県立美術館蔵）を描く。
元和元年 （1615）	【友松】	・6 月 2 日没す（83 歳）。
元和 4 年 （1618）	【等顔】	・5 月 3 日死去（72 歳）。
元和 7 年 （1621）	【宗達】	・養源院の再建に際し、宗達、襖絵および杉戸絵を描く。
元和 8 年 （1622）	【宗達】	・醍醐寺無量寿院に障壁画を描く。この頃、京都で俵屋の扇がもてはやされる。
寛永 3 年 （1626）	【探幽】	・尚信、興以、安信、長信、甚之丞、山楽ら二条城の障壁画の制作に従事。
寛永 12 年 （1635）	【探幽】	・名古屋城障壁画に「雪中梅竹鳥図」、「露台惜費図」を描く。
寛永 13 年 （1636）	【探幽】	・日光東照宮社殿、陽明門天井画を完成。大徳寺法堂天井画「蟠竜図」を描く（35 歳）。
寛永 14 年 （1637）	【光悦】	・2 月 3 日死去（80 歳）。
寛永 18 年 （1641）	【探幽】	・大徳寺本坊方丈に「山水図」襖絵を描く（40 歳）。尚信、信政、守景ら知恩院小方丈に襖絵を描く。
正保 2 年 （1645）	【武蔵】	・5 月 19 日死去（62 歳）。
正保 4 年 （1647）	【探幽】	・江戸城本丸、西の丸大広間、黒書院などに障壁画を描く（46 歳）。

慶安4年	（1651）	【山雪】	・3月12日没。泉涌寺に葬られた（63歳）。
万治元年	（1658）	【光琳】	・京都の呉服商雁金屋尾形宗謙の次男として生まれる。
寛文2年	（1662）	【探幽】	・「西湖図」（石川県立美術館蔵）を描く。
寛文3年	（1663）	【乾山】	・光琳の弟として生まれる。
寛文7年	（1667）	【探幽】	・「富士山図」（静岡県立美術館蔵）を描く。
延宝2年	（1674）	【探幽】	・10月7日没（73歳）、池上本門寺に葬られる。
貞享2年	（1685）	【白隠】	・駿河浮島原に生まれる。
元禄13年	（1700）	【光琳】	・この年より乾山焼に絵付けをする。
宝永2年	（1705）	【光琳】	・「四季草花図」を描く。
享保元年	（1716）	【蕪村】	・摂津国東成郡毛馬村(現在の大阪市都島区毛馬町)に生まれる。生家は庄屋か。本性谷口は母方の姓か。
		【光琳】	・6月2日死去。妙顕寺興善院に葬る（59歳）。
		【若冲】	・京都錦小路の青物問屋「枡源」三代目伊藤源左衛門の長男として生まれる。
享保8年	（1723）	【大雅】	・5月4日、京都西陣菱屋町に町人池野嘉左衛門の子として生まれる。
享保13年	（1728）	【玉瀾】	・京都に生まれる。
享保14年	（1729）	【大雅】	・檀王寺清光院の一井に書を学ぶ。10月、黄檗山万福寺で書を披露、第12世山主の杲堂 元昶および丈侍の大梅浄璨に神童と賞される（7歳）。
享保15年	（1730）	【蕭白】	・京都にて生まれる。（三重県芸町浄光寺壁貼付の「十六羅漢図」の落款に「宝暦九曾我氏 三十歳筆」とあったとする桃沢如水からの報告から逆算）本姓は三浦氏。
享保18年	（1733）	【応挙】	・丹波国桑田郡穴太村（現在の京都府亀山市）に生まれる。父丸山藤左衛門、母は篠山藩士 上田氏の娘か。京都生まれ説もある。幼名は与吉、のちに岩次郎。
享保20年	（1735）	【蛇玉】	・大坂に生まれる。
寛保元年	（1741）	【月僊】	・尾張名古屋に生まれる。
延享2年	（1745）	【玉堂】	・備前（岡山県）池田藩の支藩、鴨方池田藩の藩士浦上兵右衛門宗純の子として生まれる。
延享4年	（1747）	【狙仙】	・長崎または摂津に生まれる。
寛延2年	（1749）	【応挙】	・この頃、尾張屋堪兵衛の世話で石田幽汀の門下に入り、本格的に絵を学び始める（17歳）。
寛延3年	（1750）	【仙厓】	・美濃谷口に生まれる。
宝暦元年	（1751）	【大雅】	・春、上洛した白隠慧鶴に参禅し、一偈を呈す。この頃、祇園の茶屋松屋の娘徳山町（玉瀾）と結婚。 この頃、祇園下河原鳥居前神福院の内（真葛原草堂）と智恩院袋町の二カ所を住居とする（29歳）。
宝暦2年	（1752）	【呉春】	・京都に生まれる。
宝暦4年	（1754）	【蘆雪】	・山城淀に生まれる。
宝暦7年	（1757）	【若冲】	・この頃から「動植綵絵」の制作に着手か。
宝暦8年	（1758）	【蕭白】	・この年より翌年にかけ、伊勢地方へ旅に出る。三重県津市西来寺に「竹林七賢図」襖を描く （消失。落款に行年廿九歳曾我蕭白図とあったとする桃沢如水報告による）（29歳）。
宝暦10年	（1760）	【蕭白】	・**「林和靖図屏風」**（三重県立美術館蔵）を描く（31歳）。
		【蕪村】	・「倣王蒙山水図」（京都国立博物館蔵）を描く。
宝暦11年	（1761）	【抱一】	・江戸に生まれる。
宝暦13年	（1763）	【大雅】	・7月「龍山勝会・蘭亭曲水図」（静岡県立美術館蔵）、「蘭亭曲水図」（島根県立美術館蔵）、秋「青緑山水帖」 を描く（41歳）。
		【文晁】	・9月9日、江戸下谷根岸に生まれる。
明和元年	（1764）	【若冲】	・金刀比羅宮奥書院に障壁画を制作する。
		【蕭白】	・この頃再び伊勢地方へ。**「群仙図屏風」**（文化庁蔵）、「塞翁飼馬　籬史吹簫図屏風」（三重県立美術館 蔵）を制作（35歳）。また、この頃松坂市朝田寺「唐獅子図」、継松寺「雪山童子図」、斎宮永島家 障壁画「松に鷹図」、「竹林七賢図」などを描くか。
明和2年	（1765）	【若冲】	・相国寺に「釈迦三尊像」と「動植綵絵」を寄進する。
		【応挙】	・「雪中老松図」（東京国立博物館蔵）を描く。
明和3年	（1766）	【蕪村】	・妻子をのこし、讃岐に赴く（51歳）。この頃「春夜桃季園図屏風」を描く。
明和4年	（1767）	【蕭白】	・「松に孔雀図」（三重県立美術館蔵）襖絵を描く。
明和5年	（1768）	【応挙】	・『平安人物志』の画家の部の第二位に名を挙げられる。「難福図巻」「狗子図」を描く。
			・京都四条麩屋町東入ルに住む。蕪村との交流この頃よりか（36歳）。
		【白隠】	・12月11日死去（84歳）。
明和8年	（1771）	【大雅】	・与謝蕪村と「十便十宜帖」を合作する。8月「洞庭赤壁図巻」を描く（49歳）。
		【蕪村】	・大雅の「十便帖」との競作「十宜帖」を描く（56歳）。
安永2年	（1773）	【応挙】	・「花卉鳥獣人物図」を描く。
安永3年	（1774）	【応挙】	・「波上白骨座禅図　骨相図」（福岡市博物館蔵）を描く。
安永4年	（1775）	【徹山】	・大坂の舟町に生まれる。
安永5年	（1776）	【大雅】	・春より病気になり、一服の薬も飲もうとせず、4月13日真葛原の草堂に没す。
			・寺ノ内千本通の浄光寺に埋葬（54歳）。法名、大雅翁秀賢義哲居士。
安永6年	（1777）	【竹田】	・6月10日、豊後国直入郡竹田村岡藩（現在の大分県竹田市）に侍医田能村硯庵、萩野の次男として生まれる。
		【応挙】	・「双鶏図」（八坂神社蔵）を描く。
安永7年	（1778）	【応挙】	・**「仙山観花図」** 高芙蓉賛（九州国立博物館蔵）を描く。
安永8年	（1779）	【蕪村】	・「寒林孤鹿図」、「奥の細道図屏風」を描く（64歳）。

安永9年	（1780）	【蛇玉】	・10月20日死去（46歳）。
天明元年	（1781）	【蕭白】	・1月7日没（52歳）。法名―輝蕭白居士。
天明3年	（1783）	【蕪村】	・初冬より病み、12月25日未明没（68歳）。
		【梅逸】	・名古屋に生まれる。【呉春】・「柳陰帰漁図」（静岡県立美術館蔵）を描く。
天明4年	（1784）	【玉蘭】	・死去（57歳）。
		【梅関】	・仙台に生まれる。
天明5年	（1785）	【応挙】	・「雪梅図襖」（草堂寺蔵）を描く。
天明6年	（1786）	【応挙】	・**「双鶴図」**（東京国立博物館蔵）「秋月雪峡図」（千葉市美術館蔵）を描く。
天明7年	（1787）	【蘆雪】	・「牛図」「四睡図」（草堂寺蔵）を描く。「梅月図」（持宝寺蔵）を描く。
			・**「遊虎図」**「稚松丹頂図」（金刀比羅宮蔵）を描く。
天明8年	（1788）	【応挙】	・「布袋図」（名古屋市博物館蔵）を描く。
寛政元年	（1789）	【玉堂】	・『玉堂琴譜』を出版。河本立軒に自作の琴を贈る（45歳）。
寛政2年	（1790）	【応挙】	・この頃から妙法院宮真仁法親王と親しく交わる。禁裡造営の際、一門を率いて障壁画を描く（58歳）。
		【若冲】	・海宝寺に「群鶏図」の障壁画を描く。（典信）・8月16日死去（60歳）。
寛政3年	（1791）	【若冲】	・**「六歌仙図」**（愛知県美術館蔵）を描く。
寛政5年	（1793）	【崋山】	・江戸に生まれる。
寛政6年	（1794）	【応挙】	・「山水図」、「瀑布図床貼付」「竹林七賢図」（金刀比羅宮蔵）を描く（62歳）。
		【玉堂】	・春琴、秋琴の二子を伴い、但馬国城崎温泉より出奔（50歳）。
			・高松にて『玉堂琴士集』前集を出版。秋、江戸に出たか。この頃たびたび蒹葭堂を訪ねる。
寛政7年	（1795）	【応挙】	・「松に孔雀図」、「鐘馗図」、「保津川図屏風」を描く。7月17日没（63歳）。四条大宮西入ル悟真寺（現在は京都市太秦に移転）に葬られる。法名、円誉無三一妙居士。
		【蘆雪】	・「花鳥蟲獣図巻」（千葉市美術館蔵）を描く。
寛政8年	（1796）	【若冲】	・「蔬菜図屏風」を描く。
寛政11年	（1799）	【蘆雪】	・6月8日死去（46歳）。
寛政12年	（1800）	【若冲】	・9月8日没（85歳）。石峰寺に埋葬される。10月、相国寺で法要が行われる。
享和2年	（1802）	【竹田】	・「山水図」（足立区立郷土博物館蔵）を描く。
文化3年	（1806）	【狙仙】	・「蜂猴之図」を描く。
文化6年	（1809）	【竹田】	・「四季花鳥図」（大分市美術館蔵）描く。【月僊】・1月12日死去（69歳）。
文化8年	（1811）	【竹田】	・京坂遊歴の途次、神辺に菅茶山を訪ね、大坂頼山陽と初めて会う。「煙霞帖」を描く。
			・11月、藩内に農民一揆が起こり、12月「建言書」を提出（35歳）。【呉春】・7月17日死去（60歳）。
文化10年	（1813）	【玉堂】	・『平安人物志』画家の部に名が載る。京都で春琴宅に同居する（69歳）。
文化12年	（1815）	【竹田】	・「孔雀」（秋田市立千秋美術館蔵）を描く。
文政元年	（1818）	【玉堂】	・「秋色半分図」（愛知県美術館蔵）、「酔雲醒月図」（愛知県美術館蔵）、「山水図」（愛知県美術館蔵）を描く。
文政2年	（1819）	【梅逸】	・**「紅白梅図」**（島根県立美術館蔵）を描く。
文政3年	（1820）	【玉堂】	・9月4日、京都の自宅にて没す。本能寺に埋葬（76歳）。
文政4年	（1821）	【狙仙】	・7月21日死去（75歳）。
文政5年	（1822）	【竹田】	・**「高客聴琴図屏風」**（大分県立美術館蔵）を描く。
文政7年	（1824）	【義梵】	・**「富嶽図」**（東京国立博物館蔵）を描く。
文政8年	（1825）	【竹田】	・**「八仙人図」**（福島県立博物館蔵）を描く。
文政9年	（1826）	【竹田】	・「前赤壁図」（足立区立郷土博物館蔵）を描く。
文政10年	（1827）	【竹田】	・長期滞在した長崎より、鹿児島を経て12月帰藩する。「秋渓訪友図」、「清谿深遠図」を描く（51歳）。
		【義梵】	・**「滝図自画賛」**（東京国立博物館蔵）を描く。
文政11年	（1828）	【抱一】	・11月29日に雨華庵で没し、翌月築地本願寺に葬られる（68歳）。
文政12年	（1829）	【竹田】	・**「風雨渡舟図」**（東京国立博物館蔵）「梅花宿鳥図」（大分県立美術館蔵）描く。
天保2年	（1831）	【竹田】	・「暗香疎影図」（大分市美術館蔵）を描く。
		【暁斎】	・4月7日、下総古河に生まれる。
天保3年	（1832）	【竹田】	・戸次の帆足杏雨宅を訪ね、雲華と会う。9月、東上の旅の途次、山陽の訃報に接する。**「桃花流水図」**（大分市美術館蔵）、「複嶺畳嶂図」、「曲渓複嶺図」、「桃花流水図」、「梅花書屋図」、「広寿嶺図」を描く（56歳）。
天保5年	（1834）	【竹田】	・「漁樵問答図」（大分市美術館蔵）を描く。「松陰双鶴図」（大分県立美術館蔵）描く。
		【梅関】	・「墨梅」（秋田市立千秋美術館蔵）を描く。
天保6年	（1835）	【竹田】	・7月、大坂にて発病する。「吹田村寓居図」を描く。8月29日没（59歳）。同月、天王寺口縄坂上浄春寺に葬る。
天保7年	（1836）	【鉄斎】	・京都に生まれる。
天保8年	（1837）	【仙厓】	・10月7日死去（87歳）。【崋山】・
		【崋山】	・「市河米庵像」を描く。**「鷹見泉石像」**（東京国立博物館蔵）を描く。
天保9年	（1838）	【崋山】	・「風竹之図」（田原市博物館蔵）を描く。
天保11年	（1840）	【文晁】	・12月14日死去（78歳）。
天保12年	（1841）	【崋山】	・10月11日自刃（49歳）。
		【徹山】	・5月6日死去（67歳）。
天保15年	（1844）	【梅関】	・1月11日不遇のうちに死去（61歳）。
弘化4年	（1847）	【風外】	・6月22日死去（69歳）。
嘉永5年	（1852）	【梅逸】	・「四季山水図」（千葉市美術館蔵）を描く。

安政 3 年　(1856)	【梅逸】	・1 月 2 日死去（74 歳）。
明治元年　(1868)	【大観】	・9 月 18 日、水戸に生まれる。
明治 20 年 (1887)	【鉄斎】	・「普陀落迦山」（富山県水墨美術館蔵）を描く。
明治 22 年 (1889)	【暁斎】	・4 月 26 日死去（59 歳）。
明治 33 年 (1900)	【大観】	【観山】・「日・月蓬莱山図」（静岡県立美術館蔵）を描く。
明治 37 年 (1904)	【大観】	・**「木立に白鷺」**（富山県水墨美術館蔵）を描く。
明治 38 年 (1905)	【鉄斎】	・「富士遠望・寒霞渓図」（京都国立近代美術館蔵）を描く。
明治 40 年 (1907)	【大観】	・「達磨」（豊田市美術館蔵）を描く。
明治 44 年 (1911)	【大観】	・**「釈迦十六羅漢」**（東京国立博物館蔵）を描く。
大正 2 年　(1913)	【大観】	・**「松並木」**（東京国立博物館蔵）を描く。
大正 3 年　(1914)	【鉄斎】	・**「虎僊育虎子図」**（愛知県美術館蔵）、「焚火」（豊田市美術館蔵）を描く。
大正 7 年　(1918)	【鉄斎】	・**「百事如意図」**（愛知県美術館蔵）を描く。
大正 8 年　(1919)	【鉄斎】	・**「竹窓高臥図」**（富山県水墨美術館蔵）、「竹」（髙島屋史料館蔵）を描く。
大正 12 年 (1923)	【鉄斎】	・**「二神会舞」**（東京国立博物館蔵）を描く。
	【大観】	・**「生々流転」**（東京国立近代美術館蔵）を描く。
大正 13 年 (1924)	【鉄斎】	・12 月 31 日死去（89 歳）。
昭和 10 年 (1935)	【大観】	・**「五浦の月」**（東京国立博物館蔵）を描く。
昭和 16 年 (1941)	【大観】	・**「雨後之山」**（富山県水墨美術館蔵）を描く。
昭和 33 年 (1958)	【大観】	・2 月 26 日死去（89 歳）。

[画像データ提供・資料掲載協力]

愛知県美術館
秋田市立千秋美術館
板橋区立美術館
大分県立美術館
大分市美術館
大津市歴史博物館
岡山県立博物館
岡山県立美術館
北野天満宮
九州国立博物館
京都国立博物館
金刀比羅宮
齋年寺
滋賀県立安土城考古博物館
島根県立美術館
曹源寺
千葉市美術館
DNP アートコミュニケーションズ
敦賀市立博物館
天授庵
東京藝術大学大学美術館
東京国立博物館
東北歴史博物館
栃木県立博物館
富山県水墨美術館
豊橋市美術博物館
福岡市博物館
福岡市美術館
福島県立博物館
文化庁
三重県立美術館
龍泉庵
黎明教会資料研修館

[参考文献]

「日本の美術 No.13　水墨画」松下隆章・編　至文堂 1967 年
「日本の美術 No.63　雪村と関東水墨画」中村渓男・編　至文堂 1971 年
「日本の美術 No.69　初期水墨画」金沢 弘・編　至文堂 1972 年
「別冊太陽　日本のこころ 23 号　水墨画」平凡社　1978 年
「禅の美術」京都国立博物館　1981 年
「特別展観　近世水墨画展」文化庁　東京国立博物館　1985 年
「日本美術名宝展」文化庁　東京国立博物館　京都国立博物館　1986 年
「特別展　日本の水墨画」東京国立博物館　1987 年
「芸術新潮　やさしく極める水墨画」新潮社　1987 年
「岡山の絵画 500 年」岡山県立美術館　1988 年
「日本の美術 No.335 水墨画 雪舟とその流派」渡邊明義・編 至文堂 1994 年
「日本の美術 No.337 水墨画 祥啓と雪村」中島純司・編　至文堂　1994 年
「日本の美術 No.338 水墨画 能阿弥から狩野派へ」島尾 新・編 至文堂 1994 年
「奈良県立美術館　蔵品 100 選」奈良県立美術館　1994 年
「千葉市美術館所蔵作品集」千葉市美術館　1995 年
「室町時代の狩野派」京都国立博物館　1996 年
「北野天満宮神宝展」京都国立博物館　2001 年
「芸術新潮 与謝蕪村 江戸時代ルネサンス最大のマルチアーティスト」新潮社 2001 年
「芸術新潮　逸脱の画聖　ほんとうの雪舟へ！」新潮社　2002 年
「没後 500 年　特別展　雪舟」東京国立博物館　京都国立博物館　2002 年
「魅惑の水墨画　墨戯」岡山県立美術館　2002 年
「富山県水墨美術館収蔵作品集」富山県水墨美術館　2003 年
「別冊太陽　日本のこころ 124 号　水墨画発見」平凡社　2003 年
「円山応挙　写生画　創造への挑戦」毎日新聞社　2003 年
「曾我蕭白　無頼という愉悦」京都国立博物館　2005 年
「芸術新潮　水墨サイケデリック　蕭白がゆく」新潮社　2005 年
「自然をめぐる千年の旅　山水から風景へ」愛知県美術館　2005 年
「江戸絵画　木村定三コレクション」愛知県美術館　2006 年
「金刀比羅宮　書院の美」東京藝術大学大学美術館　金刀比羅宮　2007 年
「特別展覧会　狩野永徳」京都国立博物館　2007 年
「動物絵画の 100 年」府中市美術館　2007 年
「岡山県立美術館所蔵　雪舟と水墨画」千葉市美術館　2008 年
「日本の美・発見Ⅰ 水墨画の輝き　雪舟・等伯から鉄斎まで」出光美術館 2009 年
「没後 400 年　長谷川等伯」東京国立博物館　京都国立博物館　2010 年
「長沢芦雪　奇は新なり」MIHO MUSEUM　2011 年
「特別展覧会　狩野山楽・山雪」京都国立博物館　2013 年
「黎明教会資料研修館図録」黎明教会資料研修館　2015 年
『日本の美術 23　文人画』米沢嘉圃　吉沢 忠・著　平凡社　1966 年
『日本の美術 12　周文から雪舟へ』田中一松・著　平凡社　1969 年
『花鳥画の世界 2　水墨の花と鳥　室町の花鳥』金沢 弘・編　学習研究社 1982 年
『日本の美と文化　禅と水墨』衛藤 駿・著　講談社 1982 年
『新潮世界美術辞典』新潮社　1985 年
『原色図典 日本美術史年表』太田博太郎・山根有三・河北倫明・監修 集英社 1986 年
『日本絵画史図典』山根有三・監修　福武書店　1987 年
『日本文化総合年表』岩波書店　1990 年
『新潮日本人名辞典』新潮社 1991 年
『墨絵の譜　日本の水墨画家たち　1・2』小林 忠・著　ぺりかん社 1991 年
『琳派美術館（全 4 巻）』第二アートセンター・編　集英社　1993 年
『水墨画の巨匠　第 1 巻～第 14 巻』講談社　1994・1995 年
『奇想の系譜』辻 惟雄・著　筑摩書房　2004 年
『日本の笑い』コロナ・ブックス編集部・編　平凡社　2011 年
『江戸の美術大図鑑』狩野博幸・並木誠士・今橋理子・監修　河出書房新社 2017 年
『日本水墨画全史』小林 忠・著　講談社学術文庫　2018 年
『日本の水墨画 1　山水』河出書房新社　2018 年
『日本の水墨画 2　花鳥』河出書房新社　2018 年
『日本の水墨画 3　人物』河出書房新社　2018 年

日本の図像　墨のいろ
SUMI-E: The Iconography of Japan

2025 年 3 月 21 日　初版第 1 刷発行

編著	濱田信義
企画・編集	編集室　青人社
序文	畠中光亨
写真	中田 昭
デザイン	谷平理映子（SPICE design）
翻訳	マクレリー ルシー（ザ・ワード・ワークス）
校閲	廣瀬まゆ
制作進行	宮城鈴香

発行人	三芳寛要
発行元	株式会社 パイ インターナショナル

〒 170-0005　東京都豊島区南大塚 2-32-4
TEL 03-3944-3981　FAX 03-5395-4830
sales@pie.co.jp

PIE International Inc.
2-32-4 Minami-Otsuka, Toshima-ku, Tokyo 170-0005 JAPAN
international@pie.co.jp

印刷・製本 : 株式会社東京印書館

© 2025 Nobuyoshi Hamada / PIE International
ISBN978-4-7562-5982-0 C0071
Printed in Japan

本書の収録内容の無断転載・複写・複製等を禁じます。
ご注文、乱丁・落丁本の交換等に関するお問い合わせは、小社までご連絡ください。
著作物の利用に関するお問い合わせはこちらをご覧ください。
https://pie.co.jp/contact/

SUMI-E: The Iconography of Japan

Text by Nobuyoshi Hamada
Translated by The Word Works
Designed by Rieko Tanihira
Proofreading by Mayu Hirose

©2025 Nobuyoshi Hamada / PIE International

All rights reserved. No part of this publication may be reproduced, stored in a
retrieval system, or transmitted in any form or by any means, graphic, electronic
or mechanical, including photocopying and recording, or otherwise, without prior
permission in writing from the publisher.

PIE International Inc.
2-32-4 Minami-Otsuka, Toshima-ku, Tokyo 170-0005 JAPAN
international@pie.co.jp
www.pie.co.jp/english

ISBN978-4-7562-6002-4 (Outside Japan)
Printed in Japan

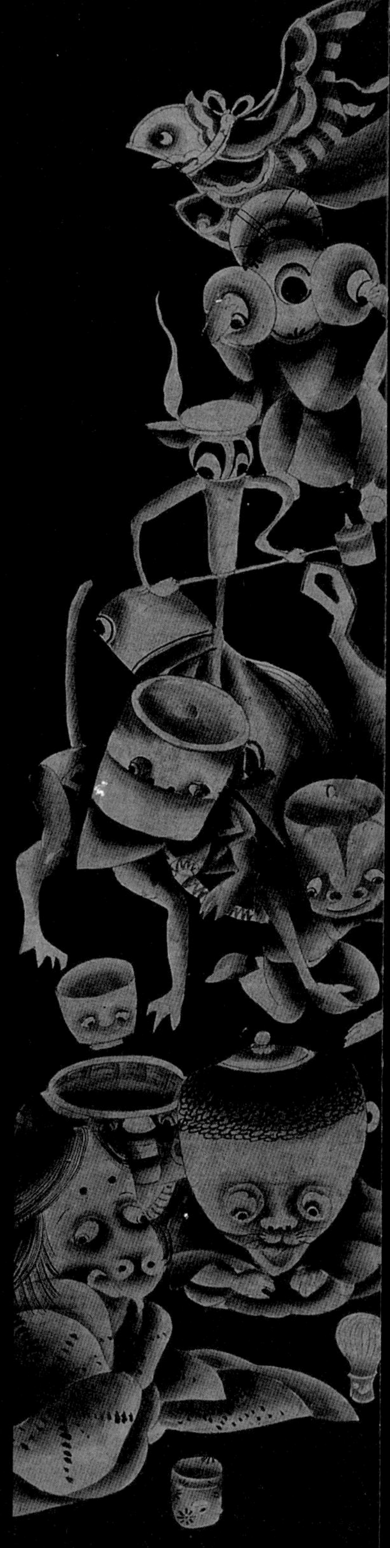